ISBN 978-1-5278-7696-5
PIBN 10906993

THE

HISTORY

OF THE

REIGN OF GEORGE III.

TO THE

TERMINATION OF THE LATE WAR.

TO WHICH IS PREFIXED,

A VIEW OF THE PROGRESSIVE IMPROVEMENT OF ENGLAND, IN PROSPERITY AND STRENGTH, TO THE ACCESSION OF HIS MAJESTY.

IN SIX VOLUMES.

By ROBERT BISSET, LL.D.

AUTHOR OF THE "LIFE OF BURKE," &c. &c.

VOL. V.

LONDON:

Printed by A. Strahan, New-street Square,

FOR T. N. LONGMAN AND O. REES, N° 39, PATERNOSTER-ROW; AND W. CREECH, EDINBURGH.

1803.

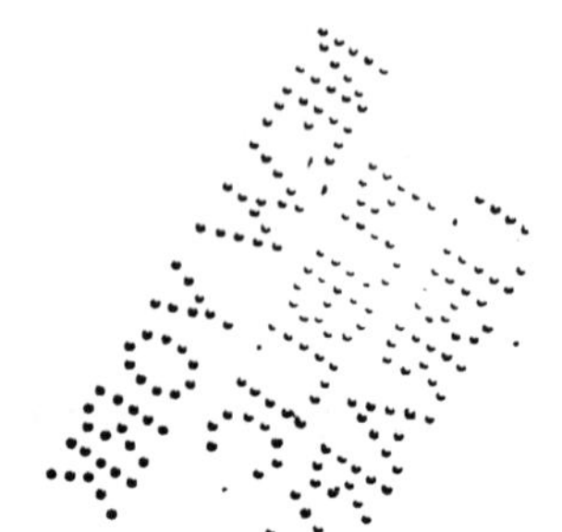

CONTENTS

OF THE

FIFTH VOLUME.

CHAP. XLIII.

CONTENTS.

CHAP. XLIV.

CONTENTS.

CHAP. XLV.

 military,

CHAP. XLVI.

CHAP. XLVII.

CHAP. XLVIII.

CHAP. XLIX.

CHAP. L.

an

CHAP. LI.

CHAP. LII.

CHAP.

CHAP. LIII.

CHAP. LIV.

HIS-

HISTORY

OF THE

REIGN OF GEORGE III.

CHAP. XLIII.

Retrospective view of France.—Old government.—Character and spirit of France under Louis XIV.—Sources of submission to arbitrary power—commencing and progressive change under Louis XV.—Beginning of infidelity.—Voltaire and his disciples.—Beginning of anti-monarchism.—Rousseau supposes man a perfectible being.—Progress of his doctrines through the efforts of literature.—Co-operating political causes.—General impolicy and burdensome expence of the French wars against Great Britain.—Enormous expenditure and distressful consequences of the war to support our revolted colonies.—Pecuniary embarrassments.—Various schemes of alleviation.—Convention of the notables—Calonne unfolds the dreadful state of the finances.—Calonne proposes an equalization of public burdens—incenses the privileged orders.—Outcry against the minister—disgraced—retires into banishment.—Brienne minister.—Trifling and inefficient reforms.—Contests with parliaments.—Attempts of the crown to overawe the refractory—unsuccessful.—Arbitrary suspension of parliaments.—National ferment.—Distressed situation of the king—abandoned by many of his courtiers—resolves to recal Mr. Neckar—who consults the convocation of the states-general.—Question concerning the consolidation of the orders.—Meeting of the states.—Commons propose to meet in one chamber—opposed by the crown.—Commons constitute themselves a national assembly, with-

out regard to the other orders.—Violence of demagogues.—Soldiers infected with the popular enthusiasm—insubordination and licentiousness.—King orders troops to approach to Paris.—Popular leaders prepare to defend the capital.—An army of volunteers immediately raised—attack the royal magazines to procure arms—assail the Bastile.—Subversion of the old government.—Declaration of rights—fundamental principle the RIGHTS OF MAN.—*First acts of the revolutionists—power—great and general object to subvert establishment—to that object all the whole energies of the French genius and character exerted.—Licentiousness of the press.—Twenty thousand literary men employ themselves in stimulating the mob to outrage.—An engine of government new in the history of political establishments—*CLUBS*—influence of—extended by association—doctrines—influence and operation.—Lawless violence in the country.—Peasants turn upon the proprietors.—Some of the nobility propose to sacrifice a large portion of their privileges and property—their example imitated and emulated.—Sacrifices of the nobles and clergy.—Admiration of the commons.—Proposition for the seizure of church property—remonstrances of the clergy—disregarded.—Parliaments annihilated.—Immunities sacrificed.—The law and policy of the kingdom overturned.—Scheme for voluntary contributions.—Gold and silver sent to the mint.—Preparations for the new constitution—the authority to be possessed by the king.—Suspensive* VETO.—*Question, if the assembly was to be composed of one or two chambers—carried, that there should be only one.—English constitution proposed as a model—rejected.—French commons inimical to mixed government—settlement of the succession.—Ferocity of the people—inflamed by scarcity.—Additional troops arrive at Versailles—entertainment given by the officers in the palace to the new comers.—The royal family visit the banqueting room.—Music describes the sufferings of a captive prince.—The queen having in her arms the infant dauphin presents him to the officers—the ladies of the court accompany her.—Effects of beauty, music, and*

wine

wine, combined.—Unguarded enthusiasm of the loyal soldiers—trample on the national cockade.—Report of this entertainment at Paris.—Rage and indignation of the revolutionists.—Activity and influence of the fishwomen and courtezans.—The mob determines to bring the king to Paris—expedition of the women for that purpose—hang priests and aristocrates—march to Versailles—overawe the legislature—break into the assembly and take possession of the speaker's chair.—Mob assault the palace—attempt to murder the queen—prevented by the heroism of her defenders.—King and queen agree to depart for Paris.—Mournful procession of a degraded monarch.—Farther proceedings at Paris.—The existing government endeavoured to quell the mob—severe prosecutions for that purpose.—Effects of the French revolution in Britain.—Detesting the old French government and not acquainted with the new, Britons approve of the revolution as friendly to liberty.—Sentiments of various classes—respectively differing, concur in favouring the French revolution.

CHAP. XLIII.

1789.

THE event which rendered the year 1789 most important to Britons and all the civilised world, was the French revolution, the causes and means of which extraordinary change it requires a retrospective view of the scene of operation to investigate and comprehend. The government of France was, in the earlier ages, one of those feudal aristocracies, which the northern conquerors established over Europe. The degree of civil and political liberty that extended to the commons was very inconsiderable in France, as in most other countries, except England and the Netherlands. The power of the king in the middle ages was extremely limited; the country consisted of a collection of principalities, in each of which the lord superior enjoyed an arbitrary sway, and held the

Old government of France.

CHAP. XLIII. 1789.

the people in a condition of abject vassalage. This state of relative power in the vicissitudes of human affairs underwent material changes. The kings had one general object, diminution of baronial authority: prudence required the barons to unite for their common advantage, yet they had respectively separate interests which much more constantly occupied their attention. By sowing discord between these turbulent chieftains, the sovereigns rendered their aggregate force less formidable. Conquests, escheats, or treaties, united several fiefs to the crown: Louis XI. considerably reduced the power of the nobility, the feudal aristocracy was entirely destroyed by cardinal Richelieu, and the separate sovereignties were consolidated into one entire mass *. As the people had been without liberty under feudal lords, they continued to be in servitude under the monarch: before the total reduction of the aristocracy, they had indeed possessed an assembly of states, but so modelled, that the commons had little real share of the power: the nobles and clergy were closely connected by immunities and other privileges, and could easily overpower the third estate. From the administration of Richelieu, France had been without even the appearance of a legislative voice; every privilege of the subject was under the control of a government habitually corrupt and tyrannical. The men of wealth and distinction were purchased either by courtly honours, presents, pensions, or a lavish waste of the public revenue, which was endeavoured to be exclusively wrung from the

* See Introduction to this History.

grasp

grasp of the poor, the weak, and the laborious. Liberty and even life were insecure, if either interfered with the will of the prince. Instead of making a part subservient to the whole; estimating either permanent regulations, or temporary measures, by the aggregate of happiness which they were calculated to produce; the old government of France administered the whole according to the pleasure and caprice of a very small part; the comfort and welfare of twenty-four millions was of little account when compared with the freak or fancy of the prince, the interest or inclination of his favourites. The suggestion of a priest or a prostitute would desolate a whole province*, and drive from that country its most industrious inhabitants. The nobility and clergy, and also the magistrates, were exempted from their share of the public burdens; the taxes, instead of being paid by the rich and the great, fell upon the poor. These tyrannical exactions were rendered more cruelly oppressive by the established mode of extortion; the revenue was farmed, and farther leased by the principal undertakers to others, and by these to subordinate collectors with advance of rent; in the various steps of intermediation between the payer of the impost and the government, much greater sums were squeezed from the commons than ever found their way to the public treasury. The farmers of the revenue principally constituted the monied class, or at least, were the greatest capitalists†; in them government had its chief resource for loans to carry

CHAP. XLIII. 1789.

* See in Render's Tour through Germany, an account of the devastation of the Palatinate.

† Annual Register, 1787 and 1789.

CHAP. XLIII. 1789.

on the projects of extravagant ambition, and infatuated aggression. Many of the nobility from their prodigality were poor notwithstanding their immunities and donatives, and from these men had the means of supply; the court, therefore, very readily connived at most flagrant extortions in the administration of the revenue, as the commons only were to suffer by the spoliation.

Character and spirit of France under Louis XIV. and XV.

The old government of France was, no doubt, liable to these and other objections, both in its principles and practice; and in the reigns of Louis XIV. and XV. it was a very arbitrary and oppressive system. Its vices appeared the more glaring to political observers, by being contrasted with the constitution of the neighbour and rival of France. Perhaps, indeed, this circumstance produced to that system still less estimation than it really deserved. To Britons it would have been an intolerable scheme of policy, and must have crushed the energy of the British character, which in a great measure results from civil and political liberty; but a greater or less degree of restraint is necessary according to the knowledge and dispositions of a nation as well as an individual. The French minds, sentiments, and habits, appeared to require a stronger curb than the British; but on the other hand the authorities which were to control the violence, regulate the vivacity, and guide the versatile instability of the Gallic character, were by no means well placed. The power was not exerted for rendering the greatest benefit to the subjects which even their tempers would admit; it was much more arbitrary than was expedient for a civilized people to tolerate. The great mass of the commons were in a ſtate of ſlavery to the prieſts, the nobles, and the officers of the crown *; ſuch a condition only profound ignorance, fear, or infatuation could ſuffer. It was natural for intelligent and ingenious men to ſee the imperfections of the arbitrary government, and to wiſh for a reform of various abuſes. The ſplendid actions of Louis XIV. notwithſtanding their real impolicy, dazzled his ſubjects; his oſtentatious diſplays to other nations of his ſuperiority ſo flattering to the predominant vanity of the French character, rendered them eager partiſans of their great monarch. Inſtrumental to the glory of the ſovereign, they thought they were promoting their own! Vanity aſſumed the diſguiſe of honour; and in gratifying the prince, and courting his approbation, they overlooked their own condition; they forgot they were bearing ſlavery, encountering war, poverty, and ſtarvation, merely as puppets in the hands of a vain-glorious tyrant †. Under Louis XIV. their ſubſerviency was very abject, but it aroſe from cauſes that could not be permanent, and, indeed, from a certain operation of paſſions and energies, which, in another direction, might readily attempt, and powerfully affect the diſſolution of their fetters. Submiſſion to arbitrary power ariſes from various cauſes, and operates differently according to the diverſities of national characters; often it may proceed from barbarous ignorance and intellectual debaſement, which mindful of only animal wants thinks not of any higher

Sources of ſubmiſſion to arbitrary power.

* New Annual Regiſter, 1789.

† Smollett's Continuation of Hume, vol. i.

 enjoy-

enjoyments than the ſupply of theſe*; a phlegmatic temper that does not feel injuſtice and oppreſſion; or from relaxation, indolence and timidity, which, notwithſtanding a knowledge of right, and a feeling of wrong, prevents ſtrenuous efforts for vindication and redreſs; ſervitude in theſe caſes is a *paſſive principle.* The French were very far from being void of knowledge, ſenſibility, courage, or active exertion: on the contrary, they were intelligent, ardent, bold, and enterpriſing, but their paſſions engaged their ingenuity and their force in ſupporting and aggrandiſing their abſolute monarch. Submiſſion to arbitrary power in them love for the ſovereign, a STRONGLY ACTIVE PRINCIPLE; theirs was implicit obedience yielded by ſtrength, not deſpotiſm forced upon weakneſs. The French animation was extremely eager in the purſuit of pleaſure as its levity was very fond of pageantry and ſhew. The magnificent profuſion of Louis and his court was well adapted for increaſing the popularity acquired by political and military atchievments; the high admiration, or rather the adoration with which his ſubjects regarded this monarch, ſoon excited in their warm and enthuſiaſtic minds an ardent affection for the whole royal family, and indeed all the princes of the blood; they aſſociated the ideas of eſtimation for royalty with military proweſs. Theſe effects were, as long as they laſted, very favourable to the continuance and extenſion of abſolute ſway, but the cauſes were perfectly compatible with totally different ſentiments.

* As in the caſe of the negroes, ſee Park's Travels, paſſim.

Under

Under Louis XV. the French long continued ardent in loyalty, and manifested their affection and reverence for the kingly name in implicit obedience to the mandates of his most christian majesty; but while energy was exerting itself in the boldest enterprise for promoting the great monarch's glory, props of his power were beginning to be impaired. From the middle of his reign the Roman catholic faith commenced its decline, and towards the close the political power of the sovereign received a considerable shake.

Commencing and progressive change under Louis XV.

Beginnings of infidelity.

The abandoned debauchery of the court under the duke of Orleans's regency had prepared the higher ranks for the infusion of infidelity which was afterwards so extensively received. The first movers of this scheme of irreligion were certain votaries of literature, who employed men of high rank as their instruments. Learning became daily moreprevalent in Europe, and having been fostered in France by the ostentatious vanity of Louis XIV. though limited during his reign to subjects of taste, sentiment, and natural philosophy, afterwards extended to theology, ethics, and politics. Voltaire was admirably fitted for impressing the susceptibility, gratifying the taste, amusing the fancy, inflaming the passions, and so misleading the judgment of lively, refined, ingenious, ardent, and volatile readers and hearers: he, therefore, was thoroughly skilled in the most effectual means of attacking the faith of Frenchmen. Vanity materially assisted the infidel's operations: the nobility having imbibed under Louis XIV. a relish for literature and still more for literary patronage, were

Voltaire.

1789.

desirous of cultivating, or appearing to cultivate, intimacy with a man of so high rank in letters, repeated his doctrines and witticisms, and abandoned their religion to pass for philosophers. Besides, the debauchery of Louis XIV., carried by his pupil the duke of Orleans to a much more profligate excess, and not much corrected under the mature age of Louis XV., established in the morals of courtiers a powerful auxiliary for spreading infidelity. The ridiculous absurdity of many of the popish doctrines was easily discernible to French sagacity when turned to such animadversions; and their various mummeries afforded scope to the French wit and satire, when permitted to take such a range. Gallic ingenuity could easily find arguments to expose the frivolity and folly of many of their priestly doctrines, rites, and observances; but as ardent as versatile, leaving their superstitions, they took the opposite and much more dangerous extreme. Some of the king's ministers, pleased with the theories of the Voltaire school, and converted by his jokes, became deists, made the king inimical to various parts of the ecclesiastical establishment, and inspired him with a desire of reforming the church. This reform both in France and other countries arose partly from a diminished regard for the established church, but principally from the love of plunder: its consequences were a degradation of the clerical character to a much lower state than was requisite for the purposes of spiritual and moral instruction. The suppression of the religious orders, and the general system of policy towards the church, from the

peace

peace of Paris to the end of the duke de Choiseul's administration tended very powerfully to second the efforts of deistical writers against the church. Indeed the of acts Louis XV. at the instigation of his favourites, were powerfully efficient causes, though not the proximate, of the downfal of religion in the reign of his successor. It is by no means a difficult undertaking for a man of genius to establish a new sect in religion or politics: if he mean to mislead the judgment, he has only by animated description to impress the imagination, or by impassioned eloquence to impel the affections *. Voltaire was very successful in the use of these instruments: other literary adventurers readily pursued a tract leading so directly to esteem and patronage. Under such influence, projects and institutions were formed for circulating their doctrines. By such influence, projects, and institutions †, infidelity made very rapid advances; except in the lower classes of people, in the latter period of the reign of Louis XV. the majority of laity in France were deists. Opinions and sentiments so inimical not only to absolute monarchy, but to every form of regular government, are indebted for their disseminations to the imbecility of Louis XV., and the narrow views of his ministers. The same spirit of free inquiry not being properly understood or wisely modified by the court of France, from exposing the absurdities of many

CHAP. XLIII. 1789.

* Whitfield, Wesley, and other adventurers of a more recent date clearly and strongly illustrate the facility with which ingenuity fashioning itself to the fancies and passions of men, may impress a new hypothesis of religion.

† See Barruel on Jacobinism, vol. i. passim.

popish

CHAP. XLIII.

1789.
Commencement of antimonarchical doctrines.

popiſh obſervances proceeded to attack chriſtianity itſelf, and ſoon extended to politics. In their efforts againſt ſuperſtition, the philoſophiſts, in the violent ardour of the French character, ruſhing to the oppoſite extreme, pulled up the wheat as well as the tares; the ſame operators, employed on the ſame materials, uſing a ſimilar proceſs in politics, produced ſimilar effects; and in both, ſeeking to avoid one evil, without diſcriminating it from the good in which it was mixed, they incurred a greater. Speculating upon the rights and happineſs of man, they eaſily ſaw that the government of France was very far from being well adapted to the ſecurity of rights or the diffuſion of happineſs. The ingenuity of Frenchmen has, in moſt ſubjects of ſtudy, exhibited itſelf much more frequently in framing hypotheſes than in collecting facts, inveſtigating principles, and deducing conſequences from actually eſtabliſhed premiſes. This mode of procedure, well adapted to the poet's invention, was employed in caſes which required the reaſoning of the philoſopher, and the wiſdom of the ſage. A poſition was aſſumed by Helvetius and many others, but above all by Rouſſeau, that man was a perfectible being, and that every change of ſyſtem was to be adapted to the perfection which he might attain. While Voltaire and his ſect were labouring to undermine exiſting eſtabliſhments, Helvetius, Rouſſeau, and their ſects, beſides rendering a helping hand to the ſcheme of demolition, were very active in propoſing new models totally impracticable, becauſe to conſiſt of perfect men, materials no where found to exiſt. The French ſtateſmen were equally blind

Rouſſeau ſuppoſes man a perfectible being,

to

to the probable consequences of the political as of the theological theories so prevalent towards the close of Louis XV.'s reign. Then was the time * to have prevented their destructive effects by gradual and progressive melioration of church and state, which both demanded correction. The systematic impolicy of France in seeking commercial and maritime aggrandisement by provoking that nation that can always ruin her trade and crush her navy, tended very powerfully to give a practical operation to the spirit of liberty. The immense expence incurred in the seven years war, causing fiscal derangements, was the chief source of those contentions with the provincial parliaments that principally distinguished the last years of Louis XV. The actual opposition of these political bodies was perfectly justifiable, but called into action the prevailing theories, and paved the way for much more unrestrained efforts against the prince's power. Louis XVI., kind and liberal by nature, was disposed to moderate in its exercise the rigour of his absolute power, and to accommodate his government to the sentiments which, without comprehending their precise nature or extent, he in general saw become prevalent among his subjects. The first years of his

Co-operating political causes,

General impolicy and burdensome expence of the French wars against Britain.

* So early as the year 1772, Edmund Burke, in the theological scepticism and political hypotheses of the French writers, saw the probable overthrow of religion and government; and even in the house of commons mentioned his apprehension of the danger, and proposed to form an alliance among believers against (he said) those ministers of rebellious darkness who are endeavouring to shake all the works of God established in beauty and order.

reign promised popularity to the prince with increasing happiness to his people. Repetition, however, of the same preposterous policy which had cost France so much blood and treasure, not only drove him to an unprovoked war with England, but to a war in which he was to support revolting subjects against their sovereign in which every argument that he could adduce in favour of the Americans might be employed with much greater force to vindicate a revolt of his own subjects. The intercourse of the French with the defenders of a republican constitution very rapidly increased an antimonarchical spirit in a country predisposed for its reception.

Enormous expences and distressful consequences of the war to support the Americans.

The enormous expences incurred in nourishing America, and endeavouring to injure Britain, plunged France into unexampled distress, and the aggression recoiled on the aggressor. An immense new debt was added to the old, the accumulation became intolerable. The multitude of the distinct loans which altogether composed this vast mass of debt, and the diversity of the conditions upon which, according to the genius of the respective projectors, they had been raised, the numberless appropriations of specific revenues to particular funds, and the frequent infractions of these to supply the immediate necessities of the state, occasioned such voluminous detailed accounts, such endless references *, explanations, and deficiencies, with such eternal crowds of figures, that the whole presented a chaos of confusion, in which the financiers themselves seemed scarcely less bewildered than

Pecuniary embarrassments.

* See Annual Register, 1787, chap. vii.

the

the public. The taxes, numerous as they were, and ruinous in the laſt degree to the people, were totally unequal to the ſupply of the current expences of the ſtate and to the diſcharge of the intereſt or annuities ariſing on the various funds; new funds could not be raiſed, but the exigencies of the ſtate muſt be ſupplied. No effectual means were deviſed, but by withholding the annuities due to the public creditors to the amount of the deficiency. This meaſure involved numbers in diſtreſs and calamity, and cauſed loud clamours: in a ſituation ſo diſaſtrous, projects and projectors of relief multiplied. The wealth of France was certainly very great, but the principal was in the private repoſitories of miniſters, contractors, commiſſioners, ſtock-jobbers, farmers general, and the minions of the court.

Schemes of extrication.

Vergennes died in 1786, and was ſucceeded by Monſieur de Calonne, who having in vain tried the experiment of new loans, the king propoſed to aſſemble the ſtates, but was diſſuaded by the court and miniſtry. If the ſtates were aſſembled, they might, inſtead of granting ſupplies, begin their deliberations with demanding a redreſs of grievances. Monſieur de Calonne wiſhed to convene the Notables, an aſſembly deriving its name from the members being men of rank and reſpectability. The miniſters had endeavoured to prevail on the nobility and clergy to contribute a ſhare ſpontaneouſly of thoſe immenſe ſums which through their exemptions they were preſumed to have accumulated. The ſame influence, it was alſo hoped, would be ſucceſsfully uſed in prevailing on the great monied capitaliſts to bring

Convention of the Notables.

CHAP. XLIII. 1789. bring forward part of their ſtores for the relief of the nation. A proclamation was acordingly iſſued the 16th of December for holding this aſſembly *.

Calonne. In an introductory ſpeech Calonne contended that the public embarraſſment aroſe from cauſes which were highly honourable to France, and the preſent reign, and, notwithſtanding the immediate exigency, ultimately beneficial as well as glorious. A marine had been formed infinitely more powerful than any ever known in France; his majeſty's fleets had ſailed triumphant over the ocean, he had humbled the rival, and terminated an honourable war by a ſolid and permanent peace: devoting his attention to the public welfare, he had, ſince peace was eſtabliſhed, invariably purſued extenſive commerce abroad, and good adminiſtration at home. He unfolds the dreadful ſtate of the finances; The miniſter had found the finances, when he was entruſted with their management, in a deplorable ſtate; a vaſt unfunded debt, all annuities and intereſt greatly in arrear; all the coffers empty, the public ſtocks fallen to the loweſt point, circulation interrupted, and all credit and confidence deſtroyed. He then ſhewed the meaſures which he had purſued, and the happy effects they had produced (ſo far as his meaſures could reach)

* It conſiſted of ſeven princes of the blood, nine dukes and peers of France, eight field-marſhals, twenty-two nobles, eight counſellors of ſtate, four maſters of requeſts, eleven archbiſhops and biſhops, thirty-ſeven judges of parliament, twelve deputies of the pays d'etat, the lieutenant civil, and twenty-five magiſtrates of different towns; in all, one hundred and forty-four. See Macfarlane's hiſtory of George III. vol. iii. p. 345.

in

in remedying theſe complicated evils. He had, he ſaid, re-eſtabliſhed public credit upon a ſound baſis, had undertaken great and expenſive works of the higheſt national importance; but notwithſtanding all thoſe favourable appearances of proſperity, there was an evil every year increaſing in magnitude, this was the great annual deficiency of the public revenue, and its inadequacy to the national expence; to eradicate this evil was beyond the reach of miniſters; additional taxes would opreſs the people, whom the king wiſhed of all things to relieve; anticipation on the revenue of ſubſequent years had already been practiſed to a ruinous extent; and the reduction of expence had been carried as far as was poſſible without weakening the ſtate and government. In the reform of abuſes, the king and his miniſter chiefly truſted to find a remedy for the evil. One of the moſt intolerable grievances which then prevailed, was the immunity of the moſt opulent claſſes from taxation; Calonne therefore propoſed to equaliſe public burdens by rendering the taxes general; to accompliſh this purpoſe, the nobility, clergy, and magiſtracies ſhould be no longer exempted, but contribute their ſhare to the exigencies of the ſtate; the officers under the crown were to be aſſeſſed; and there ſhould be a general impoſt on land, without excepting the poſſeſſions of any order or individual. Such a project, in whatſoever motives it originated, was certainly juſt in its principle, and efficient in its object, as a ſcheme of finance: as a meaſure of policy it was wiſe and equitable, ſince it propoſed to reſtore to the commons ſo great a part of their uſurped rights: but the miniſter did not

He propoſes an equaliſation of public burdens.

 ſhew

CHAP. XLIII. 1789.

ſhew much judgment and prudence in the means which he choſe for carrying his plan into execution. It was very improbable that the ariſtocratical corporations, to influence whom he had called the council of notables, would willingly recede from ſuch lucrative immunities; indeed, the notables themſelves conſiſted of members of the privileged orders, and might as a body be preſumed unfavourable to a project tending ſo much to diminiſh their corporate advantages. They actually proved very inimical to the plan, which they repreſented as merely a new expedient for getting immenſe ſums of money into the hands of government, to ſupply its extravagance and corruption; they refuſed to concur in the territorial impoſt, unleſs they were ſuffered to inveſtigate the paſt expences and accounts, and future eſtimates, as thereby only they could know how far public money had been, or was likely to be, applied for the national good. The privileged orders raiſed a general outcry againſt the man who had propoſed to aboliſh their immunities: they even perſuaded the other claſſes, that the ſole object of the miniſter was rapacity, for the purpoſes of embezzlement and peculation; that, ſo far from intending to lighten their burdens by his new ſyſtem of impoſt, he deſigned to load them with freſh taxes, and thus the ariſtocrates excited the hatred of the people againſt the miniſter, whoſe plan, if adopted and fairly executed, would have rendered to the people themſelves ſo eſſential a ſervice. Moreover, the queen was a great enemy to the miniſter, becauſe he attacked one of her favourites. The mild and compliant

He incenſes the privileged orders.

Outcry againſt the miniſter,

pliant Louis readily imbibed the prevailing ſentiment, and withdrew his confidence and regard from a man whom he ſaw diſtruſted and hated by ſo many others. Calonne, fearing a judicial proſecution while the minds of all ranks were ſo biaſſed againſt him, retired into England *. Meanwhile monſieur de Brienne †, archbiſhop of Thouloufe, a leading member of the notables, was appointed prime miniſter, and without attempting the radical reform which the exigency required, he propoſed and executed various partial improvements in the collection of taxes, and the management of the public money. It was manifeſt that a change ſo confined in principle and operation could not extricate the country from its preſent evils. By the new miniſter the aſſembly of notables was diſſolved ‡, and he thought himſelf obliged to have recourſe to the uſual mode of raiſing money by edicts. Among the meaſures was a double poll-tax, and a heavy ſtamp-duty. The parliament of Paris remonſtrated againſt the firſt ſubſidy, in terms very unlike the former language of their aſſemblies, even when they oppoſed the will of the king. Before they ſhould concur in raiſing money, they required to be informed of the real ſtate of the finances, and the purpoſes to which the new impoſts were to be applied; and they particularly ob-

CHAP. XLIII. 1789.

Diſgraced: he retires into baniſhment.

Brienne miniſter.

Trifling and inefficient reform.

Conteſts with the parliament of Paris.

* This miniſter has been charged with having amaſſed immenſe riches by plundering the public. He certainly lived in London, for ſeveral years, in magnificent ſplendor; but what his funds were, or how acquired, was never aſcertained.

† Bouillé on the French Revolution, p. 50.

‡ In the opinion of Bouillé, very unwiſely, p. 51.

CHAP. XLIII. 1789. Attempts of the crown to overawe the refractory, unsuccessful.

jected to the stamp-duty; their requisition not having been admitted, they refused to enregister the edict. The king finding them inflexible to persuasion, held a bed of justice, to compel them to registration. This procedure, hateful in the reign of Louis XV. was infinitely more odious at present, when the spirit of liberty was so much stronger and more generally diffused. The edict having been forcibly registered, the parliament PROTESTED, that not having been obtained by their approbation and consent, IT SHOULD NOT BE VALID; and that whoever attempted to put it in execution should be doomed to the gallies as a traitor. This resolute opposition was imitated by all the other parliaments. Matters now appeared to draw to a crisis; the alternative of the crown seemed to be, either to proceed to coërcion, or to relinquish for ever the long-usurped power of raising money by its own authority. On the other hand, the judicative bodies were determined to shew that they would not, without resistance, any longer permit an arbitrary invasion of property, however supported by precedent.

Remonstrance of the parliament of Paris.

On the 24th of July the parliament of Paris published a remonstrance*, highly celebrated for a forcible reasoning, a bold and animated eloquence, which clearly demonstrated and strongly impressed awful truths. After a happy peace that had lasted five years, they, from the revenue before possessed by the crown, had trusted that no fresh imposts would have been proposed; great, then was their surprise at the requisition of an additional tax so extensive, and

* See remonstrance, State Papers, July 24th 1787.

generally

generally odious. Minifters had never approached the throne with a voice of truth, but had difguifed from the king the actual ftate of his dominions, and the fentiments of his fubjects. The council of the notables had been the occafion of difcovering to the public the dreadful fituation of affairs, and the progreffive fteps of error, corruption, and vice, by which courtiers had reduced France to fuch a condition. Taxes were the contributions of citizens for their own private fecurity and the public fafety; if they exceeded thofe purpofes, they were inconfiftent with juftice and the good of the people, the fole objects of legitimate government. Neither parliaments, nor any other authority but the whole nation affembled, could fanction a new impoft. The nation only, being convened and inftructed in the true ftate of the finances, could extirpate the abufes that actually exifted, and offer refources to obviate fuch evils in future. If this remonftrance be confidered in relation to the rights of a free people, and to the actual abufes under the French government; it was firm, yet perfectly temperate and refpectful. Addreffed, however, to a monarch who had inherited arbitrary power, it appeared a prefumptuous encroachment. It was extremely natural for Louis to think himfelf rightfully entitled to the fway of his anceftors; to overlook the injuftice in which that dominion was founded, and the great change of popular fentiment from the time even of his laft predeceffor. Like Charles I. he prefumed a divine right to what his anceftors and he had poffeffed only by human fufferance; and, like Charles I. he did not difcern that the opinions and

 fentiments

CHAP. XLIII. 1789. ſentiments which had permitted thraldom, no longer exiſted among his ſubjects. Louis, however, had a much more formidable force than Charles, in which he conceived he might repoſe ſecure confidence. He therefore determined on coërcion; collected great bodies of troops round the metropolis; and ſent parties of ſoldiers to the houſe of every individual member of the parliament of Paris, to carry him in baniſhment to Troyes, about ſeventy miles from the capital, and not to ſuffer him to write or ſpeak to any perſon of his own family before his departure. Theſe orders were executed at the ſame inſtant, on the 18th of Auguſt, and by force the judicial body was prevented from proceeding in its official buſineſs. In the following month the preſident was diſpatched by the exiles to Verſailles, to repreſent to his majeſty the pernicious effects of the compulſory meaſures which he was then purſuing. After ſeveral audiences, inſtead of adhering to the hereditary maxims of arbitrary power, the king yielded to the dictates of his individual benignity and patriotiſm; he conſented to abandon the obnoxious attacks, and to ſuffer parliament to reſume its functions. Meanwhile the flame of liberty was burſting forth in various parts of the kingdom *. Other parliaments not only emulated, but ſurpaſſed the generous boldneſs of Paris, and with the right of property aſſerted the claims of perſonal ſecurity. The parliament of Grenoble declared *lettres de cachet*, or arbitrary impriſonment, to be totally unconſtitutional; and pronounced a decree,

* Annual Regiſter, 1787, chap. vii. paſſim.

rendering

rendering it capital for any perſon, under ANY authority, to attempt ſuch an act within that province. In all the populous towns, where there was the moſt ready and extenſive interchange of opinion and ſentiment; the conduct of government, once ſo ſacred in France, was openly diſcuſſed, and moſt ſeverely reprobated, both in diſcourſe and publications *. The king, in November, appeared to have changed his diſpoſition and intentions: meeting the parliament of Paris, he ſaid he had come to hear their opinions; but before they delivered them; to ſignify his own †. They ought to confine themſelves to the functions entruſted by the king to their predeceſſors: the expediency of calling public aſſemblies was a meaſure of which he was the ſole judge. He was about to iſſue an edict, creating for five ſucceſſive years a loan that would require no new impoſt. Permiſſion being given for every member to ſpeak without reſtraint, a warm debate on the regiſtration of the edict enſued in the preſence of the king; but at laſt his majeſty, ſuddenly riſing, commanded the decree to be regiſtered without delay. The duke of Orleans, firſt prince of the blood after the king's brothers, warmly oppoſed this order, as a direct infringement of parliamentary right; and proteſted againſt all the acts of the day, as thereby rendered void. His majeſty, aſtoniſhed at a proceeding ſo new to an abſolute prince, repeated his order, and quitted the aſſembly. The next day he baniſhed the duke and two of his moſt

Baniſhment of the active oppoſitioniſts.

* Bertrand de Moleville, introduction.

† State Papers, Nov. 19, 1787.

CHAP. XLIII. 1789.

active fupporters. The parliament, far from tamely fubmitting to this act of power, publifhed a very ftrong addrefs, which juftified the exiled members, avowed the higheft approbation of their conduct, and reprefented the dangerous confequences of fuch a reftriction on the neceffary freedom of fpeech. The king anfwered, that he had ftrong reafons for the banifhment of thofe members; with this affurance parliament ought to reft fatisfied; the more goodnefs he was difpofed to fhew to his parliaments, the more firmly he would approve himfelf if he faw his goodnefs abufed. Parliament replied in the bold tone of men determined to affert their freedom: "your parliament does not *folicit* favour, it DEMANDS juftice. No man ought to be condemned without a fair trial: arbitrary banifhments, arrefts, or imprifonments, conftitute no part of the legal prerogative of the French crown. It is in the name of thofe lawswhich preferve the empire, in the name of that liberty of which we are the refpectful interpreters and lawful mediators, in the name of your authority, of which we are the firft and moft confidential minifters, that we dare demand either the trial or the releafe of the duke of Orleans and the exiled magiftrates." This attack on a prerogative fo long exercifed by the court, and effential to the maintenance of arbitrary monarchy, was refifted by the king; and he told them, that what they demanded of his juftice depended on his will. This principle that would fubject the freedom and happinefs of millions to the will of an individual, though the foundation of French abfolute monarchy, the enlightened parliament totally condemned; they refufed

Bold tone of parliament, and forcible addrefs.

fused to purchase justice by concession; declared parliament would never cease to demand the impeachment or liberty of the persons in question, and would employ the same zeal and perseverance to ensure to every Frenchman the personal security promised by the laws, and due by the principles of the constitution. This patriotic assembly supported the claim in question, and urged new assertions, not for their own body alone, but for the whole nation. They published a remonstrance *, declaring that no taxes could be granted but by the consent of the people; they extended the same doctrine to the whole body of legislative power, insisting that no man ought to be imprisoned, dispossessed of his property or liberty, outlawed or banished, or in any way hurt or injured, unless through his own act, his representatives, or the law of the land †. The parliament ‡ of Paris vindicated those fundamental rights, which no time, nor precedent, nor statute, nor positive institution can abolish, which men always may reclaim when they will. They endeavoured from history

The parliament of Paris asserts the rights of a free people.

* State Papers, Nov. 23d, 1787.

† See this doctrine stated by Hume in his remarks on the great charter of England, Hist. vol. ii. p. 88.

‡ The provincial parliaments of France were originally courts of justice, possessing no share in the legislation, either as an order or as representatives of the people. From the time of cardinal Richelieu, the legislative as well as the executive authority was vested entirely in the crown. The practice of employing the parliaments to enregister the king's edicts, was never intended to convey any authority or force through these bodies; they were considered merely as notaries, to record and authenticate their existence, and thereby as well to promulgate them, as to prevent any

CHAP. XLIII. 1789.

history and authority to prove this popular consent to have been the foundation of laws in former times, before the subversion of the constitution under the house of Bourbon. The precedents which they quoted did not apply to the present situation, and indeed obscured instead of illustrating their claims. But as neither the justice or expediency of the doctrine rested upon former usage or authority, the irrelevancy of their citations affected neither the truth of their positions, nor the wisdom of their conduct.

Spirit of boundless innovation.

The spirit of liberty and reform, operating on the ingenious and volatile character of Frenchmen, and tinctured by the peculiar doctrines of late political philosophers, produced a disposition to innovation. Even at this period many reformers assumed a position, that every existing establishment was bad, and therefore that melioration consisted in a total change. The court imputed to parliaments the prevailing spirit, which these bodies rather expressed than incited; and, confounding the organs with the

any doubts being entertained by the public of their reality. The parliament, however, as their popularity and power increased, and times and circumstances proved favourable to the design, assumed a right of judging whether these edicts were injurious to the public. If they determined them to be hurtful, they by a legal fiction pretended that being contrary to the welfare of the people, and contrary to the king's wisdom, justice, or clemency, they did not believe them to be the king's real acts, but considered them as an imposition practised by his ministers; and on this ground they presented memorials or remonstrances to the king, placing in the strongest colours they could all the evil consequences which they presumed would attend their being passed into laws. See Annual Register, 1789.

cause

caufe, formed a project for annulling the authority which was recently affumed by thefe bodies. Profeffing to gratify the popular paffion for reform, minifters propofed a general amendment in the codes both of civil and criminal juftice. For this purpofe, a tribunal was to be inftituted, endowed with fuch powers as would carry back the parliaments to the original principles of their inftitution, and reduce them to the condition of mere courts of juftice*. The members of this body were all to be chofen by the king†: their number, and every circumftance relative to their meeting, was to depend on the royal will. Profound fecrecy was obferved in conducting this project: the edicts were privately printed at the royal prefs, and intended to be prefented, on on the fame day to all the parliaments in France, and the regiftration was to be enforced by foldiers. The fcheme, however, being difcovered before it was ripe for execution, by M. d'Eprefmenil, was by him communicated to the parliament of Paris, of which he was a member. This body, meeting on the 3d of May 1788, iffued a declaration, ftating a report of a confpiracy, by the court, againft the authority of parliaments, the interefts and liberties of the nation. Detailing the alleged rights of parliaments, and the purpofes both of their general be-

* Bouillé, 54.

† They were to have confifted of princes of the blood; of peers of the realm; of great officers of ftate; of marfhals of France; of governors of provinces; of knights of different orders; of members of council; and of a deputation of one member from each parliament of the kingdom, and two from the chamber of accounts and fupply. Annual Regifter, 1789, c. i.

ftowal

CHAP. XLIII. 1789.

ftowal and recent exercife, they declared their refolution of furrendering their privileges, not to minifters, or any new courts eftablifhed by their influence, but to the king himfelf, and the ftates general. Though Louis had, as an act of grace, liberated Orleans and the magiftrates, he ftill determined to fupport the principle of arbitrary imprifonment. Agreeably to this refolution, he ordered M. D'Epréfmenil, and M. De Monfambert, two of the moft active members of the parliament, to be arrefted in their houfes. Though thefe patriots evaded immediate caption, by concealing themfelves from the foldiers, they difdained to abftain from their duty in parliament. That body, informed of the attempt, fent a deputation to remonftrate with the king; but the delegates were not admitted. A regiment of guards furrounded the court of parliament; its commander entering the affembly, demanded the two magiftrates whom the king had ordered to be arrefted: a profound filence for fome time enfued; at laft, the prefident rifing, with the acclamations of the whole body, replied, every member here, is a D'Epréfmenil and a Monfambert*. Thefe magiftrates, however, furrendered themfelves, and were led off to prifon amidft the loud execrations of the people. The king, on the 8th of May, held a bed of juftice to introduce the intended reforms: he inveighed againft the undutiful behaviour of parliament, and declared his determination to fupprefs fuch exceffes, in a few

* Annual Regifter, 1789, chap. i. Mackintofh's Vindiciæ Gallicæ.

of

of the magiſtrates; yet in general he preferred prevention to penal animadverſion; he then announced the heads of the new conſtitution which his chancellor fully detailed *. Parliament the following day entered againſt theſe proceedings a proteſt, repeating the ſubſtance of their former remonſtrances, and declaring individually and aggregately that they would accept of no employment under the projected eſtabliſhment. This proteſtation was ſeconded by a great body of the members; and ſo generally was the new ſpirit now diſſeminated, that even many of the clergy declared concurrence in their ſentiments and reſolution. Thus encouraged, parliament publiſhed a ſtill ſtronger memorial than any which they had before iſſued; preremptorily declaring their inflexible determination to perſevere in their paſt meaſures. Through all the kingdom, public bodies, ſpontaneous aſſociations, and private individuals, appeared agitated by the ſame ſpirit. The court, on the other hand, proceeded to coërcive meaſures; the governor of Paris entering the parliament-houſe, took poſſeſſion of all the papers and archives; having locked the doors, and ſtamped them with the king's ſeal, he carried away the keys. All the other parliaments in the kingdom were ſuſpended from their functions, and forbidden under the ſevereſt penalties to hold any meetings. In this criſis, the queſtion now evidently lay between the eſtabliſhment of liberty, or of complete deſpotiſm *. Brienne was by no means capable of conducting affairs in ſo difficult a ſitua-

Arbitrary ſuſpenſion of the parliaments.

National ferment.

* State Papers, May 8th. † Bouillé, paſſim.

tion;

CHAP. XLIII.

1789.

Unfitness of Brienne for his office.

tion; he possessed neither the sagacity which could have discovered the force of a general spirit diffused through a people of such boldness and energy, nor the wisdom which, to a certain extent, would have gratified the national desire, in order to prevent the national violence; and moderated the regal power to preserve its essential and useful prerogative. He was no less deficient in that boldness of design, and vigour of execution, which only could have overborne the determination of the people, and crushed their rights. The ready and willing tool of arbitrary power in its usual and established exercise, he possessed neither invention nor courage to be its counsellor or champion in untried dangers. The conduct of government was a motley mixture of outrage and irresolution, violence and feebleness: for a short time the court persisted in coërcive efforts, both in Paris and other provinces; and in Dauphiny, Languedoc and Britany, the parliaments were exiled, but the rage of the people broke out in riots, which produced disorder and bloodshed. In some instances it appeared, that the soldiers being commanded to quell the disturbances, manifested an extreme unwillingness to act against their countrymen. The king was at this time in the greatest pecuniary distress, which he saw the people would not voluntarily relieve: nothing, he perceived, short of military execution would enforce the obnoxious edicts. Destitute of money, he lost a great part of the influence which through donative he had possessed; many of the nobility, from the extravagance of their ancestors, their own, or both, were mere dependents on the bounty of the

Distressed situation of the king.

crown;

crown; and in the poverty of the king they saw themselves precluded from the usual resource of titled insignificance and beggary; accustomed to luxury and splendor, and the eleemosynary fountain of their prodigality and ostentation no longer flowing, they from a special cause became infected with the general discontent; poor lords, who had subsisted by the royal dole, forsook the king when he had no dole to bestow *. The household of the monarch, extremely magnificent and expensive, had supported vast numbers of officers and attendants; in the king's distresses four hundred of these were necessarily dismissed; many of them, no longer maintained in idleness and pomp, turned against the hand which had given them food while it had food to give, and from the most despicable and unworthy motives added to the number of those who opposed the king's government from generous and patriotic principles. The discontents rising from political causes were enhanced by a physical calamity; a dreadful hurricane of wind, rain, hail, thunder and lightening, on the 13th of July, assailing the land, destroyed the fruits and corn. Want and misery were soon felt through the kingdom; and the capital itself was apprehensive of a famine. The dearness of provisions induced or compelled many families to dismiss their servants, and thus increased the number of the idle, distressed, and dissatisfied. To aggravate the danger which menaced the court from so many concurring causes, the wild theories of sophistical projectors, equally inimical to religion as to regular government, to

* Annual Register, 1789.

CHAP. XLIII. 1789. beneficial liberty as to abſolute monarchy, were faſt gaining ground. In the latter end of 1788, the opponents of the king conſiſted of two great claſſes:—firſt, the champions of rational liberty, determined not only to prevent future encroachments, but to correct paſt uſurpations; to change the government from an abſolute to a limited monarchy; to render its object the general happineſs, inſtead of the pleaſure of individuals, its rule the national voice, inſtead of the monarch's will. The other claſs conſiſted of thoſe who, not contented with an alteration of meaſures, ſought an utter ſubverſion of the eſtabliſhment, and promoted doctrines and ſchemes, which would deſtroy all government: between theſe two extremes there were various gradations, from the ſupporters of limited monarchy to the levellers of all ranks and orders. The principal actors were at this time chiefly of the former diviſion, or at leaſt more nearly allied to it than to the latter; but ſubordinate agents, eſpecially many of the literary men employed as efficacious inſtruments by the leaders, were cloſely connected with the votaries of boundleſs revolution. Many of the writers, in combatting abſolute power to aſſiſt parliaments and vindicate the rights of the people, attacked all exiſting forms and eſtabliſhments, and looſened the great cements of ſociety *.

The miniſter ſeeing his ſovereign in ſuch calamitous circumſtances, was more mindful of his own ſafety, than gratitude to his maſter; he reſigned his office, and ſought refuge in Italy. Louis finding his own diſtreſſes, and thoſe of his kingdom,

* Bertrand de Moleville on the French Revolution, v. i. c. 1.

multi-

CHAP. XLIII. 1789.

multiplying, and that the arbitrary meaſures which were ſuggeſted by his miniſters were producing effects ſo different from their predictions, and his wiſhes, reſolved to adopt a new plan, more conſiſtent with his own benignant character. To gratify the nation, and procure a counſellor likely to relieve the country and himſelf, he determined to recal the celebrated Mr. Neckar. From this gentleman, ſo univerſally popular, and, indeed, the idol of their adoration, the warm fancies of Frenchmen expected impoſſibilities. They ſeemed to have conceived that he poſſeſſed a kind of magical power, which could pay off an immenſe public debt without money, and ſupply twenty-five millions of people with corn and bread. But Neckar by no means poſſeſſed thoſe extraordinary talents which were once imputed to him by the grateful ſubjects of Louis, and by that monarch himſelf. Strict morals and integrity even his adverſaries * aſcribed to this celebrated economiſt; but the impartial philoſopher † readily diſcovered that he was a mere man of detail; a ſkilful and upright ſteward, but not a profound ſtateſman. "Neckar (ſays Bouillé) viewed France with the eyes of a citizen of Geneva." Native of a republic, he was warmly attached to the rights and intereſts of the people; of plebeian extraction, he too little regarded the diſtinctions of rank and of birth, and eſtimated them by the abſtract principles of equality, inſtead of the actual inſtitutions of an eſtabliſhed government in a great and powerful nation: his ſentiments and habits of thinking were inimical to the privileged orders.

He reſolves to recal Mr. Neckar,

* Bouillé, page 70. † Adam Smith.

CHAP. XLIII. 1789.

Neckar was, individually, a man of immenſe riches; during a conſiderable part of his life, he had been chiefly converſant with monied capitaliſts, and naturally attributed more than its due ſhare of importance to the diſtinction of wealth: hence, in every regulation which he ſhould deſire to frame, farmers of the revenue, contractors, bankers, and merchants, were likely to be more conſidered than the clergy or nobility: and from theſe various cauſes Neckar was chiefly attached to the third eſtate. With ſuch notions and predilections he came to the adminiſtration of France, at a ſeaſon which required a ſtateſman and lawgiver that could ſurvey the whole circumſtances and intereſts of the empire without leaning either to clergy or laity, nobility or plebeians, to riches or to birth; and would provide impartially and effectually for the welfare of the whole.

On Mr. Neckar's appointment, the chief perſons of Brienne's party were diſmiſſed from office. The parliament of Paris was reſtored to its functions, met in the middle of September, and cauſed all the king's late decrees, which they repreſented as unconſtitutional, to be publicly burnt. Mr. Neckar found the finances in ſo diſordered a condition, that he adviſed a convocation of the States General as the only effectual meaſure for relief. He propoſed, however, as a preliminary, to ſummon a new convocation of notables, who ſhould deliver their opinion concerning the compoſition of the States General, the qualifications of the electors, and of the elected; the mode of election, the proportion of delegates to the wealth and populouſneſs of the ſeve-

who counſels the convocation of the States General.

ral

ral diſtricts; alſo, the amount and relation of members to be ſent by the different orders, and the inſtructions which they were to receive from their conſtituents; and the 1ſt of May 1789, was the day appointed for the meeting of the States General.

CHAP. XLIII. 1789.

Queſtion concerning the conſolidation of the orders,

Two great queſtions exiſted between the three orders, the nobles, the clergy, and the commons; firſt, whether all the deputies ſhould meet in one aſſembly, wherein the concentrated power of the States General ſhould reſide, or whether they ſhould be divided as they had been at the laſt meeting in 1614, into three chambers, through which a reſolution muſt be carried (at leaſt two of them) before it became the acknowledged act of the States *. Secondly, whether the number of deputies from each of the orders ſhould be three hundred, as in 1614, or the clergy and nobles ſhould retain their former numbers, and the commons ſend ſix hundred, ſo as to equal the amount of the other two eſtates: this was called the double repreſentation of the people. Theſe two queſtions agitated the public with great violence: if they voted by orders, a double repreſentation would be of no effect, as the two eſtates could out-vote the three; therefore, the double repreſentation was propoſed on the ſuppoſition that they were to vote by numbers. The arguments for three aſſemblies were founded on ancient uſage; for one, upon juſtice and expediency. By the ſupporters of the

* Voting *by heads* was the term applied to the firſt of theſe alternatives, and voting *by orders* to the ſecond.

CHAP. XLIII. 1789.

last it was contended, that unless there was but one assembly the power of the commons would really be nugatory. The clergy and nobles would coalesce together to defend their immunities against the commons, who, in their own, maintained the general interests of the people. If their numbers were not equal to those of the other two orders, they could effect no purpose of important improvement. The aristocratical estates prevailing among the notables, that council voted for separate chambers. In their opinion concurred the Parliament of Paris, which, though desirous of repressing the power of the crown, was inimical to the exaltation of the commons. Mr. Neckar inclined to the third estate, but at the same time professed a desire to preserve the necessary and useful prerogatives of the crown; but the means were not wisely adapted to the end. Neckar reasoned like an accountant rather than a statesman, and treated a question for constituting the legislation of a mighty nation, as if he had been summing up the items of a day-book in order to make an entry into a ledger: he thought that by equalizing the *numbers* of the commons and the two privileged orders, the one would balance the other; the States General, like the parliament of England, would consist of two great branches of law-givers, which, together with the king, might produce mutual support and reciprocal controul, therefore he promoted the double representation. But though there would be thus an *arithmetical* equality between the two first orders and the third, perfectly satisfactory to an auditor of accounts, there was by no means that POLITICAL equality

and the double representation

equality which would have satisfied a wise law-giver, who proposed to establish an effectual balance in a constitution. If Neckar had discerned the actual state and party, he would have found that the partizans of the privileged orders among the commons were very few, that the partizans of the commons among the privileged orders were very many *, and therefore, that if they were equal in number, the commons would engross the power which he proposed to be separated. Intending that the aristocracy and democracy should be a mutual equipoise, Mr. Neckar, to whose opinion the king implicitly resigned himself, in no small degree contributed to the destruction of the one and predominancy of the other. The minister entirely neglected the question concerning the consolidation of the orders; an omission which prevented a corrective of the power which the commons were to obtain by the double representation. The parliament of Paris found they had lost their popularity by taking the side of the other privileged orders, and that they might regain the favour of the commons, published a decree which vindicated as the rights of a Frenchman, all the leading objects that have been attained, or indeed sought, by the best and most admired constitutions. The rights claimed, nearly the same as those secured to Englishmen, were such as must have contented all who understood both the extent and bounds of useful liberty. The chief heads of the decree were, that no assembly could be considered as national, unless it ascertained the following points in favour of the people: the periodical returns of the States

* See Annual Register 1789.

CHAP. XLIII. 1789.

General; no ſubſidy to be allowed, unleſs granted by the States; no law to be executed by the courts of juſtice, unleſs ratified by the States; the ſuppreſſion of all taxes which marked the exemption of certain orders; equalization of impoſts; the reſponſibility of miniſters; the right of the States General to bring accuſations before the courts of juſtice for crimes; the abolition of arbitrary impriſonment, by bringing before the proper judges every man who was detained; and confirming the lawful freedom of the preſs. Theſe claims were far from anſwering the ideas of liberty now ſpread through France. The decree was regarded with indifference, and the parliament henceforward dwindled into inſignificance. The year 1789 began with very great diſſenſions between the orders. The nobility and clergy, which, in 1787, had refuſed to part with their immunities, now expreſſed their willingneſs to take an equal ſhare of the public burdens. The commons, far from being ſatisfied with this ſubmiſſion, propoſed to overthrow all privileges whatſoever; to reject every claim founded on ancient uſage, or on compact; to make general equality the ſtandard of private or public right. The writers of the time employed their ſeparate and joint ingenuity in attacking the rank and titles of the nobles, and the tenure by which many of them held their eſtates; and French liberty, in the beginning of 1789, was mingled with principles ſubverſive of rank and of property. Until the meeting of the States, the queſtion concerning the amalgamation of the orders agitated the nobles and commons, while the clergy appeared undecided, and ready to join the party which ſhould prevail. It had been cuſtomary in France, in former times, when

The commons of France already deſire a licence too great for uſeful liberty.

CHAP. XLIII. 1789.

when the States General met, for the orders in each district to deliver instructions to their respective delegates. This practice being now revived, the directions given to the deputies of the nobles, and to the deputies of the commons, by their respective constituents, very fully manifested the diversity of the spirit which actuated the three bodies. The instructions of the nobility enjoined their representatives to urge a reform of the constitution; to strengthen the securities for property, liberty, and life; and to surrender their pecuniary exemptions, but not resign their feudal rights, nor to consent to a consolidation of the orders. The commons, in their mandates to their commissioners, instructed them to insist on the abolition of all distinctions, the abandonment of feudal rights, and the resolution of the different states into one mass. The injunctions of the nobility tended, if followed, to establish a moderate and limited government, securing civil rights to all classes of subjects, but preserving a distinction of orders and a subordination of ranks. The injunctions of the commons, previous to their first assembly, tended to overturn the other states under the weight of a democracy *.

Instructions from constituents to delegates.

On the 1st of May 1789, after a cessation of 175 years, the States General of France met for the first time. The parties which had prevailed through-

Meeting of the states.

* Mr. Lally Tolendal, in exhibiting the different views of the parties of this time, observes, the commons wished to conquer, the nobles wished to preserve what they already possessed; the clergy waited to see which side would be victorious, in order to join the conquerors.

CHAP. XLIII. 1789.

out the kingdom, appeared in the States General, and ranged themſelves into three great diviſions. The firſt was the ariſtocratic party, determined to ſupport the ancient form and mode of procedure, by a ſeparation of the States into three chambers. This claſs was conſiderable from the rank, talents, and ſituation of its members. The ſecond diviſion was that of the moderate party; its members were, on the one hand, averſe to aſſemblies of three ſeparate orders, as tending to throw the legiſlative power too much into the hands of the privileged ſtates, and, inſtead of an unlimited monarchy, to eſtabliſh an uncontrouled ariſtocracy; on the other, they were inimical to the confuſion of the orders, as tending, inſtead of reforming, to ſubvert the government. Theſe were deſirous of forming the nobles and clergy into one houſe, upon a principle of reciprocal controul, analogous to the Britiſh conſtitution. The third diviſion was the great and formidable democratic party, ſeeking and tending to overbear all ranks and diſtinctions. In this claſs were to be numbered ſome of the moſt conſpicuous men of the other orders. The extraordinary abilities of Mirabeau were employed againſt that eſtate to which he himſelf belonged. The firſt prince of the blood was active in promoting factions tending to ſubvert the monarchy from which he derived his elevated rank and immenſe poſſeſſions *. Againſt the

* The yearly income of the Duke of Orleans was eſtimated at half a million ſterling. A conſiderable part of this revenue was employed in acquiring popularity, and forming, from the idle and profligate rabble through the provinces, but eſpecially in

the clergy appeared the Bishop of Autun, carrying with him a great body of his brethren, and prepared to join the most violent commons in their democratic excesses. The Abbe Sieyes, an eminent disciple of the new philosophy, penetrating, crafty, and versatile, brought all his ability and address to support the faction which his discernment easily perceived about to be paramount. The literary men, a great and powerful class in circumstances that so much depended on public opinion, ranged themselves under the standard of the commons, pursuing measures so inimical to that tranquillity and prosperity which best nourish the pursuits of literature. The monied capitalists, proud of their wealth, and envious of the rank which their opulence could not attain, were foremost in instigating measures tending to the destruction of that property which only could prevent them from insignificance. Besides these classes, the third division included numbers of profligate spendthrifts, abounding in France, as in all luxurious countries, who wished for a change by which they hoped to be better, and knew they could not be worse.

Speech of the king.

The States being met, his majesty, in a speech from the throne, mentioned his reasons for convoking the assembly; he noticed the restless spirit of innovation, and the general discon-

in the city of Paris, a numerous body of retainers, ready to undertake any service, however desperate, at his instance. If his views, as has been often asserted, were directed to the highest pinnacle of ambition, by a fatality which often accompanies wickedness, the measures, which he pursued for the destruction of another, destroyed himself.

tent

CHAP. XLIII. 1789.

tent which prevailed among his people. A great object of the ſtates, he truſted, would be to remove thoſe evils; and they would manifeſt in their proceedings that loyalty and attachment to the monarchy from which France derived ſuch glory and benefit. The chancellor ſpoke of the advantages which accompanied a limited government, equally diſtant from deſpotiſm and anarchy. Mr. Neckar then riſing, excited in the audience the higheſt expectation. From him all parties truſted for the moſt full and accurate information concerning every important department of public affairs; ſtrong practical reaſoning, which would demonſtrate what was wiſe and right to be done at ſuch a criſis; with manly eloquence to inculcate the neceſſity of correſpondent conduct; but all were totally diſappointed: his ſpeech was looſe and declamatory, abounding in general maxims of morality and politics, which were obviouſly true, but in no way illuſtrated the momentous ſubjects of deliberation; and ſentimental effuſions, that aſſerted the wiſhes of the ſpeaker for the happineſs of France, without explaining any means for its attainment. On the great ſubject of conſolidation he ſaid nothing deciſive, he merely expreſſed a deſire that the matter might be accommodated. Appointed by his ſovereign to addreſs the national repreſentatives, who were aſſembled to deliberate on great public difficulties, he neither ſtated facts, nor propoſed means leading to extrication; his harangue was totally inadequate to the office which he was choſen to diſcharge. The miniſtry were no leſs feeble and indeciſive in their conduct than their language. The king at this time poſſeſſed

Of Neckar.

all the legal authority of the kingdom; and though the ſtates were met, they were not yet conſtituted, as the writs of election had not been examined. He, by his eſtabliſhed authority might have inſtituted concerning their ſeſſions, any regulations which ſhould be conformable to ancient precedent and uſage; and to have refuſed compliance with his directions would have been rebellion. Notwithſtanding his poſſeſſion of this power, his miniſters moſt impolitically neglected the exerciſe of it to prevent the confuſion of the orders, and thereby ſuffered the ſtates to become a democratical aſſembly. The verification of their powers* afforded the firſt occaſion to the commons of inſiſting that they ſhould meet in one chamber. Encouraged by their own ſtrength, and the backwardneſs of the miniſters, they very boldly aſſerted, that unleſs the writs were verified in their preſence, they could not admit their holders to a ſeat in the aſſembly, and that both nobles and clergy would be illegal meetings. The clergy wavered; many of the nobility were firm in maintaining the rights of a ſeparate verification, but there were great diſſenſions in that body. The commons, on the other hand,

Diſunion and indeciſion of the nobles and clergy.

* Each member was obliged, before the commencement of public buſineſs, to preſent his writ of election upon the table of the chamber to which he belonged. Commiſſaries were then appointed by each order to examine the authenticity of all the writs immediately belonging to itſelf; and until this buſineſs was finiſhed, which uſually took up ſeveral days, the States General were deſtitute of all legal authority whatſoever. The ſanction of theſe commiſſaries to the authenticity of the writs, afforded what was called the *verification of powers.*

were

CHAP. XLIII. 1789.

The commons declare themselves a national assembly.

were united. Mr. Neckar proposed conciliatory measures, which, from their indecisiveness, satisfied neither party. The nobles remaining inflexible, the commons, by a still bolder stretch of their power and influence, declared that they would constitute themselves into an active assembly, and proceed to legislative business. Many of the clergy, seeing the commons prevalent, flocked to their hall, and were most joyfully received. The commons executed the bold design which they had formed, and constituted themselves into a meeting which they denominated the NATIONAL ASSEMBLY. This body so formed by its own act, rapidly advanced in the assumption of power. On the 17th of June they published a decree, intimating that they possessed the sovereign authority, and exercised the same by a very popular act, declaring all existing taxes to be illegal*. The king was alarmed at proceedings which changed the constitution, and tended speedily to draw the supreme authority into the democratic vortex; and began to be dissatisfied with his ministers, to whose irresolution and inaction, he now imputed the progress of ambitious violence. The princes and other votaries of the old government, exhorted him to vigorous measures †; they advised him to hold a royal session in the hall of the States General, which by assembling would suspend the meeting of that body. The king agreed to follow the advice, and on the 20th of June he issued a proclamation appointing the

* Bertrand, vol. I. 69.

† Bertrand, chap. II.

22d for that purpose. The majority of the clergy having now agreed to join the commons, the members of the third estate repaired to the hall. The king having appointed the same day for the royal session, the guards were ordered to keep that apartment clear until the arrival of his majesty. As the members of the assembly came to the door, they were refused admittance by the soldiers; the commons, from so violent an act, apprehending an immediate dissolution, retired to an old tennis-court, where they bound themselves by a solemn oath never to part until the constitution was completed. The majority of the clergy now joined the commons, and met them in St. Louis's church, on the 23d. The royal session being opened, his majesty proposed the outlines of a new constitution: he engaged to establish no fresh tax, nor to prolong an old impost beyond the term assigned by the laws, without the consent of the representatives of the nation; he renounced the right of borrowing money, unless with the approbation of the states; there should be an end of pecuniary exemptions; and *lettres de cachet* should cease, with some modifications. He condemned the late decree of the commons, which assumed by their own sole act, the whole legislative power of the kingdom; and concluded that none of the laws established in the present States General could ever be altered, but by the free consent of future States General, and that they should be considered as equally sacred with all other national properties. On the other hand, he declared that all tithes and feudal rents should

CHAP. XLIII. 1789.

ſhould be accounted property, and therefore ſacred; and that the ſtates ſhould be aſſembled in three chambers inſtead of one. The manner of the addreſs by no means ſuited the conciliatory profeſſions, nor indeed the ſubſtance of the propoſition. It frequently introduced the king's will as the foundation of grants which in a government intended to be free were RIGHTS, not *favours*. In themſelves, however, the propoſitions were ſuch as a few years before, political ſagacity could have not conceived that a king of France would offer to his ſubjects. His majeſty commanded them to ſeparate, and to meet the next day in the halls of their reſpective orders. Equitable as the plan was in itſelf, it required little penetration to perceive, that it would by no means meet the ideas of the commons; that the magiſterial expreſſions would render it ſtill more unpalatable, and were therefore extremely unwiſe. The commons liſtened in haughty ſilence, while the plan was reading; and as ſoon as the king departed, abſolutely refuſed to break up their ſeſſion. The king's attendants having reminded them of his majeſty's order, the preſident anſwered, THE NATION ASSEMBLED HAS NO ORDERS TO RECEIVE*. They paſſed a reſolution declaring the adherence of the aſſembly to its former decree; and another pronouncing the perſons of the deputies

* Mirabeau, who through ſome acts and ſome ſuſpicions had nearly loſt his popularity, had the fortune upon this occaſion to recover it with increaſe, by the impetuoſity with which he told the king's attendants, that nothing but the points of bayonets ſhould force them out of their chamber.

ſacred and inviolable. The populace at Verſailles became violent in behalf of the commons. At Paris the ferment was ſtill more outrageous †, and increaſed in proportion to the attempts of either the nobles or the court, to oppoſe or controul the pretenſions of the third eſtate. The commons now found themſelves ſo ſtrong in the public ſupport, that they affected to treat the king's ſyſtem and declaration as too inſignificant to merit conſideration or anſwer. On the 24th of June, the Count de Clermont moved, that the nobles ſhould unite with the commons, and was ably joined by Monſieur de Lally Tollendal; but the majority of nobles, would not bend to a propoſal which the natural prepoſſeſſion of birth, rank, and cuſtom, taught them to deem humiliating. Many of that body, however, were either connected with the popular party, or convinced that inflexibility would anſwer no purpoſe; and therefore joined the aſſembly. The people became hourly more

Popular violence.

Firmneſs in the nobles.

† No claſs of rioters was more active in the French capital than the (poiſſardes) fiſh-women; who, in addition to the violence of their ſiſters in our own metropolis, poſſeſſed all the Gallic vivacity. Far exceeding the Billingſgate fair, inſtead of confining themſelves to volubility of invective, from time immemorial they had acted a diſtinguiſhed part in Pariſian mobs, and were noted for their ferocious actions. On ſo great an occaſion they were not ſlow in diſplaying their zeal and their talents. The ſex likewiſe afforded another claſs of auxiliaries, more inſinuating, leſs ſavage in appearance, but not leſs effective. Theſe were the courtezans, whoſe numbers were immenſe in that profligate city. One of the chief ſcenes of diſorder and enormity was the garden of the Duke of Orleans, whither the mob daily reſorted, where hired orators inflamed them to every act of atrocious violence.

CHAP. XLIII. 1789. violent against the majority of the nobles, whom they deemed refractory: outrage and bloodshed were expected. The members of this self-created assembly had far exceeded the instructions of their constituents; in assuming the legislative power, they were not the representatives of the people; they were a strong and numerous faction, that usurped the office of lawgivers by force; by force only could usurpation have been opposed. Concession never did nor can avert the encroachments of determined ambition. This was the language which the princes of the blood*, and all the firmest friends of the monarchy held; it was indeed not the language of choice, but necessity. From the attempt of the popular faction to seize the direction of the empire, the simple question with the votaries of monarchy was, shall we defend ourselves or be overwhelmed? There was no alternative. The king was uniformly impelled by humanity, and in the mildness of his disposition, seeking the good of his people, he deviated from that firmness by which only their welfare could have been effectually secured. To avert the dangers whch he conceived to impend over the unyielding nobles, he entreated that order to give up their judgment and determination to the wishes of the governing faction. On the 27th of June he sent the following message to the nobles, by their president the Duke of Luxemburgh: "From the fidelity and affection of the order of which you are president, I expect its union with the other two. I have reflected upon it, and am determined to make every sacri-

The king exhorts them to yield.

* See Bertrand.

fice,

fice *rather than that a single man should perish on my account.* Tell the order of the nobility, therefore, that I entreat them to join the other two estates; and if this be not enough, I command them to do it as their king—it is my will. If there be one of its members who believes himself bound by his instructions, his oath, or his honour, to remain in the chamber, let me know: I will go and sit by him, and die with him if it be necessary!" A long and violent debate took place, in which the Duke of Luxemburgh read a letter from the Count d'Artois, intimating that the king's person might be exposed to immediate danger, if the popular fury was roused by their refusal. The question of union was at last carried in the affirmative, and the nobles repaired to the hall of the commons that evening. The proposed meeting of the orders became a popular convention; and, from this moment, the constitution of France may be considered as actually changed, although the commencement of the revolution be dated from a subsequent period. The popular leaders now saw that imperious demand would extort concession; and on this discovery they formed their judgment, and regulated their conduct.

CHAP. XLIII. 1789. At his majesty's instance they unite with the commons.

The people, seeing the orders united, believed the happiness of France on the eve of completion. All parties agreed on the necessity of correcting the ancient government; the only difference appeared to be respecting the extent to which the reform should be carried, and the means that should be employed. It was hoped that the presence of the nobility and clergy, containing, besides rank, so

CHAP. XLIII. 1789.

much of talents and of learning, might reftrain the intemperate heat of republicans, while the ardent zeal and bold freedom of the commons might infpire and invigorate the other ftates; and that thus they fhould eftablifh liberty without licentioufnefs; but thefe expectations were entirely difappointed. The conduct of the court, having before exhibited fuch a mixture of rafhnefs and timidity, violence and irrefolution, confiftent in weaknefs and fluctuation only, foon prefented appearances that excited confiderable alarm, but much greater fufpicion. The ftates-general, fince their confolidation, had been more moderate than at any other period of their feffion. They had already appointed a committee to prepare materials for the new conftitution: Monfieurs Lally Tollendal, and Mounier, two of the moft able and temperate leaders, were of this committee; and entertained flattering hopes that the moderation would prove general. The demagogues very early endeavoured to cultivate a clofe connection between their votaries and the foldiers, and fuccefsfully inftilled the popular doctrines into thefe troops. In feducing the army from obedience to their king, the democrats very liberally employed wine, gold, and women, of which laft article they had an abundant fupply by their alliance with the harlots of Paris. The foldiers now having their profeffional daringnefs and debauchery, without the profeffional reftraints of fubordination and military difcipline, totally difregarded their officers; left their barracks without leave, repaired to the Palais Royal, joined and even headed the mob in their

The foldiers are infected with the popular enthufiafm.

1789. Infubordination and licentioufnefs.

their moft enormous exceffes, while hand bills and ballads were compofed and difperfed, to fpread the flames. The foldiers vied with the populace in their democratic exclamations and other exceffes: the moft daring and refractory being committed to prifon, the people flew in crowds to the jail, forced the gates, liberated the captives, and demanded for them a free pardon. The national affembly endeavoured to accommodate the matter, by exhorting the Parifians to tranquillity, and the king to clemency. His majefty having no efficient force at hand was obliged to comply, and thus ended military difcipline and civil government at Paris.

The king orders troops to approach Paris.

The diforderly ftate of the metropolis, and the unfitnefs of the guards for re-eftablifhing tranquillity, were oftenfible reafons for bringing a great armed force from the different provinces. In the beginning of July about thirty-five thoufand men drew near Paris and Verfailles. On the 10th of the month the national affembly prefented very ftrong remonftrances to the king on the approach of the forces. He anfwered that he had no other motive for his conduct, than the neceffity of eftablifhing and maintaining good order in the capital. He was fo far from intending to interrupt the proceedings of the affembly, that if the prefence of the foldiery gave them umbrage, he was ready to transfer the ftates-general to Noyon, or Soiffons, and repair himfelf to fome place in its vicinity, where he could maintain a ready communication with the legiflative body. The moderate members were willing to accede to this propofal; but the popular leaders

CHAP. XLIII. 1789.

were aware of the ſtrength which they derived from the capital, and would not leave its vicinity. They either repoſed, or profeſſed to repoſe, no confidence in the king's aſſurances, and gave out that a plot was formed by the court to cruſh the naſcent liberties of Frenchmen. The king now appeared evidently to liſten to the ſupporters of the old government, and withdrew his confidence from thoſe counſellors who had been favorable to popular meaſures. The partizans of the ancient monarchy ſeverely reprobated the conduct of Neckar, to whoſe republican ſentiments and counſels they imputed the degraded ſtate of royal authority: and ſtrongly urged the king to diſcharge a ſervant who from either deſign or imprudence* had endangered the monarchy. Accordingly on the 11th of July Mr. Neckar was diſmiſſed † from adminiſtration, and ordered to quit the kingdom, and with him the other members of the cabinet were alſo diſcharged from their employments. Mr. de Breteuil, a zealous friend of the old government, was appointed prime miniſter, and Marſhal Broglio, who maintained

M. Neckar diſmiſſed.

* Bertrand, vol. 1, p. 191.

† Mr. *Neckar* kept his diſgrace a profound ſecret, even from his wife, and received company that day at dinner, as uſual. Thoſe who dined with him did not perceive the leaſt alteration in his countenance. After dinner his wife and daughter invited him to take a ride to the Val, a country houſe ſituated in the foreſt of *St. Germain*, belonging to Madame *de Beauvais*, an intimate friend of Mrs. Neckar's. He conſented, and went into the carriage with his wife, but inſtead of going to the Val, he took the road to Bruſſels, in order to be the ſooner out of the kingdom.

the

the fame fentiments, commander in chief. On Sunday the 12th of July, thefe changes being reported at Paris, caufed the greateft defpair and fury, and riots prevailed in every quarter. The rafhnefs of the prince de Lambefe, who, endeavouring to difperfe a riotous body of populace, wounded with his own hand one who was faid to be only a fpectator, not only increafed the tumult, but haftened the general infurrection for which the people were fo ripe. The mob, with clubs, fpits, and fuch weapons as they could procure, rufhed upon Lambefe's troops, and put them to flight, not without killing fome of the number*. The following night Paris was filled with a dread of flaughter from the army, and of general plunder

* This tranfaction of Lambefe's appears to have been without any orders from the minifters, or any concert with the other military commanders. Though there were feveral regiments of foot ftationed clofe to Paris, none of them ftirred to affift and protect Lambefe's corps. The total inaction of the troops, both on the fucceeding day and night, during all which time, critical as the feafon was, and notwithftanding the preparations they knew to be making in Paris, they never attempted to enter the city, feems to exculpate the court and minifters from the bloody defigns imputed to them by the popular party. If fuch a fcheme had been propofed, this would have been the feafon for its execution, when prevalent confufion and terror would have prevented any effectual plan of refiftance. Weaknefs and folly, indeed, chiefly characterized the minifterial councils of the time. Knowing that in former periods the very appearance of troops had intimidated the Parifian populace, they without adverting to the total change of fentiments and circumftances, feem vainly to have expected the fame effect at prefent.

 from

CHAP. XLIII.

1789.

An army of volunteers is immediately raised. The national cockade.

from the multitudes of miſcreants with which that vaſt metropolis abounded; but prompt in expedient, they next day generally armed, formed themſelves into one great body with the profeſſed intention of ſecuring internal order, and defending themſelves againſt external enemies. They adopted a peculiar cockade for the purpoſe; and thirty thouſand citizens totally unaccuſtomed to arms, were ſoon ſeen completely accoutred, and in a few hours aſſumed the appearance of order and diſcipline. The national volunteers came in a body to proffer to the people their ſervice, which was moſt joyfully accepted. Directed by the popular leaders, and inſtructed by their military auxiliaries, the armed citizens prepared to defend the capital againſt the approaching troops. They threw up entrenchments, and formed barricadoes in different parts of the ſuburbs. A permanent council was appointed to ſit night and day at the Hotel de Ville; and a communication was eſtabliſhed between this body and the national aſſembly. In the courſe of this day, various robberies being committed, the multitude ſeizing ſome of the thieves in the fact, dragged them inſtantly to the Greve, the common place of execution, and hanged them by the ropes which were uſed to faſten the lantherns. Hence originated that moſt horrid practice of the French mob, making themſelves judges and executioners in the ſame inſtant, without the ſmalleſt regard to law or juſtice, rank, age, or ſex.

They attack the royal magazines to procure arms.

The next day was the celebrated 14th of July. The new army, early in the morning, attacked the Hotel des Invalids, and taking it by ſurprize, ſeized feized a large magazine of arms and ammunition; thence they proceeded to the *Garde Meuble*, or ancient armoury, forced it open, and diftributing the contents among their own body, completed their means for defenfive and offenfive operations. They now conceived a much bolder defign, which was to feize the Baftile; but aware that this fortrefs was very ftrong, and amply fupplied with provifions for ftanding a fiege, they bethought themfelves of attempting ftratagem; they accordingly negociated with the marquis de Launay, and coming to the gates, demanded arms and ammunition. The governor appearing to comply with this requifition, the gates were opened; a great number being admitted over the firft bridge, the bridges were drawn up; in a fhort time a difcharge of mufketry was heard; but whether from a pre-concerted fcheme of De Launay, or provoked by the intemperate violence of the citizens, has never been afcertained*. But whoever might

* The teftimonies on this fubject are fo extremely contradictory, that an impartial judge would find very great difficulty in developing truth, amidft the exaggerations of infuriated paffions. Where we can place no reliance on the declarations of witneffes, our opinions muft be formed from probability. De Launay could expect no advantage to the royal caufe from this partial maffacre. Inftead of intimidating, he muft have feen that it would enflame the Parifians to ftill more violent outrages. The cruelty imputed by the popular hypothefis was not found in any one authenticated inftance to be a part of the royal policy. What purpofe could it ferve, from what motive could it fpring? On the part of de Launay, this hypothefis implies, that from mere wanton barbarity he perpetrated

CHAP. XLIII. 1789.

might be the aggreffors, when the firing was heard, the paffions of the populace were inflamed to fuch enthufiafm and fury, that the Baftile, the citadel of Paris, with its feemingly impaffable ditches, and its inacceffible towers and ramparts, covered with a powerful artillery, was, after an attack of two hours, carried by ftorm. De Launay was immediately dragged to the Place de Greve, and miferably murdered. M. de Lofme, the major of the Baftile, met with a fimilar fate, and equal cruelty. When the place was captured, the Parifians loudly exclaimed, let us hang the whole garrifon; but the prifoners were faved by the interceffion of the national troops. The popular rage now manifefted itfelf in a fpecies of favagenefs long unknown in civilized Europe. They infulted and mutilated the remains of the dead, and exhibited their heads upon pikes to applauding multitudes; fo dreadful were the ingredients already mingled with Gallic liberty. The victorious Parifians, exploring the

petrated mifchief tending moft powerfully to ruin himfelf, and injure his mafter's caufe. Such a fuppofition is, no doubt, within the verge of poffibility, but another view appears much more probable. The Parifians were in a ftate of the moft violent rage and indignation againft every fupporter of government, and gave full vent to their paffions both in words and actions. The Baftile they confidered as a great bulwark of defpotifm, and the receptacle of its moft miferable victims: entered into that gloomy manfion, whofe horrors had fo much occupied their imaginations, and ftimulated their paffions: and viewing its guards, whom they confidered as the minions of atrocious tyranny, nothing could be more likely than that their conduct to the foldiers would be abufive, infulting, and furioufly intemperate, and that thence quarrels might arife leading to a bloody cataftrophe.

gloomy dungeons of oppreſſion, in expectation of delivering numbers of unfortunate victims, to their great ſurprize and diſappointment, found only ſeven captives, four of whom were confined on charges of forgery, and three only were ſtate criminals. So little was this engine of tyranny employed under the mild and humane Louis XVI. When the capture of the Baſtile was reported at Verſailles, the miniſters at firſt treated it as an extravagant fiction of the democratic party, but they were ſoon too well aſſured of the fatal truth. In this ſituation they formed the abſurd reſolution of keeping the king in ignorance of what had paſſed, and urged Broglio to proceed immediately to the reduction of Paris; but he anſwered, that his troops were infected with the popular ſpirit, and that he could not rely on their efforts. The miniſters and the princes were ſoon convinced that oppoſition would be ineffectual, and began to provide for their own ſafety. The Count de Artois had hitherto uſed every effort to inſpirit the king, and to prevent the downfal of the whole fabric; but he now ſaw that the attempt was hopeleſs. At midnight, the Duke de Liencourt, who was maſter of the wardrobe, forced his way into his majeſty's apartment, and informed him of the whole. The king reſolved on the moſt unconditional ſubmiſſion to the national aſſembly; and repairing thither without guards, early in the morning, he declared he reſigned himſelf into their hands; and thus, deſerted by its moſt efficacious ſupporters, attacked by the combined efforts of thepeople, and relinquiſhed by its poſſeſſor, fell the abſolute monarchy of France; and here

CHAP. XLIII. 1789.

here the historical reader may date the commencement of the French revolution *.

Louis arrived in the national assembly, and having declared that his sole reliance was on their wisdom and patriotism, intreated them to use their power for the salvation of the state. He informed them, that he had ordered all the troops to quit the neighbourhood of Paris and Versailles; the Parisians however being still afraid of sieges and blockades, proceeded with preparations for defence. They appointed M. La Fayette commander of their armed corps, to which they gave the name of national guards. The capital was now a great republic, and it soon was so sensible of its power, as to give the law, not only to the unfortunate sovereign, but to the national assembly and the whole kingdom. The national assembly sent a deputation, consisting of eighty-four members, with a view of restoring tranquillity. The Parisians received the deputies with every mark of respect and applause, but expressed a desire that the king himself should visit the city of Paris. This humiliating measure Louis carried into execution on Friday the 17th of July, under a full conviction

* The susceptibility of the French character renders that people very easily impressed by any address to their senses, imagination, or passions. A song that was composed about this time had a still stronger effect than even that which is ascribed by our historian to the celebrated air Lillibullero *: this was the famous *Ca Ira*, both in the words aud music skilfully adapted to the impetuous ardour of impassioned Frenchmen: in rapid strains and expressions, it announced the immediate downfall of existing establishments.

* See Hume, vol. viii. p. 300.

that

that he thereby encountered the peril of inſtant aſſaſſination. He was received by a body of twenty-five thouſand national guards; and thus led in a melancholy proceſſion, amidſt the loud and continual acclamations of *Vive la nation*, while the ancient favourite cry of *Vive le roi* was not once heard. Being conducted to the hotel, he was obliged to accept the new cockade, and to hear an harangue from the popular leaders, charging the court with all the cruel deſigns that were reported to have been formed againſt the city of Paris. Having ſo clearly and poſitively denied this imputation, as to impreſs conviction on the moſt democratical of his hearers, he returned ſafely to Verſailles, to the great joy of his friends, many of whom never expected to ſee him again. Meanwhile the princes, and ſome of the chief nobility, with many of the inferior courtiers, perceiving the popular party paramount, ſought ſafety in flight. The national aſſembly having ſignified a wiſh that Mr. Neckar * ſhould be recalled, that miniſter was invited to return to Paris, and other popular miniſters were appointed. Some degree of tranquillity having been re-eſtabliſhed at Paris, the national aſſembly proceeded to the formation of a new conſtitution. As the ground work on which they were to build a fabric, they began with forming a declaration of rights. This maniſeſto was introduced by a remark tending to

* Mr. Neckar was welcomed both at Verſailles and Paris, with ſuch demonſtrations of general and exceſſive joy, that democratic writers compared it to the tranſports of the Romans on the return of Cicero from baniſhment.

CHAP. XLIII. 1789.

ſhew, that the ignorance, neglect, or contempt of human rights, are the ſole cauſes of public misfortunes, and to avoid theſe evils, that it was neceſſary to define and explain thoſe rights. The declaration contains the outlines of the doctrines afterwards held out by the various revolutioniſts, and, indeed, is the text that has given riſe to the principal claſs of the comments ſo long the ſubject of literary and political diſcuſſion. Here was the noted principle brought forward which founded legitimate government upon the NATURAL RIGHTS OF MAN. This theory, however, ſuppoſing mankind ſuſceptible of perfection, deduces its inferences from an aſſumption which it neither did nor could prove, and which daily experience diſproved. Many of the remarks are, no doubt, abſtractly true; but they are uſeleſs, becauſe they do not apply to circumſtances either exiſting or likely to exiſt *: on this baſis they proceeded to raiſe the new conſtitution.

Declaration of rights: its fundamental principle the Rights of Man.

The

* The following is a copy of the declaration of rights, conſiſting of ſeventeen articles:

I. Men were born, and always continue, equal in reſpect of their rights; civil diſtinctions, therefore, can be founded only on public utility.

II. The end of all political aſſociations is the preſervation of the natural and impreſcriptible rights of man; and theſe rights are liberty, property, ſecurity, and reſiſtance of oppreſſion.

III. The nation is eſſentially the ſource of all ſovereignty; nor can any individual, or any body of men, be entitled to any authority which is not expreſsly derived from it.

IV. Political Liberty conſiſts in the power of doing whatever does not injure another. The exerciſe of the natural rights of every man has no other limits than thoſe which are neceſſary

to

1789. First acts of the French revolutionists. Great object to subvert establishment.

The practical operation of the principles immediately manifested itself in the acts and proceedings of the national assembly, and the various classes of the French revolutionists. Manifold were the subjects of consideration; but the great and general object was subversion of establishment. In prosecuting this purpose, the energy, susceptibility, and violence of the French character, were clearly displayed.

to secure to every other man the free exercise of the same rights; and these limits are determinable only by the law.

V. The law ought to prohibit only actions hurtful to society. What is not prohibited by the law should not be hindered; nor should any one be compelled to that which the law does not require.

VI. The law is an expression of the will of the community. All citizens have a right to concur, either personally, or by their representatives, in its formation. It should be the same to all, whether it protects or punishes; and all being equal in its sight, are equally eligible to all honours, places, and employments, according to their different abilities, without any other distinction than that created by their virtues and talents.

VII. No man should be accused, arrested, or held in confinement, except in cases determined by the law, and according to the forms which it has prescribed. All who promote, solicit, execute, or cause to be executed, arbitrary orders, ought to be punished: and every citizen called upon or apprehended by virtue of the law, ought immediately to obey, and renders himself culpable by resistance.

VIII. The law ought to impose no other penalties than such as are absolutely and evidently necessary; and no one ought to be punished, but in virtue of a law promulgated before the offence, and legally applied.

IX. Every man being presumed innocent till he has been convicted, whenever his detention becomes indispensable, all rigour to him, more than is necessary to secure his person, ought to be provided against by the law.

CHAP. XLIII. 1789.

played. Freed from all the restraints which not only superstition and despotism, but religious and salutary controul, had formerly imposed, they now gave full vent to their dispositions. Their natural ardour was farther goaded to fury by demagogues.

Licentiousness of the press.

The licentiousness of the press even exceeded the licentiousness of the mob, and most powerfully prompted its atrocity.

Twenty thousand literary men stimulate the mob to outrage.

Twenty thousand literary men were daily and hourly employed, not as be-

X. No man ought to be molested on account of his opinions, not even on account of his religious opinions, provided his avowal of them does not disturb the public order established by the law.

XI. The unrestrained communication of thoughts and opinions, being one of the most precious rights of man, every citizen may speak, write, or publish freely, provided he is responsible for the use of his liberty in cases determined by law.

XII. A public force being necessary to give security to the rights of men and of citizens, that force is instituted for the benefit of the community, and not for the particular benefit of the persons to whom it is entrusted.

XIII. A common contribution being necessary for the support of the public force, and for defraying the other expences of government, it ought to be divided equally among the members of the community, according to their abilities.

XIV. Every citizen has a right, either by himself or his representatives, to a free voice in determining the necessity of public contributions, the appropriation of them, and of their amount, modes of assessment, and duration.

XV. Every community has a right to demand of all its agents an account of their conduct.

XVI. Every community in which a separation of powers and a security of rights is not provided for, wants a constitution.

XVII. The right to property being inviolable and sacred, no one ought to be deprived of it, except in cases of evident public necessity, legally ascertained, and on the condition of a previous just indemnity.

came

came ſuperior ability and knowledge, in reſtraining vicious paſſions, and in teaching the ignorant the way to virtue and happineſs, but in exhorting and ſtimulating them to outrageous actions. Never was intellectual ſuperiority more diſgracefully debaſed by the venal panegyriſt of corrupted courts, or the hired encomiaſt of titled ſtupidity and inſignificance, than by theſe adulators of an infuriate populace. But even in ſcheming and promoting anarchy and diſorder, the inventive, bold, and ready genius of Frenchmen appeared. A confederacy was framed which in its inſtitution and effects, exhibited a new phenomenon in the hiſtory of political organs. A combination was firſt formed of literary men, to aſſociate under the name of a *club*, at their meetings to concert meaſures which might give the tone to the mob, and through their overbearing influence direct the decrees of the national aſſembly, and the acts of all municipal, judicial, and executive bodies, and thus make the whole power of France ultimately depend upon their reſolves. Theſe demagogues invited into their ſociety ſuch of the populace as they conceived likely to become uſeful inſtruments, and exhorted them to conſtruct other clubs, both in Paris, and through all the provinces; and that ſuch Meetings ſhould be connected, or to uſe a new revolutionary metaphor, *affiliated* together. Theſe conventicles conſiſted firſt of literary votaries of the new philoſophy, who promulgated and inculcated ſuitable doctrines, ſentiments, and conduct. One of the clubs meeting in a convent formerly bolonging to the Jacobins, aſſumed the name

An engine of government new in the hiſtory of political eſtabliſhments. CLUBS.

CHAP. XLIII.

1789. Their influence extended by affiliation.

name of Jacobin Club*, which afterwards extending to appendant ſocieties, gained a ſuperiority over the reſt, and became ſo noted throughout the world. In the firſt deliberations of the national aſſembly, theſe ſocieties, guided by literary demagogues, and directing the populace, had a powerful influence. Many of the lawgivers were indeed members of the new inſtitutions; and thoſe who were moſt inimical to the exiſting eſtabliſhments, and to rank and property, were held in the higheſt eſtimation, and were really the directors of the revolutioniſts. Various in detail as were the precepts of theſe innovators; in principle and object they were ſimple and uniform. Their leſſons of inſtruction, or exhortations to practice, may be compreſſed in a few words. Religion is all folly; diſregard religion and its miniſters. Every eſtabliſhment is contrary to natural right; pull down eſtabliſhments. Order is an encroachment upon natural freedom; overturn all order. Property is an infringement upon natural equality; confiſcate all property†. Such was the ſyſtem generally received in the enthuſiaſm of reform, through a moſt extenſive and populous nation, diſtinguiſhed for promptneſs and fertility of genius, for boldneſs and activity of character, and by its very virtues rendering its errors more extenſively pernicious. To follow through the various and manifold details, the doctrines and objects which guided the national aſſembly, would be

* Annual Regiſter, 1790. Chap. I.

† See revolutionary publications at Paris 1789, paſſim.

foreign

foreign to our hiſtory; but aſſuredly it belongs to our ſubject to ſketch the ſpirit and principal operations of a revolutionary ſyſtem by which Britain was ſo eſſentially affected.

Lawleſs violence in the country.

The licentiouſneſs of Paris ſpread through the provinces; and the peaſants, having been long ſeverely oppreſſed by ſeignorial tenures and privileges, conceived themſelves now emancipated, and turned upon the proprietors with the moſt outrageous violence*. Reports of robberies, rapes, and murders, daily reached the aſſembly. Landed proprietors apprehended the plunder of their property; and ſome of the nobility, whoſe poſſeſſions were very great, were ſeized with a ſudden impulſe of ſacrificing a large portion to ſecure the reſt. On the 4th of Auguſt, the Viſcount de Noailles, and the Duke d'Aguilon, propoſed an equalization of taxes, and an abolition of feudal ſervices. This offer ſtriking the aſſembly and galleries with the warmeſt admiration, excited in the other proprietors a wiſh to emulate conduct which was ſo highly applauded. The nobles and clergy vied with each other in ſurrendering privileges of their orders, and both theſe eſtates concluded with ſacrificing their manerial juriſdictions. So far there was nothing but voluntary ceſſion, directed by preventive policy, and ſtimulated by praiſe, or flowing from enthuſiaſm. The next day it was propoſed that tythes ſhould be aboliſhed, and church property ſhould be ſeized by the ſtate. This propoſition the clergy eagerly combated, but

The peaſants turn on the proprietors.

Some of the nobility propoſe to ſacrifice a large portion of their privileges and property. Admiration of the commons.

Propoſition for the ſeizure of church property. Remonſtrances of the clergy diſregarded.

* Bertrand, vol. i. c. 11.

their

CHAP. XLIII.

1789.

their remonſtrances were ineffectual; and at one blow all the immenſe property of ſuch a numerous body was confiſcated, without the leaſt allegation of delinquency. The Abbe Sieyes, though a friend to the revolution, ſtrongly remonſtrated againſt this forfeiture, as commencing freedom with iniquity*. But the ſound reaſoning, even of a partizan, was unavailing againſt determined rapacity. Equality being the profeſſed object of the revolutioniſts, it was propoſed that all the provincial diſtinctions, the peculiar rights and privileges of each diſtrict ſhould be aboliſhed, and that, without any local diverſity and immunity, or any regard to particular cuſtoms, uſages, and preſcriptions, the whole nation ſhould be conſolidated into one compact body. The deputies of privileged towns and diſtricts ſurrendered the immunities of their conſtituents, all excluſive claims in every part of France were reſigned; and the provinces which had poſſeſſed the right of taxing themſelves, renounced the power of taxation. The parliaments which had ſo long held the judicial authority of France, and had been conſidered as the able, upright, and intrepid guardians of the public welfare, were annihilated. All the canon, eccleſiaſtical, and political codes of law, all the claims of the court of Rome, all the fees or taxes which it heretofore received, were aboliſhed. Even the very ſyſtems of theology and metaphyſics, which had prevailed for ſo many ages, fell, not under the regular and well-conducted force of reaſon, but the furious rage of innovation. In

Parliaments are annihilated.

Immunities are ſacrificed.

The law and policy of the kingdom are overturned.

* Bertrand, vol. i. chap. xii and xiii.

a few days the whole law and policy of the nation were changed, a great part of its property was disarranged; and every thing had altered its ancient form and aspect. A revolution more comprehensive and complete in its objects, as well as more minute and particular in its details, than any which is recorded in the annals of mankind, was carried into effect by an assembly of men professing to deliberate, with little more reflection or discussion, than in a senate of prudent lawgivers and statesmen, would have been bestowed on the most ordinary municipal or local regulation. The nobility and clergy in the provinces, not having been impressed with the impassioned enthusiasm from which their delegates in the national assembly had so lavishly surrendered their rights of tythe, without their concurrence, very generally condemned a bounty that bestowed what did not belong to the donors. They were greatly enraged and grieved at the confiscation of their property, and could not think highly of a new system of government, the first specimens of whose character were irreligion and robbery. Resistance, however, they saw would be vain; and they were therefore compelled to acquiesce in the humiliating and plundering decrees. But the pecuniary pressure, the proximate cause of the present crisis, still continued. The peasants considered taxes as an infringement upon liberty, and refused payment; others followed their example, and there was no money to support government, or carry on the public business. After stating the national wants, Mr. Neckar asked for a loan of thirty millions of livres, but the subscription

 was

CHAP. XLIII.

1789. Scheme of voluntary contributions.

not filled. A ſcheme for voluntary contributions was adopted, and from its novelty eagerly embraced by this volatile people. All ranks vied in bringing their ſilver and gold to the public treaſury, nor was coin only produced, but alſo plate, and the minuteſt articles of dreſs. The members of the aſſembly themſelves, in their bountiful patriotiſm, agreed to ſacrifice their ſhoe-buckles to the exigencies of the community. The king and queen ſent their gold and ſilver plate to the mint for coinage. Theſe offerings, however, were very inadequate to the ſupply of the public wants. A ſcheme was propoſed by Mr. Neckar, and after many ſtrong objections and remonſtrances, embraced by the national aſſembly, for applying one FOURTH of every man's annual income to the wants of the ſtate*.

Gold and ſilver utenſils carried to the mint.

Preparations for the new conſtitution.

Having made theſe very momentous changes reſpecting corporate and private property, they proceeded now to new model their conſtitution, according to the declaration of rights. The aſſembly was divided into ſections and committees†; to each of which was aſſigned a ſpecific part of the new polity, to be prepared, and grooved with the reſt. The firſt queſtion conſidered reſpecting the conſtitution was of the very higheſt importance; what ſhare of authority the king ſhould poſſeſs in the new legiſlature? On the ſolution of this problem it was to depend whether the royal power ſhould be ſtrong enough to reſtrain the

Authority to be poſſeſſed by the king.

* Annual Regiſter, 1790. Chap. ii.

† Bertrand, vol. i. chap. 13.

violence

violence of democracy. On the one hand, it was proposed that the king should possess a veto, or negative, in the passing of a law; on the other, that he should be merely the chief executorial magistrate, without any voice in the legislation. For the negative voice were ranged, not only all the friends of the ancient monarchy, but the majority of the nobility and clergy; now sensible that they had conceded too much; apprehensive that their total ruin was intended, and desirous in the kingly prerogative to preserve a bulwark which might afford some defence to the remaining rights, to resist the torrent of democracy. Against it was opposed the whole body of the commons, who containing many subordinate divisions, agreed in the general desire of reducing the monarchy. The question was agitated with great force and violence on both sides. The opposition of the privileged orders was represented by demagogues to arise from an intention of attempting a counter revolution; and the people were transported into fury and alarm. Louis himself, ever desirous of accommodating differences, satisfying all parties, and maintaining tranquillity, made a proposal of a compromise, by which he should have a power of suspending a law during two legislatures; but that if the third assembly persisted in its support, he should be obliged to give it his sanction. This proposal proving satisfactory to both parties, a decree passed, conferring these prerogatives on the king, under the denomination of *a suspensive veto**. Another question was now dis- *Suspensive veto.*

* Bertrand, vol. ii. chap. xiv.

CHAP. XLIII.

1789.

Question if the assembly was to be composed of one or two chambers.

cussed, also of very great importance. Whether the national assembly should be composed of one or of two chambers. Lally Tolendal, Clermont, Mounier, and other leaders of the moderate reformers, were equally zealous with the republicans for the establishment of a free government; but, considering a limited monarchy as affording the fairest prospect of beneficial and permanent liberty, they ardently recommended a senate, and a house of representatives, which should controul the proceedings of each other, agreeably to the principle, and nearly after the model of the British constitution. From the narrow and interested impolicy of many of the nobles and clergy, who vainly hoped for the re-establishment of the three chambers, together with the predominance of the republicans, this proposal was entirely overruled. The commons reprobated every species of mixed government, and steadily abstaining from imitation of England, proposed, and carried, that the duration of the French legislative assembly should be only two years. Notwithstanding the rage for innovation, they confirmed the hereditary succession of the crown according to the Salic law. The friends of the Duke of Orleans eagerly contended that the assembly, by confirming the renunciation of the first Bourbon king of Spain,* should render their patron next heir after the king, his son, and brothers. But the assembly, however violent and precipitate in what concerned France only, cautiously refrained from giving umbrage to other

Carried that there should be only one. The commons reprobate the example of Britain. Settlement of the succession.

* Bertrand, vol. ii. chap. xiv.

powers;

powers; and avoided the diſcuſſion. Meanwhile the furious republicans, both in the clubs and the national aſſembly, reſolved that the reſidence of the royal family, and the legiſlature, ſhould be changed from Verſailles to the capital, where they would be ſtill more completely under the controul of democratic direction. The court, and eſpecially the queen, conceived the greateſt horror at the idea of a compulſory abode, among ſo tumultuous, bloody, and ferocious a people. A tranſaction which took place in the beginning of October, accelerated the removal of the king and his family to a ſcene which they had ſo much reaſon to dread.

Ferocity of the people

Among other cauſes of popular violence, famine ſtill raged throughout France, but particularly in Paris and Verſailles. To repreſs the tumults, additional troops were ordered to march to the royal habitation. The king himſelf was ſtill allowed to have about his perſon a regiment of his own life-guards; and the newly arrived corps was the regiment of Flanders. The gentlemen of the ſtationary forces, on the arrival of the ſtrangers, according to the eſtabliſhed cuſtom of military hoſpitality, gave their brother officers an entertainment. In the courſe of their feſtivity, when both hoſts and gueſts were heated by wine, the king and queen, with the infant dauphin, viſited the banquetting room. The royal mother carried the infant prince completely round the table. Meanwhile the muſic played an air* which the ladies of the court accompanied with the appropriate ſtanzas pathetically

enflamed by ſcarcity.

Additional troops arrive at Verſailles.

Entertainment given by the officers in the palace to the new comers.

The royal family viſit the banquetting room.

The queen preſents the infant dauphin to the officers.

Muſic deſcribes

* Bertrand, vol. ii. chap. xiv.

CHAP. XLIII.

1789. The sufferings of a captive king. Effects of beauty, music, and wine.

describing the feelings and sufferings of a captive king*. The power of music and the charms of beauty, combining with inherent loyalty, inspired the company with an enthusiasm which wine drove beyond all bounds of caution. Drawing their swords, they drank copious bumpers to the august health of their illustrious visitors and their family, successively†, while the chief personages, having expressed their warmest gratitude, retired. In such a disposition of mind, no moderation could be expected. A scene of complete intoxication ensued, and exhibited without disguise, and with augmented fervour, the sentiments with which it commenced. All the extravagance followed which wine could produce on romantic fancies and impassioned hearts. The national cockades were by the offi-

* Taken from a dramatic work founded on the story of Richard Cœur de Lion's captivity when returning from the Holy Land, and beginning, "O Richard, O mon Roi"

† Bertrand, who gives a very particular account of this entertainment, mentions the following circumstance, which I do not recollect to have seen in any other publication. "I have (he says) been assured by two persons who were present at this entertainment, that the words *to the health of the nation* were also pronounced feebly by one of the guests, or one of the spectators, and that the not repeating or seconding this toast, was attended with no consequences. The custom of drinking to the health of the nation had not been then established, and one may be allowed, without a crime, to think that was not the moment for introducing such an innovation; yet one of the greatest crimes imputed to the *gardes-du-corps*, was their not being willing to drink to the health of the nation, that is to say, to their own health, for they were indisputably a part of the nation."

cers

cers of Flanders torn from their hats, and trampled under foot*; and in their place were substituted old royal cockades, supplied by the ladies of the court, who took white ribbands from their own head-dresses, to decorate the loyal officers, while the three coloured cockade was treated with contempt and scorn. This banquet was really no more than an excess of conviviality, at a season when prudence would have dictated reserve; but being exaggerated by all the circumstances which malicious invention could devise, filled Paris with the most violent rage. The innovating leaders pretended that the conduct of the officers and courtiers arose from counter-revolutionary projects, with exulting joy from the confident expectations of success: a conspiracy, they affirmed, was matured for the restoration of despotism, and that the queen was at its head. The carousal of the royalists, at the time that the people wanted bread, was a flagrant insult to the nation. These sentiments were disseminated by the various classes and factions that were friendly to innovation; but were spread with peculiar activity by the adherents of the Duke of Orleans.

CHAP. XLIII. 1789. The officers trample the national cockade. Report of the entertainment at Paris. Rage and indignation of the revolutionists.

Louis Philip Bourbon, Duke of Orleans, was the descendant and representative of the only brother of Louis XIV., and after the posterity of that monarch, next heir to the throne of France. In such an elevated rank, with riches far beyond the measure of any other European subject, he had devoted his youth to the most profligate debauchery: his vices, by their coarseness, excited the indignant contempt of a gentleman almost as much

Character and projects of the Duke of Orleans.

* Annual Register 1789.

CHAP. XLIII. 1789.

as the enormity of his crimes called on him the detestation of every virtuous man. His wealth affording him the means of very extensive depravity, enabled him to corrupt great numbers of the youth, and even to make considerable advances in vitiating the metropolis; and his habitation at the Palais Royal, far exceeded any other part of the French capital in variety, extent, and flagrancy of wickedness. Such was the mode of life by which this prince was distinguished by the time he had reached his fortieth year. His reputation, however, did not rest solely on uniform and habitual debauchery: other species of turpitude concurred in rendering him at once flagitious and execrable. Opulent as Orleans was, he was boundless in avarice. The Duc de Penthiévre, high admiral of France, was one of the wealthiest noblemen of his country. Orleans cast his eyes on the daughter of this minister, but the son Lamballe intervened: with this youth he cultivated a close intimacy, and according to the concurrent accounts of various writers *, was the means of shortening the brother's life, after which he married the sister, now heir of her father's possessions. He moreover proposed to secure the reversion of Penthiévre's very lucrative post. With this view he entered the navy, and the first time he saw an enemy, a descendant of Henry IV. betrayed the despicable degeneracy of personal cowardice †.

* See Playfair on Jacobinism.—Adolphus's memoirs.—Picture of Paris, &c.

† In D'Orvillier's running fight with Admiral Keppel. See this History, vol. iii. p. 81.

Such

Such an exhibition effectually destroyed all his pretensions to naval promotion; and he conceived the blackest vengeance against the royal family, because the king would not entrust the supreme direction of his navy to a person who was afraid to fight: various circumstances also rendered the queen the peculiar object of his hatred. The commencing discontents in France opened to him prospects not only of revenge, but ambition: he hoped by fomenting disaffection to pave the way for the overthrow of the royal family, and his own advancement to the regency, if not to the throne. Weak as well as wicked, in seeking the downfall of the reigning sovereign, he promoted and headed attacks upon the monarchical authority; and what he sought by villany, by folly laboured to impair. He did not reflect that the doctrines which he promoted tended to overturn the crown which he pursued. He was so infatuated as to suppose that the bold and able leaders of a revolution which annihilated all adventitious distinctions, would labour to exalt a person, who, destitute of genius and of courage, had none but adventitious distinctions to boast. Since the subversion of the old government, he had abetted the most violent and licentious proceedings of the revolutionary mobs. Sagacious agitators at once saw his designs, and their futility, and professing to be his agents, used him as their dupe. The most eminent of his declared partisans at this time was Mirabeau, who at certain periods appears to have desired the promotion of Orleans to be regent of the kingdom,

in

CHAP. XLIII. 1789.

in the expectation of being the supreme director himself. Mirabeau very actively promoted the rage of the Parisians: he and his agents pretended to impute the scarcity to the machinations of the aristocrats, and the absence of the royal family, and encouraged the popular cry for the removal of the king to Paris. He promoted the belief of a conspiracy by the queen, and even intimated an intention of impeaching her Majesty*, as a conspirator for destroying the freedom of the people, and keeping bread from the Parisians. These topics being repeated in the capital, the malignity of the Orleans faction, revolutionary enthusiasm, and popular licentiousness, concurred with the scarcity in producing a determination to hasten to Versailles to demand of the king bread, punishment of the aristocrats, and especially the guards. A multitude of the lowest women undertook this expedition; these amazons broke open the town-house, seized the arms there deposited, and meeting on the stairs a priest, required no farther proofs of his guilt than his dress; and commenced their orgies by hanging him to a lamp-post. With the yell of infuriate savages they set out for Versailles, joined by Maillard, a creature of Orleans, and a favourite spokesman in the Palais Royal, with a few of his associates. They proceeded on their march: and meeting two travellers in the dress of gentlemen, they concluded them to be aristocrats, and hanged them without further enquiry. Arriving at Versailles, they sent Maillard to the national assembly,

The mob determines to bring the king to Paris.

Movement of the women for that purpose. They hang priests and aristocrats.

Expedition to Versailles.

* Bertrand, vol. ii. chap. 17.

to demand the immediate punifhment of the ariftocrats and the life-guards. The affembly fent their own prefident with a deputation of the women to wait upon the king. The deputies being thus employed, their conftituents fet about drinking—an operation for which their hafty departure in the morning had not allowed them time, and the road had not afforded materials. In half an hour the greater number of them were completely intoxicated. Thus prepared, they broke into the national affembly, not only filled the galleries, but took their feats among the lawgivers, overwhelmed them with the groffeft and loudeft obfcenity and imprecations. At laft two of them, obferving the prefident's chair to be empty, took poffeffion of it themfelves, and dictated the fubjects of difcuffion. Such, even then, was French liberty; fuch were the affeffors who controuled the deliberations of men affembled on the moft momentous bufinefs that could occupy legiflators. While the female army was thus employed at Verfailles, the fermentation at Paris rofe to an extraordinary pitch, and all claffes of the populace burned with anxiety to know the refult of the expedition. The national guards became fo impatient, that they compelled their officers to lead them to Verfailles, and declared their refolution to join in obliging the king to repair to Paris. La Fayette, the commander, though a friend to the new conftitution, was favourably difpofed to the perfon of Louis *, as well as to the authority † which the new fyftem had conferred on the fovereign, and was

The women overawe the legiflature, break into the affembly, and take the prefident's chair.

* Bertrand, chap. xvi. † Bouillé's Memoirs.

the

CHAP. XLIII. 1789.

the adverfary of violent republicans on the one hand, and of the Orleans faction on the other. He endeavoured to diffuade his foldiers from this expedition but found that the attempt would be impracticable; he therefore tried to moderate its operation. As the guards made no fcruple of publicly proclaiming their opinions and fentiments on national affairs, La Fayette and his officers eafily difcovered whence their prefent thoughts and intentions originated. The grenadiers informed the general, without referve, they underftood the king to be an ideot, therefore they (the grenadiers) would not hefitate to declare, that matters muft go on much better by the appointment of a regent. As this was the peculiar language and doctrine of Mirabeau and other directors of the Orleans faction, there could be little doubt where either the politics or the march of the guards originated *. Many of the foldiers alfo declared an intention of maffacring the queen. The Parifian guards arrived at Verfailles late in the evening, and were moft cordially received by the national guards at Verfailles, the mob of the fame place, and the amazons of Maillard †. The moft ferocious of the guards and other mob in the morning furrounded the palace, and, with dreadful howlings, denounced the murder of the queen; and the palace was filled with confternation. But Marie Antoinette was not frightened. Amid crimes, (fays Bertrand), alarms,

* Annual Regifter 1790, page 48.

† Bertrand informs us, that this man was rather turbulent than malignant, and even tried to preferve fome degree of moderation among his troop; which was certainly, in their prefent condition, no eafy tafk.

confufion,

CHAP. XLIII. 1789.

confusion, and general stupor, the queen majestically displayed the sublimest and most heroic character. Her constant serenity, her countenance, firm and ever full of dignity, transfused her own courage into the soul of all who approached her. On that day she received a great deal of company. To some who expressed uneasiness she replied, "I know they are come from Paris to demand my head; but I learned of my mother not to fear death, and I will wait for it with firmness." Her answer to the advice given to her, to fly from the dangers that threatened her, does not less deserve to be recorded.—"No, no," said she; "never will I desert the king and my children: I will share whatever fate awaits them." Some hours of sleep happily came to repair her exhausted strength, and to enable her to encounter on the next day, with equal magnanimity, dangers still more horrid. About half past five in the morning, the repose of the princess received a frightful disturbance. An immense croud endeavoured to break down the palace gate, and after murdering two of the life-guards, effected their purpose. Dreadful howlings announced their entrance into the palace: they soon arrived at the foot of the great staircase, and ran up in crouds, uttering imprecations and the most sanguinary threats against the queen*. Before six they forced their way to the apartments of the royal consort. The centinel, Monsieur de Miomandre, perceiving the ruffians, called out, "Save the queen; her life is sought: I stand alone against two thousand tigers." Her majesty escaped by a private

The mob assault the palace;

* Bertrand, vol. ii. p. 112.

passage

CHAP. XLIII.

1789.

attempt to murder the queen; prevented by the heroism of her defenders.

passage into the king's apartment. Louis, flying to her relief, was met by his own guards, who escorted him back to his apartments, where he found his queen and children arrived. The ruffians now endeavoured to force the antichamber, which a body of loyal guards defended with heroic courage; but their number was decreasing under the murdering hands of the banditti. The assassins had almost entered the apartment when the persuasions and supplications of Fayette and his officers induced them to desist. Meanwhile, the furious mob in the outer court demanded the appearance of the king and queen: the royal pair was persuaded to present themselves on the balcony. An universal cry arose, To Paris, to Paris. Refusal or remonstrance would have been instant death: the king's assent was immediately notified, and the furious rage converted into the most tumultuous joy. Within an hour began the procession, more melancholy and humiliating to the king and queen than any which history records of captive princes exhibited as spectacles to triumphant enemies. The sovereign of a mighty and splendid monarchy; so long and so recently famed for learning, arts, sciences, and civilization; renowned for the generosity, honour, and valour of its nobility; the courage and discipline of its numerous and formidable armies; their zealous and enthusiastic affection for their king and his family; the ardent loyalty of the whole people; was now, without foreign invasion or war; without any avowed competitor for his throne; even without any acknowledged rebellion of his subjects, with his queen and family, dragged from his

The king and queen agree to depart for Paris.

Mournful procession of a degraded monarch.

his palace, and led in triumph by the offscourings of his metropolis, the loweſt and moſt deſpicable of ruffians, the meaneſt and moſt abandoned trulls.

Farther proceedings at Paris.

From the 6th of October 1789, the king is to be conſidered as a priſoner at Paris. Mounier, equally the friend of liberty and of monarchy, from theſe horrid tranſactions augured the downfal of both. He and other penetrating obſervers ſaw that the outrages were not the mere accidental ebullitions of of a temporary and local frenzy, but the effects of a general cauſe. He, Lally Tolendal, and others of the moderate party, who had been the vigorous and ardent advocates of a limited monarchy, now ſeeing their efforts unavailing, ſeceded from the aſſembly. But the juſt and virtuous Mounier, before his retirement, eſtabliſhed an enquiry into the recent maſſacres. The national aſſembly followed the king to Paris. The republican party now began to expreſs ſuſpicions of the Duke of Orleans, which they had before entertained; though finding him and his creatures inſtrumental to their deſigns, they had made uſe of his agency as long as it was wanted. Become now ſo powerful, they thought proper to drop the maſk, and intimated to him through Fayette, that his preſence in France was incompatible with the public good: he was accordingly compelled to retire into England. At this time the Pariſian mob promulgated its reſolution to take the adminiſtration of juſtice into its own hands; and accordingly hanged* ſeveral ariſtocrats (eſpecially bakers) at the lamp-poſt. The aſſembly, from regard to its own ſafety, reſolved to

The exiſting government endeavours to quell the mob.

* Annual Regiſter, 1790.

 prevent

CHAP. XLIII. 1789. Severe prosecutions for that purpose.

prevent so summary proceedings. They passed a very effective decree, by which the municipal magistrates were obliged to proclaim martial law whenever the mob proceeded to outrage. They instituted a criminal inquiry into the late murders; several ring-leaders were hanged, and terror thus was struck into the rest. Some degree of tranquillity was established in the metropolis; and the assembly proceeded with less interruption and greater security in its schemes of legislation.

Effects of the French revolution in Britain. Detesting the old government, and not acquainted with the new, Britons approve the change as friendly to liberty.

Such were the leading features and principal acts of the French revolution in 1789. Britons rejoiced at the overthrow of the old French government because so contrary to the liberty which they themselves enjoyed. A change from such a system they concluded must certainly be an improvement. They trusted that the alterations in France would generate a government similar to the British constitution. Presuming beneficial effects from the French revolution, the greatest part of the people rejoiced at this event. The generous feelings of Englishmen sympathized with the assertors of liberty, before they had time and opportunity to ascertain its effects on the situation and characters of its new votaries. Men whose classical erudition had a greater influence in forming their opinions than experience and reason; who judged of political wisdom more from the practice of the ancient republics than from history, investigation of character, and circumstances, admired what they conceived to be approaches to the democratic institutions of Greece and Rome. Scholars, chiefly eminent for philology, were, with very few exceptions, admirers of a system

Sentiments of various classes.

system * that they supposed similar to those which they found delineated and praised in their favourite languages. Literary men of a higher class than mere linguists; persons of profound metaphysical and moral philosophy, but of more genius and speculative learning than conversancy with practical affairs, commended the lawgivers of France for taking for their guide the "polarity of reason, instead of following the narrow and dastardly ‡ coastings of usage, precedent, and authority." There were many who, forming their ideas of civil and political liberty from their own abstractions more than from experience, admired the French for declaring the equality of mankind, and making that principle the basis of government, instead of modifying it according to expediency. This latter class comprehended the greater number of eminent projectors of civil and ecclesiastical reform, who long had considered even Britain herself deficient in the liberty which their fancies represented as deducible from the rights of man. Various political societies had been constituted for different purposes of reform, but of late years the most active of them had manifested principles too abstract and visionary † to be practicably consistent with the British constitution, or indeed, any form of government founded upon an opinion that human nature is imperfect, and requires controuls proportioned to the prevalence of

* The instances are numerous, as the observing reader can easily recollect without particularization.

‡ See Vindiciæ Gallicæ.

† See Price's Discourse of the love of our country, November 4, 1789, in Priestley, passim; also, Writings of their votaries, passim.

 from

CHAP. XLIII. 1787. passion. These societies * praised the French revolutionists, and recommended their example as a glorious pattern for the human race. They sent congratulations to the French leaders. A regular official correspondence was carried on between the members of private clubs in England, and the leaders of the republican revolution in France. Statesmen of high rank, and of the highest talents †, venerating liberty in general, presumed French liberty would render its votaries happy; and imputing the aggressions of France on this and other nations to the corrupt ambition of her court, anticipated tranquillity from her renovated state, and rejoiced at a change that appeared to them to forebode peace to Britain and to Europe. These admirers of the French revolution were stimulated by British patriotism as well as love of freedom. The excesses they saw and lamented, but tracing them to their source, they imputed them to enthusiasm; which, reasoning from experience, they trusted, though furiously violent in its operation on such characters, would gradually subside, and leave only the ardour of useful reform and improvement. The ablest men on the side of administration, abstained from delivering any opinion concerning the internal proceedings of a foreign state which had not then interfered with ours. At the end of 1789, by far the greater number of all classes and parties in Britain

* Revolution Club and Society for Constitutional Information.

† See Speeches of Messrs. Fox and Sheridan in session 1790.

was

CHAP. XLIII. 1789.

was friendly to the French revolution; and its favourers included a very great portion of genius and learning, while none was hitherto exerted by our countrymen on the opposite side. Such was the impression which this extraordinary change of Gallic polity produced in the most liberal and enlightened of neighbouring nations.

CHAP. XLIV.

Meeting of parliament.—At the beginning of the session little debate or discussion.—Mr. Fox takes an opportunity of praising the French revolution—commends the conduct of the French army in supporting the cause of the people against an arbitrary court—likens them to the English army supporting the Prince of Orange—deems the French revolution, in many respects, similar to the deliverance of England.—His friend and political associate, Mr. Burke, manifests a different opinion—unfolds his view of the French revolution—considers its principles, and the characters on which they are operating—points out its first effects, and deduces the outrageous excesses from its nature and doctrines—deprecates the French system as a model for England—denies the allegations of similarity between the French and British revolution—praises the excellence of the British constitution, as contrasted with the French system.—Mr. Sheridan concurs in Mr. Fox's praises of the French revolution.—Mr. Pitt, praising the British constitution, delivers no opinion on the French system.—Dissenters again propose to seek the repeal of the test act.—Circumstances apparently favourable to the hopes of the dissenters—they are strenuously opposed by the members of the church.—Work entitled, Review of the case of the Protestant Dissenters.—Dissenters trust their cause to the transcendent talents of Mr. Fox—his view of the subject, and answers to objections.—Mr. Pitt continues to treat admissibility to offices as a mere question of expediency—deems the leaders of the dissenters inimical to our establishment—adduces from the conduct of the dissenters, and the situation of political affairs arguments against the repeal.—Mr. Burke speaks on the same side—Majority against the proposed repeal.—Mr. Flood proposes a plan for a parliamentary reform—his subtle theory is controverted by Mr. Windham—withdraws

withdraws his motion. - Petitions from manufacturers of tobacco, praying to repeal the law subjecting them to excise.—A motion to that effect by Mr. Sheridan—is negatived.—Financial statements.—Prosperous situation of the country.—Mr. Dundas presents an account of our East India possessions.—Libels against the commons on account of the management of Hastings's trial—censured.—Dispute with Spain.—Nootka Sound.—Insult offered by Spain—satisfaction demanded.—Conduct of Spain—King's message to parliament.—Parliament unanimously pledge their support of the king in vindicating the rights of Britain.—Dissolution of parliament.—Warlike preparations.—Diplomatic discussion between Britain and Spain.—Spain attempts to interest France.—The French nation is inimical to war with England.—Spain, hopeless of aid, yields to the demands of Britain.—The disputes are adjusted in a convention.

CHAP. XLIV.

1790. Meeting of parliament.

THE British parliament had sitten so late in the preceding year, that it did not meet till the 21st of January 1790. In the opening speech, his majesty mentioned the continuance of the war in the North and East of Europe, and informed the house that the internal situation of different parts of the continent engaged his majesty's most serious attention. Concerned as he was at the interruption of tranquillity, he was persuaded his parliament would join him in entertaining a deep and grateful sense of the favour of providence, which continued to his subjects the increasing advantages of peace, and the uninterrupted enjoyment of those invaluable blessings which they had so long derived from our excellent constitution. His Majesty informed them, that during the recess of parliament, he had been under the necessity of adopting measures for preventing the exportation, and facilitating the import-

 ation

CHAP. XLIV. 1790.

ation, of corn. The addresses were voted without opposition or debate; an act of indemnity was proposed, and unanimously carried, respecting the order of council about grain.

At the beginning of the session there is little debate or discussion

During the first weeks of the session, there was scarcely any parliamentary discussion, but afterwards some of the most striking efforts of eloquence arose from a subject which was not properly before the house. Such a momentous event as the French revolution, interesting all enlightened men, had very early engaged the ardent mind of Mr. Fox. This illustrious senator venerated and admired liberty; and contemplating the Gallic change, estimated its nature and value by the happiness which, he conceived, from overturning an arbitrary government, it would bestow upon many millions. He spoke with transport and exultation of a great people breaking their chains on the heads of their oppressors, and celebrated the particular acts, both civil and military, that had been most instrumental in effecting the change. As a man, he rejoiced in the subversion of despotism, and as a Briton, in a state from which he foreboded tranquillity to this country. When the army estimates were under consideration*, this distinguished orator first promulgated to parliament his opinions concerning the French revolution. The military establishments proposed were nearly the same as in the former year. Messrs. Pitt and Grenville contended, that though there was no reason to apprehend hostilities from any foreign power, yet the unsettled state of Europe, and the internal situation of several parts of it made it necessary for us to keep

Mr. Fox takes an opportunity of praising the French Revolution;

* February 9th, 1790. See parliamentary reports.

ourselves

ourselves in such a condition as might enable us to act with vigour and effect if occasion should require our exertions. It was (they argued) a preposterous economy to tempt an attack by our weakness, and for a miserable present saving to hazard a great future expence. Our foreign alliances had been approved by all parties, as necessary for the preservation of that balance of power in Europe upon which the permanence of its tranquillity depended; but they could only be rendered effectual for their purpose by our ability to support them with an adequate force. Mr. Fox argued, that our ancient rival and enemy, by her internal disturbances, probably would be disabled from offering us any molestation for a long course of years; and the new form that the government of France was likely to assume would make her a better neighbour, and less propense to hostility, than when she was subject to the cabal and intrigues of ambitious and interested statesmen*. He applauded the conduct of the French soldiers during the late commotions: by refusing to obey the dictates of the court, that army had set a glorious example to all the military bodies of Europe; and had shewn, that men, by becoming soldiers,

commends the conduct of the French army in supporting the people against an arbitrary court. Likens them to the

* Mr. Fox's expectation of tranquillity to other states from the prevalence of freedom in France, even had there been nothing peculiar in the nature of that freedom, and the habits and dispositions of its votaries, seems to have arisen more from theory than from the actual review of the history of free countries. Had the comprehensive and full mind of this philosophical politician called before him his own extensive knowledge of the actions of mankind, he would have immediately perceived that free nations have been as propense to hostility as the subjects of an arbitrary prince. See the several histories of the ancient republics in the Greek, Latin, or modern languages: in our own tongue Ferguson, Gillies, and Mitford.

did

CHAP. XLIV.

1790 the English army supporting the Prince of Orange.

did not ceafe to be citizens. Their conduct (he faid) refembled the behaviour of the patriotic foldiers of England when the Prince of Orange landed to affift in preferving our civil and religious liberties: the French revolution, indeed, in many refpects was like to the glorious event which eftablifhed and fecured the liberties of England.

His friend and political affociate, Mr. Burke, manifefts a different opinion;

To thefe doctrines Mr. Fox found an opponent in a very eminent fenator, with whom he had coincided during the greater part of his parliamentary life. Habituated to profound meditation on important queftions in political philofophy, and thoroughly converfant with hiftory, Mr. Burke had applied himfelf, with the moft watchful attention, to obferve the details, and to ftudy the principles, of this extraordinary change. He had reprobated the old government of France; and although he thought it, in the reign of Louis XVI. foftened in its exercife by the progrefs of civilization, and the perfonal character of the monarch, ftill he deemed the welfare of the people to reft on an unftable bafis, and to require very confiderable reform before it could be a beneficial fyftem. But efteeming arbitrary power a great evil, he knew that unwife efforts to fhake it off might produce more terrible calamities. He venerated the fpirit of liberty as, when well-directed and regulated, a means of human happinefs; his refpect for it, in every individual cafe, was proportionate to his opinion of its probable tendency to produce that end, where he had not actual experience to afcertain its effects. It was not merely the poffeffion of it that conftituted it a bleffing, but the enjoyment of it to fuch an extent, and with fuch regulations as could make it fubfidiary to virtue and happinefs. Its operation,

ration, as a blessing or a curse, depended, he thought, on its intrinsic nature, compounded with the character of its subjects, and, in a certain degree, extrinsic causes; and he uniformly controverted* those doctrines of the rights of man which would allow the same freedom to all persons, and in all circumstances. Neither did he conceive, that every one state, though refined, was equally fit for the beneficial exercise of liberty as every other state, which was not more refined. The controul, he thought, must be strong in the direct ratio of passion, as well as the inverse ratio of knowledge and reason. Having long viewed, with anxiety, the new philosophy become fashionable in France, he bestowed the most accurate attention on the designs of its votaries, as they gradually unfolded themselves. A sagacity, as penetrating as his views were comprehensive, discovered to him the nature of those principles which guided the revolutionists, as well as the characters on which they were operating. The notions of liberty that were cherished by the French philosophy he accounted speculative and visionary, and in no country reducible to salutary practice: he thought they proposed much less restraint than was necessary to govern any community, however small, consisting of men as they are known from experience; he conceived also that the volatile, impetuous, and violent character of the French, demanded in so great a nation, much closer restraints than were requisite in many other states. From the same philosophy which generated their extravagant notions

unfolds his view of the French revolution; considers its principles, and the characters on which they were operating.

* See Life of Burke, passim.

of

CHAP. XLIV.

1790. points out its first effects,

of freedom proceeded alſo infidelity. He had many years before* predicted that the joint operation of theſe cauſes, unleſs watchfully and ſteadily oppoſed, would overturn civil and religious eſtabliſhments, and deſtroy all ſocial order. The compoſition of the national aſſembly, the degradation of the nobility, the abolition of the orders, the confiſcation of the property of the church, and many other acts, tended to confirm the opinion which he had formed. Much as he deteſted the outrages, he reprobated the principles more, and foreſaw that in their unavoidable operation, they would lead to far greater enormities: in the ſpirit and details of the new conſtitution, he did not expect either happineſs, or even permanent exiſtence. The vicinity of France to England made him apprehenſive leaſt the ſpeculations of that country ſhould make their way into this, and produce attempts againſt a conſtitution founded on obſervation and experience, and not on viſionary theories. The approbation manifeſted by many Britons, both of the doctrines and proceedings of the French revolutioniſts, increaſed his apprehenſion. When he found that his friend, of whoſe wiſdom and genius he entertained ſo very exalted an opinion,

and deduces its outrageous exceſſes from its nature and doctrines.

* This was the opinion which he had maintained of infidelity and ſpeculative politics in general, in his vindication of natural ſociety, and in his letter to the Sheriffs of Briſtol, and of French infidelity and ſpeculative politics in particular, in his ſpeech after returning from France in 1773;* and in all his ſpeeches and writings, whenever the occaſion required his admonition.

* Life of Burke, p. 161.

was

1790. He reprobates it as an example to England.

was among the admirers of the recent changes in France; he was anxious lest a statesman to whose authority so much weight was due, should be misunderstood to hold up the transactions in that country as a fit object of our imitation. Our patriotic ancestors had with cautious wisdom guarded against the contagion of French despotism, which had not only infected our sovereigns Charles and James, but also made some impression on many of their subjects. The danger in the last ages, he observed, was from an example of tyranny in government, and intolerance in religion. The disease was now altered, but far more likely to be infectious. Our present danger arose from atheism instead of bigotry, anarchy instead of arbitrary power. Through an admiration of men professing to be the votaries of liberty, those who did not thoroughly examine the real features of the French revolution, might be led to imitate the excesses of an irrational, unprincipled, proscribing, confiscating, plundering, ferocious, bloody, and tyrannical democracy*. He severely reprobated the conduct of the army: the abstract proposition that soldiers ought not to forget they were citizens, he did not combat; but applied to any particular case, it depended entirely on the circumstances: in the recent conduct of the French guards, it was not an army embodied under the respectable patriot citizens of the state, in resisting tyranny; it was the case of common soldiers deserting from their officers, to join a furious and licentious populace. The conduct of the

* See Parliamentary Debates, Feb 9, 1790.

British

CHAP. XLIV. 1790.

British soldiery in 1688, was totally different from the conduct of the French soldiery in 1789. William of Orange, a prince of the blood royal of England, was called in by the flower of the English aristocracy to defend its ancient constitution, and not to level all distinctions. To this prince, so warmly invited, the aristocratic leaders who commanded the troops, went over with their several corps, as to the deliverer of their country: military obedience changed its object; but military discipline was not for a moment interrupted in its principle. After enumerating the constituents and acts of the French revolution, he contended that in almost every particular, and in the whole spirit of the transaction, that change differed from the alteration effected by Britain. "We," said Mr. Burke, "took solid securities; settled doubtful questions; and corrected anomalies in our law. In the stable fundamental parts of our constitution, we made no revolution; no, not any alteration at all; we did not weaken the monarchy; perhaps it might be shewn that we strengthened it very considerably. The church was not impaired; the nation kept the same ranks, the same privileges, the same franchises, the same rules for property. The church and state were the same after the revolution that they were before, but better secured in every part."

He controverts the allegation of similarity between the French and British revolutions, and praises the British constitution as contrasted with the French system.

Mr. Sheridan concurs in Mr. Fox's views of the French revolution.

Mr. Sheridan declared that he entirely disagreed from Mr. Burke concerning the French revolution, and expressed his surprize that a senator whose general principles had been uniformly so friendly to liberty, and to the British constitution, could declare

clare or feel an indignant and unqualified deteſtation of all the acts of the patriotic party in France. He conceived theirs to be as juſt a revolution as ours; proceeding upon as ſound a principle, and a greater provocation. Abhorring their exceſſes, he imputed them to the depravity of the old government, the ſentiments and characters which deſpotiſm formed. He himſelf regarded the French revolution as a glorious ſtruggle for liberty, and wiſhed its ſupporters the fulleſt ſucceſs. Concerning the Britiſh revolution, he no leſs differed from Mr. Burke. That event was founded on the ſame principle with the French change; regard for the rights of man. It overturned tyranny, gave real efficient freedom to this country, which he would wiſh to ſee diffuſed throughout the world*. Mr. Pitt teſtified his high approbation of the principles laid down concerning our excellent

* Mr. Sheridan's admiration of the French revolution appears to have ariſen firſt from conſidering it as a triumph of liberty over deſpotiſm, in which eſtimate he had not paid an adequate attention to its peculiar nature and principles; and ſecondly, from an idea that in principle it reſembled our revolution, though diſſimilarity had been very clearly and ſtrongly ſtated by Mr. Burke, and that ſtatement, though not admitted, had not been overturned by Mr. Sheridan, or any of his ſupporters*. His ardent wiſh for the general diffuſion of a liberty producing the greateſt bleſſings to Britain, overlooked the diverſities of national characters in different countries. From a partial conſideration of the caſe, inſtead of an accurate and complete view of every circumſtance, and its whole character, appeared to ariſe the prepoſſeſſions of many men of genius and patriotiſm in favour of the French revolution.

* See Parliamentary Debates, February 1790.

conſtitution

CHAP. XLIV.

1790.

Mr. Pitt, praising the British constitution, delivers no opinion on the French system.

constitution; for these he declared this country to the latest posterity ought gratefully to revere the name of Mr. Burke. With that caution which, advancing all that was necessary, abstained from declarations not required by the occasion, Mr. Pitt confined his applause to that part of Mr. Burke's speech which referred to the constitution of Britain. That was a subject of discussion that could never be foreign to a British parliament: concerning the French revolution, as affecting, or likely to affect France itself, he delivered no opinion.

Colonel Phipps and Sir George Howard, as military men, strongly objected to the panegyric pronounced by Mr. Fox, on the French guards, as a model of military conduct, and contrasted their desertion of their master, and junction with rioters, with the behaviour of the British troops, during the disturbances of 1780. Our soldiers did not, in violation of their oaths, and of their allegiance, join anarchy and rebellion, but feeling as citizens and soldiers, patiently submitted to the insults of the populace; in spite of provocation, maintained the laws, and acted under the constituted authorities of the realm.

Dissenters again propose to seek the repeal of the test act.

The dissenters, encouraged by the smallness of the majority which had rejected Mr. Beaufoy's motion of the former year, persevered in their application to parliament, and spared no efforts, either by general appeals to the public, or by canvassing particular members of the legislature; nor were grounds wanting to excite their sanguine hopes of success. The French revolution was favored by a considerable

1790.

considerable number of Britons, who venerating the principles of liberty that were enjoyed by themſelves, regarded with pleaſure the ſuppoſed diffuſion of freedom to their neighbours. This approbation of the Gallic ſyſtem, in many was not without a tinge of their peculiar doctrines; and they began to think that the higheſt perfection of a free government conſiſted in exemption from reſtraint. Hence great numbers, totally unconnected with the diſſenters, and before quite indifferent about their peculiar views and intereſts, became zealous advocates for the repeal of the teſt and corporation acts, as inimical to the rights of man, lately promulgated in the neighbouring nation. On theſe viſionary theories the claims of the diſſenters were maintained in periodical publications*, which were employed in promoting their cauſe, and in other occaſional works produced for their ſervice. The leaders of the nonconformiſts having declared their enmity to the national religion, found ready and willing auxiliaries among thoſe who had no religion at all. The deiſts, encouraged by the aſpect of affairs in France to hope for the ſpeedy diffuſion of infidelity, or as they phraſed it, *light*, eagerly joined in a meaſure tending to weaken the great bulwark of national faith. From the time of the French revolution, we may date a coalition between the deiſts and the Socinian diſſenters, which, in its political or religious effects, afterwards extended to many others. Republicans, aware of the cloſe connection between the church and monarchy, moſt readily joined a claſs of men

Circumſtances apparently favourable to it.

* See Analytical Review, paſſim.

 who

CHAP. XLIV. 1790.

who were alleged to ſeek the downfal of our eccleſiaſtical eſtabliſhment; a change, which they well knew, would tend to the overthrow of the monarchy. Beſides this new acceſſion of ſtrength, the circumſtance of an approaching election appeared alſo favourable to the attempt of the diſſenters, on account of their great weight and influence in many counties and corporations, and their avowed determination to exert them on the enſuing occaſion, in the ſupport of ſuch candidates only as were known, or ſhould promiſe to be their ſupporters*. Farther to ſtrengthen their cauſe, they propoſed to conſolidate with their own, the intereſts of the Roman catholic diſſenters, and from the various conſtituents of their force, they had ſanguine expectations of ſucceſs.

They are ſtrenuouſly oppoſed by members of the church.

On the other hand, the friends of the church, though not ſo early in their preparations, were fully as vigorous when they did commence. Leſs numerous, but more forcible, literary efforts were made in defence of our eccleſiaſtical eſtabliſhment. The caſe was argued from the probable tendency of diſſent, from actual experience of the general conduct of diſſenters, and from the preſent ſtate of political affairs. On the firſt head it was obſerved, that ill-will to the eſtabliſhment† muſt in

Work entitled *Review of the caſe of Proteſtant Diſſenters.*

* This mode of proceeding is much blamed by eminent, but moderate members of their own body, whoſe opinion I have heard very lately in perſonal converſation.

† See *Review of the caſe of proteſtant diſſenters*; a celebrated pamphlet imputed to Dr. Horſeley.

all

all governments belong to the character of the dissenter, if he be an honest man, however it may be softened by his natural good disposition, or restrained by political sagacity. A dissenter may occasionally support an establishment which he hates, if he foresee that its ruin would raise another from which his party would meet with less indulgence*. But a preference to his own sect is in itself a virtuous principle; every dissenter must be inclined to use any influence or authority with which an imprudent government may entrust him, to advance his sect in the popular esteem, and to increase its numbers. He will employ all means that appear to himself fair and justifiable, to undermine the church, if he hope that its fall may facilitate the establishment of his own party, or some other more congenial to his own. In all this, the crime is not in the man, but in the government entrusting him with a power, which he cannot but misuse. The man himself, all the while, supposes he is doing good, and his country service; and the harm which he may effect under the notion of doing good, will be the greater in proportion to his abilities and virtues: on these undeniable principles the policy of a test is founded. To confirm arguments from probable tendency, appeals were made to facts; and the history of dissenters was traced from the first germs of puritanism to the present time. Under certain restrictions, they had

* The dissenters often cited their fidelity to the house of Hanover, and enmity to the Stuarts. This remark was probably intended to account for their zeal.

CHAP. XLIV. 1790.

been beneficial to the community, but without these restrictions, they had been hurtful. This position was illustrated by views of their proceedings during the last century; from the attainment of partial advantage, to the overthrow of the church and monarchy, the destruction of rank, confiscation of property, cruel persecutions, and massacres. The principles which had produced such enormities were now cherished and supported, and wanted only predominant power to give them effect. Dr. Priestley, followed by a numerous tribe of votaries, had published his enmity to the church; while Dr. Price had no less publicly proclaimed his enmity to monarchy. They and their disciples had, from the downfall of the orders in France, become more eager in their expectations, more confident in their boasts, and more incessant in their efforts. For these and other reasons founded on the same principles, the most eminent of the prelates, the body of the clergy, and the friends of the church, called to the people to assist them in defending the ecclesiastical establishment. The dissenters, to have an advocate of abilities proportioned to their conception of the importance of the question, entrusted the discussion of their cause to the brilliant and powerful talents of Mr. Fox; and on the 2d of March the orator brought the subject before the house of commons. Acquainted with the arguments employed by Dr. Horsely, and other champions of the church, he directed his reasoning chiefly to impugn their allegations, and pursued nearly the order of those whom he wished to confute. It was, he contended, unwarrantable to infer *a priori*, and contrary to the profes-

Dissenters entrust their cause to the transcendent talents of Mr. Fox.

sions

ſions and declarations of the perſons holding ſuch opinions, that their doctrines would produce acts injurious to the common weal. Men ought not to be judged by their opinions, but by their actions. Speculative notions ought never to diſqualify a man for executing an office, the performance of whoſe duties depends upon practical abilities, diſpoſitions, and habits. The object of the teſt laws at firſt had been to exclude anti-monarchical men from civil offices; but ſuch conduct proceeded upon falſe pretences, it tended to hypocriſy, and ſerved as a reſtraint on the good and conſcientious only. Inſtead of a formal and direct oath of allegiance, they reſorted, by means of a religious teſt, to an indirect political ſtandard. The danger of the church aroſe only from the ſupine negligence of the clergy, and the ſuperior activity and zeal of the diſſenters, in diſcharging the duties of their ſacred functions. Hiſtory exhibited the diſſenters ſupporting the principles of the Britiſh conſtitution, while the high church promoted arbitrary power. When this country had been diſtracted with internal troubles and inſurrections, the diſſenters had with their lives and properties ſtood forward in its defence. Their exertions had powerfully contributed to defeat the rebellions in 1715 and 1745, to maintain the conſtitution, and eſtabliſh the Brunſwick family on the throne: in thoſe times every high churchman was a Jacobite, and as inimical to the family of Hanover, as the diſſenters were earneſt in their ſupport. An attempt had recently been made, with too great ſucceſs, to raiſe a high-church party: the diſcipline of the church, and the abſtract duties which ſhe

His view of the ſubject,

CHAP. XLIV. 1790.

prefcribed, he admired and revered, as fhe avoided all that was fuperftitious, and retained all that was effential: he therefore declared himfelf her warm friend. Individual members of the body he efteemed for their talents, learning, and conduct; but as a political party, the church never acted but for mifchief. Objections had been raifed for the repeal, from the French revolution; but this great event was totally irrelevant, as an argument againft the claims of the diffenters: it had, indeed, a contrary tendency; the French church was now paying the penalty of former intolerance. Though far from approving of the fummary and indifcriminate forfeiture of church property, in that country, he could not but fee that its caufe was ecclefiaftical oppreffion. This fhould operate as a warning to the church of England; perfecution may prevail for a time, but ultimately terminates in the punifhment of its abettors. He was aware that the caufe which he had undertaken, was not at prefent popular; fome of thofe whom he moft highly valued differed with him upon this fubject. So far was he individually from having any connection with the diffenters, that in them he had experienced the moft violent political adverfaries; but regarding their caufe as the caufe of truth and liberty, he fhould give it his warmeft fupport both on the prefent and every future occafion. He concluded with propofing a more fpecific motion for the revifion of the teft act, than any which was formerly made.

and anfwer to objections.

Mr. Pitt, after arguing that eligibility to offices in any community, was a queftion not of right but expediency,

Mr. Pitt continues to treat admiffibility

expediency, conſidered the teſt act upon that ground. Preſuming the utility of the eccleſiaſtical eſtabliſhment to be generally granted, he enquired whether the principles of the diſſenters did not aſpire at the ſubverſion of the church, and whether their conduct did not manifeſt an intention of carrying theſe principles into practice. Mr. Fox had propoſed to judge men, not by their opinions, but by their actions. This was certainly the ground for procedure in judicial caſes; but in deliberative, thepolicy of prevention was often not only wiſe but neceſſary; opinions produced actions, therefore provident lawgivers and ſtateſmen muſt often inveſtigate opinions, in order to infer probable conduct. Leading diſſenters, from their principles inimical to the church, had indicated intentions immediately hoſtile; and favourite arguments in their works were the uſeleſſneſs of an eſtabliſhment, and the probability that by vigour and unanimity it might be overthrown. Againſt ſuch avowed deſigns, it became all thoſe who deſired the preſervation of the church, firmly to guard. Admiſſibility into offices of great truſt would obviouſly increaſe the power of the diſſenters: the aſſertions of their advocates, that their theological opinions had no influence on their political conduct, were moſt effectually confuted by their own declarations. At a general meeting they had ſubſcribed reſolutions recommending to voters to ſupport, at the election, ſuch members only as favoured the repeal. Thus while they themſelves reprobated a religious teſt eſtabliſhed by the conſtituted authorities of the kingdom, they wiſhed to enforce a political teſt by their own

CHAP. XLIV.

1790.

to offices as a mere queſtion of expediency.

and deems the leaders of the diſſenters inimical to our eſtabliſhment.

CHAP. XLIV. 1790.

ſole authority. Perceiving their general principles practically operating in conduct hoſtile to the church, he ſhould vote againſt a repeal, which in the preſent circumſtances he deemed injurious to our eſtabliſhment.

Mr. Burke, from various details and documents, endeavoured to prove, that the diſſenters anxiouſly deſired, and confidently expected, the abolition of tithes and the liturgy; and that they were bent on the ſubverſion of the church *. The arguments recently and now employed in the writings and ſpeeches of the friends of the church, the conduct of the diſſenters, and the downfal of the French hierarchy, placed in the moſt ſtriking light by Mr. Burke, added powerfully to the effect of Mr. Pitt's reaſoning, and made a deep impreſſion on members of parliament. In a meeting conſiſting of about four hundred, there was a majority of near three to one againſt the projected repeal.

The arguments againſt the application.

Great majority againſt the the repeal.

The ſpirit of change extended itſelf to our political conſtitution; two days after the rejection of Mr. Fox's motion, Mr. Flood propoſed a reform in the repreſentation of the people in parliament. This propoſition, like the reaſoning for the eligibility of diſſenters, was grounded upon abſtract theories concerning the rights of men. In a ſpeech replete with metaphyſical ſubtlety, he endeavoured to prove, that in the popular branch of our government, the conſtituent body was inadequate to the purpoſe of elections.

Mr. Flood propoſes a reform in parliament;

* To eſtabliſh theſe poſitions, he quoted paſſages from the reſolutions at the public meetings; their catechiſms; the writings of Doctors Price and Prieſtley, and other ſupporters of the cauſe.

elections. Electoral franchises ought to be formed on principles both of property and number. Electors should be numerous, because numbers are necessary to the spirit of liberty; possessed of property, because property is conducive to the spirit of order. Pursuing these principles through various theoretical niceties, and applying them to the actual state of representation, he endeavoured to evince the necessity of a reform, which should extend electoral franchise to every householder. In answer to this theory, Mr. Windham argued from plain fact and experience. Mr. Flood had proved by an arithmetical statement, what no one denied, that the representation was unequal, but he had not proved from political history and reasoning, that it was inadequate. Statesmen and lawgivers should argue from experience, and not from visionary theories; we had no *data* to ascertain the operation of such fanciful projects. Our representation as it stood, answered its purpose, as appeared in the welfare of the people, and the prosperity of the country. According to the present system, it was evident that the influence of the people was very extensive and powerful. It was their voice that sanctioning, permitted the most important acts of the executorial government; the commencement and continuance of war; the conclusion of peace, and the appointment of ministers were most frequently dictated by the people. Their weight was fully as great as expediency, their own security, and happiness admitted. Besides were parliamentary reform generally desirable, the present æra of speculation, change, and ferment, was totally unfit for the purpose. Messrs. Burke, Pitt, and others

1790. his subtle theory

is controverted by Mr. Windham.

CHAP. XLIV.

1790. He withdraws his motion.

others maintaining the ſame ground, and a great majority appearing inimical to Mr. Flood's plan, he withdrew his motion. Theſe were the only great political queſtions which engaged the Houſe of Commons that ſeaſon; and there they reſted without extending to the Peers.

Petitions from dealers in tobacco, praying to repeal the law ſubjecting them to the excife. A motion to that effect by Mr. Sheridan.

Subjects of revenue occupied the chief attention of parliament, during the remainder of the ſeſſion. Dealers in tobacco preſented a great number of petitions, praying for the repeal of the act, which ſubjected that commodity to the exciſe. Mr. Sheridan took the lead in this ſubject, and, having in a ſplendid ſpeech directed his eloquence againſt the whole ſyſtem of exciſe laws, by the fertility of his genius, in his illuſtrations, he gave an appearance of novelty to ſo very trite a ſubject. He came at laſt to the peculiar hardſhips of the tobacco bill, enforced the objections made the preceding year, and propoſed a reſolution, that the ſurvey of the exciſe is inapplicable to the manufactory of tobacco. It was contended by miniſters, that the arguments againſt this application of exciſe, reſted on the teſtimony of dealers, who had derived a great profit from fraudulent traffic, of which they were now deprived by the new mode of collection. It could be no juſt argument againſt a plan for the prevention of illicit trade, that it was not ſanctioned by the approbation of contraband dealers. Was it unfair or illiberal to doubt the veracity and honour of a ſmuggler, when he gives teſtimony concerning his forbidden articles. The extent of former frauds was obvious in the productiveneſs of the late preventive means. Since its ſubjection to the exciſe, the revenue from tobacco

had

had increaſed upwards of three hundred thouſand pounds a-year *. For theſe reaſons, Mr. Sheridan's motion was negatived by a majority of a hundred and ninety-one to a hundred and forty-ſeven. CHAP. XLIV. 1790. is negatived.

Financial ſtatements.

In the month of April, Mr. Pitt opened his ſcheme of finance for the year; having in general ſtated the proſperous ſituation of the country, to prove and illuſtrate his poſition, he recapitulated the extraordinary expences, defrayed in 1789, in addition to the regular eſtabliſhment. Notwithſtanding theſe unforeſeen demands, though we had borrowed only one million, we had paid ſix millions of debt. The increaſe of revenue, which had thus liquidated ſo many and great charges, originated in two permanent cauſes, the ſuppreſſion of ſmuggling, and the increaſe of commerce †. Our navigation

* From the ſtatement of the tobacconiſts, it appeared, that the manufacturers were about four hundred in number; eight millions of pounds were annually ſmuggled. The revenue of which amounted to four hundred thouſand pounds ſterling; this ſum purloining from the public they divided among themſelves, ſo that each manufacturer on an average gained a thouſand a year, by cheating the public.

† The exports for the year 1789, as valued by the Cuſtom-houſe entries, amounted to no leſs a ſum than £18,513,000 of which the Britiſh manufactured goods exported, amounted to £13,490,000 Upon an average of the exports ſix years prior to the American war, which average he took on account of thoſe years being the period in which our commerce flouriſhed moſt, it appeared, that the Britiſh manufactured goods exported, amounted to no more than £10,343,000 The imports for that year, amounted to a higher ſum than was ever before known, being valued at £17,828,000 This increaſe of import, which might at firſt appear diſadvantageous, as it might ſeem to leſſen the balance of trade in favour of the country, Mr. Pitt, having traced

CHAP. XLIV.

1790.
Prosperity of the country.

tion* had increased in proportion to our commerce. This prosperity arose from the industry and enterprize, and capital, which are formed and protected under the British constitution. A system productive of so momentous benefits, it was our most sacred duty to defend against all innovations. Mr. Sheridan endeavoured, as in the preceding year, to controvert the minister's calculations, and through the same means, by including in a general average, the year 1786, that had been unproductive from causes peculiar to itself. The supplies for the army, navy, and ordnance, were nearly the same as in the former year: no new taxes were imposed; but there was a lottery as usual.

Mr. Dundas presents an account of our East India possessions.

Mr. Dundas about the same time, presented an account of the financial state of India. The result of his statement was, that the revenue considerably exceeded the product of the former year †; and that the

traced to its real source, shewed to arise from circumstances demonstrating the wealth and prosperity of the nation. It issued in remitted property from the East and West Indies, from the increased products of Ireland, shewing the growing prosperity of the sister kingdom, from the Greenland and South Wales fisheries, being wealth poured in from the ocean.

* In the year 1773, there belonged to British ports, 9,224 vessels, and 63,000 seamen; and in the year 1785, 11,085 vessels, and 83,000 seamen, shewing an increase of seamen in 1788, above the number in 1773, of no less than one third.

† The revenues of Bengal amounted to		£5,619,999
— of Madras		1,213,229
— of Bombay		138,228
		£6,371,451
Charges of Bengal	£3,183,250	
of Madras	1,302,037	
of Bombay	568,710	5,053,997
	£5,053,997	£1,297,454

To

the increafe though, in fome particulars, owing to temporary circumftances, was chiefly the effect of of permanent caufes. The fyftem of juftice and moderation adopted from the time that the territorial poffeffions were fubjected to the controul of the Britifh government, had produced the moft beneficial confequences both to the natives and to this country. The landed revenues being much more willingly paid, were much more eafily collected. The friendly intercourfe between the Hindoos and the Britifh, had fuggefted various improvements in the collection. Foftered by a humane and equitable adminiftration, the internal commerce of our India fettlements had greatly increafed. Obferving rigid faith with the Indian natives, we had to encounter no formidable confederacies, which fhould at once diminifh territorial improvement, aud caufe enormous expences. Profperity arifing from a general fcheme of policy at once wife and liberal, muft increafe with accelerated rapidity. In a few years the Company would be enabled to pay off their arrears*: Britifh India would be more flourifhing in wealth, in commerce, manufactures, and in every enjoyment, than any other part of the whole continent of Hindoftan. In the prefent ftate of our

To this amount of the net revenue was to be added £230,361 for exports; and the fum of £65,000 charges for Bencoolen and the Prince of Wales's ifland; leaving on the whole, a net fum of £2,147,815 applicable to the difcharge of debts, and the purchafe of inveftments.

* The debts of the company for the laft year were £7,604,754 thofe of the prefent year £6,501,385 giving a decreafe of £1,103,369.

power,

CHAP. XLIV. 1790.

power, we certainly had no danger to apprehend from any European nation. Holland was in alliance with us, and the French were not in a ſituation to diſturb Britiſh India. We had ſtill one enemy in the country, but without European auxiliaries, unſupported by the other native powers, Tippoo Saib could not be formidable to the Britiſh force. Mr. Francis endeavoured to controvert Mr. Dundas's allegations reſpecting both the territorial and commercial ſituation of affairs, and reſted his objections chiefly upon extracts from letters. Theſe Mr. Dundas inſiſted, being garbled, were partial and incomplete evidence; and reſolutions formed on Mr. Dundas's ſtatement, were propoſed and adopted. The houſe voted ſeveral ſums as a recompence for ſervice, and an indemnification for loſſes ſuſtained in the cauſe of the public. On a meſſage from his majeſty, parliament beſtowed an annuity of a thouſand pounds for twenty years, on Dr. Willis, who, under providence, had been ſo inſtrumental in reſtoring to the country ſo valuable a bleſſing*. The ſalary of the ſpeaker was augmented from three thouſand to ſix thouſand a year. In a committee upon American claims, Mr. Pitt repreſented to the houſe the loſſes ſuſtained by the family of Penn; their caſe was different from that of any of the other American loyaliſts, and therefore could not be governed by the rules which the houſe had eſtabliſhed reſpecting the generality of caſes. He propoſed to grant to them and their heirs four thouſand per annum out of the conſolidated fund. Mr. Wilberforce moved for the conſideration of the ſlave-trade; moſt of the time allotted to that ſubject was

* See vol. 4. chap. 41.

occupied

occupied in hearing evidence, and no bill was introduced during this sessſion.

CHAP. XLIV.

1790.

Libels againſt the commons on account of Haſtings' trial.

The trial of Mr. Haſtings made but little progreſs during the preſent ſeſſion. The court ſat but thirteen days, in which the managers of the houſe of commons went through the charge relative to the receipt of preſents, which was opened by Mr. Anſtruther, and ſummed up by Mr. Fox, in a ſpeech which laſted two days. Mr. Burke detailed the circumſtances which retarded the trial: the appointed mode of procedure had increaſed the difficulties and delays; the managers had propoſed in the written evidence, to confine recital of letters and papers to ſuch extracts as related to the charges; but the counſel for Mr. Haſtings inſiſted on reading the whole of ſuch documents, though many of them were extremely long; and the Lords had agreed that no partial quotation from any paper could be received as evidence; that either the whole contents, or no part ſhould be adduced; and the reſolution evidently tending to promote impartial and complete enquiry, Mr. Burke complained of as an obſtacle to the proſecution. It was however, he contended, the duty of the houſe of commons, and their managers, to perſevere in the trial, without regarding any hindrances which might occur. He moved two reſolutions to that effect, and the motions were both carried. Mr. Haſtings continued to have a moſt zealous and ardent advocate in Major Scott, who very frequently employed not only his tongue but his pen in the cauſe. Scott had indeed a great propenſity to literary exhibitions; and ſundry letters to editors of newſpapers, and ſeveral

CHAP. XLIV. 1790.

ſeveral pamphlets, manifeſted his zeal as a pleader, and his fruitfulneſs as an author. Among his other effuſions was a letter ſubſcribed with his own name, in a newſpaper called the Diary; this eſſay contained many injurious aſſertions againſt the managers, and alſo blamed the houſe of commons for ſupporting the impeachment. On the 17th of May, General Burgoyne complained of the letter as a groſs libel. Major Scott avowed himſelf the author; but declared that he meant no offence to the houſe. If he had been guilty of an error, he had been miſled by great examples; Meſſrs. Burke and Sheridan had publiſhed *ſtronger* * libels than ever he had written. After offering this defence, Scott withdrew from the houſe; ſeveral motions of cenſure were made, and various modifications were offered: Mr. Burke was very urgent that an exemplary puniſhment ſhould be inflicted; the conduct of Mr. Scott, he averred, had been extremely reprehenſible: from the commencement of the proſecution he promoted libels againſt the managers, and their conſtituents†. After a long conſideration it was agreed, that the letter ſhould be voted a groſs libel, and that the author ſhould be cenſured in his place.

* If either of theſe gentlemen publiſhed libels, few will controvert the Major's opinion, that they muſt be *ſtronger* than any which he wrote.

† Mr. Burke ſaid, he was well aſſured, that not leſs than twenty thouſand pounds had been expended in libels ſupporting Mr. Haſtings; that Major Scott was his agent in all theſe caſes, and the common libeller of the houſe.

While

1790. Dispute with Spain about Nootka Sound.

While the nation flourished in the enjoyment of peace, an alarm arose that so beneficial a tranquillity would be speedily interrupted. On the 5th of May Mr. Pitt delivered a message from his majesty to the commons, and the Duke of Leeds to the peers; intimating an apprehension that the peace, during which Britain had so greatly prospered, might be broken. The following were the circumstances in which the message originated. During the last voyage of the celebrated Cook, the Resolution and Discovery having touched at Nootka (or Prince William's) Sound, the crews purchased a considerable number of valuable furs, which they afterwards disposed of to very great advantage in China; and Captain King, who published the last volume of Cook's voyages, recommended the traffic with those northern coasts, as very lucrative. In consequence of this advice, some mercantile adventurers settled in the East Indies*, and having consulted Sir John Macpherson the governor general, with his consent they undertook to supply the Chinese with furs from those regions, and also ginseng, an article that was likewise plentiful: for this purpose they fitted out two small vessels. The trade proved so advantageous, that in the year 1788 the adventurers determined to form a permanent settlement. With this view Mr. Mears, the gentleman principally concerned, purchased ground from the natives,

* The statement of the grounds of the dispute is compressed from the memorial of Lieutenant Mears, presented to Mr. Secretary Grenville, which see in State papers, 1790.

and

CHAP. XLIV. 1790.

and built a house which he secured and fortified, as a repository for his merchandize. The following year the settlement was enlarged; more land was bought from the country proprietors, and about seventy Chinese, with several artificers, constituted the establishment. In the month of May, two Spanish ships of war arrived in the Sound; for some days they made no hostile attempt, but on the fourteenth, one of the captains seized an English vessel, conveyed the officers and men on board the Spanish ships, and afterwards sent them prisoners to a Spanish port. He also took possession of the lands and buildings belonging to the new factory, removed the British flag, and declared that all the lands between Cape Horn, and the sixtieth degree of north latitude, on the western coast of America, were the undoubted property of the Spanish king. Another vessel was captured afterwards under the same pretence; the crews of both were thrown into prison, and the cargoes were sold for the captors, without the form either of condemnation or judicature. The Spanish ambassador first informed the court of London that the ships had been seized; and at the same time expressed his master's desire, that means might be taken for preventing his Britannic majesty's subjects from frequenting those coasts, which he alleged to have been previously occupied by the subjects of the Catholic king. He also complained of the fisheries carried on by the British subjects in the seas adjoining to the Spanish continent, as being contrary to the rights of the crown of Spain. His Britannic majesty immediately demanded adequate satisfaction to the individuals

Insult offered by Spain.

individuals injured, and to the British nation for the insult which had been offered. The viceroy of Mexico had restored one of the vessels*, but had not thereby satisfied the nation; on the contrary, the court of Spain professed to give up the ships as a favour, not as a right, and asserted a direct claim to exclusive sovereignty, navigation, and commerce, in the territories, coasts, and seas in that part of the world. His majesty, far from admitting this allegation, made a fresh demand for satisfaction, and having also received intelligence that considerable armaments were equipping in the ports of Spain, he judged it necessary to prepare on his side for acting with vigor and effect, in supporting the rights and interests of Britain. The message from the king stated the injury and insult, the satisfaction demanded, the reply, the second demand, the subsequent conduct of Spain, and the measures of Britain arising from that conduct: it farther recommended to his faithful commons, to enable him to make such augmentations to his forces as might be eventually necessary. His majesty earnestly wished that the wisdom and equity of the Catholic king might render the satisfaction which was unquestionably due, and that this affair might so terminate as to prevent future misunderstanding, continue and confirm harmony and friendship between the two nations,

CHAP. XLIV.

1790.

Satisfaction demanded. Conduct of Spain.

The king's message to parliament.

* The ship and crew (they said) had been released by the viceroy of Mexico, on the supposition, as he declared, that nothing but ignorance of the rights of Spain could have induced the merchants in question to attempt any establishment on that coast.

CHAP. XLIV. 1790.

which his majesty would ever endeavour to maintain and improve by all means consistent with the dignity of the crown, and essential interests of his subjects*.

The message being taken into consideration, Mr. Pitt declared, whatever the House must feel on the subject of his majesty's communication, he was too well assured of the public spirit of every member, to conceive that any difference of opinion could arise as to the measures which such circumstances would make it necessary to adopt. From the facts stated in the message, it appeared that British subjects had been forcibly interrupted in a traffic which they had carried on for years without molestation, in parts of America where they had an incontrovertible right of trading, and in places to which no country could claim an exclusive right of commerce and navigation. Ships had been seized, restitution and satisfaction demanded, but without effect: the court of Madrid had advanced a claim to the exclusive rights of navigation in those seas, that was unfounded, exorbitant, and indefinite: in its consequences aiming destruction at our valuable fisheries in the southern ocean, and tending to the annihilation of a commerce, which we were just beginning to carry on to the profit of the country, in hitherto unfrequented parts of the globe; it was therefore necessary and incumbent upon the nation to adopt measures which might in future prevent any such disputes. Much as we wished for peace, we must be prepared

* See State Papers, May 25, 1790.

for

for war, if Spain continued to refuse satisfaction for the aggression, and to assert claims totally inconsistent with the rights of independent navigators, to lands which being before unappropriated, they should make their own by occupancy and labour. He therefore moved an address conformable to the message.

On a subject which involved both the interest and honour of the country, there was but one sentiment in both houses of parliament. No British senator could bear without indignant resentment, such an imperious assumption by any foreign power; and in the commons, the first to declare his cordial support was Mr. Fox; he however blamed the minister for having so very lately afforded such a flattering prospect of the continuance of peace, when before that time he had known from the Spanish ambassador, the principal grounds of his majesty's message. It was replied, that this animadversion was founded on a misapprehension of fact; at the period mentioned, government did not know the extent of the Spanish claims, nor the preparations that were carried on in the Spanish ports. An unanimous address was presented by parliament, assuring his majesty of their determination to afford him the most zealous and effectual support for maintaining the dignity of his crown, and the essential interests of his dominions*. This address was soon followed by a vote of credit of a million, for the purpose of carrying into effect the warlike preparations that might be necessary. Motions were

Parliament unanimously pledge their support of the king in vindicating the rights of Britain.

* See State Papers, May 26, 1790.

CHAP. XLIV. 1790.

afterwards made in both houses, for papers that might illustrate the grounds of the dispute, but they were resisted upon an established rule, founded in wise policy, and sanctioned by uniform precedent, that no papers relating to a negociation with a foreign power should be produced while such negociation is pending.

On the 10th of June, his majesty closed the session with a speech, in which he acquainted the two houses that he had yet received no satisfactory answer from Madrid, and was therefore under the necessity of continuing to proceed with expedition and vigour in preparations for war, in the prosecution of which he had received the strongest assurances from his allies, of their determination to fulfil the engagements of the existing treaties. His majesty announced his intention of immediately dissolving the present parliament; and in signifying this determination, he thanked them for the proofs they had given of affectionate and unshaken loyalty to his person, their uniform and zealous regard for the true principles of our invaluable constitution, and their unremitting attention to the happiness and prosperity of the country. In a very concise, but comprehensive and strong summary, his majesty exhibited the effects of their exertions. "The rapid increase (he said) of our manufactures, commerce, and navigation, the additional protection and security afforded to the distant possessions of the empire, the provisions for the good government of India, the improvement of the public revenue, and the establishment of a permanent system for the gradual reduction of the national debt, have furnished

furnished the best proofs of your resolution in encountering the difficulties with which you had to contend, and of your steadiness and perseverance in those measures which were best adapted to promote the essential and lasting interests of my dominions." His majesty farther emphatically added, "The loyalty and public spirit, the industry and enterprize of my subjects, have seconded your exertions. On their sense of the advantages which they at present experience, as well as on their uniform and affectionate attachment to my person and government, I rely for the continuance of that harmony and confidence, the happy effects of which have so manifestly appeared during the present parliament, and which must at all times afford the surest means of meeting the exigencies of war, or of cultivating with increasing benefit the blessings of peace." The parliament was dissolved the following day by proclamation.

Dissolution of parliament.

Warlike preparations.

The preparations for maintaining our rights against aggression were carried on with vigor and expedition, proportioned to the resources of so potent a nation. But it being the intention of the British government to avoid hostilities, unless absolutely necessary for the national honour and security, Mr. Fitzherbert was sent to Madrid with full powers to settle the disputes between the Spanish and British nations, in a decisive manner. The grounds of the Spanish claims were set forth in a declaration to all the European courts, dated the 4th of June, 1790*, and more specifically detailed in a memorial delivered

Diplomatic discussion between Britain and Spain.

* State Papers, 1790.

CHAP. XLIV. 1790.

the 13th of June to Mr. Fitzherbert, the British ambassador*. According to these statements, Spain had a prescriptive right to the exclusive navigation, commerce, and property of Spanish America and the Spanish West Indies. The various treaties with England had recognized that right: in the treaty of Utrecht, which was still in force, Spain and England had agreed, that the navigation and commerce of the West Indies, under the dominion of Spain, should remain in the precise situation in which they stood in the reign of his catholic majesty Charles II. It was stipulated that Spain should never grant to any nation permission to trade with her American dominions, nor cede to any other power any part of these territories †. These rights extended to Nootka Sound; and though Spain had not planted colonies in every part of these dominions, still they were within the line of demarkation that had been always admitted. On the part of England it was answered‡, that though the treaty of Utrecht, and subsequent conventions, recognized the rights of Spain to her dominions in America, and in the West Indies, to be on the same footing as in the reign of Charles II. and we were still willing to adhere to that recognition, the admission by no means proved that Nootka Sound made part of those territories. By the plainest maxims of jurisprudence, whatever is com-

* State Papers, 1790.

† The object of this stipulation was, to exclude France, which was become so closely connected with Spain, from any share in her American trade or possessions.

‡ State Papers, 1790; Mr. Fitzherbert's answer to the Spanish memorial.

mon

[illegible] to the first occupiers; but the right to exclusive occupancy is by occupancy determined: every nation, like every individual, has a right to appropriate whatever they can acquire without infringing on the previous appropriations of others. The English had a right to possess as much of the desert coast of America as they could occupy or cultivate. The Spaniards not having established their claims by either occupancy or labour, proved no right to the exclusive property of Nootka Sound. The seizure, therefore, of the British vessels and British effects, was an injury and an insult for which Britain demanded restitution and satisfaction. The language of British justice, demanding what British power could so easily enforce from any aggressor that dared to provoke its vengeance, was represented by Spain as haughty and menacing; and various difficulties occurred before matters were brought to a decision. The Spaniards professed a desire of conciliation, but were really endeavouring to interest the French government in their behalf; and the royal family of France was sufficiently disposed to support the Bourbon compact; but the king had now lost the power of giving effect to this agreement. The national assembly decreed an armament of fourteen ships of the line, but avowedly to protect their own commerce and colonies, and to embrace no measures that were not purely defensive; and this resolution highly gratified the people, who were not then disposed to go to war with England. Though the preparations of Spain were vigorous as far as her power and resources admitted, yet her fleets

Spain attempts to interest France.

The French nation is adverse to war with England.

CHAP. XLIV. 1790.

fleets consisting of seventy ships of the line, by such sailors as she could collect, was lit to cope with the navy of England, amour one hundred and fifty-eight ships of th manned by British seamen. Finding no pro effectual assistance from France, and consc her own inability to contend with England, began to mingle proffers of concession with her declarations of pacific intention. Mr. F bert having persisted in his demands, relaxing the claims, the Spanish court, on the July, issued a declaration testifying their willi to comply fully with the demands of his nic majesty, by rendering satisfaction and pensation. In order to mitigate to the peo Spain the bitterness of a just concession, extor fear, the declaration* set forth that his Cathol jesty was fully persuaded the king of Britain act to him in the same manner, under simil cumstances. Mr. Fitzherbert having accept declaration, all differences between the Cou Madrid and London were terminated with formality and precision, by a convention † be his Britannic majesty and the king of Spain, sig the Escurial, on the 28th of October, 1790. The ment at Nootka Sound was restored, a full l of trade to all the north-west coasts of Am and navigation and fishery in the southern pacifi confirmed to England. Both nations were eq restricted from attempting any settlement near Cape Horn than the most southerly plant

Spain, hopeless of aid, yields to the demands of Britain.

The disputes are adjusted in a convention.

* State Papers July 24, 1790.
† State Papers, October 28, 1790.

al

already established by Spain. It was agreed, that should any ground of complaint thereafter arise, no violence should be committed, but the case should be reported to the respective courts, who would bring it to an amicable termination.

CHAP. XLIV. 1790.

The declaration of the 24th of July having been received in England, and the result communicated by the Duke of Leeds, secretary of state, to the lord mayor, and published in the Gazette extraordinary, afforded great pleasure to the nation; but the convention completed the satisfaction of the people, who deemed it equally honourable and advantageous to Britain; as the minister without involving the country in a war, had obtained every compensation which justice could demand; and had shewn to other powers, that BRITISH SUBJECTS WERE NOT TO BE MOLESTED WITH IMPUNITY.

CHAP. XLV.

Continental affairs.—Measures of Britain and her allies for counteracting the ambition of Joseph and Catherine.—Poland friendly to the defensive alliance.—Death of Joseph II. emperor of Germany; and character.—Leopold his successor moderate and pacific.—He agrees to open a congress at Reichenbach.—Military operations between the Austrians and Turks; bloody but indecisive.—Habitual prepossessions of Kaunitz and Hertsberg.—Liberal and wise policy of Britain, and ability of Ewart.—Peace between Austria and Turkey, under the guarantee of the defensive alliance.—Operations between Russia and Turkey.—Siege of Ismail.—Desperately valiant defence.—Stormed.—Cruel and dreadful slaughter.—Campaign between Sweden and Prussia.—Peace between Russia and Sweden.—State of affairs in the Netherlands.—Rise of a democratical spirit.—Its votaries propose to subvert the constituted authorities.—Contests between the aristocratical and democratical revolutionists.—Leopold proposes to avail himself of their dissensions.—He offers to redress their real grievances, but vindicates his right to the sovereignty.—Britain and her allies mediate between the Flemings and Leopold.—Under their guarantee the Netherlands are restored to their ancient privileges.—They obtain further concessions from Leopold.—They find their security in their ancient mixed government.—Proceedings of the French revolutionists in forming the new constitution.—Qualification of active citizens.—preclude universal suffrage.—Division into departments.—New and comprehensive principle of financial legislation.—Confiscation of clerical property.—Civic oath.—Scheme for converting the spoils of the clergy into ready money.—Boundless power of the mob.—The multitude, civil and military

military.—Destitute of religion.—Mixture of ridiculous levity and serious iniquity.—Anarcharsis Cloots, ambassador from the whole human race.—Abolitition of titles and hereditary nobility.—Summary of changes within the year.—Anniversary celebration of the 14th of July in the Field of Mars.—Federal oath.—Violent proceedings against those who refused it.—Britain.—The French revolution is better understood.—Mr. Pitt and his friends forbear discussion of its merits.—Majority of literary men favour the new system though they censure its excesses.—Sentiments of Mr. Fox.—The clergy are alarmed by the infidelity and confiscation of the revolutionary system.—Burke's work on the subject—effects.—General election.

CHAP. XLV.

1790. Continental affairs.

WHILE Britain was thus successfully employed in securing the blessings of peace to herself, she was desirous of also extending them to others. The grand scheme of confederacy which was formed by Kaunitz for uniting the great continental powers, had been discomfited by the co-operating talents of William Pitt the English minister, and Frederic the Prussian king. The alliance having since been renewed between the two empires, and endangering the balance of power, had stimulated the son of Pitt, and Frederic's counsellors, to form a new plan of defensive confederation, to counteract the ambitious designs of Russia and Austria *. Their project was so extended as to embrace all those states which were likely to be affected by the imperial aggressors.

Measures of Britain and her allies for counteracting the ambition of Joseph and Catharine.

Poland, Sweden, and Turkey, were equally interested in forming a part of this confederacy. Mr. Ewart, British ambassador at Berlin, a man of great abilities,

* Segur's History of Frederic William, vol. ii. p. 136.

CHAP. XLV. 1790.

abilities, and extensive political knowledge, having attained very considerable influence with the Prussian court, employed it in promoting the purposes of the defensive alliance. This minister, viewing the situation and productiveness of Poland, saw that it might be rendered the source of immense political benefit to the confederacy, and might ultimately produce important commercial advantages to Great Britain. Poland might be rendered a formidable barrier to the designs of Russia; and the acquisitions which Prussia might obtain by another dismemberment of Poland, would not contribute so essentially to her security as the independence of the Polish monarchy; it was, therefore, the interest of Prussia to support and strengthen that neighbour *. The Poles themselves were made sensible that it would be mutually beneficial to Prussia and their country to be closely connected. Having long nourished the most indignant resentment against the Russians, their rage was recently inflamed by the insolence of the imperial confederates, who, without asking their consent, had stationed large bodies of troops in their territories, and even urged them to enter into an alliance against Turkey, a power which had been always friendly to Poland; induced by these considerations, they readily acceded to the defensive union, and made vigorous preparations. This confederacy, when joined to the belligerent opposers of the two empires, constituted a sextuple † alliance, comprehending Great Britain, Prussia, Holland, Sweden,

Poland friendly to the defensive alliance.

* Otridge's Annual Register 1791.—Segur, vol. ii. passim.

† Otridge's Annual Register 1791, chap. i.

Poland,

Poland, and Turkey. Its first and principal object was to save the Ottoman empire from the grasp of the imperial confederates; and to afford to the contracting parties reciprocal protection from the boundless ambition of the combined aggressors. Not only to liberate Poland from its subjection to Catharine, but to draw to the English ports the numerous productions, naval and commercial, of that extensive and fertile country, formed a secondary, but essential, object of British policy. As negotiation was the first purpose of the powers which were not actually engaged, they made overtures for a congress, which, though rejected by Russia, they, from a recent change in the sovereignty of Austria, expected to meet with a more favourable reception from that power.

Death of Joseph II. emperor of Germany,

Joseph II. emperor of Germany, whose life had been chiefly distinguished for extent and variety of project terminating in disappointment, had long laboured under bodily distemper; if not caused in its origin, increased in its operation, and accelerated in its effects, by the distresses of a mind impatient of crosses encountered from its own injustice, precipitancy, and folly. The gleam of success from Turkey was soon forgotten in the gloomy prospect which opened from the Netherlands. The unbounded spirit of reform had produced subversion; the attempt to govern without controul had, in the most valuable part of his dominions, left him no subjects to command. In Hungary also, his innovations generated discontent, discontent demands of redress; demands of redress were first haughtily refused, but at length extorted concession. Indeed, his imperious [illegible] and his ambition weakened

CHAP. XLV. 1790.

weakened as he approached that period when earthly power and glory could no longer avail. In his last illness, he sought consolation in that religion which for so great a part of his life he had disregarded, and learned on his death-bed, how absurd and pernicious the attempt was to suppress in his subjects that principle which only could restrain turbulent passion, and heal a wounded breast. In the languor of illness, and the awful hour of dissolution, he saw that his policy had been as unwise as unjust; and that disgrace and disaster awaits the prince who attempts to enslave a free and gallant people. Being now weaned from the ambition which had so much agitated his life, he acquired tranquillity, and preserved it to the last. On the 20th of February he expired, in the forty-ninth year of his age, the twenty-fifth of his imperial reign as the successor of his father, and the ninth of his sovereignty over the Austrian dominions as the heir of his mother.

and character.

Joseph II. was by nature ardent in spirit, active in disposition, and fond of distinction. His situation cherished in such a mind the love of power which he had so much the means of gratifying. With lively feeling, but without strength of understanding and originality of genius, in his objects and undertakings he was the creature of imitation. From the splendor of Frederic's character, his illustrious exploits, and his immense improvements of his dominions, as well as the vicinity of their situation, and personal and political intercourse, he chose for a model the Prussian king, without discrimination to understand the peculiar features of his supposed archetype; acuteness to discern the principles and rules of that monarch's

narch's conduct, or compass of mind to comprehend the general system of his measures and actions. He also was an admiring imitator of Catharine, and supposed himself the confident of her counsels when he was only the tool of her schemes. From both he copied infidelity *, but did not copy from them that prudent policy which cherished religion in their subjects, adapted themselves in appearance to the popular prepossessions, and made their respective churches engines of state. He imitated their ambitious projects without possessing the wisdom of plan, or the consistent and well-directed vigour of execution, which accomplished their designs. Springing from a variety of causes, and encouraged to a certain extent by these sovereigns, there prevailed in Europe a great disposition to reform. Frederic clearly apprehending what was right or wrong, innovated wherever change was improvement. Joseph was a reformist because innovation was the favourite pursuit of the times; and on the same principles, by which private votaries of some favourite fashion are often actuated, sought distinction by being a leader of the reigning mode, without considering how far it was wise, prudent, or suited to the circumstances in which he was placed. His pursuit of reform being neither accommodated to the habits nor to the sentiments of its objects, was the primary end of his conduct; and from the violence of his temper, and the total want of moderation, the principal source of his manifold disasters. In his wars, as well as his internal politics, Joseph was a factitious and imitative character.

* See Abbé Barruel, vol. i.

 Without

CHAP. XLV. 1790.

Without military talents or inclinations, without well-founded prospects of advantage, he appears to have sought hostilities from the desire of rivalling his warlike neighbours. Joseph's misfortunes arose entirely from his incapacity of directing himself, and from not being counselled by able and upright men. Without sound judgment himself, he wanted wise and faithful advisers * to oppose projects which were evidently hurtful to the projector. Qualities apparently contrary, indecision with precipitation, obstinacy with fickleness and inconstancy, openness, and benignity of manner and countenance, with duplicity and faithlessness, arose from the same source; an understanding which judged without examination; and a will directed by temporary impulse, without any fixed principles of conduct. The character of Joseph, from his condition, was very conspicuous in its operation, and very pernicious in its effects; but instead of being, as has been often represented, *singular*, is, in its springs and constituents, EXTREMELY COMMON. Whoever observes, in private life, vivacity of fancy without soundness of judgment; ardour of disposition and eagerness of pursuit, without just appreciation of end, or skilful selection of means; emulation in mere fashion; multiplicity of project formed without wisdom, and carried on without constancy, beholds, in a confined scene, the same character exhibited which the world contemplated

* The ruling principle of Kaunitz being the elevation of the House of Austria, successful as he had been as the counsellor of the prudent Maria Theresa, yet he soothed and abetted the impetuous Joseph, in projects that eventually tended to its depression.

templated on the great European theatre, performed by Joseph II. emperor of Germany.

1790. Leopold, his successor, moderate and pacific.

Joseph was succeeded by his brother Leopold, Grand Duke of Tuscany, a prince of a very different character. Accustomed to the pleasurable regions of Italy, and the enervating refinement of Italian manners, Leopold, presiding at Florence, was chiefly distinguished for luxurious softness; and having no incentives to war, or opportunities of ambition, was habitually pacific, and actually indolent. Both from nature and circumstances, and perhaps also from contemplating the effects of his brother's violence, he was remarkable for moderation. When, instead of being an Italian prince, he became head of the house of Austria, he demonstrated that his apparent indolence arose from the want of motives to action, and not from an inherent inertness of character; he shewed himself firm and efficient, but retained his moderation and pacific disposition; and though he did not possess superior talents, was, by his mixed steadiness and prudence *, well qualified to remedy the evils which had proceeded from the capricious and violent Joseph. Averse himself from war as an *adventure of ambition*, he saw, in the circumstances of his affairs, and his relation to foreign powers, strong reasons for promoting his disposition to peace. He was involved in hostilities with his own subjects: at variance with the principal electors, he was in danger of being excluded from the imperial throne: the conquests on the desolated borders of Turkey, obtained at an immense ex-

* See Otridge's Annual Registers for 1791 and 1792. Passim; also Segur, vol. ii.

pence,

CHAP. XLV. 1790.

pence, were of little value. The supplies for carrying on the war had lost, in the Netherlands, their most productive source. A hundred thousand disciplined Prussians hovered over the frontiers of Bohemia, while three other armies were prepared to act in different quarters. England would pour her wealth, and Prussia her troops, to support the revolted Netherlands. From war Austria had little to gain, and much to lose. For these reasons Leopold was disposed to pacification, and acceded to a proposal for opening a congress at Reichenbach in Silesia. Meanwhile the campaign was opened on the frontiers of Turkey. Selim, to compensate the impolicy, and consequent losses of the former year, chose for his vizier Hassan Aly, a man of great ability. The Turks, who imputed the adverse events of the last campaign to the misconduct of the late vizier, were ready and eager to renew the contest, and a great army was prepared. The sultan spared no aid, which superstition could afford, to inspirit his troops. He clad them in black, to denote their readiness to meet death in defence of their cause; and, in concurrence with his chief priests, proclaimed a remission of their sins to all who should die in battle: these incentives, co-operating with the native valour of the Turks, early in the season he had four hundred thousand men ready to take the field. The campaign on the Danube was opened by the capture of Orsova, which having been blockaded during the whole winter by the Austrians, was suddenly reduced through the misapprehension of the garrison. The Turks conceiving a shock of an earthquake to be the explosion of

He agrees to open a congress at Reichenbach.

Military operations between the Austrians and Turks;

of a mine, were ſtruck with a panic, and ſuppoſing themſelves about to be blown up, immediately ſurrendered. A detachment of the Auſtrians beſieged Guirgewo, but the Ottomans, reſuming their wonted courage, marched to its relief. Encountering the Auſtrians they fought with the moſt deſperate valour, threw thoſe brave and diſciplined troops into confuſion, and defeated them with the loſs of three thouſand men. Among the killed was Count Thorn the general, whoſe head the Turks, agreeably to the cuſtom of thoſe ferocious barbarians, diſplayed in triumph through the army. This was the laſt act of hoſtilities carried on between the Turks and the Auſtrians.

bloody, but indeciſive.

At Reichenback the ambition of Kaunitz, which, for forty years, had been chiefly directed to aggrandize the houſe of Auſtria, ſtill entertained hopes of acquiring advantages from the Ruſſian confederacy, and the proſecution of the Turkiſh war, and was averſe to the peace. Count Hertſberg, the Pruſſian miniſter, formed under Frederic, and conſidering every maxim of that illuſtrious monarch's policy as the rule of conduct, without adverting to the change of circumſtances, deſired to attack Auſtria when weak and exhauſted; diſpoſſeſs her of the reſt of Sileſia, abet the revolt in the Netherlands, and prevent the elevation of Leopold to the imperial throne. A more comprehenſive and liberal policy, however, originating in the wiſe councils of Britain, and urged by Mr. Ewart, inculcated the neceſſity of ſacrificing hereditary enmity to ſolid intereſt, and influenced the Pruſſian king. Leopold being no leſs diſpoſed to conciliation, tranquillity was, without

Habitual prepoſſeſſions of Kaunitz and Hertſberg.

Liberal and wiſe policy of Britain, and ability of Ewart.

CHAP. XLV. 1790.

Peace between Austria and Turkey, under the guarantee of the defensive alliance.

difficulty, established; and on the 27th of July a convention was concluded. The king of Hungary agreed to open a negociation for peace, on the basis of reciprocal restitution under the umpirage of the defensive alliance *. The empress of Russia was to be invited to accede to these conditions; but if she should refuse, Leopold was to observe a perfect neutrality between the contending potentates. The king of Prussia would co-operate with the maritime powers to allay the troubles in the low countries, and restore them to the Austrian dominions, on condition that their ancient privileges and constitution were re-established. The English and Dutch ministers engaged in behalf of the respective courts, to guarantee those stipulations; and an armistice for nine months was, not long after, concluded between Leopold and the Turks, which, notwithstanding various obstacles, arising from the artifices of Catharine, terminated in a peace. The war between Russia and Turkey was this year languid in its operations, as Catharine's attention was chiefly directed to the congress in Silesia, and also to schemes of policy in various quarters: some desultory engagements took place, both by land and on the Black Sea, but without any important event. To facilitate her favourite objects of driving the Turks from Europe, and raising her grandson to the Byzantine throne, the empress persevered in a plan of detaching the Greek subjects of Turkey from their obedience.

* Segur, who shews himself well acquainted with continental politics, betrays gross ignorance of the views of Britain, when he deems this league to spring from offensive ambition. See vol. ii, chap. i.

dience. By her encouragement, and pecuniary assistance, a rebellion was fomented in Albania: the leader of the insurgents defeated a Turkish governor; and acquired such power and confidence as to form a regular and extensive plan for emancipating themselves from the Turkish yoke, and offering the sovereignty of Greece to the Russian prince. A memorial *, not unworthy of the descendants of ancient Greeks, stating both the object and plan, was presented to Catharine, and very graciously received; but before it could be matured, Russia had been induced, if not to relinquish, to postpone, her plan of subjugating Turkey. It was the latter end of autumn before Prince Potemkin was in motion: his tardy commencement of the campaign was not without policy and design. The Russian troops, inured to the colds of the North, were much less adapted to the summer heats even of their own southern frontiers. The Asiatic Turks, on the contrary, could easily bear the solstitial season in countries so much colder than their own as the banks of the Danube and the confines of Tartary; but even the autumnal cold of those countries they could not endure; and on the approach of winter it was their uniform practice to leave the army and return to warmer latitudes. Potemkin, knowing the number and valour of those troops, deferred his military operations until they had taken their departure. His plan was, first to reduce Ismail, then Braicklow, which would complete the Russian

Operations between Russia and Turkey.

* The reader will find a translation of this ingenious and eloquent performance in Otridge's Annual Register for 1791, page 278.

conquest

CHAP. XLV. 1790.

conqueſt to the Danube; paſſing that river, to place himſelf between the Turkiſh army and Conſtantinople; and thus compel the vizier either to riſk an engagement, or to accept of a peace on terms preſcribed by Ruſſia. Abandoned by the Aſiatics, the Turkiſh army did not exceed forty thouſand men. Diſſenſions and conſpiracies prevailed in Conſtantinople, and the affairs of the Turks were in the moſt critical and dangerous ſtate; but the Divan, unbroken by theſe diſtreſſing circumſtances, had reſolved to maintain the Ottoman independence to the laſt extremity; and for the accompliſhment of his purpoſe, Selim truſting not only to the reſources which ſtill remained, but to the vigorous mediation of the defenſive alliance, cheriſhed and ſupported the firmneſs of his council. The town of Iſmail had always been deemed the key of the lower Danube: it was ſurrounded by two walls, covered by their reſpective ditches, of conſiderable depth and breadth, and capable of being filled with the waters of the Danube. A ſelect and numerous garriſon had been early appointed, with an artillery amounting to more than three hundred pieces, and lately reinforced by thirty thouſand men. The Ruſſian forces on the Danube were formed into three diviſions; one commanded by Prince Potemkin, a ſecond by Prince Repnin, the third by General Suwaroff. To this laſt body, covered and ſupported by the two others, the ſiege of Iſmail was entruſted. Suwaroff ſurrounded the place with batteries conſtructed on every ſpot of ground which would anſwer the purpoſe; and theſe were loaded with forges for heating the balls, with the heavieſt battering artillery

Siege of Iſmail.

lery and mortars and every other engine of destruction hitherto invented. On the 22d of December the besiegers made a general assault in eight columns: the Turks received them with intrepid valour. Five times were the Russians repulsed: five times they renewed the attack; and at the last onset were discomfited with a slaughter which seemed to render all farther effort hopeless. The besiegers now began to think of nothing but to sell their lives as dearly as possible, when Suwaroff, having dismounted his cavalry to supply the slain infantry, snatched a standard, and running up a scaling ladder, planted it with his own hand on a Turkish battery.

Desperately valiant defence.

Stormed.

Re-animated to enthusiasm by the personal prowess of their general, the Russians not only withstood the attack of the pursuing enemy, but repulsed them, and again became the assailants. The Turks disputed every inch of ground; but the Russians being reinforced by fresh troops from the covering armies, by numbers overpowered the valiant defenders of Ismail, carried post after post till they reduced the whole.

Cruel and dreadful slaughter.

With the fury of enraged barbarians, they effected a merciless, horrid, and undistinguishing slaughter, which spared neither age nor sex. The annals of Attila or of Gesneric, in the benighted ages of Northern Europe, furnish no record of savage butchery which surpasses the carnage at Ismail, by troops employed, according to their mistress's professions, to expel barbarism from this quarter of the globe, and instead of the bloody superstition of Mahomed, to establish the mild and peaceful religion of the meek and benevolent Jesus: such was the Russian mode of making converts to the

CHAP. XLV. 1790.

the Greek church, and extending christianity. The inflexible endurance * of the vanquished was as great as the inflicting cruelty of the conquerors; as the Russians would give, the Turks would receive no quarter: they either rushed on the bayonet, plunged into the Danube, or sought death by some means equally efficacious. Twenty-four thousand of the Turkish soldiers perished in this bloody contest: the governor of Ismail was found covered with wounds; the whole number of massacred Turks, including inhabitants of all ages, sexes, and conditions, amounted nearly to thirty-one thousand †. The slain on the side of the Russians exceeded ten thousand men, among whom were many of their officers.

Campaign between Sweden and Russia.

The king of Sweden, having entirely conciliated the affections of his people, and excited their admiration, by his conduct in the preceding year, was, through their unanimous efforts, enabled to open the campaign of 1790 early in the season. In the beginning of April, putting himself at the head of three thousand

* The suffering fortitude of the Turks illustrates the very ingenious reasoning of Dr. Smith, in his Theory of Moral Sentiments, wherein he accounts for the unconquerable firmness of savages.

† About three hundred Circassian women, consisting partly of those belonging to the Governor's haram, and partly of others who had fled thither for refuge from other harams, were preserved and protected by an English gentleman, in the Russian service, Colonel Cobley, who commanded the dismounted cavalry, when they were on the point of throwing themselves into the Danube to escape violation from the Cossack and Russian soldiers. See Otridge's Annual Register for 1791, page 101.

thousand forces in Finland, he penetrated into the Savalax, a district of Russia not far from Wiborg. Alarmed by the approach of the enemy within a hundred miles of Petersburgh, Catharine sent ten thousand troops to obstruct his progress. They found their enemy entrenched in a very strong position. Trusting to their superior numbers, the Russians attacked the Swedish lines; but the cool intrepid courage of the Swedes, headed by the personal valour and genius of their sovereign, repelled the attack: it was soon, however, renewed by the impulse of national pride, rivalry, indignation, and shame of being defeated by such a handful of men. The engagement, for about two hours, was most desperate, obstinate, and bloody; but rage, fury, and superior numbers, gave way, at last, to calm and determined valour. The Russians left about two thousand dead upon the spot, and Gustavus, encouraged by this success, advanced farther into Russia. Meanwhile, the fleet under the Duke of Suddermania sailed up the gulph of Finland. The prince projected the destruction of the Russian squadron lying in the port of Revel, the great naval arsenal, along with its docks and magazines. The ships were, eleven of the line, three of which carried a hundred guns each, and five frigates; and they were protected by numerous batteries. The Swedish fleet, notwithstanding all these obstacles, on the 13th of May penetrated into the harbour, and in the midst of the hostile fire, maintained for four hours a doubtful conflict; but towards the evening a violent storm arose, which obliged the Swedes to retreat. They afterwards fell in with a Russian fleet

CHAP. XLV. 1790.

fleet from Cronstadt, and an engagement ensued, in which the Swedes at first appeared superior, when night intervening interrupted the contest. The next day battle being renewed, while the Swedish fleet was engaged with the enemy in front, the squadron from Revel appearing in the rear, the duke was in extreme danger of being surrounded, but by judicious manœuvres and bold exertions, assisted by a favourable wind, he extricated himself from the danger, and joined his royal brother not far from Wiborg. Against this city the land and naval force of Sweden directed their efforts; but while they were making dispositions for the purpose, the Russian fleet came in sight. The Swedes were now hemmed in between the united squadrons of Russia and the garrison of Wiborg. His majesty and his army were accompanied by a fleet of gallies, which were likewise enclosed; the only alternative, therefore, was, to force their way through the enemy or to surrender: the former was of course chosen: they effected their escape, but not without incurring very great loss of ships and troops, that were either taken or sunk: the whole number of men either killed or captured, amounted to seven thousand. The genius of Gustavus, stimulated by difficulty, soon refitted his shattered fleet, and recruited his diminished army. On the 9th of July, with his armament, he encountered a large Russian fleet, commanding his own squadron in person, he immediately offered them battle, and conducted his operations with so masterly skill, that, after a very obstinate conflict, he gained a decisive victory. The loss of the Russians amounted to four thousand five

hundred

hundred prisoners, and nearly as many killed and wounded. This defeat astonished and alarmed Catharine: in the great talents of Gustavus, she was at last convinced, she had to encounter a formidable foe, which she had not apprehended in a contest with Sweden. Such an antagonist was not to be subdued either by overwhelming numbers, or the adversity of fortune. Being now abandoned by the Austrians, and threatened by the English and Prussians, she saw her projects respecting Turkey had little chance of being accomplished, if she continued at war with Sweden: she therefore directed the chief efforts of her policy to the attainment of a peace; she accordingly signified to Gustavus a pacific disposition. The Swedish king, finding his country greatly exhausted by her extraordinary efforts, and not doubting that the defensive alliance would repress the ambitious projects of Russia as far as general security required, was not averse to these overtures of amity. Neither Catharine nor Gustavus communicated to their allies their pacific intentions, but concluded between themselves an armistice, which, in the middle of August, terminated in a peace.

Peace between Russia and Sweden.

State of affairs in the Netherlands.

Freed from a Turkish war, Leopold had leisure to turn his chief attention to the affairs of the Netherlands. The Flemings had begun their opposition to Joseph from a desire of preserving existing establishments. They limited their wishes and designs to the maintenance of that constitutional liberty, which they inherited from their ancestors. Their principle of conduct was totally different from that of the French. Dislike of innovation, ecclesiastical, civil, and

CHAP. XLV. 1790.

and political, was the leading feature of the Flemish character at the time they renounced their allegiance to Joseph of Austria. But the vicinity of the Netherlands to France produced a close intercourse between the two countries, and opened the way to the French doctrines, which various causes now cooperated to disseminate. Since the revolt the States General had exercised the supreme authority: the composition of that body was, in a considerable degree, aristocratical, as the states of the nobility and clergy had a greater share in the representation than the commons: this inequality was very soon remarked by the members of the third estate, and strongly reprobated by those who either had imbibed democratical notions; or from ambition, by raising the commons proposed to aggrandize themselves. So early as January 1790, a number of individuals, professing such sentiments, formed themselves into an association, which they called a patriotic assembly. After passing various resolutions of partial and subordinate reform, they framed a general and comprehensive system of revolution, which, subscribed by two thousand persons, they published as an address to the states, in the name of the people. They therein decreed the permanent exercise of sovereign authority, an aristocratical despotism, equally contrary to the rights of the people as the imperial tyranny of Joseph. The States General they allowed, with propriety, exercised the sovereign power on the *dismission* of the emperor, and the declared independence of the Belgic provinces. But this authority, arising from a temporary cause, could only endure until a legitimate constitution,

Rise of a democratical spirit.

formed

formed and ratified by the people, could be established. The ancient constitution of the Austrian Netherlands was no more. It fell by the stroke that cut off its head Joseph II. of Austria, representative of the Dukes of Burgundy, in whom the functions of the other branches of the legislature centered: they were not original and absolute, but relative and conditional. The States General were therefore responsible to the people for all which they had done since the deposition of the emperor: a national assembly only could insure tranquillity and security to the commonwealth. These principles and claims were very offensive to the two higher orders, as they were totally inimical to the power which they wished to retain without controul. Knowing the influence of the parish priests among the people, they attempted to employ these in persuading their respective parishioners to sign a counter-address, requesting the states to seize and punish all those disturbers who wished to introduce innovations in their religion and constitution. Those clergymen, however, connected by the closest intimacy and friendship with their flocks, were by no means zealous and active in recommending a measure so very unpopular. The states farther endeavoured to prevent the sentiments which they wished to inculcate from being counteracted through the press. They issued a decree, that this great engine of public opinion should be limited to the same restrictions as under the sovereignty of the emperor; that all literary works should be subject to the scrutiny of censors, before they were republished; and that all publishers should be responsible for the contents

Its votaries propose to subvert all the constituted authorities.

CHAP. XLV.
1790.

Contests between the aristocratical and democratical revolutionists.

tents of the books which they presented to the world. These attempts to restrain the actions, and even controul the thoughts, of the people, gave great dissatisfaction to those who wished for a larger portion of democracy in the constitution. The two higher orders, joined by a common opposition to the democratical schemes, formed one party, while the third, and all those who were inimical to privileged orders, formed another party. The nobility, on their side, possessed great inheritances, and were reverenced on account of their ancient families, and many of them highly esteemed for their personal characters: but the clergy, in a country distinguished for extreme bigotry, possessed peculiar influence: these circumstances prevented democratic turbulence from rising to the pitch which it would have otherwise attained. But the discontented restlessness of innovation soon triumphed in the minds of the populace over the submissive acquiescence of superstition. The higher orders attempted to awe the multitude by force, but soon found that here, as in France, the army had embraced the popular side. The commander of the Flemish troops was General Vandermersch, who, after having long served under the emperor, on the first dawnings of the revolution had returned to his native country. This gentleman was distinguished for his military talents and recent successes: he embraced the popular side, and spread his sentiments through the army. In March an attempt was made by the aristocratical party to remove the commander from his office, and deputies were sent by the states for this purpose. In this situation the general

neral adopted very bold meaſures: being nominated by the army commander in chief of the Belgic forces, in defiance of the ſtates, he ordered the deputies to be committed to priſon. He iſſued a proclamation, declaring that he was placed at the head of an army for the purpoſe of defending the civil and religious rights of the people, which he was determined to protect from all invaſion. Officers of ſimilar ſentiments were placed at the head of the war departments; and next to Vandermerſch in the command of the army were the Duke of Urſel and the Prince of Arenberg. The ſtates ordered the troops which were ſtationed at Bruſſels to march againſt the general. A civil war appeared on the eve of commencement between the ariſtocratic and democratic parties; but the army, by ſome ſudden impulſe of paſſion, the cauſes of which have never been aſcertained, abandoned that general whom they had ſo highly valued and recently exalted, and gave him up to the rage of his enemies. The congreſs of the ſtates at this time was chiefly directed by Vandernoot and Van Eupen; the former a lay nobleman, the latter an eccleſiaſtic. Under their direction, charges were drawn up againſt the general; and alſo againſt the Duke of Urſel, hereditary chief of the nobles in Brabant, a man of large fortune and popular character. Vandermerſch was doomed to a dungeon at Antwerp: Urſel was arreſted and confined for five weeks, without any form of juſtice: but being tried and acquitted, he was ſtill retained in confinement until a ſtrong body of volunteers forcibly reſcued him from this tyranny. Theſe unjuſt and violent proceedings of the ariſtocratic

 party

CHAP. XLV. 1790.

party excited the severest reprobation of their adversaries. Priests and feudal tyrants (they said) had seized the sceptre and sword, and used them as instruments of injustice and cruelty against the most patriotic and exalted characters.

A government which had, in a few months from its formation, manifested such discord, was not likely to be permanent. The army having lost its honour as well as its general, became disheartened, and was now not unfrequently defeated. Great supplies were wanted for maintaining and paying the troops; but the congress had so disgusted the principal cities, that their applications for a loan were totally unsuccessful. Attempts were made in Holland and in England, but to no purpose; and it was evident that the Belgic states were every day, from their internal dissensions, becoming weaker in power, and less important in the estimation of foreign countries.

Leopold prepares to avail himself of their dissensions.

He offers to redress their real grievances, but vindicates his right to the sovereignty.

Leopold, aware of these circumstances, sent a memorial to the people of the Netherlands, which professed sincere regret for the despotic proceedings of the Austrian government; and declared the disposition of the prince to redress all their real grievances, but vindicated his undoubted right to the sovereignty of the Netherlands, and announced his resolution to maintain his claim. This address, together with the situation of affairs, revived the loyalists, or friends of the house of Austria; who, before overawed by the prevailing power, had made no efforts to resist. As the folly and violence of the present government became more evident and more hateful, this party increased: many moderate men, who had at first favoured the revolution, compared

the

the present miserable situation with the tranquillity and contentment enjoyed under Maria Teresa. A coalition of priests and nobles (they observed) was formed, obviously for the purposes of self-interest and ambition. If the States General should continue to govern, the Belgic nation must groan under a two-fold aristocracy. If a republic were attempted on democratical principles, the first probable consequence would be anarchy; which, after producing all its horrible evils, would terminate in a single despotism. An hereditary monarchy, properly limited and modified, appeared most suitable to the character and habits of the Flemings. These considerations induced many considerate men to favour a reconciliation with Leopold. The populace, without examining matters so deeply, but actuated by the impulse of resentment and indignation, against the usurpers of sovereignty, very readily joined the loyalists. That party now displayed a force which, even without the assistance of Austrian troops, was formidable and rapidly increasing. The king of Prussia, intimating that he had acknowledged Leopold as Duke of Brabant, the aristocratical party saw their hopes of foreign assistance totally vanished, whilst their internal power was fast declining: Leopold, now Emperor of Germany, immediately after his coronation, issued a manifesto, engaging himself, under an inaugural oath, and the guarantee of Britain, Prussia, and the United Provinces, to govern the Belgic Netherlands according to the constitution, charters, and privileges, which were in force during the reign of Maria Teresa. He offered a general amnesty to all who,

Britain and her allies mediate between the Flemings and Leopold.

Under their guarantee the Netherlanders are restored to their ancient privileges.

 before

CHAP. XLV. 1790.

before the 1ſt of November, ſhould return to their duty. The mediating powers notified to the Belgic ſtates their approval of theſe terms; but that body ſtill refuſed to acquieſce, and publiſhed a counter-manifeſto, denying Leopold's right to the ſovereignty of that country, derived from his anceſtors; and aſſerted, that though many of them had enjoyed the ſovereignty of the Netherlands, they owed it entirely to the free choice of the people, who had a right to chooſe for their governors whomſoever they pleaſed. This doctrine, inimical to hereditary right, and favourable to popular election of ſovereigns, combined with their enmity to monarchical power, to bring back the democratical party to ſome concert with the other revolutioniſts. The congreſs uſed various endeavours to animate the people to a general combination, but without effect. Willing to catch at every twig to ſave their ſinking power, they propoſed to confer the ſovereignty on the Arch-duke Charles of Auſtria, and his heirs of that family, but with the perpetual excluſion of its head: theſe terms were rejected. Various engagements, uniformly unſucceſsful, intimated that reſiſtance was hopeleſs. The allied powers repreſented to them the futility of their efforts, and in its uſeleſſneſs the cruelty of their warfare. The Auſtrian troops preſſed on all ſides, the Flemiſh people without exception ackowledged the authority of the Auſtrian prince, heir and repreſentative of their ancient rulers. The members of the congreſs, and other leading partiſans of the revolt apprehending ſevere reſentment from the Emperor, eſpecially after the refuſal of his recent offers, ſought ſafety in flight.

The

1791.

They obtain further concessions from Leopold.

The Auſtrians uſed their ſucceſs with wiſe moderation; the general, by obſerving the ſtricteſt diſcipline among his victorious troops, protected the perſons and property of all men. In a convention guaranteed by the defenſive alliance, and executed at the Hague, the 10th of December 1790, the Belgic provinces were not only reſtored to the rights and privileges which they enjoyed at the death of Maria Tereſa, but obtained ſeveral advantages tending to render them more ſecure in the enjoyment of their ancient conſtitution. Thus the Catholic Netherlands having with reaſon and juſtice, to preſerve their conſtitutional rights, reſiſted Joſeph's tyranny, after they had experienced within two years deſpotical oppreſſion, ariſtocratic uſurpation, and democratic violence, at laſt found refuge and tranquillity in the mixed government that had deſcended to them from their anceſtors.

They find their ſecurity in their ancient mixed government;

Proceedings of the French revolutioniſts in forming the new conſtitution.

We left the national aſſembly on the eſtabliſhment of ſome degree of tranquillity, proceeding in the formation of the new conſtitution. Operoſe as this object muſt have appeared to perſons who intended to frame a ſyſtem of legiſlation on principles juſtified by experience, a knowledge of human nature, and an accurate acquaintance with the character of the people for whom the conſtitution was intended, theſe revolutioniſts found the attainment of their purpoſe neither tedious nor difficult. Their ſyſtem was free from complexity; equality was to be the baſis of the polity to be formed; the means were ſimple and expeditious, perſeverance in the courſe which they had ſo effectually begun, by reducing every inequality. In the application of this ſimple maxim they ſtruck a very effectual blow,

CHAP. XLV. 1790.

by a decree, announcing that there was no longer any diſtinction of orders in France, and thus cruſhed the nobility and clergy. Having equalized rank, the next buſineſs was to model elections agreeably to this new ſyſtem. The choice of repreſentatives was ultimately veſted in primary aſſemblies, compoſed of men to be diſtinguiſhed by the appellation of active citizens. The activity was to conſiſt in contributing to the public exigencies, an annual ſum not leſs than half-a-crown. By requiring this qualification in electors, they contravened their own principles of equality, and precluded univerſal ſuffrage; they excluded from legiſlation, beggars and many other citizens, not only effectually active in their reſpective vocations, but active by their tumults in the ſtreets and galleries, in controuling the national aſſembly itſelf. It farther debarred from the legiſlation, the deliberative wiſdom of fiſh-women and proſtitutes, whoſe executorial efforts, had ſo powerfully promoted the revolutionary ſchemes. The primary aſſemblies, conſtituted with theſe exceptions to equality, were to chuſe electoral aſſemblies; the electoral aſſemblies delegates to the legiſlative, judges, and executive adminiſtrators. That no veſtige of antiquity might remain, they proceeded in the abolition of provincial diſtinctions; and dividing the whole kingdom into eighty-three departments, conſolidated the diverſities into one maſs: as a geographical arrangement, this change was executed with great ſkill and ability, the departments chiefly took their names from mountains, rivers, and ſeas, which ſhape and bound countries; and as a political alteration, it certainly tended to render

Qualifications of active citizens,

precludes univerſal ſuffrage.

Diviſion into departments.

the

the government more uniform. A plan was eſtabliſhed of municipal juriſdictions, to conſtitute a fourth aſſembly, to be choſen by the ſame electoral aſſembly which, conſtituted by the primary, appointed the members of the legiſlature. Financial legiſlation next occupying their attention, they began this branch of politics, as they had begun others, by eſtabliſhing a ſimple and comprehenſive principle, which would apply to every poſſible caſe. They enunciated a theorem totally new in juriſprudence, that *all property belongs to the nation.* Having declared their ſovereign power over property, the next queſtion was, how private and corporate wealth was to be forth coming. They ſaw it would be prudent to augment the pay of the army which was ſo very ſerviceable to the revolutioniſts, and which would become more and more attached to ſyſtems of confiſcation, by ſharing in the proceeds. There were many and numerous demands upon the public, and it was farther expedient to have a governmental bank, which would be able to accommodate the nation by advances, but a capital was wanting. Whatever their lawgivers were in wiſdom and virtue they certainly manifeſted the national ingenuity in fertile invention and prompt expedient. They ſoon diſcovered a very efficient fund for the exigency, in the landed eſtates of the clergy; ſome politicians oppoſed the ſeizure of clerical property, not as unjuſt, becauſe they knew its juſtice had been already eſtabliſhed in the new code of ethics; but as impolitic. The appropriation would enrage the clergy, who ſtill retained great influence among the leſs enlightened people; and would alſo diſpleaſe and alarm fo-

New and comprehenſive principle of financial legiſlation.

CHAP. XLV. 1790.

Confiscation of clerical property.

reign powers, who might not only reprobate a confiſcation, but dread the principle: theſe admonitions however were of little avail. A decree was paſſed declaring the eccleſiaſtical eſtates to be at the diſpoſal of the nation. The clergy expoſtulated on the robbery, and excited great diſcontents among their votaries, which were farther increaſed by the nobility indignant at their own degradation. To counteract the growing diſaffection, the aſſembly ſpread reports of plots and conſpiracies, and thus by alarming their fears, diverted the attention of the people from the iniquities of government. Rumours were ſpread, that the princes were now in exile at Turin, and the ariſtocrats both in and out of the kingdom were confederating with foreign princes to effect a counter revolution. Aware that the king was conſidered by their adverſaries as a priſoner, and that his acts could in that ſuppoſition be no longer binding, than the compulſion laſted, they endeavoured to procure from him an approbation of their proceedings which ſhould appear voluntary; they attempted to prevail on his mild and compliant diſpoſition, to come to the aſſembly and explicitly declare himſelf the head of the revolution, and ſatisfied with all their proceedings; but this application his Majeſty reſolutely refuſed. Finding the king inflexible, the republicans diſſeminated reports of new plots and conſpiracies, for reſcuing Louis from his preſent ſituation. To deter ariſtocrats and loyaliſts from ſuch an attempt, it was very frequently declared in common converſation, and in the clubs, that an endeavour to extricate the king would certainly produce his death.

The

The queen was very openly and loudly threatened as the inſtigator of his majeſty's refuſal; the benignant Louis from tenderneſs for his wife and children was induced to make a conceſſion, which no apprehenſions for his perſonal ſafety could have extorted; and he repaired to the national aſſembly, and ſpoke to the purport deſired by the republicans. The democratic party ſeeing the anti-republicans overwhelmed with diſmay by the acquieſcence of the king, reſolved to take advantage of the conſternation, and iſſued a decree obliging every member to take a newly deviſed civic oath, under the penalty of excluſion from voting in the aſſembly. They now publiſhed a general addreſs to the nation, ſtating their acts and meaſures for the ſake of public liberty, and their farther intentions in order to complete the great work of regenerating France. Various tumults having ariſen, and murders and other outrages having been committed both at Paris and Verſailles, the ringleaders were ſeized and puniſhed by the aſſembly, which with conſiderable vigour chaſtiſed ſuch riots and diſorders, as did not promote its own purpoſes. Having again re-eſtabliſhed nearly as much quietneſs as they wanted, and attained their object from the king, they reſumed the affairs of the clergy. In February, they ſuppreſſed all monaſtic eſtabliſhments, and for ever confiſcated the lands. By another decree in April, they forfeited all the territorial poſſeſſions of the church, for the payment of the public debts, but generouſly allowed the plundered proprietors a ſmall annual pittance from the booty. As the ſpoils were not immediately convertible into ready money, they employed

CHAP. XLV. 1790.

Civic oath.

Scheme for converting the ſpoils of the clergy into ready money.

CHAP. XLV. 1790

ployed them as *pledges*. They iſſued out a ſpecies of notes under the name of *aſſignats*, being aſſignments to the public creditor of confiſcated property; and payable to bearer, that they might ſerve the purpoſe of a bank paper currency. About this time, they began to affect an imitation of the Roman republic, and adopting its phraſeology with one of its cuſtoms, decreed that mural crowns ſhould be publicly preſented to the conquerors of the Baſtile.

Boundleſs power of the mob.

The legiſlature were not without experiencing inconveniences from the diffuſion of their own doctrines. They had found it neceſſary to idolize the mob; to talk of the majeſty of the people; their ſupreme authority; their uncontroulable ſway to which all things muſt bend. Theſe ideas with the experience of their own force, operating on the ardent fancies and combuſtible paſſions of the French populace, meetings, clubs, parties, and individuals conſidered themſelves as collectively and ſeparately, rulers of the empire. They indeed regarded the national aſſembly as a neceſſary, legiſlative, and executive organ, but ſubject to their own general and ſupreme controul. As force was the great ſpring of government, the ſoldiers with reaſon claimed an important ſhare in the direction of affairs; and by the laws of equality deemed themſelves exempted from every degree of ſubordination and obedience, excepting ſo far as ſuited their wiſhes or convenience.

The multitude civil and military destitute of religion.

Both the populace and ſoldiers conceived, that by their political regeneration, they were entitled without reſtraint to gratify every paſſion. The moſt active of the revolutionary leaders had ſpared no pains to baniſh from the people, that ſalutary moderator

derator of passion, the christian religion*. In extent of despotic power, the French mob equalled the Turkish sultan; the army the Janissaries; and the national assembly the Divan, despotic under the despot and his soldiers, but totally dependant upon these for its own sway. But the horrible tyranny of Turkish rule was mitigated by the Alcoran, whereas the despotic licence of France was devoid of any such corrective. A great portion of the vulgar both civil and military were rank infidels. Thus destitute of moral restraint, all the energy of a most ingenious people, all the French force and versatility of intellect and temperament, were the instruments of moral depravity. A great object of the republicans in the assembly had uniformly been to identify in the opinion of the civil and military vulgar, their interests and views with their own; and like other demagogues, while they professed to admit the rabble as their associates, really to employ them as their tools, and they in a great measure accomplished their purpose. There was under the direction of the national assembly, an army much more numerous than ever had been commanded by the French monarchs.

Many of the nobility, as we have seen, had been the zealous votaries of reform, while they conceived it tending to limited freedom and limited monarchy. But they had always been deficient in point of concert;

* Mirabeau laid it down as an axiom in the science of politics, that if they would have an effectual reform, they must begin by expelling christianity from the kingdom. This maxim was loudly praised, and generally followed by the republican partizans.

by

CHAP. XLV. 1790.

by suffering separate and subordinate views to occupy their attention, they had facilitated the progress of republicanism. They had already felt the fatal effects of disunion, among the opponents of jacobinism militant, they were destined to feel them more severely from jacobinism triumphant. There was in the proceedings of the French democrats, a strange mixture of ridiculous levity with the most serious iniquity. Paris at this time overflowed with adventurers from all countries. Among these was a Prussian of the name of Clootz *, who having left his own country for reasons recorded in the journals of the police, had resorted to Paris, and assuming the name of the antient Scythian sage, Anacharsis, set up as a philosopher, and by his lectures instructed the Parisians. But not having hitherto attained notoriety equal to his ambition, he bethought himself of the following expedient to become conspicuous: collecting a great number of his companions and other vagabonds who swarmed about the streets, and hiring all the foreign and grotesque dresses from the opera and play-houses, he bedecked his retinue; and proceeding to the national assembly, he introduced his followers, as strangers arrived from all countries of the globe, being the virtual ambassadors of all those enslaved nations who wished to be free, and were therefore disposed to enter into fraternity with France, for the glorious purpose of establishing universal liberty. This deputation was most graciously received by the assembly, of which it being evening sitting, many of the members were

Mixture of ridiculous levity and serious iniquity.

Anacharsis Clootz, ambassador from the whole human race.

* Otridge's Annual Register, p. 148.

in

CHAP. XLV. 1790.

in a condition † ſuited to a frolic. The legiſlature after ſome decrees and reſolutions ſuitable to this contemptible farce, followed their deliberative levity, by a very ſerious act. A decree was propoſed for the abolition of titles, and hereditary nobility, with all the heraldic monuments, which would recal to deſcendants the diſtinction and merits of their anceſtors. In vain the nobles oppoſed ſo haſty and violent a propoſition, it was immediately paſſed into a decree. Thus in one year, the national aſſembly cruſhed rank and diſtinction, confiſcated property, annihilated hierarchy and ariſtocracy, left monarchy only an empty name, and perfected their levelling efforts; they now propoſed that the 14th of July, the anniverſary of the captured baſtile, and of the birth of liberty, ſhould be ſolemnized by a general confederation of Frenchmen, pledging themſelves to maintain the new conſtitution, and to bind the king, the aſſembly, and the people civil and military in one general fraternity. This ſpectacle was exhibited in the field of Mars, appointed to be called ever after, the field of confederation. The king, the aſſembly, the people, and the army, were reciprocally ſworn. The ſame oath was taken the ſame day through the whole kingdom.

Abolition of titles and hereditary nobility.

Summary of changes within the year.

Anniverſary celebration of the 14th of July in the field of Mars.

Mr. Neckar friendly as he had been to the popular ſide, diſapproved very highly of the late democratical proceedings, and eſpecially the confiſcations. Being now received with great neglect and diſplea-

† Drunkenneſs, a vice formerly ſo little known in France, was ſince the revolution become extremely prevalent even among the lawgivers. Annual Regiſter.

ſure,

CHAP. XLV. 1790.

ſure, and being apprehenſive of his perſonal ſafety, he quitted the kingdom, and retired to Switzerland. In proſecuting their ſyſtem of reform, the aſſembly thought it expedient to render the clergy ſtill more dependant on their will. They accordingly paſſed a decree, impoſing on clergymen a new oath, by which they were bound to ſubmit to the conſtitution as decreed by the aſſembly, in all caſes whatever. This oath was a direct breach of the oath taken at ordination; and great numbers of the clergy refuſed to ſwear contrary to their engagements and principles. All the recuſants were immediately ejected from their benefices; and their livings filled by others. Thus a republican aſſembly endeavoured to force mens conſciences to be guided by its decrees, and not ſatisfied with exerciſing tyranny over perſons and property, attempted by the ſame deſpotiſm to enchain their minds.

Federal oath.

Violent proceedings againſt thoſe who refuſed it.

Britain.

This year the French revolution began to be better underſtood in Britain, and to produce more definite and ſpecific opinions, either of approbation or cenſure, or of a mixture of both. Many Britons ſtill continued upon Britiſh principles to admire the French revolution, and though they regretted the exceſſes which had accompanied its operations, yet expected that the violence would ſubſide, and that a ſyſtem of rational and beneficial liberty would be eſtabliſhed. They ſaw that the plan of polity would conſiderably deviate from the Britiſh conſtitution. The greater number of literary men continued to favour the changes, and imputed the enormities to the vitiating ſyſtem of government

under

under which the French had so long lived, joined with the enthusiasm of new liberty. But the most experienced and discriminating of philosophical politicians perceived that the Gallic revolution in its nature, principles, and effects, was different from any former case, and avoided unqualified opinions concerning either its merits, or probable duration. They considered it as a composition of extraordinary phenomena, not yet sufficiently investigated to become the foundation of a just theory; but they saw that, the rapidity of French change far exceeded the progressive variations of circumstances, and the human character *. Writers of genius and erudition attached to certain visionary principles and doctrines, prized the French revolution more for its particular acts and innovations, than for the general assertion of liberty; and celebrated most highly those measures which overthrew hierarchy, reduced monarchy, and degraded aristocracy. Dissenters of very high literary reputation, and unimpeached private character, were so transported by their peculiar doctrines and sentiments, as to praise the lawless violence of the Parisian mob, and the abduction of the royal family in triumph, because these acts tended to overthrow the existing orders; and even recommended the example of the French to the imitation of the English. The able and eminent Dr. Price, and his many votaries in civil and religious dissent, manifested in 1790, an unqualified admiration of the French changes, and proposed a close connection between the revolutionists of France,

CHAP. XLV.

1790. The French revolution is better understood.

Majority of literary men favour the new system, though they censure its excesses.

* See Dr. William Thomson's letter to Dr. Parr.

CHAP. XLV. 1790.

Mr. Pitt and his friends forbear discussion of its merits.

France, and the people of England. Certain members of parliament, at the head of whom was Mr. Fox, continued to admire the principles of the French revolution, as tending eventually to produce a moderate and rational liberty, that would in time fit the circumſtances and character of the people, and promote the tranquillity of Europe. The great miniſterial leaders, cheriſhing the principles of conſtitutional liberty, could not reprobate in another country an attempt to procure that bleſſing, the enjoyment of which made this nation proſperous and happy; and when they diſcerned the peculiar nature and tendency of the new ſyſtem, conceiving that it became ſtateſmen leſs to ſpeculate than to provide, inſtead of delivering judgment on the meaſures of the French, vigilantly watched the conduct of Britons. The ſentiments of the miniſter and his principal ſupporters concerning the affairs of France, were not hitherto declared. The firſt open cenſurers of the French revolution, were courtiers, who being the votaries of pageantry and ſhew, under a kingly government, regarded the pomp and ceremony of the palace more than the vigour and efficacy of the monarchy; who regretted Louis's loſs of royal trappings and appendages, more than the ſeizure of his power; who conſidering the king's friends and attendants as no longer enjoying the balls and proceſſions of Verſailles, ſaw grievances, which being thoroughly conceived by their fancies, could attract their ſympathetic feelings. But a ferocious confiſcating democracy, overturning religion and property, did not equally affect their ſenſibility, becauſe they by no means ſo clearly underſtood

ſtood the nature, or comprehended the extent of the evil. One claſs, indeed, eminent for ability and learning, venerable for profeſſion and aggregate character, in the early ſtages of the French revolution, obſerved its leading principles with horror, and its conduct with dread. The clergy augured ill from a ſyſtem guided by profeſſed infidels, and ſympathizing with plundered brethren, beheld not without apprehenſion, the contagion of confiſcation ſo very near themſelves. In this country, they knew there were men as willing to plunder the church as the moſt rapacious revolutioniſts of Paris. But though they diſapproved of the French ſyſtem, they did not deem it expedient to declare an alarm. Such an avowal, they thought, might imply an imputation of diſloyalty, and enmity to the church, which could not be juſtly charged to the majority of Britons. Engliſh clergymen, therefore, did not decry the revolution, which many other literary men praiſed. In autumn 1790, the declared ſentiments of Britons, with ſeveral modifications, were on the whole favourable to the French revolution. One man, however, was deſtined to effect a ſpeedy and important change. Edmund Burke, having formed and delivered in parliament the opinions already recorded, with increaſing anxiety continued to beſtow the cloſeſt attention on revolutionary proceedings. He had many correſpondents at Paris, of different nations, abilities, and ſentiments. Through them he completed his acquaintance with the French ſyſtem. While attending to its progreſs, and its operation within the country which it immediately affected, he carried

The clergy are alarmed by the infidelity and confiſcation of the revolutionary ſyſtem.

Burke's work on the ſubject.

 his

CHAP. XLV. 1790.

his views to the impressions that it had made in his own country. Penetrating into the various grounds of the praise which it had procured in England, his sagacity perfectly distinguished between those who rejoiced at what they conceived the emancipation of France, and those who in the destruction of the orders, and forfeiture of property, found a model which they wished to be copied in England. In considering the admirers and supporters of the French revolution, he, from the authority of Dr. Price among his votaries, apprehended that the late promulgation of that gentleman's political opinions in a sermon, might be very hurtful, unless precautions were used to expose the tendency of his doctrines. To convince mankind, especially Britons, that the French revolution did not tend to meliorate but to deprave the human character, to promote happiness, but to produce misery, to be imitated and copied, but to be reprobated and abhorred, Mr. Burke composed and published his work. To establish his position, he analyzed the intellectual principles by which the revolutionists reasoned; the religious, moral, and political principles by which the revolutionists acted; and contended that the effects which had proceeded, and were proceeding, were natural and necessary consequences of the principles and doctrines. He predicted the completion of anarchy and misery from the progressive enormity of the French system. Profound wisdom, solid and beneficial philosophy, enforced by all the powers of Mr. Burke's eloquence, produced a very great change in public opinion. From this time many men of talents, learning, and political

CHAP. XLV. 1790.

political consideration, openly declared sentiments unfavourable to the French revolution. The nobility, with few exceptions, were apprehensive of the danger which awaited their order if French principles became prevalent in Great Britain. The clergy publicly testified the opinion which they before held. Ministers, cautious as they were in avowing any sentiments concerning the French revolution, did not conceal the high estimation in which they held Mr. Burke's production. The public opinion, which at first had been so extremely favourable to the French revolution, was at the end of 1790 greatly divided.

and effects.

The most important transactions belonging to the internal history of Britain in the recess of 1790, was the general election. The contests were not, however, carried on with the violence of former times. The country was in a state of progressive, and rapidly augmenting prosperity; the minister possessed the public confidence, and no great political question agitated the public mind. The election, which was most warmly disputed, did not owe the contest to the contention of parties. Of the elective bodies in Great Britain, none is of importance equal to Westminster; the seat of government, the royal family, and for half the year the principal nobility and gentry: hence there had usually been a very warm competition in this city. The dispute in 1788 between Lord Hood and Lord John Townsend, had been carried on with extreme eagerness on both sides; and with an expence calculated to have exceeded even the costly election of 1784. It was tacitly understood between the two parties, that at the

General election.

CHAP. XLV. 1790.

general election there should be no contest, but that Lord Hood and Mr. Fox should be jointly chosen. This apparent determination was represented to many electors of Westminster, as a coalition between the candidates to insure themselves the choice, and thus deceive the inhabitants. Mr. Horne Tooke a gentleman of great and deserved literary eminence, and also of very conspicuous political conduct, which was variously interpreted, proposed himself as the representative; he disavowed all connection with any party, and assuming an independent tone, procured a respectable number of supporters; he every day exhibited from the hustings a series of acute and poignant observation; clear, direct, and vigorous reasoning, not unworthy of being opposed to the vehement and forcible oratory of his illustrious competitor; his efforts however were unsuccessful. Though there were several disputed elections, yet there was none that attracted so much attention as the poll for Westminster, in which Horne Tooke was pitched against Charles James Fox.

CHAP. XLVI.

Meeting of the new parliament.—Convention with Spain is approved by parliament.—Expences of the late armament.—Unclaimed dividends.—Measures of Britain for repressing the ambition of Russia—submitted to parliament—Mr. Fox opposes hostilities with Russia—argument of Mr. Pitt on the importance of Oczakow—principle of British interference in continental politics—hostilities with Russia unpopular through the nation—war with Russia avoided.—New constitution of Canada—political principles introduced into the discussion.—Mr. Fox incidentally mentions the French revolution—Mr. Burke inveighs against that event, and the new constitution—Mr. Fox explains the extent and bounds of his approbation—declares the British constitution the best for this country—quotes Mr. Burke's speeches and writings favourable to liberty—rupture between these friends, and their final separation.—Question whether impeachments by the Commons before the Lords, abate with the dissolution of parliament—precedents and arguments for and against—determination of the house that impeachments do not abate by a dissolution.—Liberty of the press—motion of Mr. Fox for ascertaining and declaring the law of libels, and bill for that purpose—arguments for and against—postponed for the present, but is afterwards passed into a law.—State and conduct of the English catholics—they renounce the most dangerous moral and political doctrines of popery.—motion for their relief—modified and corrected by Dr. Horseley, it is passed into a law.—Petition of the church of Scotland respecting the test act—is rejected.—Full discussion of the slave trade—motion of Mr. Wilberforce for the abolition—arguments for and against—continuance of the trade defended on the grounds of humanity, justice, and expediency—Messrs. Pitt and Fox agree in supporting the abolition---the motion is negatived.

negatived.—Settlement at Sierra Leone.---Finance.---Supplies.---Indian finance.---Trial of Hastings, evidence for the prosecution closed---impressive speech of the defendant.---Session rises.

CHAP. XLVI. 1790. Meeting of the new parliament.

THE British parliament opened the 26th of November; and his majesty stated that the dispute between this country and Spain had been brought to an amicable termination. The first subject of parliamentary consideration was the convention * with the Catholic king. In a question concerning an injury, the great objects to be regarded were reparation for the past, and prevention of future aggression. In the present case, according to opposition, the restitution promised was incomplete, and the promises were not performed. Before the commencement of the dispute, we had possessed and exercised the free navigation of the Pacific Ocean, as well as the right of fishing in the South Seas, without restriction. But the admission of a part only of these rights was all that had been obtained by the convention. Formerly we had claimed the privileges of settling in any part of south or north-west America, from which we were not precluded by previous occupancy. Now, we consented to limit our right of settlement to certain places only, and even in these under various restrictions. What we had retained was vague and undefined, and consequently liable to be again disputed. We had reserved what was insignificant to ourselves, and resigned what was very beneficial to Spain.

Convention with Spain is approved by parliament.

* See page 124 of this volume.

Spain. To these arguments ministers answered; if we had not acquired new rights, we had obtained new advantages. Before the convention, Spain had denied our right to the southern whale fishery, and to navigate the Pacific Ocean; but now she had ratified those claims. In the convention, the wisdom and energy of ministers had vindicated the honour of the British flag, preserved the rights of private citizens, and established the glory of the British name over all the world, without shedding a drop of blood. On these grounds the majority in both houses approved of the terms of the adjustment. The liquidation of the expences incurred by the late armament, the minister proposed to separate from the general financial arrangements for the season; and to pay off in four years the incumbrances now incurred, by a distinct plan of finance. The first resource was the balance of the public money, which had accumulated in the hands of the bank of England from *unclaimed dividends**. The bank was agent for the public; received an adequate allowance for its services, and was therefore not entitled to retain a balance greater than the probable demand. Since public creditors forbore punctually demanding their interest, not the bank, who were agents for the payment of that interest, but the nation, their employers, should profit by that forbearance. The balance had been gradually increasing

Expences of the late armament.

Unclaimed dividends.

* Many of the public creditors had omitted to demand their dividends when due; the money, therefore, issued for their payment, was used by the bank until the proprietors should demand the payment.

CHAP. XLVI. 1790.

from the year 1727, and now amounted to £660,000. Of this ſum the miniſter moved that £500,000 ſhould be applied to the public ſervice, and that the creditors ſhould have ſecurities in the conſolidated fund for payment, whenever the demand ſhould be made. In addition to this ſum, he propoſed temporary duties upon ſugar, Britiſh ſpirits, brandy, rum, malt, aſſeſſed taxes, and bills of exchange. Mr. Fox, and ſome other members, objected to the miniſter's propoſition as unjuſt to public creditors, and alſo unfair to the bank. But it appearing to the majority of both houſes that the creditors poſſeſſed the ſame ſecurity of prompt payment as before, and that no injury could accrue to an agent from his employer withholding money which was not neceſſary to the tranſactions which he was appointed to manage: notwithſtanding various petitions from the bank, deprecating the application, a bill agreeable to the miniſter's project was paſſed into a law.

Meaſures of Britain for repreſſing the ambition of Ruſſia;

The conteſt with Spain being thus concluded, another very important ſubject of foreign politics occupied the attention of parliament. At the congreſs of Reichenbach, the defenſive alliance had propoſed to Ruſſia to accede to the peace which Auſtria was concluding, and that all conqueſts ſhould be reſtored; but Catharine conſtantly replied, that ſhe would admit of no interference between her and the Turks. Deprived, however, of the aſſiſtance of Auſtria, in the ſtrength and determination of the allies ſhe ſaw the impracticability of ſubjugating Turkey for the preſent, and now offered to reſtore all her acquiſitions by the war, except the town and dependencies of Oczacow. This poſſeſſion, ſhe conceived, would on the one hand ſecure her dominions againſt the irruptions of the Tartars, and on the other command an entrance into Turkey, whenever circumſtances ſhould prove more favourable to the execution of her ambitious deſigns. The allied powers perfectly comprehended the objects of Catharine, and deemed them incompatible with that tranquillity which it was the purpoſe of the confederacy to inſure. There was, beſides, an unfriendly diſpoſition long manifeſted by Ruſſia towards Great Britain. During our difficulties, ſhe had headed a confederation for the expreſs purpoſe of reducing the naval power of this country. When the commercial treaty between England and Ruſſia was expired, Catharine not only declined renewal, but obliged our merchants to pay in duties twenty-five per cent more than ſhe exacted from other countries, though they gave half a year's credit for their exports, and were always a whole year in advance for their imports. At the ſame time ſhe concluded commercial treaties with France* and Spain, on terms that were advantageous to both theſe countries. Such indications of enmity to this country, joined to her ambitious projects, ſtrongly impelled the Britiſh government to prevent the encroachments of the empreſs's court. Britain and her allies ſtill adhered to their purpoſe, of inducing or compelling Catharine to reſtore the conqueſt. Finding pacific negociations unavailing, the defenſive alliance projected more

* See State Papers, and Segur's hiſtory of Frederic William.

effectual

effectual interference. Having concerted forcible mediation for the security of Europe, his majesty, on the 24th of March, sent a message to both houses, stating his unsuccessful efforts for the establishment of peace, and that from the progress of the war, consequences so important might arise, as to render it necessary for this country to be prepared to meet them by an augmentation of our naval force. The message coming under consideration of Parliament, Mr. Fox opposed hostile interference on the following grounds: all wars were to Britain unwise, as well as unjust, that did not originate in self-defence. Too much latitude was given to the construction of defensive alliances, and treaties comprehended under that denomination had at present a very offensive tendency. By including in the objects of defensive resistance not only actual, and even probable, but possible injury, the professed defenders of Europe proposed to carry on war wherever they thought it expedient to any of the confederates. We had received no injury from Russia that could justify hostilities: her demands upon Turkey could not so materially affect Great Britain as to render a bloody and expensive war prudent to prevent their attainment: expediency as well as justice, forbade war with a power which neither directly attacked Britain, nor pursued any other object by which she could be endangered: the present plan of ministers tended merely to second the ambitious policy of Prussia, in whose intrigues and projects we were lately become too much involved: Was the protection of a barren district in the barbarous recesses of Tartary, a reason for exposing

1791. submitted to parliament.

Mr. Fox opposes hostilities with Russia.

CHAP. XLVI. 1791.

exposing Great Britain to the evils of war? Was our trade with Russia, which employed eight hundred and fifty ships, trained in that hardening service thousands of seamen, afforded materials for our manufactures to the amount of two millions sterling, received our manufactured goods of more than a million, and yielded two hundred thousand pounds to our revenue, to be all foregone for the sake of a Turkish fortress? Even were Russia to succeed in conquering Turkey, instead of becoming more formidable to her neighbours, she would become weaker, and spread over a more extensive surface. Could wisdom and policy justify Britain in going to war, for preserving an empire inhabited by a barbarous and savage race, habitually connected with our rival; a race that for the sake of religion, humanity, civilization, and commerce, ought to be exterminated from the continent of Europe*.

Arguments of Mr. Pitt on the importance of Oczacow.

Ministers argued that the aggrandizement of Russia, and the depression of Turkey, would injure both our commercial and political interests. While Russia was confined to the Baltic, her naval exertions would be inconsiderable; but if her fleet were suffered to range through the Mediterranean, she would become a great maritime power, and a formidable rival. The possession of Oczakow would facilitate not only the acquisition of Constantinople, but of Alexandria, and all lower Egypt. The object of Britain in opposing Russia was conformable to her general policy in continental interference.

* See parliamentary reports, 1791.

CHAP. XLVI. 1791.

ference. Britain had herſelf no ambitious end to purſue; we had nothing to gain; we wiſhed only to remain as we were; our alliances could only have the tendency of maintaining the balance of power.

Principle of Britiſh interference in continental politics.

It was known to Europe, that our principles were pacific*. Standing on the high eminence which we occupied, we exerted our power only for the maintenance of peace. It was a glorious diſtinction for England, that, placed on a pinnacle of proſperity, having in her reſources and power ſuch motives to ambition, ſhe exerted her ſtrength not as the diſturber, but the protector of her neighbours†: this had ever been her character and principle. In endeavouring to repreſs Ruſſia, ſhe purſued the ſame line of conduct which ſhe had always choſen.

Hoſtilities with Ruſſia unpopular through the nation.

The ſupreme director of a free country, and eſpecially of Great Britain, is PUBLIC OPINION. The forcible eloquence of Mr. Fox, coinciding with the immediate intereſts of merchants and manufacturers, impreſſed thoſe bodies of men very powerfully. Their ſentiments were rapidly and widely diffuſed through the nation, and rendered the people in general inimical to a Ruſſian war.

War with Ruſſia avoided.

Miniſters, feeling the due and conſtitutional reverence for the voice of the people, ſacrificed their own counſels and meaſures to dictates ſo deſervedly authoritative. Although Britain was thus prevented from compelling Ruſſia to reſtore the key of Turkey, yet it was the energy of the

* See ſpeeches of Mr. Pitt and Mr. Grenville. Parliamentary Reports.

† Speech of Mr. Grenville.

defenfive alliance which induced Catharine to relinquifh all the other acquifitions of the war.

C H A P. XLVI. 1791. New conftitution of Canada.

The circumftances of one of our provinces called on parliament to frame a new conftitutional code, that required difcuffions at all times important, but peculiarly momentous when they were combined with the queftions which from the French revolution agitated the public mind. After the acquifition of Canada, a proclamation, as we have feen*, had been iffued by his majefty, promifing that meafures fhould be adopted for extending to that country the benefit of the Britifh conftitution. Encouraged by this affurance, many Britifh fubjects had fettled in the new province; and in confequence of the American revolution, great numbers of royalifts had emigrated into a country fo near to their own, and which contained inhabitants of congenial principles and fentiments; thefe readily coalefced with the Britifh fettlers, and joined them in frequent applications to remind government of the royal promife. The native Canadians readily admitted the excellence of the Britifh conftitution; but deprecated its unqualified extenfion to themfelves, as tending to interfere with privileges which they had inherited from their anceftors. The Canadian nobleffe, efpecially, enjoyed many feudal rights and immunities, which they feared the introduction of a new form of government might infringe or abolifh. The minifter, confidering the diverfity of character, fentiment, cuftoms, and privileges, between the French Canadians on the

* See vol. I.

one

CHAP. XLVI. 1791.

one hand, the British and Anglo-American colonists on the other, proposed a separate legislature to each, that might be best suited to their respective interests, and social situation. With this view he purposed to divide Canada into two distinct provinces, upper and lower; and introduced a bill for this arrangement, and for the establishment of distinct legislatures. The division was to separate the parts which were chiefly inhabited by French Canadians, from recent settlers. For each of the provinces, a legislative council was to be hereditary, or for life, at the option of the king; and a provincial assembly was to be chosen by freeholders possessing lands worth forty shillings of yearly rent, or renters of houses paying ten pounds in six months. The provincial parliament was to be septennial, to assemble at least once in a year: the governor, representing the sovereign, might refuse his sanction to any proposed law, until the final determination of Britain were known. The British government renounced the right of taxation, and though it asserted the right of regulating external commerce, yet left the imposts to the provincial legislatures. All laws and ordinances of the whole province of Canada at present in force, were to remain valid until they should be altered by the new legislature. The bill passed through both houses without any material alterations. But in the house of commons its discussion gave rise to a debate concerning the French revolution, between Messrs. Burke and Fox, who respectively delivered their principles, sentiments, and doctrines on this momentous subject, more clearly, specifically, and categorically,

Political principles introduced into the discussion.

categorically, than in the disquisition of the former year. In considering the constitution which the legislature was preparing for Canada, Mr. Fox proposed to confer as much freedom as was possibly consistent with the ends of political establishments, instead of mere suitableness to any existing form. The scheme for the government of Canada adhered, he conceived, too closely to the British constitution, which though the most perfectly adapted to the character, habit, and circumstances of Britons, was not the best that possibly could be framed for any case. The United States in North America would have afforded a better model, more fitted both to the character and social situation of the Canadians, than the model which had been followed. Hereditary distinctions, possessions, and powers, ought not to be abolished where they had been long established; and were interwoven with the manners and sentiments of the people, as well as the laws*; but it was unwise to create them in countries not fit for their establishment. There was not in Canada either property or respectability sufficient to support an hereditary nobility. Mr. Pitt, in defending his own plan, confined himself to its adaptation to the proposed ends, and without entering into

* These were nearly the words of Mr. Fox, at least this was certainly the substance, as appears after a careful comparison of the several reports of parliamentary debates. Yet he was misrepresented as having declared himself, without qualification, the enemy of hereditary rank and distinction. Far was he from asserting that an order of nobility was useless in any circumstances; he merely declared his opinion, that in its present state it did not suit Canada.

abstract

CHAP. XLVI. 1791.

abstract speculations upon government, contended that a polity formed for any part of the British dominions, should be as nearly as possible modelled according to the British constitution; that such being his object, he conceived it effected by the present system for the government of Canada. In the reciprocation of debate, Mr. Fox still reprobated the council of nobles; said he could not account for the zeal in its favour, unless by the supposition that an opportunity was eagerly embraced of reviving in Canada, formerly a French colony, those titles and honours, the extinction of which some gentlemen so much deplored, and of awakening in the west that *spirit of chivalry* which had so completely fallen into disgrace in a neighbouring country. Mr. Burke, by these expressions, conceived that his opinions, and indeed his writings on the French revolution were attacked; he also heard doctrines advanced which he deemed repugnant to the British constitution; to controvert such opinions, he drew a contrast between that admirable system, and the new order of things in France. The Canada bill (he said) called forth principles analogous to those which had produced the French revolution. There was a faction in this country inimical to our constitution of church and state. It became parliament to watch the conduct of individuals or societies, which were evidently disposed to encourage innovations. Mr. Fox conceiving that Mr. Burke intended to implicate him in the censure passed on the admirers of the French revolution, replied to his animadversions. Mr. Burke's object appeared to be (Mr. Fox said) to stigmatize

Mr. Fox incidentally mentions the French revolution.

Mr Burke inveighs against that event, and the new constitution.

Mr. Fox explains the extent and bounds of his approbation.

ſtigmatize thoſe who thought differently from himſelf on the French revolution, and who had expreſſed their opinions in parliament; and to repreſent them as the ſupporters of republican tenets. To vindicate himſelf from this charge, he diſtinctly and explicitly declared his own ſentiments. The praiſe that he had beſtowed, was given to the French revolution, which had aboliſhed the old arbitrary government; and not to the ſyſtem which was ſubſtituted in its ſtead. As a ſubverter of a tyranny that had enthralled twenty-five millions of people, he ſtill would maintain that it was one of the moſt glorious events in the whole hiſtory of mankind. The new polity remained to be improved by experience, and accommodated to circumſtances. The excellence of forms of government was relative, and depended on the ſituation, ſentiments, and habits of the people *: the Britiſh conſtitution he thought the beſt and fitteſt for this country, and would to the utmoſt of his power oppoſe republicaniſm among Britons; but it was contrary to ſound logic to infer, that becauſe Britiſh liberty was moſt effectually ſecured by a government of three eſtates, therefore ſuch an arrangement muſt be the fitteſt for France. He conſidered the late great change as the precurſor of freedom and happineſs to twenty-five millions, and therefore rejoiced at its ſucceſs. From Mr. Burke himſelf he derived thoſe principles, and imbibed thoſe ſentiments which Mr. Burke now cenſured: he quoted various paſſages from the ſpeeches and writings of that

declares the Britiſh conſtitution the beſt for this country;

quotes Mr. Burke's ſpeeches and writings favourable to liberty.

* Theſe obſervations are conformable to Ariſtotle, as the Engliſh reader will ſee in his Politics, tranſlated by Dr. Gillies, book iv.

 eloquent

CHAP. XLVI. 1791. Rupture between these friends, and their final separation.

eloquent and philosophical senator, and referred to measures which he had either proposed or promoted, and comparing them with the sentiments now or recently delivered, endeavoured to fix on him a charge of inconsistency. Mr. Burke complained of this allegation, and declared it to be unfounded: his opinions on government, he said, had been the same during all his political life. His conduct would evince the truth of his assertions: his friendship with Mr. Fox was now at an end; deep must be his impression of truths which caused such a sacrifice to the safety of his country; he gave up private friendship and party support, and separated from those he esteemed most highly. His country, he trusted, would measure the sincerity of his avowals, and the importance of his warnings, by the price which they had cost himself. He was far from imputing to Mr. Fox a wish for the practical adoption in this country of the revolutionary doctrines; but thinking and feeling as Mr. Fox and he now did, their intercourse must terminate. With great emotion, Mr. Fox deprecated the renunciation of Mr. Burke's friendship; and tears for several minutes interrupted his utterance*. When the first ebullitions of sensibility had subsided, he expressed the highest esteem, affection, and gratitude for Mr. Burke, whom, notwithstanding his harshness, he must still continue to love. Proceeding for some time in a strain of plaintive tenderness, he gradually recovered his usual firmness, and afterwards contracted no small degree of severity,

* This account is chiefly compressed from parliamentary debates, and partly taken from a gentleman who was present.

when

when having vindicated the reſiſtance of France, on Whig principles, he renewed his charge of inconſiſtency againſt Mr. Burke, for deviating from thoſe principles. This repetition of the charge of inconſiſtency, prevented the impreſſion which the affectionate and reſpectful language and behaviour, and the conciliatory apologies might have probably made: the breach was irreparable; and from this time Mr. Fox and Mr. Burke never reſumed their former friendſhip. In this diſcuſſion, the impartial examiner cannot find a ſingle ſentence, or even phraſe, of Mr. Fox, which was not highly favourable to the Britiſh conſtitution; ſo that the political difference between theſe illuſtrious men, aroſe entirely from their oppoſite apprehenſions concerning the French revolution, which hitherto was to a Britiſh ſenator a queſtion of ſpeculative reaſoning, and not of practical contention; but Burke had already conceived ſuch an abhorrence of the Gallic ſyſtem, that he could not bear any expreſſion of approbation reſpecting a change which he deemed deſtructive to the beſt intereſts of ſociety.

Queſtion whether impeachment by the commons before the lords abate with the diſſolution of parliament.

With colonial policy, parliament this year conſidered alſo important queſtions of domeſtic law. One of theſe aroſe from the trial of Mr. Haſtings: it was doubted whether an impeachment brought by the commons of England abated by the diſſolution of parliament. Several members of high note in the profeſſion of the law, and among the reſt Sir John Scott, the ſolicitor general, were of opinion, that the renewal of the impeachment was neither juſtified by law, precedent, nor equity.

CHAP. XLVI. 1791. Precedents and arguments for and against.

It was a queſtion, they ſaid, concerning which there was no ſtatute; we muſt therefore be governed by the law of parliament, that is by the orders of the lords, and by uſage. The lords in 1678, had affirmed, that diſſolution did not preclude the renewal of an impeachment; but that order was not ſanctioned by former practice. They had ſuffered the impeachment of Lords Danby and Stafford to proceed from the ſtage in which they had been left by the old parliament; but at that time the nation was in a ferment about the Popiſh plot; deteſted Stafford as a catholic, and execrated Danby as the ſuppoſed promoter of arbitrary power and a connection between the king and Louis XIV. Both peers and commons were ſeized with the ſame enthuſiaſm againſt popery and France, and under its influence continued the impeachment, contrary to law and uſage. From theſe caſes, therefore, which were peculiarly circumſtanced, no precedent could be drawn. In 1585 Lord Danby was by the houſe of lords freed from the impeachment, which in fact reverſed the precedent of 1678. Lords Saliſbury and Peterborough being accuſed of high treaſon, pleaded a diſſolution, and in 1690 were liberated. On the ſame grounds the Lords Somers and Halifax, Sir Adam Blair, and others, were releaſed. To ſupport their poſition, they alſo adduced ſeveral analogies, and concluded with arguments from equity; by continuation of an impeachment the accuſers might be changed, and even not a few of the judges. If a trial is to laſt beyond one parliament, may it not be prolonged to an indefinite term, or even during life: a court of juſ-

tice

tice ſhould be free from bias and prejudice; but how could this be the caſe with a tribunal in which there were ſo many new judges; and ſome of them even accuſers from the lower houſe. The ſupporters of continued impeachment reaſoned in the following manner. If the alledged precedents exiſted, they would be extremely prejudicial, becauſe they would enable the ſovereign to ſave a favourite ſervant, and to defeat the purpoſes of national juſtice; and it would become the legiſlature ſpeedily to remedy ſuch an evil, by a law enacted for the purpoſe. This remedy, however, could only be applied to future caſes, without including preſent or paſt; but ſuch a ſeries of uſages does not exiſt*. There is no evidence of parliamentary practice to juſtify the ceſſation of a trial before the truth or falſehood of the charges be aſcertained. Parliamentary records demonſtrate that in ancient times impeachments were continued after diſſolution. But without ſearching into remote monuments, in the reign of Charles II, in 1673, when there was no ferment either on the one ſide or the other, the houſe of Lords declared their writs of error, petitions of appeal, and other judicial proceedings, ſhould be narrowed as to the portion of time which they were to occupy during a ſeſſion, but ſhould extend from parliament to parliament, if they were not decided. The reaſon of this order evidently was, that on the one hand judicial proceedings might not employ any part of the time which was required by legiſlative, on the other, that the objects either

* See Speeches of Mr. Pitt and of Mr. Fox.

 of

CHAP. XLVI. 1791. of civil or criminal juftice might not be defeated by difcontinuance of procefs. The precedents, it was contended, did not apply: and in the various cafes alleged, the proceedings had been difcontinued by a general pardon, admiffion to bail, or fome other caufe, and not from the diffolution of parliament. Thefe pofitions their fupporters endeavoured to evince by a confideration of the very cafes that were quoted by the advocates of the oppofite doctrine. They further argued, that decifions of courts of law, and the authority of judges, with few exceptions, fanctioned the fame opinion; and cited cafes to prove their pofition: the general analogy of judicial proceedings illuftrated the conformity of their conception of the law of parliament with the eftablifhed modes of procefs before fubordinate tribunals: the commons are the public profecutors, and in this refpect analogous to the attorney or folicitor general in ordinary cafes of criminal profecutions. The removal of an attorney general does not quafh an information or indictment; and the procefs is carried on by his fucceffor. The public profecutors before the houfe of peers, are the fucceffive houfes of commons, as before the inferior courts, they are the fucceffive attornies general. The houfe of peers are the judges in caufes carried on at the inftance of the houfe of commons; the peers may be not all the fame in fucceffive parliaments, as the judges of the inferior courts may be changed while the trial is pending. Equity and expediency coincide with analogy; impeachments are calculated for bringing to condign punifhment criminals too

5 exalted

exalted for the inferior courts; criminals, who to secure themselves or their friends from all responsibility as ministers of the crown, might advise a dissolution, as often as it should be required for their safety. Hence parliament would be no longer able to controul either the civil or judicial administration of the kingdom. The cabinet and courts of law would remain equally without a check; it is therefore clear from the weight of precedents, the authority of the greatest luminaries of the law, the principles of the constitution, the analogy of public trials, the immutable rules of equal justice, and the dictates of expediency and common sense, that impeachments continue notwithstanding the dissolution of parliament. On these grounds a great majority in both houses voted that the impeachment of Warren Hastings was still depending.

Determination of the house, that impeachments do not abate by solution.

An enquiry concerning the judicial power of parliament was soon followed by a discussion of the powers of juries. One of the chief engines of that moral and political knowledge, of those sentiments and privileges of rational and beneficial liberty which prevail in Britain, is a FREE PRESS. By this vehicle a writer may communicate to the public his observations, thoughts, and feelings, and according to his talents, learning, and dispositions, may inform and instruct mankind; and thus the press bestows all the knowledge and wisdom which cannot be imparted by oral delivery. But as all persons who address the public through this vehicle are not both capable and disposed to inform and instruct society, an instrument of general good is

Liberty of the press.

CHAP. XLVI. 1791. frequently productive of confiderable, though partial evil. The liberty of the prefs has often permitted feditious, treafonable, immoral, and blafphemous libels; and generated mifchiefs that were followed by very pernicious confequences. For a confiderable time after the invention of printing, government poffeffed the means of preventing noxious publications, as the prefs was liable to the infpection of a licenfer; but the preventive was much worfe than the evil; and the fubjection of writings to a previous examination, being found totally incompatible with the purpofes of beneficial freedom, ceafed foon after the revolution. Precluded by the law from preventing the publication of hurtful works, certain judges endeavoured to deter writers by increafing the punifhment: to avoid one extreme running into its oppofite, they attempted to attach criminalty to productions, that before would have been reckoned innocent; and to fupply the fuppofed deficiency of preventive juftice, they tried to enlarge the precincts of penal law. They alfo endeavoured to change the judicial rules eftablifhed by the conftitution. For a feries of years it had been maintained by very high legal authority, as we have already feen*, that the truth of an allegation could not be pleaded in bar of an indictment for a libel, and alfo that in cafes of libel juries were to inveftigate the fact only; to return a verdict relative to the proof of the allegations, but to leave the criminalty to the judge; and though thefe doctrines had been queftioned by very high legal autho-

* See vol. ii. c. ix.

rity,

rity*, yet they were most frequently followed in recent practice. Various cases occurred in which guilt had been found on grounds, that in the popular estimation were inadequate, or punishment had far exceeded the criminalty that was evinced. Mr. Fox having adopted the same sentiments respecting some late decisions, and disapproving of the interposition of crown lawyers, introduced a bill declaring the power of the juries to decide upon the law as well as the fact in trials of libels. Where any special matter of law is pleaded (said Mr. Fox) the judge and not the jury is to decide; but where a general issue is joined, and the law is so implicated with the fact that they cannot be separated, the jury must, as in all other criminal processes, bring in a general verdict of guilty or not guilty. The decision of this important question greatly depended on the import of the word *meaning*, used in all indictments for libels. The different senses annexed to this term Mr. Fox explained, and marked with discriminating precision. The term to *mean* might, he observed, be understood to imply a proposition according to strict *grammatical and logical construction*, or to express the MORAL INTENTION of a writer or speaker. In the former sense it had been received for many years by judges and crown lawyers; in the latter it ought to be interpreted by a candid and impartial English jury, who were to investigate the intention of the accused, as a part of the fact to be proved or disproved. It is the intention that must constitute guilt, if any guilt existed.

Motion of Mr Fox for ascertaining and declaring the law of libels, and bill for that purpose. Arguments for and against.

* See vol. ii. chap. ix.

The

CHAP. XLVI. 1791.

The bill was oppofed as an innovation on the laws of the kingdom, that was agitated at prefent by the dangerous maxims which were embroiling our neighbours. In fuch circumftances we ought to avoid novelties, civil and political. The prefent procefs had been the practice for a long courfe of years, without producing any oppreffion to the fubject; the judges were independent of the crown, and could have no motive to unfair and partial decifions. This bill was not debated as a party queftion, but as a fubject of exifting law, juftice, and conftitutional right. Mr. Pitt was no lefs vigorous in its fupport than Mr. Fox, or Mr. Erfkine. In the houfe of lords, Lord Grenville fupported the motion with no lefs zeal than Lord Loughborough, and Lord Camden took the lead in promoting its fuccefs. After paffing the commons by a great majority, it was rejected by the peers; but the following feffion, being again propofed, it paffed into a law.

Poftponed for the prefent; is afterwards paffed into a law.

Mr. Fox alfo propofed a law for depriving the attorney general in right of the crown, and every other perfon in his own right, of a power to difturb the poffeffor of a franchife in a corporation, after having quietly exercifed it for fix years. The end of this propofition was, to fecure the rights of election, and prevent vexatious profecutions for political purpofes: the bill was paffed into a law.

State and conduct of the Englifh catholics.

Parliament, endeavouring to remove all reftrictions upon natural freedom, as far as was confiftent with fecurity, directed its attention to the Catholics. The Englifh catholics were now totally

changed,

changed, and no longer refembled the Romanifts of the feventeenth century; nor even thofe who, at a later period, wifhed to exalt a popifh pretender to the throne. They were now quiet and peaceable fubjects, friends to the prefent government, and favourable to our conftitution of church and ftate, which was fo mild and tolerant to every religious fect that worfhipped God according to their own confcience, without difturbing the public tranquillity. Many of the catholics, as they mingled with proteftants, imbibed a great fhare of their mildnefs and moderation; and, without relinquifhing the fenfible rituals, prefcribed obfervances, or the metaphyfical theology of the popifh church, were really proteftants in their moral and political principles and conduct. A confiderable body of them had recently protefted in exprefs terms againft doctrines imputed for near three centuries to papifts. They denied the authority of the pope in temporal concerns, his right to excommunicate princes, and to abfolve their fubjects from their oaths of allegiance. They difavowed the lawfulnefs of breaking faith with heretics; and denied that any clerical power could exempt man from moral obligations. The penal laws againft catholics arifing from circumftances and conduct fo totally different from the prefent, were ftill extremely fevere. To render the law more fuitable to their prefent fentiments and character, Mr. Mitford propofed to repeal the ftatutes in queftion, fo far as to exempt from their penal operations thofe who had renounced the hurtful doctrines above-mentioned, under the denomination of the PROTESTING CATHOLIC DISSENTERS, upon thefe catholics taking an

They renounce the moft dangerous moral and political doctrines of popery.

Motion for their relief:

CHAP. XLVI.

1791.

modified and corrected by Dr. Horfley, it is paffed into a law.

an oath conformable to the proteft. The principle of the bill was generally approved; and the bench of bifhops difplayed the moft liberal zeal in its favour. Dr. Horfely efpecially exerted his great abilities, not only in promoting its fuccefs, but in removing a claufe which was neither agreeable to its principles nor conducive to its objects. In the propofed oath, the doctrine that princes excommunicated by the pope might be depofed and murdered by their fubjects, was declared to be impious, heretical, and damnable. The catholics felt no reluctance to exprefs their own rejection and difapprobation of fuch doctrine; but from fcruples founded on a tender regard for the memory of their progenitors, they could not induce themfelves to brand it with the terms which the oath prefcribed. To remove this objection, he propofed the oath which had been adopted in 1778: this alteration was admitted, and the bill was paffed into a law.

Petition of the church of Scotland refpecting the teft act,

The church of Scotland perceiving a difpofition in parliament to grant relief to non-conformifts, tranfmitted from the general affembly a petition praying for the repeal of the teft act as far as it applied to Scotland; and on the 10th of May Sir Gilbert Elliot made a motion conformably to the petition. The fupporters of the motion endeavoured to prove that the law, as it now ftood, was inconfiftent with the articles of the union. Scotland, by her conftitution, and by treaty, had a feparate church, and a feparate form of religion. By the treaty of union fhe was to have a free communication of civil rights; but a teft which, as a condition for attaining thofe civil rights, impofed on her a neceffity of departing from her own eſtabliſhed theology, and ſubmitting to the ſyſtem of England, either abridged her religious liberty by means of the civil attainments, or obſtructed the civil attainments through the religious obligations. When the two kingdoms entered into a treaty of union, being independent nations, they meant to ſtipulate and contract on terms of perfect equality. Was it not an infringement of that equality, that a Scotchman entering into any Britiſh office in England ſhould ſolemnly profeſs his attachment to the church of England, which a ſcrupulous man might deem a dereliction of his native church; while an Engliſhman appointed to an office in Scotland incurred no ſimilar obligation. The oppoſers of the motion argued, that the teſt muſt have been underſtood as a ſtipulation at the time of the union, and had never been repreſented as an hardſhip till the preſent time. The grievance was merely imaginary; the teſt was not a dereliction of the church of Scotland, but a pledge of amity with the church of England. The general ſentiment of members of the Scottiſh church was affection and reſpect for the ſiſter eſtabliſhment: but in Scotland there were, as in England, ſectaries of various denominations, whoſe ſentiments were leſs liberal. Againſt ſuch ſectaries it was juſt as well as expedient, that the teſt ſhould operate; otherwiſe the church of England would incur a danger from them, to which from the ſectaries of England ſhe was not expoſed. Since there was no teſt in Scotland, the propoſed exemption would let in upon the church of England diſſenters and ſectaries of every denomination; and thus break down the fence

which

CHAP. XLVI. 1791.

which the wisdom and justice of parliament had so often and so recently confirmed. This petition, in reality, arose ultimately from the English dissenters. These had operated on the church of Scotland by representing themselves as Presbyterian brethren. Many of the Scottish clergymen, not discovering the total diversity of political sentiments that subsisted between them and many of the English dissenters, were, from supposed religious sympathy, induced to give them their support. The majority of the house being impressed by these arguments, voted against the proposition.

Is rejected.

Full discussion of the slave-trade.

The slave-trade underwent this year a much more complete discussion than when it was formerly agitated. The facts on both sides had now been very thoroughly examined: there was fulness of information; so that the public and parliament had the amplest means of viewing the subject in every light. Mr. Wilberforce, on the 18th of April, proposed a bill for preventing the farther importation of slaves into the British colonies in the West Indies. In his prefatory speech he considered, as he had done two years before, first humanity, and secondly policy. He traced the condition of the Africans from their native country to the West India plantations; and, according to the information which he had collected, in more copious detail, with more numerous instances, repeated his former statements of the causes of slavery, the treatment of the negroes on their passage, and their sufferings under the planters. On the ground of policy he strongly argued that the abolition of the slave-trade was expedient for the West India planters and the British nation. Compelled

Motion of Mr. Wilberforce for the abolition.

Arguments for

pelled to promote multiplication among the ſlaves, the planters would ſoon find that their preſent negroes, in a climate ſo congenial to their native Africa, would, if well treated, people the plantations; and if allowed to acquire ſome little intereſt in the ſoil, would be ſtimulated to much greater exertions. The loſs of ſeamen which Britons ſuſtained in the negro trade was immenſe. From Liverpool, in one year, three hundred and fifty ſhips, having on board twelve thouſand two hundred and fifty men, loſt two thouſand four hundred and fifty, being one fifth. The commercial profits were to be totally diſregarded, when acquired by ſuch a violation of humanity, and at the expence of ſo many valuable lives of Britiſh ſailors.

and againſt it.

The continuance of this trade was defended on the grounds of juſtice, policy, and even humanity. Slavery had been eſtabliſhed time immemorial in various parts of the earth, eſpecially in Africa and the adjacent countries. So far was it from being reckoned a crime, that the Old Teſtament frequently mentions male and female ſlaves under the names of bondſmen, handmaids, and others of ſimilar import, and never cenſures mancipation, but ſpeaks of all its offices as juſt employments. The characters held up to imitation had ſlaves themſelves, and endeavoured to acquire ſlaves to others *. The habits and

* Joſeph, a patriarch ſo highly favoured by God, when he became prime miniſter to Pharoah in conſequence of the foreſight conferred on him by the divine gift, having laid up ſtores of proviſions againſt the ſeaſon of ſcarcity, purchaſed with the king's corn the liberties of his ſubjects; and nothing in this procedure is blamed by the ſacred hiſtorian. It appeared, indeed, perfectly fair and reaſonable to the ſubjects of an African prince.

ſentiments

CHAP. XLVI. 1791. ſentiments of Africans render this condition by no means ſo grievous to them as it would be to people unaccuſtomed to the daily contemplation of ſlavery. The aſſertion of the abolitioniſts, that the hope of acquiring priſoners to be ſold to Europeans is the chief cauſe of war, is far from being generally true. Wars in Africa, as well as wars in Europe, ariſe from pride, reſentment, envy, jealouſy, emulation, ambition, and other paſſions, beſides avarice alone. As an accurate knowledge of the interior country increaſed, it was more clearly comprehended that captives, though a conſequence of war, were far from being its moſt frequent objects. The purchaſer of ſlaves taken in war preſerves the lives of captives that would be otherwiſe butchered. Their ferocious conquerors would give way to the ſavage gratification of rage and cruelty, if the thirſt of blood were not changed into the thirſt of gain. The extreme indolence of the Africans, notwithſtanding the fertility and even ſpontaneous productiveneſs of the ſoil, renders their ſupplies of the neceſſaries of life very ſcanty. Priſoners taken in war, therefore, are great burthens upon the captors; and unleſs there was a market for vending them, they would be immediately maſſacred, not merely from cruelty, but from the ſavage economy of thoſe barbarians; and the European traders ſaved many a life. Our merchants, on the faith of parliament, had embarked property to a great amount in this trade; the total loſs of which would immediately follow the abolition. The legiſlature had invited them to engage in the traffic, that Britain might be furniſhed from their plantations with thoſe commodities which habit has

now

CHAP. XLVI. 1791.

now rendered universally neceſſary, and if not ſupplied by them, muſt be purchaſed from other countries. It invited them alſo to engage in this commerce, that the carriage of their productions might rear up a navy; yet now, when they have a capital of ſeventy millions embarked, when ſeveral iſlands lately occupied, and therefore thinly peopled, require a conſtant ſucceſſion of freſh ſupplies; and when twenty millions of debt in mortgages and deeds of conſignment, preſs heavily on the Weſt India proprietors, the abolition is propoſed in contradiction to ſo many acts of parliament, and without compenſation of the only means by which they can be relieved from the enormous load. Is it conſiſtent with Britiſh juſtice to depreciate, and even deſtroy, property, engaged in a commerce which the legiſlature pledged itſelf to protect, and repeatedly declared its diſpoſition to improve? But private property would not alone be affected; from this trade the revenue would ſuffer a very material diminution. The evidences adduced to prove the horrid cruelties practiſed upon ſlaves were repreſented to be in ſome inſtances falſe, in many partial, in almoſt all exaggerated. It is the intereſt both of the tranſporting owners of ſlaves, and their purchaſers in the Weſt Indies, to treat them humanely, and eaſy to deviſe regulations for enforcing this treatment, and puniſhing the contrary. But were Britain from an impulſe of benevolent enthuſiaſm to aboliſh the ſlave-trade, under a ſuppoſition that it ſubjected the Africans to the moſt poignant miſery, would not other European nations engaged in the trade ſupply the vacancy left by our relinquiſhment of a traffic neceſſary for raiſ-

Continuance of the ſlave-trade defended on the grounds of humanity, juſtice, and expediency.

CHAP. XLVI. 1791.

ing commodities naturalized to the European palates? Would the purchaſers, the venders, or the ſubjects ſold, be leſs numerous? Would fewer ſlaves be exported from Africa? Reſpecting the effects of this commerce on our navy, the friends of the abolition were totally miſinformed. A naval commander of the very higheſt eminence, Lord Rodney, had declared that the power of obtaining from Guinea ſhips, ſo numerous a body of men inured to the climate, whenever we wiſhed to ſend a fleet to the Weſt Indies on the breaking out of a war, was, in his opinion, a conſideration of great moment. His Lordſhip's opinion was illuſtrated, and his authority confirmed, by concurring teſtimonies of other officers, both of the army and navy. The abolition would be equally contrary to the commercial and political intereſts of the public, as to the rights and well-founded expectations of private individuals. On this queſtion Meſſrs. Pitt and Fox took the ſame ſide, and ſupported the abolition with every argument that genius could invent; but their united eloquence was not effectual: on a diviſion it was carried in the negative by a majority of one hundred and ſixty-three to eighty-eight. The benevolent ſpirit which prompted the abolition of the ſlave-trade directly, produced an attempt gradually to demonſtrate its inefficacy and inutility. For this purpoſe its impugners projected to try an experiment whether Africa could not be civilized, and rendered more lucrative as a vent for manufactures, than as a nurſery for ſlaves. Mr. Devaynes, who had long reſided at Sierra Leone, on the coaſt of Africa, in the eighth degree of north latitude, atteſted that the ſoil is ex-

Meſſrs. Pitt and Fox agree in ſupporting the abolition.

The motion is negatived

cellent,

cellent, and produces cotton, coffee, and sugar, with the slightest cultivation. There a society proposed to establish a colony in hopes of effecting the desired change in the character and condition of the Africans. A bill for the establishment of such a company was introduced by Mr. Henry Thornton, and passed through both houses without opposition.

CHAP. XLVI.

1791. Settlement at Sierra Leone.

Finance.

Previous to the production of his financial plan, Mr. Pitt proposed to appoint a committee to consider and report the amount of the public income and expenditure during the last five years; also, to inquire what they might respectively be in future; and what alterations had taken place in the amount of the national debt since January 5th, 1786. The report stated that the annual income, on the average of the three last years, was sixteen millions, thirty thousand, two hundred and eighty-six pounds; and the annual expenditure fifteen millions, nine hundred and sixty-nine thousand, one hundred and seventy-eight pounds, including the annual million for liquidating the national debt: the balance, therefore, in favour of the country, was sixty-one thousand, one hundred and eight pounds *. Mr. Sheridan, as usual, took the lead in combatting the financial conclusions of Mr. Pitt, and moved no less than forty resolutions, which were intended to shew that the past revenue had been considerably inferior to ministerial calculations; and that in calculating the future income, the minister had overlooked contingencies which recent experience demonstrated to

* 16,030,286
15,969,178
£ 61,108

CHAP. XLVI. 1791.

be probable. The greater number of these propositions were negatived, and others were amended. Various resolutions were framed by ministers, confirming, in detail, the report of the new committee, and maintaining the calculations which were founded on their enquiry. The supplies were nearly the same as in the usual peace establishment, and no fresh taxes were imposed. Mr. Dundas produced his annual statement of Indian finance, which had been in a state of so progressive prosperity ever since the establishment of Mr. Pitt's plan of territorial government, and the commencement of Mr. Dundas's executive direction. It appeared from the documents which he presented, that the British revenues in the East Indies, amounting to seven millions, after defraying all the expences of government, left a clear surplus of near a million and a half, either to be laid out in investments, or applied to contingent services. Among the pecuniary grants of this year was an annuity of twelve thousand pounds, bestowed on his majesty's third son, Prince William Henry, created about two years before Duke of Clarence.

Supplies.

Indian finance.

Trial of Hastings. The evidence for the prosecution closed.

This year the prosecution of Mr. Hastings closed its evidence (May 30). The managers proposed an address to the king, praying him not to prorogue the parliament until the trial was finished; but this address was negatived. Mr. Hastings, when the prosecution was closed, addressed the court in a speech of singular acuteness, force, and eloquence, exhibiting his view of the result of the prosecutor's evidence, contrasting the situation in which he found with the situation in which he left British India; explicitly, but not arrogantly, detailing the counsels

and

CHAP. XLVI. 1791.

and conduct by which he had effected these great ends: he appealed to the commons, his accusers, in the following dignified and striking peroration. "To the commons of England, in whose name I am arraigned for desolating the provinces of their dominions in India, I dare to reply, that they are, and their representatives persist in telling them so, the most flourishing of all the states of India. It was I that made them so: the value of what others acquired I enlarged, and gave shape and consistency to the dominions which you hold there: I preserved it: I sent forth its armies with an effectual but economical hand, through unknown and hostile regions, to the support of your other possessions; to the retrieval of one from degradation and dishonour, and of another from utter loss and subjection. I maintained the wars which were of your formation, or that of others, not of mine: I won one member of the great Indian confederacy from it by an act of seasonable restitution; with another I maintained a secret intercourse, and converted him into a friend: a third I drew off by diversion and negociation, and employed him as the instrument of peace. I gave you all, and you have rewarded me with confiscation, disgrace, and a life of impeachment." Of Mr. Hastings's hearers, even those who could not admit a plea of merit as an abatement of special charges, were very forcibly impressed by this energetic representation. The defence of the accused was, by the direction of the court, postponed till the following session, and on June 10th the parliament was prorogued.

Impressive speech of the defendant.

Session rises.

CHAP. XLVII.

Peace between Russia and Turkey—on moderate terms.—Reasons of Catharine's apparent moderation.—Poland attempts to recover liberty and independence.—Wise, moderate, and patriotic efforts for that purpose.—New constitution, an hereditary, mixed, and limited monarchy—effected without bloodshed.—Rage of Catharine at the emancipation of Poland.—She hopes to crush the new system of Poland.—Impression made by the French revolution on other countries—on sovereigns.—Circular letter of the emperor to other princes.—Equitable and prudent principle of British policy respecting the French revolution.—Paris—ejectment and banishment of the clergy who refused the civic oath.—Progress of confiscation.—Forfeiture of the estates of emigrants.—Abolition of primogeniture.—Invasion of the rights of German princes.—The emperor remonstrates against this violation of national engagements.—Proposed jaunt of the king to St. Cloud—is prevented by the populace.—Memorial of Louis delivered to foreign powers.—Flight of the king.—He is arrested at Varennes.—Proceedings of the legislature during his absence.—He is brought back to Paris.—The monarchical party adopts a vigorous system, but too late.—State of parties.—The king's friends advise him to accept the constitutional code.—He accepts it in the national assembly.—Honours paid to infidel philosophers.—Want of money.—Inspection of accounts.—Dissolution of the national assembly.—Review of the principal changes effected by this body.—How it found and left France.—In all its excesses it manifested the genius and energy of the French character.—Progress of political enthusiasm.—Britain.—Certain ingenious visionaries expect a political millennium.—Thomas Paine.—Rights of man—Dexterous adaptation of to the sentiments and passions of the vulgar—astonishing popularity of among the lower ranks.—Commemoration

moration of the French revolution at Birmingham.—Riots.—Destruction of Dr. Priestley's library—the Doctor's conduct. Comparison between Priestley and Paine.—Rapid and extensive diffusion of democratic principles —Wide diffusion of superficial literature—favourable to revolutionary projects. Mary Anne Wollstonecroft.—Debating Societies.—Cheap editions of Tom Paine's works.—One able and profound work in favour of the French Revolution.—Vindiciæ Gallicæ.—Marriage of the Duke of York to the Princess of Prussia.

CHAP. XLVII.

1791. Peace between Russia and Turkey,

CATHARINE perceived her grand object of subjugating the Ottomans, for the present to be impracticable, and now satisfied herself with endeavouring to compel the Sultan to a peace, before the interference of the confederates could prevent her from dictating the terms. With this view her armies took the field early in spring, repeatedly defeated the enemy, and compelled them to retire nearer to Constantinople; and to enhance their danger, several symptoms began to appear in Asiatic Turkey of a disposition to revolt: menaced by most imminent perils both in Asia and Europe, and apprized that the co-operation of Prussia and of Britain, was now obstructed, Selim began to listen to the proposals of the Empress; the negotiation was not tedious; and a peace was concluded on the 11th of August at Galatz, by which Russia retained Oczakow, and the country between the Bog and the Dnieper, which had belonged to Turkey before the war. The latter of these rivers was to be the boundary of both powers: each to be equally entitled to the free navigation of the river; and each to erect fortifications on its respective shores. However important this acquisition might be to Russia, it was certainly

on moderate terms.

1791. Reaſons of Catharine's apparent moderation.

certainly much inferior to the expectations which ſhe entertained at the commencement of the war; and during its ſucceſsful progreſs: but other circumſtances combined with the exertions of the defenſive alliance to induce Catharine to content herſelf, for the preſent, with Oczakow and its dependencies. Frederic William agreeably to the general objects of the confederacy, as well as his own particular intereſt, cultivated the friendſhip of Poland. Encouraged by their connection with this powerful prince, and beginning once more to conceive themſelves of weight in the ſcale of Europe, reviving ſelf-eſtimation re-kindled in the Poles that courage and patriotiſm, which though ſmothered, had not been extinguiſhed; and thus once more they entertained hopes of freeing themſelves from the thraldom in which they were held by the imperious Catharine.

Poland attempts to recover liberty and independence;

In 1788 and 1789, various efforts were made to eſtabliſh the independent intereſt of Poland in the diet, and to overturn the power which Ruſſia had aſſumed. A party of generous patriots ſtimulated their countrymen to emancipate themſelves from a foreign yoke; the ſpirit of liberty was ſtudiouſly diffuſed through all claſſes of the community; and in 1790 had riſen very high. Its leading votaries ſaw, that the only method of ſecuring the attachment and fidelity of the people to thoſe who were projecting ſuch alterations, was to accompany them with ſuch benefits to the middling, and even to the inferior claſſes, as might deeply intereſt them in their ſupport. But though deſirous of changes, which would terminate the oppreſſive power of the great, the Poles were ſincerely inclined to be

ſatisfied

satisfied with a moderate degree of freedom; and at present bounded their wishes to deliverance, from the personal thraldom in which, for so many ages, they had been tyrannically held. Conformably to this disposition, the popular leaders exerted their influence, with so much wisdom and prudence among the commons, that they made no claims but those that were strictly equitable and consistent with legal subordination. On these moderate principles of freedom, the people of Poland drew up an address to the diet, amounting to a declaration of rights. This representation, instead of recurring to the *natural rights of man*, antecedent to political establishment, considered *what was most expedient for the character and circumstances of the Polish people.* The constitution of Poland having been extremely defective in various constituents of liberty and security, the address in its claims, proposed such changes only as would remedy the defects, without subverting the existing orders. The nobles, clergy, and commons, should continue distinct, and the nobility retain their rank, dignity, and all the privileges which were compatible with public freedom; they should only be deprived of the power of oppression and tyranny. The commons should not only be exempted from civil thraldom, but have all the political power that was consistent with the balance of the estates. Requisitions so discriminately moderate, tending to produce the balance of the parts, as well as the welfare of the whole, were most graciously received by the Polish nobility, who shewed themselves desirous of promoting a new system, conformable to the wishes of the people. The Polish patriots were eager

CHAP. XLVII.

1791. wise, moderate, and patriotic efforts for that purpose.

CHAP. XLVII. 1791. eager to complete their reform, before Russia should be in a condition to give them any effectual interruption. Reports were spread and suspicions entertained, that there was a new partition in comtemplation: the only way to prevent such a calamity and disgrace, was without delay to establish a system of polity, which should produce an union of the whole strength and energy of the Polish nation, resist the interference of foreigners in its domestic affairs, and preserve its natural independence and dignity. With these views the patriots formed a system, which had for its basis, the rights claimed in the address of the people; and they presented their plan to the diet at Warsaw. The new constitution proposed two objects; the external independence, and internal liberty of the nation. The Roman Catholic religion was to continue to be the national faith, with a toleration of every other which should peaceably submit to the established government. The clergy should retain their privileges and authority; the nobility their pre-eminence and prerogatives; the commons including the citizens and peasants, should participate of the general liberty; and the peasants were to be exempted from the predial servitude, under which they had so long groaned. Stipulations between the landholders and the peasants should be equally binding on both parties and ontheir respective successors, either by inheritance or acquisition: all property of every rank, order, or individual should be sacred, even from the encroachments of the supreme national power. To encourage the population of the country, all people, either strangers who should come to settle, or

natives

1791. New constitution, an hereditary, mixed, and limited monarchy;

natives who having emigrated should return to their country, might become citizens of Poland, on conforming to its laws. The constitution should be composed of three distinct powers, the legislative power in the states assembled; executive power in the king and council; and judicial power in the jurisdictions existing, or to be established. The crown was declared to be elective in point of families, but hereditary in the family which should be chosen. The proposed dynasty of future kings, was to begin with the Elector of Saxony, and to descend to his heirs. The king at his accession must engage to support the new constitution, and was to command the army, and preside in the legislature: the legislation was to be vested in two houses, the nobility and commons, meeting by their representatives; and the judicial power was to be vested in a gradation of courts, rising to one general and national tribunal. Such are the outlines* of the constitution of Poland, which appeared to steer a middle course between aristocratic tyranny, and democratic violence. It seemed well calculated to maintain internal liberty, encourage the industry of the great mass of the people, improve the immense advantages of their soil and situation, and invigorate their energy by the newly infused spirit of personal freedom; to confirm subordination of rank, which best guides the efforts of the people, and by diffusing harmony and force throughout the nation, to afford the disposition and means of maintaining the independence

* See Otridge's Annual Register for 1791. Appendix to Chronicle, page 88.

of

CHAP. XLVII. 1791.

of Poland. There were members of the diet who not only oppofed thefe proceedings, but drew up a proteft againft them in the form of a manifefto. Their conduct excited univerfal diffatisfaction, and though the moderation of the patriotic party offered no infult to their perfons, yet the people could not forbear to view them with indignation. The king and the other leaders of the popular party were extremely vigilant in reftraining every appearance of violence. Indeed a fingular and happy circumftance of this revolution, was the peaceable manner in which it was effected: Poland attained the end which it propofed, without the lofs of a fingle life. In framing this fyftem, Staniflaus himfelf had difplayed great ability: he had confulted the Englifh and American conftitutions, and with acute difcrimination had felected fuch parts as were beft adapted to the circumftances of Poland. The Polifh patriots aware of the difpofitions of Catharine, and apprehending other neighbouring ftates to regard the project with a jealous eye, urged the fpeedy adoption of the new conftitution; and they exerted themfelves fo ftrenuoufly, that on the 3d of May 1791, it was accepted by the eftates, and all orders and claffes of men, and ratified by fuitable oaths, and inaugural folemnities.

effected without bloodfhed.

Rage of Catharine at the emancipation of Poland;

The fituation of Poland, freed from the Ruffian yoke, and rifing to independence and refpectability, galled the pride, and alarmed the ambition of Catharine; fhe was enraged, that the Poles, over whom fhe for many years had imperioufly domineered, now afferted a right of managing their own affairs:

fhe

she saw in the power of Poland, if allowed to be confirmed, under her present constitution, a bar to the accomplishment of her vast projects: she was therefore eager to conclude the peace of Galatz, on terms less humiliating to the vanquished Ottoman, than from her successes she might have expected.

CHAP. XLVII. 1791.

There were circumstances which afforded her hopes of not only resuming her dictation in Poland, but also rendering her power over that country more arbitrary than ever.

She hopes to crush the new system of Poland.

At the commencement of the French revolution, the other great powers of the continent were so much engaged in their own several projects, as not to bestow an adequate attention on the character and spirit of the Gallic proceedings. Spain was by far too feeble to entertain any hopes of interfering with effect in favour of fallen monarchy. The king of Sardinia afforded refuge to the exiled princes and nobility, but could supply no important aid. The refugee princes and their party, though anxiously eager to interest foreign powers in the cause of the privileged orders, yet during the year 1790, had little success; but when Leopold had restored tranquillity in the Low Countries, after having concluded peace with Turkey, and being on terms of amity with the defensive alliance, he turned his attention* to the situation of France. Though moved by consanguinity, he was yet more deeply impressed by kingly sympathy: he considered the present ruling party in France as inimical to all monarchy, and holding up an example which he apprehended the

Impression made by the French revolution on other countries;

on sovereigns.

* See Annual Register 1791, ch. iv.

CHAP. XLVII. 1791.

ſubjects of neighbouring ſovereigns might imitate: and in theſe ſentiments other princes of Germany coincided. Leopold however was aware of the danger which would attend ſpeedy hoſtilities, unleſs he ſhould have more effectual auxiliaries than the petty princes of the Germanic empire. His own reſources were impaired by the war from which he had ſo recently extricated himſelf. France under her monarchical government had been always too powerful for the German empire; the preſent ſyſtem would afford her additional energy. From theſe conſiderations ſo early as the ſpring of 1791, he endeavoured to intereſt other potentates in his objects; and with his own hand * wrote a letter to the Empreſs of Ruſſia, the King of England, and the King of Pruſſia, alſo to the King of Spain, the States General, the Kings of Sardinia and Naples; propoſing to form an union and concert of counſels and plans, for the purpoſes of aſſerting the honour and liberty of the king and royal family of France, and ſetting bounds to the dangerous exceſſes of the French revolution; to inſtruct their miniſters at Paris to declare the concert which ſhould be ſo formed; and recommend to the reſpective princes to ſupport their declarations, by preparing a ſufficient force. Should the French refuſe to comply with the joint requiſition of the crowned heads, the confederated powers would ſuſpend all intercourſe with France, collect a conſiderable army on the frontiers, and thereby compel the national aſſembly to raiſe and maintain a great military force at a heavy expence. The inter-

Circular letter of the Emperor to other princes.

* Annual. Regiſter as above.

ruption

ruption of trade, and general induſtry, would bring the people of France to more ſober thoughts; and might tend to the evaporation of their preſent enthuſiaſm. On ſo great an undertaking, the Emperor could not venture alone; the concurrence of the other great powers, eſpecially Pruſſia and Great Britain, was neceſſary to give efficacy to the project.

Equitable and prudent principle of Britiſh policy reſpecting the French revolution.

Whatever effect this application might have on the powers ſeverally, to whom it was addreſſed, it did not ſucceed in producing the propoſed concert. The principle of Britain manifeſted not only in her declarations, but uniform conduct, was that an internal change in the political ſyſtem of any country did not juſtify the interference of neighbouring nations, unleſs that internal change led its votaries to aggreſſion: that it did not belong to England to determine whether the government of France ſhould be monarchical or republican; and that in changing her conſtitution, humbling her monarch, degrading her nobility, plundering her church, and even committing various acts of atrocity, in her own provinces or metropolis, ſhe did no act which it belonged to Britain to avenge: ſhe inflicted no injury on Britain. As impartial obſervers, Britons might individually cenſure French proceedings, as unwiſe, unjuſt, or impious; but the Britiſh nation neither poſſeſſed nor aſſerted a right of dictation to the French concerning the management of their own internal affairs, ſo long as their conduct did not produce aggreſſion againſt this country.

Paris— ejectment and baniſhment of the

While ſymptoms of enmity againſt the French revolution were manifeſting themſelves in ſome of the

CHAP. XLVII.

1791.

Clergy who refused the civic oath.

the neighbouring countries, its votaries were proceeding in their career. With great expedition they ejected from their livings the refractory priests who would not swear contrary to their belief and conscience, and filled their places with more complaisant pastors, who were willing to submit to the powers that be; and in a few months there was a new set of spiritual teachers, most eagerly attached to the revolution to which they were indebted for their benefices. Besides this body of staunch auxiliaries, the national assembly, by robbing the church, procured another set of very active assistants in the holders of the assignments. These were, indeed, a kind of revolutionary pawn-brokers, who advanced money on plundered effects, and depended on the stability of the new system for payment. By the spiritual influence of the new priests, and the temporal influence of the new brokers, who consisted of great monied capitalists, the people became still more attached to the revolution, and its engine the national assembly.

Progress of confiscation.

This body of legislators, finding confiscation so productive a source of revenue, deemed it unwise to confine it to the property of the church.

Forfeiture of the estates of emigrants.

A new fund they provided in the estates of the refugee princes and nobility*; and with their usual dispatch they passed a decree sequestering the principal estates, and threatening to confiscate them all if the proprietors did not immediately return.

Abolition of primogeniture.

Farther to equalize property, they passed a decree abolishing primogeniture, and ordaining that the property of parents should be

* See proceedings of the national assembly.

equally,

equally divided among their children. But the national aſſembly now extended its ſyſtem of confiſcation to the properties of foreigners. Several German princes, ſecular and eccleſiaſtical, held great poſſeſſions in Alſace, by tenures repeatedly ratified under the moſt ſolemn treaties; and guaranteed by the great neighbouring powers. Yet theſe rights the national aſſembly overthrew by a mere act of lawleſs robbery*. This flagrant aggreſſion on the rights of independent powers, not only excited the indignant reſentment of the princes who were actually deſpoiled, but the diſpleaſure and apprehenſions of others. The confiſcation of French property by the government was an invaſion of the rights of French ſubjects. But the invaſion of foreign property was a declaration of intended hoſtilities againſt all nations to which their plundering arms could reach. The emperor remonſtrated on this violation of exiſting treaties, requiring compenſation for the paſt, and ſecurity againſt future attacks on the rights of princes of the empire. The national aſſembly imputed this requiſition to hoſtile intentions, and affirmed that there was a concert of foreign ſovereigns, French princes, and ariſtocrats, to effect a counter revolution: Louis, they ſaid, had acceded to this confederation, and was preparing to eſcape from France.

Invaſion of the rights of German princes.

The emperor remonſtrates againſt this violation of national engagements.

His majeſty at Eaſter had taken the ſacrament from the hands of a refractory † prieſt, and had thereby given great offence and alarm to the Pariſians. It was alſo remarked that he had recently

* See proceedings of the national aſſembly.

† Thoſe clergymen who would not take the preſcribed oath were, by the revolutioniſts, ſtyled refractory prieſts.

CHAP. XLVII.

1791.

Proposed jaunt of the king to St. Cloud, is prevented by the populace.

promoted officers inimical to the revolution. On the 18th of April, being Easter monday, his majesty and family intended to repair to St. Cloud, a palace about three miles from the city, there to spend the holidays. In the morning, as the family was stepping into their coaches, an immense crowd surrounding the carriages, refused to suffer them to proceed, and insisted that they should remain at Paris. The national guards, joining the multitude, exclaimed that the king should not be suffered to depart; and the sovereign found it necessary to comply with the requisition of the populace. After several discussions, the Parisians represented their apprehension of dangers assailing them from various quarters, and especially the king's intimate counsellors. His majesty, to gratify the populace, dismissed various royalists from their places at court, and employed other means to remove the popular dissatisfaction.

Memorial of Louis delivered to foreign powers.

One step which he took for this purpose, was to send a memorial to the French ministers in foreign countries, with orders to deliver a copy at each court where they respectively resided. This document recapitulated the events which produced and followed the revolution, and described that great change as having importantly improved the condition both of the monarch and the people. It extolled the new constitution, reprobated the efforts employed to overthrow that beneficial fabric, most clearly and unequivocally expressed the royal approbation of the present system, and declared that the assertions of those Frenchmen in foreign parts, who complained that he was obliged to disguise his sentiments, were unfounded in truth. This dispatch

being

being communicated on the 23d of April to the national aſſembly, was received with the loudeſt applauſe, and ordered to be poſted up in the moſt conſpicuous places of every municipality in the kingdom, to be read at the head of every regiment and company in the army, and on board of every ſhip in the navy. For ſeveral weeks the greateſt harmony appeared to prevail between the king and the aſſembly. Meanwhile the royaliſts, without being diſmayed by the power of the revolutioniſts, expreſſed their ſentiments with an aſperity, which increaſed the more that in oppreſſion, they ſaw the injuſtice of the predominant principles, and felt the miſery of their effects. Attachment however to the king's perſon and family deterred them from meaſures which they had reaſon to conclude, would endanger his ſafety; ſhould they make any deciſive movement towards a counter revolution, they did not doubt, a maſſacre of the royal captives, would be the ſacrifice to popular fury. The deliverance of their majeſties and the family from a ſtate of real captivity, by whatever name it might be called, would enable them to begin their attempts without hazarding the royal ſafety. They believed that the majority of the nation ſecretly cheriſhed the ſame ſentiments with themſelves, and would readily co-operate in attempting the reſtoration of royalty, when they ſaw hopes of ſupport and ſucceſs. Under this conviction, his majeſty's friends employed their utmoſt dexterity to effect his eſcape from Paris. The enterprize appeared arduous, but not impracticable; his majeſty was accompanied by a national guard, and alſo by a Swiſs guard; the latter corps was warmly

 attached

CHAP. XLVII. 1791.

judicial examination; and to manifest their sentiments respecting kings, quoted the trial of Charles I. of England. A deputation of three members was appointed to receive the king's deposition: his majesty refused to answer any interrogatories, but avowed his willingness to make known the motives for his late departure. His intention (he said) was not to leave the kingdom, but to repair to Montmedi, a fortified town on the frontiers, where his personal liberty would be secure, and his public conduct under no restraint; and where he could have transacted business, together with the assembly, without the imputation of force. He did not object to the constitution, but only to the small degree of liberty allowed to himself, which so impaired the sanction of his voice, as to give it the appearance of compulsion. A memorial which he left at his departure, more fully detailed the various grounds of his dissatisfaction with the national assembly; recapitulated their various acts, and very ably exposed the despotic usurpation of the revolutionary party. The assembly answered this memorial by a manifesto which was intended to prove that their conduct had been directed by regard to the public good, that its effect was internal prosperity, and a strength that would resist every attempt at a counter-revolution. From the unsuccessful effort of the king to escape from thraldom, the republicans derived a great accession of strength. They, however, thought it prudent to assume in the assembly the appearance of moderation, while their emissaries and associates in the clubs were occupied in increasing among the people the prevailing hatred of of monarchy. No faith could be reposed, they affirmed, in the king or any of his adherents, who were all plotting a counter-revolution. Under pretence of guarding against the designs of the royalists, the assembly assumed the organization of the army, and, indeed, the chief part of the executive power, which, at the confederation, they and the people had sworn to leave in the hands of the king. The monarchical party now adopted a system of open, resolute, and vigorous opposition, which, if chosen at a less advanced stage, might have saved their country from the despotism of paramount democracy. They declared that they never would relinquish the defence of the monarchy: no less than two hundred and eighty joined in a bold and explicit protest against the decrees by which the assembly acted independently of the crown; but now their firm boldness was too late. The national assembly, to guard against foreign invasion, gave directions for fortifying the frontiers. Meanwhile they proceeded with the constitutional code; and the king's late attempt caused the insertion of several articles which had not been before proposed. It was decreed by a great majority, that a king putting himself at the head of an armed force, hostile to the state, should be considered as having abdicated the crown. The same penalty was denounced against him were he to retract his oath of fidelity to the constitution, or incur the guilt of conspiracy against it by a criminal correspondence with the enemies of the nation. It was farther decreed, that after such abdication he should be treated as a simple citizen, and subjected, like all other individuals, to the common

The monarchical party adopt a vigorous system, but too late.

 course

CHAP. XLVII.

1791. State of parties

course of law. There was a very warm debate about the inviolability of the king's perſon. At this time there were four parties in the national aſſembly, and throughout the French empire: the royaliſts, whoſe object was the reſtoration of the monarchy in its former power and ſplendor; the moderates, who wiſhed a mixed kingly government, conſiſting of different eſtates, uniting ſecurity and liberty with ſocial order, and ſubordination: the third was the conſtitutionaliſts, the ſupporters of the exiſting polity, which, levelling all ranks and diſtinctions of ſubjects, ſtill retained the name of king, and were by far the moſt numerous: fourthly, the republicans, who were gaining ground in number and ſtrength. The royaliſts and moderates were eager for the inviolability of the royal perſon; the conſtitutionaliſts were divided; the republicans were ſtrenuouſly inimical to the propoſition: but after a long and animated conteſt, perceiving that by perſiſting in their oppoſition in this point they would loſe the ſupport of many conſtitutionaliſts, in order to conciliate the different parties, they propoſed certain proviſional modifications to accompany the inviolability of the royal perſon. Their opponents thought it expedient to accede to a compromiſe; and it was accordingly decreed, that the king's perſon, with certain reſtrictions and limitations, ſhould be inviolable. A decree was paſſed, intruſting the education of the dauphin to a governor appointed by the national aſſembly, in order to form him to conſtitutional principles. The moderate party endeavoured again to introduce two ſeparate chambers, and enlarged on the bleſſings of the

Inviolability of the king's perſon, carried in the aſſembly.

British

British constitution, but their propositions were rejected. The constititutional code being finished, sixty members were appointed to present it to the king: these waited on his majesty with great solemnity, and were very graciously received. When they presented the code, he informed them, that the importance of the subject required his most attentive and serious examination; and that as soon as he had acquitted himself of this duty, he would apprize the assembly of his intentions. The violent republicans hoped that the king would refuse the constitution, and thereby justify a different system. The king and his friends were well informed of their wishes and schemes: the people in general, however, were not yet disposed to establish a commonwealth, and the greater number of them were most strenuous constitutionalists. His friends, aware of the designs of the republicans, advised the king to accept the constitutional code. Being prevailed upon, he, on the 13th of September, wrote a letter* announcing his acceptance, and declaring the motives of his former, recent, and present conduct. The following day, repairing to the national assembly, he verbally declared his acceptance of the constitution; and in presence of the assembly, signed his declaration. He was received with great respect, and attended by the whole assembly on his return to the Thuilleries, amidst the acclamations of all Paris. On the 28th of September the constitution was formally proclaimed at Paris. The substance of the proclamation was, that the important work of the constitution being at length perfected by the assembly, and accepted by the king, it was now entrusted to the

CHAP. XLVII. 1791.

The king's friends advise him to accept the constitutional code.

He accepts it in the national assembly.

* See State Papers, September 13th, 1791.

protection

CHAP. XLVII. 1791.

protection of the legislature, the crown, and the law; to the affection and fidelity of fathers of families, wives, and mothers; to the zeal and attachment of the young citizens, and to the spirit of the French nation*. While the assembly had been thus engaged in completing the new constitutional code, it bestowed the highest honours on the memory of those revolutionizing philosophers who had contributed so powerfully to the change. As Voltaire had been so efficacious an enemy to christianity and the church, the assembly conferred signal honours on his remains, which they ordered to be transported from his burial place, and deposited in the church of St. Genevive, the place appointed for receiving the ashes, and perpetuating the memory, of those who had deserved well of the French nation. Equal honours were decreed to Rousseau: he had been the object of almost constant persecution by priests and their votaries. France, that had now dispelled the clouds of superstition, and broken the fetters of tyranny, after having profited so much by his labours, ought to pay that veneration to his memory when dead, which ignorance and superstition had denied to him while he was alive. The public joined with the assembly in doing homage to the characters of these writers, and also to Helvetius and others, who had distinguished themselves by their exertions against christianity. To gratify the prevailing sentiment, the theatres were, as usual, accommodated: plays were represented in which infidel writers and doctrines were held up to admiration: religion, and the various establishments and orders by which it had been maintained, were exposed to ridi-

Honours paid to infidel philosophers.

* See State Papers, September 28th, 1791.

cule

cule and contempt. That they might contribute as much as possible to the perpetuation of their system, the revolutionists endeavoured to instil such sentiments concerning the relations of domestic and private life, as would best correspond with their political establishments *.

Want of money.

Amidst the many plans for regenerating France, there was one evil which ingenuity could not remedy, this was the scarcity of money. Notwithstanding the immense forfeitures, there was still a great deficiency of income compared with expenditure. The army required to support the new liberty was more numerous, and much more expensive, than the armies of the old monarchy had been at the most extravagant periods. The populace considered exemption from taxes as one of the sacred rights which they ought to enjoy, and therefore paid very sparingly and reluctantly. The boldest and most ardent champions of religious, moral, civil, and political regeneration, neglected no opportunity *of committing theft*. The assembly had declared that all property belonged to the state: from this comprehensive theorem they deduced a corollary †, that whatever was thus acquired by the state belonged to any lawgiver or statesman that could get it into his possession. Though these peculators publicly celebrated the credit of the national paper, in their own accumulations they gave the preference to gold and silver. Many other monied men who had amassed their riches by fair means, being doubtful

* See Burke's Letter to a Member of the National Assembly.

† See Playfair's history of Jacobinism.

concerning

CHAP. XLVII. 1791.

concerning the ſtability of the new government, hoarded the greater part of their caſh. All who were diſaffected to the revolutionary ſyſtem, to diſcourage aſſignats as well as to ſecure their own property, concealed as much as poſſible their gold and ſilver. A great part of the hidden treaſures was lodged in foreign countries, eſpecially the Britiſh funds, which even the French patriots practically acknowledged to afford the beſt ſecurity for property *. As ſilver and gold diſappeared, the paper money was proportionably depreciated; and great pecuniary diſtreſs prevailed. The indigent now became a more numerous body than ever, and made deſperate through want, broke into every receſs where they thought money was hoarded, and exerciſed their depredations with ſuch dexterity, that numbers of individuals loſt immenſe ſums, notwithſtanding the carefulneſs and extraordinary precautions with which they had been concealed *. As a conſiderable part of pecuniary diſtreſs was imputed to the adminiſtrators of the revenue who were the moſt zealous members of the popular party, the ariſtocrats very minutely inveſtigated and ſeverely ſcrutinized their conduct; and when the accounts were preſented for inſpection, declared openly, that they conceived them falſe, and the documents and vouchers by which they were ſupported fabricated for the pur-

Inſpection of accounts.

* So great was the influx of French money into England during the year 1791, that whereas ſeventy-five had been the average price of the conſolidated annuities of three *per cent.* during the five preceding years of peace and proſperity, from midſummer 1791 the average price was about eighty-eight.

* See Playfair on Jacobiniſm.

poſe

pose of covering fraud and depredation. The arguments and statements were very strong and clear, but the assembly overthrew arithmetical results by a majority of votes; and *so far* the patriots were cleared from the charges. The purgation of these patriotic financiers was the last important act of the national assembly: on the 30th of September 1791, this body was dissolved by a speech from the king, in which he solemnly repeated his promises to maintain the constitution.

Dissolution of the national assembly.

Revision of the principal changes effected by this body.

Thus terminated the first national assembly of France, which in little more than two years had effected a more complete change in the government, ranks, orders, laws, religion, doctrines, opinions, sentiments, and manners of the people, than any legislative body ever before effected in a series of ages. It found an absolute monarchy; left an uncontrouled popular legislature, with a king nominally limited, actually subdued. It found the laws, which emanating from the Roman code, and intermingled with the feudal institutions, had spread over the greater part of Europe, and subsisted in France for twelve centuries; it left a new code, which originated in a metaphysical fiction of universal equality; vindicated to man, when member of a community, all the rights which might belong to him in a state of separation from his fellow men, and applied to a constituted society principles that presuppose no society to exist. It found disparity of rank, a political result from inequality of ability and character, extending itself to descendants: it left all rank and eminence levelled with meanness and obscurity; seeing that in the progress of hereditary transmission there might be

How it found and left France.

CHAP. XLVII. 1791.

be degeneracy, instead of correcting the abuse, it abolished the establishment. It took away one of the strongest incentives to splendid and beneficial actions, in the desire of a parent to acquire, maintain, or extend, honour or dignity, which he may not only enjoy himself, but transmit to his children. It found the people, though turbulent, and reluctantly submitting to arbitrary power, well inclined to a free system, which should include order and subordination. Expelling monarchical despotism, instead of stopping at the middle stage, which wisdom dictated, it carried the people to the opposite extreme of democratic anarchy. Impressing the multitude with an opinion that the general will was the sole rule of government, it induced them to suppose that their wills jointly and individually were to be exempt from restraint; and that the subjection of passion to the controul of reason and virtue, was an infringement of liberty. It found property secure, and left arbitrary confiscation predominant. It found the people christians; left them infidels.

In all its excesses it manifested the genius and energy of the French character.

But whatever opinion impartial posterity may entertain of this legislative body, either in the revolution which they effected, or the new system which they established, it must be admitted that uncommon ingenuity, skill, vigour, and perseverance, were displayed in the means adopted to give to the projected changes the desired effect. Their great and fundamental principle was, to revolutionize the minds of their countrymen, as the only sure means of civil and political revolution. In the clubs, the populace, and the army, modelled by their pleasure, they formed most effectual instruments for carrying their

1791.

their schemes into execution, and rendering their will the paramount law. The first national assembly manifested ability and genius, which, unfortunately for their country, were neither guided by wisdom nor prompted by virtue.

Progress of political enthusiasm.

The revolutionary leaders did not confine their efforts to their own country. They employed emissaries in other nations to disseminate their principles and co-operate with champions in the same cause. A spirit of political enthusiasm had, indeed, been spread through a great part of Europe. In Germany, and particularly in the Prussian dominions, a set arose, though under different denominations, who, ascribing the greater part of human calamities to bigotry, superstition, arbitrary power, and error, endeavoured to awaken their cotemporaries to the most animated hopes, of the advantages that were to flow from political improvement, philosophical education, and, in all things, a vigorous exercise of reason. They professed, at the same time, the warmest sentiments of humanity, and a spirit of universal philanthropy. In Britain, as we have seen, the leading doctrines of the French revolution were maintained from various causes, and to different extents, by numbers of writers, more especially by those of the unitarian dissenters. In the beginning of this year Dr. Priestley employed his rapid and indefatigable pen in answering Mr. Burke. After repeating his usual arguments against the existing establishments, the doctor confined himself to a prophetic vision of the manifold blessings which *were to flow* through the world from the glorious French revolution. This event was to diffuse liberty, to meliorate society, and to increase *virtue and happiness.*

Britain.

CHAP. XLVII. 1791.

Certain ingenious visionaries expect a political millennium.

piness. A political millennium was about to be established, when men should be governed by the purity of their own minds, and the moderation of their own desires, without external coercion, when no authority should exist but that of reason, and no legislators but philosophers, and disseminators of truth. But a work soon after made its appearance, which, however little entitled to historical record for its own intrinsic merits, is well worthy of mention, as the cause of very important and alarming effects; this was a treatise entitled, *The rights of man*, by Thomas Paine; already mentioned as the author of a violent pamphlet written to prevent re-union between Britain and her colonies.

Thomas Paine.

Paine having gone to Paris soon after the commencement of the revolution, and thoroughly imbibed its doctrines and sentiments, undertook to induce the English to copy so glorious a model. Perhaps, indeed, there never was a writer who more completely attained the art of imposing and impressing nonsense on ignorant and undistinguishing minds, as sense and sound reasoning; more fitted for playing on the passions of the vulgar; for gaining their affections by gratifying their prejudices, and through those affections procuring their assent to any assertions which he chose to advance. His manner was peculiarly calculated to impress and effect such objects.

Rights of Man—dexterous adaptation of to the sentiments and passions of the vulgar.

The coarse familiarity of his language was in unison with vulgar taste; the directness of his efforts and boldness of his assertions passed with ignorance for the confidence of undoubted truth. It was not only the manner of his communication, but the substance of his doctrine, that was peculiarly pleas-

ing

CHAP. XLVII.

1791.

ing to the lower ranks. Vanity, pride, and ambition, are paſſions which exiſt with as much force in the tap-room of an ale-houſe as in a ſenate. When peaſants, labourers, and journeymen mechanics, were told that they were as fit for governing the country as any man in parliament, it was a very pleaſing idea; it gave an agreeable ſwell to their ſelf-importance: when farther informed, that they were not only qualified for ſuch high appointments, but alſo, if they exerted themſelves that they were within the reach, they were ſtill more delighted. Through a book ſo popular, very great additions were made to the Engliſh admirers of the French revolution. Societies and clubs, in imitation of the French Jacobins, faſt increaſing in number and diviſions, teſtified the higheſt approbation of Paine's *Rights of Man*; and very induſtriouſly, through their affiliations, ſpread cheap editions of it among the common people, in all parts of the kingdom.

Aſtoniſhing popularity of among the lower ranks.

On the 14th of July a party of the admirers of the French revolution met at Birmingham to commemorate its commencement, under the auſpices of its great champion Dr. Prieſtley. Previous to the meeting, a hand-bill * was circulated outrageouſly ſeditious, ſtigmatizing all the eſtabliſhed orders, and urging inſurrection againſt church and ſtate. As the majority of the inhabitants were warmly attached to the conſtitution, this miſchievous production excited very great alarm and rage. The celebrators having aſſembled, the populace ſurrounded the tavern where they were met; and as Dr. Prieſtley had ſo

Commemoration of the French revolution at Birmingham.

* See Gentleman's Magazine for July 1791, and Chronicle of Annual Regiſter for the ſame month.

CHAP. XLVII. 1791.

often and openly avowed his enmity to the church, they very unfortunately ſuppoſed that the preſent paper, dooming our eſtabliſhment to deſtruction, was compoſed and diſperſed by him and his votaries.

Riots.

Under this apprehenſion they became extremely riotous, burnt one of the conventicles, deſtroyed

Deſtruction of Dr. Prieſtley's library.

ſeveral private houſes, and, among the reſt, the library of Dr. Prieſtley, containing a moſt valuable apparatus for philoſophical experiments, and alſo many manuſcripts. The tumults raged for two days ſo violently that the civil magiſtrates were inadequate to their ſuppreſſion. A military force arriving the third day, diſperſed the mob; and the magiſtrates, thus aſſiſted, re-eſtabliſhed tranquillity. All friends to our king and conſtitution ſincerely regretted theſe lawleſs proceedings, though evidently originating in a zealous attachment to our eſtabliſhment. Men of ſcience lamented the deſtruction of Dr. Prieſtley's library, of his collection, machinery, and compoſitions on phyſical ſubjects, *in which department* the exertions of his talents and learning were ſupremely valuable.

The doctor's conduct.

The conduct of Dr. Prieſtley himſelf upon this occaſion, though it could not diminiſh the public abhorrence of ſuch outrageous violence, by no means increaſed ſympathy in the ſufferings of its principal object. Haſtening to London, he wrote an addreſs to the inhabitants of Birmingham, in which, though he juſtly expoſed the lawleſs diſorder of the inſurgents, and naturally complained of the miſchiefs that they had perpetrated, yet the main ſcope of his letter was to attack the church, and impute the riots to its principal ſupporters in the vicinity. The tumultuous

exceſſes

excesses he illogically and falsely ascribed to the badness of the cause; as if the intrinsic merits of any system could be lessened by the madness or folly of its defenders. Various addresses of condolence sent to Dr. Priestley by societies of dissenters, and other clubs, very clearly demonstrated the sanguine hopes of the writers, that the downfall of our establishments was approaching. Mr. Benjamin Cooper, secretary of the revolution society, hoped that the church which he (Mr. Benjamin Cooper) pronounced *an ignorant and interested intolerance*, was near its end. Dr. Priestley's reply chimed with this Mr. Benjamin Cooper's tune. The young students at Hackney college, expressed their conviction of the folly of existing establishments. Priestley's answer* to their letter may be considered as a *recitation of his political creed*. The hierarchy (he said) equally the bane of christianity and of rational liberty, was about to fall: he exhorted these young men strenuously to use their efforts in so glorious a cause, and to shew by the *ardor* and *force* of their exertions against the constituted authorities, how much more *enlightened* understandings, and liberal sentiments were formed by the plan and instructions of their academy, than those that were imbibed in national institutions, fettering and depressing the mind. The doctrines so earnestly inculcated by Priestley and his class of enemies to our establishments, tended to promote the success of Paine's political lessons. Priestley was more fitted for forming visionary and sophistical speculatists among men of superficial literature,

* See Gentleman's Magazine, for November 1791, p. 1024, and Annual Register, 1791. Appendix to Chronicle, p. 86.

 whereas

CHAP. XLVII.

1791.

Comparifon between Prieftley and Paine.

whereas Paine was beft qualified for effecting a change on the vulgar and ignorant. Prieftley dealt chiefly in prefcription; his noftrum to be applied to every cafe was *alterative*: Paine was operatical and propofed *immediate incifion.* From Prieftley proceeded fuch philófophers as Godwin and Holcroft, from Paine fuch practical reformers as Watt and Thelwall. Prieftley, to ufe his own words, had laid the train, Paine's defire was to light the match. Republican, and even democratic principles, continued to make a rapid progrefs during the remainder of the year. It would be extremely unjuft and illiberal to impute to Unitarian diffenters indifcriminately, the principles and intentions fo obvious in the herefiarch. It is however well known, that if not all, very many of that clafs of diffenters were at this time inimical to the Britifh conftitution of church and ftate. Befides the diffenters, there were other

Rapid and extenfive diffufion of democratic principles.

fets of men who regarded the French revolution as a model for imitation. From caufes purely political, without any mixture of theology, fome of the votaries of a change in parliament, and other departments of the ftate, conceived the diffufion of French principles highly favourable to their plans of reform. In the metropolis, befides men of genius and learning, well affected to the French revolution, there was another fet of adventurers in literature and politics, very eager in maintaining and

Wide diffufion of fuperficial literature,

fpreading its doctrines. If learning be not more profound in the prefent than in former ages, it is certainly fpread over a much wider furface. The commercial opulence of the country encourages the manufacture and fale of literary commodities of every

every value and denomination. The demand extending to a vast variety of productions, which require neither deep learning nor vigorous genius, the number of authors multiplies in proportion to the moderate qualifications that are necessary. All these, down to translators of German novels, and collectors of paragraphs for the daily papers, deem themselves *persons of genius and erudition, and members of the republic of letters.* In France, literary men possessed great direction; many of this class in England conceived, that if the same system were established here, they might rise to be directors in the new order of things. There were in the literary class, as in other bodies, persons who, from a benevolent enthusiasm, hoped that the French constitution would extirpate vice and misery, and diffuse over the world philanthropy and happiness. Among the literary producers, there was one set who thought the highest perfection of the human character was sensibility; and that the restraints of religious and moral precepts, as well as of political establishments, were harsh and tyrannical, because they so often contradicted the impulse of sentimental feeling; these praised the French revolution in the belief that it was inimical to austere restrictions. Under this class were to be ranked various female votaries of literature, and at their head Mary Ann Wollstonecraft, who produced, as a counterpart to the Rights of Man, a performance entitled the Rights of Woman; vindicating to the sex an exemption from various restrictions to which women had been hitherto subjected from the tyranny and aristocracy of men; but first and principally from the restraint

CHAP. XLVII. 1791. favourable to revolutionary notions.

Mary Ann Wollstonecraft.

 of

CHAP. XLVII.

1791.

Debating societies.

of chaſtity; and claiming the free and full indulgence of every gratification which fancy could ſuggeſt, or paſſion ſtimulate. Beſides theſe claſſes, there was a great and multiplying variety of clubs for political diſcuſſion and debate. To theſe reſorted many mechanics, tradeſmen, and others, from a deſire extremely prevalent among the lower Engliſh, of diſtinguiſhing themſelves as *ſpokeſmen*. By degrees, from hearing ſpeeches and reading pamphlets, they ſuppoſed themſelves politicians and philoſophers, and thought it incumbent on ſo enlightened men, to drop the prejudices of education; and ſacrificed religion, patriotiſm, and loyalty, at the ſhrine of vanity. From ſo many cauſes, and through ſo many agents, the revolutionary doctrines were diſſeminated very widely. To facilitate circulation, opulent votaries publiſhed cheap editions of the moſt inflammatory works, eſpecially Paine's *Rights of Man*, which contained the eſſence of all the reſt.

Cheap editions of Tom Paine's works.

But men of high rank, and of the higheſt ability and character, ſtill admired the French revolution as likely to produce, when corrected by time and experience, the extenſion of moderate and rational liberty; and beſides Dr. Prieſtley, a few others of eminent genius celebrated the French changes, in literary works. Of theſe, by far the moſt diſtinguiſhed production that appeared in England in vindication of the French revolution, was Mr. Mackintoſh's anſwer to Mr. Burke. The obvious purpoſe of this learned and philoſophical writer is the melioration of the condition of man; convinced that men habitually guided by reaſon, and determined

One able and profound work in favour of the French revolution.

mined by virtue, would be happier under ſmall than conſiderable reſtraints, he propoſed a controul too feeble for the actual ſtate of men now exiſting; much more of a people whoſe national character, from the old deſpotiſm, and other cauſes, required a greater degree of controul than ſome of their neighbours. The erroneous concluſions of this forcible and profound writer, appear to have ariſen from two ſources; firſt he argued from a ſuppoſition of an attainable perfection in the human character, inſtead of an accurate eſtimate of the degree of perfection which it had actually attained. Secondly, he appears to have been miſinformed concerning the principles, ſpirit, and character of the French revolutioniſts.

1791. Vindiciæ Gallicæ.

Marriage of the Duke of York to the Princeſs of Pruſſia.

Great and important as the progreſſions of public opinions were in 1791, to arreſt the attention of the philoſophical obſerver, the actual events in England to employ the pen of the annaliſt, were not numerous. His highneſs the Duke of York, in the cloſe of the year 1791, married the eldeſt Princeſs of Pruſſia, between whom and the Engliſh prince a mutual affection had ſubſiſted ever ſince the royal youth's reſidence at the court of Berlin. The arrival of the fair ſtranger, the many feſtivities that enſued on ſo auſpicious an occaſion, and the appearance of the new married couple in public, agreeably relieved the political diſcuſſions which had long abſorbed the attention of the public.

CHAP. XLVIII.

Meeting of Parliament.—Oppoſition cenſure the conduct of miniſtry reſpecting Ruſſia.—Incidental but intereſting debates about the French revolution.—Real difference between Meſſrs. Burke and Fox.—Motion of Mr. Whitbread reſpecting the riots at Birmingham.—Petition of the Unitarian diſſenters—rejected.—Multiplication of political clubs.—Society of the friends of the people—rank, character, and property of the members.—Mr. Grey.—The Earl of Lauderdale.—Addreſs of the ſociety to the people of Great Britain.—Intention good, but tendency dangerous.—Mr. Pitt oppoſes this engine of change.—Riſe and progreſs of corresponding ſocieties.—Second part of Thomas Paine's Rights of man.—Ferment among the populace.—The lower claſſes become politicians and ſtateſmen.—Proclamation againſt ſeditious writings—diſcuſſed in parliament.—Schiſm among the members of oppoſition.—The heir apparent teſtifies his zeal for ſupporting the Britiſh conſtitution.—General ſatisfaction from the manifeſtation of the prince's ſentiments.—Bill for the amendment of the London police.—Humane and diſcriminate propoſitions of Lord Rawdon for the relief of debtors and benefit of creditors.—Abolition of the ſlave trade is carried in the houſe of Commons.—Subject diſcuſſed in the houſe of Lords.—Duke of Clarence oppoſes the abolition.—His highneſs exhibits a maſterly view of the various arguments.—The queſtion poſtponed.—State of the crown lands—eſpecially foreſts.—Mr. Pitt's bill for encloſing parts of the New Foreſt—diſapproved—rejected by the peers.—Mr. Dundas's bill for facilitating the payment of wages and prize money to ſailors—paſſed.—Finances.—Proſperous ſtate of commerce and revenue.—Proſpect of farther reducing the debt, and diminiſhing

the

the taxes.—Flourishing state of India finances.—Political state and transactions in India.—Beneficial effects of Mr. Pitt's legislative measures, and Mr. Dundas's executive management.—Sir John Macpherson, governor general.—Able and successful administration—succeeded by Lord Cornwallis.—Wise plans of comprehensive improvement.—Tippoo Saib recruits his strength.—His ambitious projects revive—attacks our ally the Rajah of Travancore.—The British council remonstrates to no purpose.—The English armies invade Mysore from the East and West coasts.—Campaign of 1790—indecisive.—1791 Lord Cornwallis himself takes the field—reduces the greater part of Mysore—comes within sight of Seringapatam—prevented by the overflow of the Cavery from investing the metropolis of Mysore.—In 1792 besieges Seringapatam.—Tippoo Saib sues for peace, and obtains it at the dictation of Lord Cornwallis.—Generous conduct of his Lordship respecting the prize money.—Measures for the improvement of British India.

CHAP. XLVIII. 1792.

PARLIAMENT met January 31st, 1792. His Majesty's speech mentioned the marriage of his son, and the peace concluded between Russia and Turkey; but dwelt chiefly on the rapidly increasing prosperity of the British nation, which must confirm steady and zealous attachment to a constitution that we have found, from long experience, to unite the inestimable blessings of liberty and order; and to which, under the favour of Providence, all our advantages are principally to be ascribed. Members of opposition arraigned the conduct of ministers concerning Russia. Both the accusation and defence necessarily repeated former arguments. The British government thought interference necessary for the balance of power; and though they had sacrificed their own counsels to the voice of the public, the armament

CHAP. XLVIII. 1792.

Incidental but interesting debates about the French revolution.

armament prepared upon that occasion had not been useless, as it had prevented the Turks from being obliged to make such concessions as would have been otherwise extorted *. Mr. Fox, conceiving himself, and those who coincided in his sentiments respecting the French revolution, indirectly censured by the praises of the British polity, clearly and forcibly demonstrated the compatibility of satisfaction at the downfal of French despotism, so inimical to human rights, and destructive to human happiness, with the highest veneration and warmest attachment to the British constitution, the preserver of rights, and promoters of happiness. He rejoiced at the overthrow of the French despotism because it was bad, but would use every effort to support the British constitution because it was good. In subsequent discussions Mr. Fox, more explicitly than ever, exhibited to the house his sentiments and views on this momentous subject. The French, with characters formed by the old despotism, now emancipated from slavery, are actuated by a most impetuous enthusiasm, which drives them, as it has driven every other votary, to violent excesses. But enthusiasm, like every ardent passion, must, as knowledge of human nature and history inform us, 'ere long subside. It is illogical to impute to the principles of the French revolution the excesses which really arise from a sublimated state of passion that cannot last. Enthusiasm accompanied the reformation; enthusiasm marked the efforts of the puritans, which vindicated British liberty from kingly and priestly tyranny. But the free principles and beneficial establishments subsist many ages after the passion subsided. Do not therefore pro-

* See Parliamentary Debates January 31st, 1792.

scribe

ſcribe the French revolution becauſe a fury that muſt be temporary has inſpired many of its votaries. Let the noxious fumes evaporate, you will retain the genuine ſpirit of liberty ſalutary to mankind. Such was the opinion of one perſonage, not leſs profound as a political philoſopher than forcible as an orator, deciſive and energetic as a ſtateſman. Many and various in detail as were the ſubjects of difference between him and Mr. Burke upon French affairs, the principle was ſimple. Fox eſteemed the outrages incidental effects of an enthuſiaſm which muſt be temporary, and which formed no part of the eſſential character of the revolution : Burke reckoned the exceſſes neceſſary and eſſential parts of the revolution, which legitimately deſcended from its nature and principles ; and increaſed as they advanced, and which could never ceaſe to operate until the revolutionary ſyſtem ceaſed to exiſt. Fox thought the French to be men in the ardent purſuit of what was good, and tranſported by paſſion beyond the bounds of moderation and wiſdom ; as men purſuing what was really good have often been tranſported : Burke conſidered the whole nation as actuated by a ſpirit of diaboliſm, eagerly bent on perpetrating all poſſible miſchief ; a phenomenon never before known in the hiſtory of mankind ; and therefore, if true in that particular caſe, requiring, from its contravention to probability, the ſtronger evidence. From the oppoſite theories which they formed as political philoſophers, theſe illuſtrious men deduced very oppoſite practical ſyſtems, which they recommended as ſtateſmen. Burke very early* recommended

Real difference between Meſſrs. Burke and Fox.

* See his Hints for a memorial to be delivered to the French Ambaſſador ; and Thoughts on French affairs, both written in 1791.

CHAP. XLVIII. 1792.

commended and inculcated a confederacy, which, upon his hypothesis, was not only wise, but absolutely necessary. If the French were devils incarnate, to prevent the diabolical spirit from operation, neighbouring nations must overwhelm the power of beings so possessed, or perish themselves from the frenzy. Fox, not regarding them as a multitude of dæmons, but as the votaries of enthusiasm, recommended to encourage their spirit of liberty, and suffer their passions to subside through time, the surest corrector. Hostile interference in their internal concerns, would support instead of extinguishing their enthusiasm, turn its efforts to external defence, and give them an energy that would prove fatal to those who had roused it into action. These were the leading diversities in the theoretical and practical systems of Messrs. Fox and Burke, which account for the whole series of their respective counsels and conduct concerning France. Ministers still avoided the delivery of opinions on events and systems which had not interfered with the interest of Great Britain. Though the French revolution was never directly before the house, yet many of its proceedings arose from questions of liberty and reform which that great event was instrumental in suggesting. Mr. Whitbread, a new member, of good talents, respectable character, and immense fortune, who had joined the party of Mr. Fox, reviewing the riots at Birmingham, imputed these outrages to the encouragement given by government to persecutors of the dissenters, because they were inimical to civil and ecclesiastical tyranny. The magistrates were not sufficiently active; the government had been dilatory in sending troops; and several rioters had been

Motion of Mr. Whitbread respecting the riots at Birmingham.

been acquitted: ſome, after being condemned, were pardoned. Mr. Dundas, now ſecretary of ſtate, ſaid, that on enquiry by the attorney-general, there appeared no grounds for cenſuring the magiſtrates. From a detail of dates, and military ſtations, he proved that no time had been loſt in diſpatching troops to Birmingham. The rioters pardoned, had experienced the royal mercy on the recommendation of the judges.

The Scotch epiſcopalians perceiving a diſpoſition in parliament to extend toleration as far as political ſecurity would admit, petitioned for a more ample and unreſtrained indulgence, than that which they had hitherto enjoyed. The former motives for laying them under legal diſcouragements, ſubſiſted no longer: the houſe of Stuart, to which their attachment was known, was extinct; and their fidelity to the actual government was not liable, on that account, to be ſuſpected. A petition for exemption from reſtraints, the reaſons of which no longer exiſted, was favourably received by a legiſlature at once indulgent and diſcriminating. A bill was accordingly introduced into the houſe of lords, and paſſed both houſes. The Unitarians alleging this law as a precedent, applied for a repeal of the penal ſtatutes; and in addition to the uſual reaſons for refuſing their application, their recent practices were ſtated as inimical to church and ſtate, eſpecially their active diſſemination of Paine's works, and other democratical performances, and their formation of political clubs and ſocieties.

Petition of the Unitarian diſſenters, rejected.

While various ſubjects of alleged defect, or projected amendment, either in meaſures of government, or

Multiplication of political clubs.

CHAP. XLVIII. 1792.

or the exifting laws were agitated, a project was formed by a fociety of gentlemen, for making an important change in the compofition of the legiflature; this affociation, confifting of men eminent for talents, for character, for political, literary, and profeffional ability; for landed and mercantile property, for rank and importance in the community, took to themfelves the name of the *Friends of the people.* The following were the general objects which they profeffed to feek:—To reftore the freedom of election, and to fecure to the people a more frequent exercife of their right of electing their reprefentatives. For the purpofe of thefe reforms in parliament and the country, they inftituted their fociety, but though determined to promote them, refolved to confine their purfuit rigoroufly to fuch means, as fhould be confiftent with the exifting conftitution. A fhort declaration of thefe objects and means, was framed by a committee, and figned by the fociety, with an addrefs to the people of England tending to prove; firft, that reform was wanted; fecondly, that the prefent, a feafon of peace and profperity, was the beft fitted for commencing and eftablifhing that reform; and that if there exifted fome degree of difcontent, the propofed reform was well fitted for its removal: that the projected means were calculated to promote the good without incurring any danger; thirdly, the objection arifing from recent events in France, could not apply to a cafe fo very different, as the Britifh conftitution, with fome abufes, was from the old defpotifm of France. The object of the fociety was to recover and preferve the true balance of the conftitution. They announced the

Society of the friends of the people,

the determination of the ſociety, to move a reform in parliament early the enſuing ſeſſion. On theſe avowed principles of their union, they looked with confidence for the co-operation of the Britiſh nation: theſe are the outlines of an addreſs which may be conſidered as the manifeſto of the *only* reſpectable body, which, ſince the commencement of the French revolution, undertook the cauſe of parliamentary reform. The ſociety included the greater number of eminent oppoſitioniſts in the houſe of commons with one member of the houſe of lords: This was James Earl of Lauderdale, a nobleman of very conſiderable abilities, and deeply converſant in moral and political philoſophy and hiſtory, who had diſtinguiſhed himſelf, firſt as Lord Maitland in the houſe of commons, and afterwards made a no leſs conſpicuous figure in the houſe of peers. Mr. Grey was appointed to take the leading part for the ſociety in the houſe of commons. Mr. Grey had been educated an Engliſh whig, and conſidered the oppoſition party as the ſupporters of whig principles; and in his preſent meaſure conceived himſelf paving the way for a truly whig parliament. The rank and fortune of this peer and commoner, independent of their reſpective characters, and alſo the talents, character, and ſituation of other members, afford very ſatisfactory grounds for believing them actuated by conſtitutional motives. It is indeed not impoſſible to ſuppoſe, that ſubordinate to patriotiſm mere anti-miniſterial conſiderations might have ſome weight, and that, as Mr. Pitt had once been the advocate of reform, and was not likely to be ſo in the preſent circumſtances, they might hope to reduce him to ſome embarraſment, and expoſe him to the

rank, character, and property of the members.

The Earl of Lauderdale.

Mr. Grey.

charge

CHAP. XLVIII. 1792.

charge of inconsistency. But though such intentions perhaps operated in some degree with some of the members, there is much reason to be convinced that the friends of the people, as a society, desired only what they conceived to be moderate reform, without having the least design to invade the fundamental parts of the constitution. Their association however was liable to weighty objections: these were not incidental, but resulted from the nature, constitution, and proceedings of the society, combined with the circumstances of the country; their two declared objects, extension of suffrage, and abridgment of the duration of parliament, were both expressed in vague terms; so that they might be, and in fact actually were, construed differently by the different votaries of reform: By very many they were interpreted with so great latitude, as to comprehend universal suffrage and annual parliaments. An address to the people of Great Britain, severally or aggregately respectable, as they were desiring them to co-operate in producing an undefined change in the legislature was a measure, however pure in its motives, very doubtful in its tendency. Presuming the existence of great and radical abuses, it either supposed the incompetency of parliament to remedy evils, and consequently its insufficiency for its constitutional purposes; or was futile in desiring from the people a co-operation which was not wanted. It afterwards appeared that this society proposed to the people, to form themselves into associations to petition parliament for reform. They thereby afforded a colourable pretext for framing associations composed of very different members,

Address of the society to the people of Great Britain.

Intention good, but tendency dangerous.

bers, and entertaining very different sentiments: the friends of the people eventually produced the affiliated political clubs, which are since so well known under the name of the Corresponding Society, and proved so dangerous in their operations.

CHAP. XLVIII. 1792.

To sound the disposition of parliament, Mr. Grey intimated his intention of urging parliamentary reform early in the next session. Mr. Pitt totally regardless of the imputations which might be made against himself personally, most unequivocally, reprobated the design of the society; he was friendly to reform peaceably obtained and by general concurrence, but deemed the present season altogether improper; and was therefore inimical to the attempt. The object of the society was to effect a change by the impulse of the people; he would strenuously oppose the movement of so formidable an engine; the operations and consequences of which was so much calculated to out-go the intentions of the mover. Mr. Fox did not join a society whose objects and proposed means were so extremely indefinite; and the notice was received with very strong and general disapprobation. The affiliated clubs now imitating the French jacobins, rapidly multiplied; the principal assemblage of this sort, was the *London Corresponding Society*; the secretary of these politicians was one Thomas Hardy a shoemaker, their ostensible plan was under the auspices of this shoemaker, and others of equal political ability, and importance in the community, to effect a change in parliament. The great preceptor of these disciples was Thomas Paine, whose second part was now published, and strenuously exhorted the practical application of the doctrines, which he had promulgated in his first; it directed

Mr. Pitt opposes this engine of change.

Rise and progress of corresponding societies.

Second part of Thomas Paine's rights of man.

CHAP. XLVIII.

1792. Ferment among the populace.

his votaries to pull down every eſtabliſhment, and level all diſtinctions, in order to enjoy the Rights of Man; by far the greater number of the lower ranks and a conſiderable portion of the middling claſſes were infected with the revolutionary fever which operated in the wildeſt and moſt extravagant ravings. Thomas Paine was repreſented as the miniſter of God, diſpenſing light to a darkened world*: the moſt induſtrious and uſeful claſſes of the ſtate were ſeized with a furious deſire of abandoning their own courſe of beneficial and productive labour, and taking the management of public affairs into their own hands. All the levelling notions of John Ball, John Cade, and the fifth monarchy men appeared to revive with an immenſe addition of new extravagance. Government had conſidered the theories of Thomas Paine's firſt part, as ſuch deviations from common ſenſe, that they expected their intrinſic abſurdity would prevent them from doing any actual miſchief, and had therefore forborne a judicial animadverſion which might have given them adventitious importance. But when they found, that attempts were made to reduce the theories into practice, and that a ſecond part of the ſpeculative jargon, added direct exhortations to ſubvert the conſtitution, that they were very generally read by the vulgar and ignorant claſſes, and producing other works of a ſimilar tendency, they adopted means both for a penal retroſpect and for future prevention. A proſecution was commenced againſt Paine; and a proclamation iſſued May 21ſt, warning the people againſt ſuch writings and alſo ſuch correſpondencies with foreign parts,

The lower claſſes become politicians and ſtateſmen.

Proclamation againſt ſeditious writings.

* See a ſeditious morning paper of thoſe days, called the Argus; alſo democratical pamphlets, and the Analytical Review for 1791 and 1792, paſſim.

as

as might produce the ſame or ſimilar effects; and enjoining all magiſtrates to exert their utmoſt efforts to diſcover the authors, printers, and publiſhers of ſuch pernicious works. A copy of the proclamation being laid before the houſes of parliament was taken into conſideration on the 25th of May: and the diſcuſſion which it underwent ſhewed that a very conſiderable ſchiſm had taken place among members of oppoſition. Mr. Grey and the friends of the people, took the moſt active ſhare in cenſuring the proclamation as neither neceſſary nor uſeful for its oſtenſible purpoſe. Their arguments were that the ſeditious writings which it profeſſed an intention to reſtrain had prevailed for more than a year, and if they were ſo noxious ought to have been proſecuted at common law; and on their own hypotheſis that the works in queſtion were dangerous, miniſters deſerved ſevere cenſure for not having before employed proper means to remove this danger. But the prevention of ſeditious writings, was not the real object of the proclamation: its purpoſe was to diſparage the friends of the people, to prevent parliamentary reform, and to diſunite the whigs; and it was farther intended to increaſe the influence of government by ſubjecting to ſpies and informers, all who ſhould differ from adminiſtration. Theſe ſentiments were by no means general, even among the uſual adverſaries of Mr. Pitt: in both houſes, many members accuſtomed to vote with oppoſition joined the miniſter upon this occaſion.* Conſidering precaution againſt the preſent rage of innovation as neceſſary to preſerve the conſtitution, and their reſpective rank, property, and diſtinctions, they joined in ſupporting a meaſure cal-

Diſcuſſions in parliament.

Schiſm among members of oppoſition.

* See Parliamentary Debates of May 25th, 1792.

culated

CHAP XLVIII. 1792.

culated, they conceived, to repreſs ſo alarming a ſpirit. The overthrow of the ariſtocracy, abaſement of rank, and confiſcation of property under the new French ſyſtem, impreſſed on their minds by the glowing eloquence of Mr. Burke, had alarmed many of the chief nobility, and great landed proprietors for their own privileges and poſſeſſions. Theſe with their friends and adherents, and others who entertained or pretended to entertain ſimilar ſentiments without forming a junction with the miniſters, voted on the ſame ſide, on ſubjects that reſpected the French revolution or any of its doctrines. In the houſe of peers, the earl of Lauderdale and the marquis of Lanſdown only ſpoke againſt the proclamation: from this time ceaſed the great whig confederacy, which during the principal part of the two former reigns had been predominant; and during the preſent was ſo powerful as to have repeatedly ejected the Miniſters agreeable to the crown.

The heir apparent teſtifies his zeal for ſupporting the Britiſh conſtitution.

On this occaſion the heir apparent for the firſt time delivered his ſentiments in parliament. His highneſs conſidering the critical ſtate of affairs, as requiring from every friend to his country, a manifeſtation of the principles which he was reſolved to ſupport, and the more ſtrongly in proportion to his rank and conſequence in the country, ſpoke to the following effect:—“ When a ſubject of ſuch magnitude is before the houſe, I ſhould be deficient in my duty as a member of parliament, unmindful of that reſpect which I owe to the conſtitution, and inattentive to the welfare, the peace, and the happineſs of the people if I did not ſtate to the world my opinion on the preſent ſubject of deliberation. I was edu-

cated

cated in the principles of the British conſtitution, and ſhall ever preſerve its maxims: I ſhall ever cheriſh a reverence for the conſtitutional liberties of the people; as on thoſe conſtitutional principles carried uniformly into practice, the happineſs of theſe realms depends, I am determined as far as my intereſt can have any force, to give them my firm and conſtant ſupport. The queſtion at iſſue is in fact, whether the conſtitution is or is not to be maintained; whether the wild ideas of untried theory are to conquer the wholeſome maxims of eſtabliſhed practice; whether thoſe laws under which we have flouriſhed for ſuch a ſeries of years, are to be ſubverted by a reform unſanctioned by the people. As a perſon nearly and dearly intereſted in the welfare, and I ſhall emphatically add the happineſs of the people, it would be treaſon to the principles of my own mind, if I did not come forward and declare my diſapprobation of the ſeditious writings, which have occaſioned the motion before your lordſhips. My intereſt is connected with the intereſt of the people; they are ſo inſeparable, that unleſs both parties concurred, the happineſs of neither could exiſt. On this great and this ſolid baſis, I ground my vote for joining in the addreſs which approves of the proclamation. I exiſt by the love, the friendſhip, and the benevolence of the people, and their cauſe I will never forſake ſo long as I live." The patriotic ſentiments, ſo forcibly and impreſſively declared in the manly and dignified eloquence of the royal ſpeaker, conveyed very great and general ſatiſfaction to all his hearers, who loved their country, to whatever party they might adhere.

General ſatisfaction from the manifeſtation of the prince's ſentiments.

Among the applicants for reform this year were the

CHAP. XLVIII. 1792.

the royal boroughs of Scotland, from which certain petitioners ſtated flagrant abuſes in the adminiſtration of the revenues, and alſo other grievances, that, if proved, would have demanded redreſs; but the allegations not having been ſupported by proof, the motions ariſing from the petitions were negatived by a great majority.

State of the police in the metropolis.

Great complaints very generally and juſtly prevailed at this time of the police of London. The Britiſh capital ſurpaſſes in populouſneſs all European cities; in opulence any city throughout the known world. With wealth comes luxury, which frequently extends beyond the poſſeſſors of riches, pervades many of the poorer claſſes, and produces habitual wants, that cannot be ſupplied but by criminal means. In a city abounding with every pleaſure that can captivate the human heart, exceſs and debauchery naturally exiſt. The freedom of the country does not permit the ſame means of prevention as under abſolute governments; hence diſſipation ripens into profligacy, profligacy riſes into criminal enormity. In London the temptations are powerful and ſeductive to thoſe indulgences which corrupt principle, vitiate character, and waſte property. Thence ariſes the deſire of ſeizing by fraud, theft, or force, the ſubſtance of others as the means of vice. The practicability of plunder is much greater, and the materials of depredation much more numerous, valuable, and acceſſible *, than in any other city known in the hiſtory of mankind. Beſides the profligate of our own country, London, like ancient Rome †, is the receptacle of exotic wick-

* See Mr. Colquhoun's Treatiſe on the Police, paſſim.

† See Juvenal, ſatire iii.

edneſs.

edness. Every adventurer who, from the poverty of his own country, personal incapacity, idleness, or dissipation, cannot earn a competent subsistence at home, flocks into England, and preys upon the metropolis. Hence arises a very great increase of vice and depredation, in their various departments, but, above all, in that parent of crime, gaming. This destructive propensity within thirty years far surpassed the most extravagant excesses of former times: descending from the great, it pervaded the middle and lower conditions of life, and generated many enormities. Akin to this propensity, and originating in the same desire of acquisition without industry, is the spirit of chimerical adventure in lotteries, funds, and other subjects of hazardous project. Though this spirit enriched several votaries, it impoverished many more; and sent them, with the habits of indulgence which had been cherished during the season of temporary success and aerial hopes, to increase the number of those who find in fraud and rapine the means of luxurious enjoyments. From these and many collateral causes, sprang a vast and increasing variety of crimes against the police of the country; against the persons, habitations, and property of the inhabitants. A multiplicity of rules and ordinances had been enacted at divers periods and different occasions, but had experimentally proved unequal to the ends proposed, for want of sufficient powers being lodged in the magistracy and its agents, to discover and suppress, in a summary and expeditious manner, whatever had a visible tendency to disturb the public tranquillity. The justices of the peace were formerly men of rank,

 property,

CHAP. XLVIII. 1792. Justices of the peace.

property, character, and consideration in the country where they were commissioned to act: such gentlemen gratuitously administered justice. The simplicity of life and manners prevalent among our ancestors did not afford that complication of misbehaviour and of transgressions for which such a multiplicity of laws in modern times, have been provided. But with the modes of artificial life, and the improvements of civilized society, the modes of crime also multiplied; and the once venerable office of justice of the peace became at last too fatiguing and burdensome for people of opulence and distinction. Their unwillingness to accept of so heavy a charge obliged the ruling powers to apply to individuals of inferior character, who, in accepting of it, had an eye to the profits and emoluments arising from the exercise of their judicial powers. From the period when that honourable and weighty office was thus degraded, it lost, by degrees, the reverence in which it had been held. Venal and mercenary persons were appointed, whose base practices became so notorious, that they drew general odium and contempt both upon themselves and their functions. Hence the vilifying appellation of *a trading justice* was at last applied, with too much reason, to many of those who exercised that office. To rectify the abuses imputed to these, and to place the office itself on a footing of respectability proportionate to its importance, in the beginning of March a bill was introduced, with the countenance and approbation of government, into the lower house. Different offices were to be established in the metropolis, at a convenient distance from each other for the prompt administration of

Bill for the amendment of the London police.

those

1792.

those parts of justice which are within the cognizance of justices of the peace. Three justices were to sit in each of these offices, with a salary of £300 a year to each: they were to be prohibited from taking fees individually; and the money from the fees paid into all the offices, was to be collected and applied to the payment of their salaries and official expences. That the law might have a preventive operation as well as a penal, a clause was inserted vesting in constables a power to apprehend people who did not give a satisfactory account of themselves, and empowering the justices to commit them as vagabonds. There were, it appeared from evidence, large gangs of the most desperate villains, who were notorious thieves, lived by no other means than plunder, infested every street of the metropolis, and put the person and property of every individual passenger in danger every hour of the day and night. Various objections were made to the bill as an entrenchment on the liberty of the subject, and an increase of the power of the crown; but on investigation and enquiry, the necessity of it was found so strong as to over-rule the arguments of its opponents, and it was passed by a considerable majority.

Humane and discriminate propositions of Lord Rawdon for the relief of debtors and benefit of creditors,

While these measures were adopted to secure the innocent and industrious against the profligate and atrocious, the wisely generous Rawdon resumed his efforts for affording relief to the unfortunate, by a revision of the laws relating to debtors and creditors. His lordship's general object was, on one hand to compel the debtor to give up all that he possessed, on the other to prevent the creditor, after such a cession

of

CHAP. XLVIII. 1794. of effects, from confining the debtor in jail for life. His lordſhip, with diſcriminating juſtice equal to the benevolence of his ſpirit, ſought the reciprocal benefit of both debtor and creditor. He propoſed that no man, to gratify a malignant diſpoſition, ſhould have it in his power to keep his fellow-creature in perpetual impriſonment, merely on chooſing to pay him four-pence a day; and that no man ſhould continue in priſon to the injury of his creditor, to revel in luxury on property which might pay his debts. As the ſubject was of very great importance, and required a full and minute diſcuſſion of principles, and a very nice diſcrimination of circumſtances and caſes, it was recommended to his is postponed. lordſhip to poſtpone its introduction till the following ſeſſion, by which time it might be maturely weighed; his lordſhip conſenting, for the preſent withdrew the bill.

Abolition of the ſlave-trade is carried in the commons; The ſlave trade this ſeſſion again occupied the commons, and was alſo conſidered by the lords. In the lower houſe, the aboliționiſts having ſucceeded in the main queſtion, were divided as to the time when the ſuppreſſion ſhould take place. At laſt, at the inſtance of Meſſrs. Dundas and Addington, it was agreed that the trade ſhould ceaſe from is oppoſed in the lords. the 1ſt of January 1796. In the houſe of lords, the ſame arguments were uſed that had been employed The Duke of Clarence exhibits a maſterly view of the various arguments, and oppoſes the abolition. on both ſides by the commons. The Duke of Clarence, who now, for the firſt time, ſpoke in the houſe of peers, made a very able, comprehenſive, and impreſſive ſpeech, againſt the abolition of the ſlave-trade. This royal ſenator rejected all fanciful theories, argued from plain and ſtubborn facts, and

took

took for his guide experience, the only unerring director of the ſtateſman and lawgiver. Indeed his repeated orations on this ſubject exhibited and enforced every argument, from either humanity, juſtice, political and commercial expediency, that could be adduced; and his clear and manly reaſonings conſtitute the moſt ſatisfactory and complete treatiſe which has hitherto appeared on that ſide of the queſtion. The majority of the peers concurred with his highneſs in oppoſing the abolition, but the final determination of the queſtion was poſtponed to the ſucceeding year.

State of the crown lands, eſpecially foreſts.

Among the national objects which engroſſed this ſeſſion of parliament, was the ſtate of our foreſts. Commiſſioners appointed to inſpect the crown lands reported that the principal reſervoir of materials for our navy, the New Foreſt in Hampſhire, was in ſuch a condition, that unleſs proper attention were beſtowed immediately, there would be no timber fit for public ſervice for many years; but that if adequate care were employed, in a ſhort time it might yield a conſiderable quantity. Impreſſed by their repreſentations, Mr. Pitt propoſed a bill to encloſe certain parts of the New Foreſt, for promoting the growth of timber. Very ſtrong objections were made to this propoſition in the houſe of commons, of which many of the members profeſſed to think it a job for the private emolument of Mr. Roſe ſecretary to the treaſury, inſtead of a national object. In the houſe of peers it was ſtrongly reprobated, particularly by the lord chancellor, and was finally relinquiſhed.

Mr. Pitt's bill for incloſing the New Foreſt, is rejected by the peers.

Mr.

CHAP. XLVIII.

1792
Bill of Mr. Dundas for facilitating the payment of wages and prize money to sailors.

Mr. Dundas having in his official capacity, as treasurer of the navy, learned the many difficulties which, through their thoughtlessness and ignorance of business, our gallant supporters often experience in the recovery of their wages and prize money, introduced a bill to remove the obstacles, and prevent the frauds. When the bill was passed, Mr. Dundas sent a printed account of the spirit, tendency, and provisions of this new act, to all the parochial clergy in Britain, to be read from the pulpits, and explained to sailors and their connections. Since that time the impostures which before were so frequently practised by personating individuals, forging wills, and other criminal artifices, are very rarely attempted.

Finance.

In bringing forward his plan* of finance, Mr. Pitt shewed the national revenue to be in such a favourable state, that a diminution of the public burdens might be reasonably expected. The taxes for the year 1791 had produced £ 16,730,000, exceeding the average of the last four years £ 500,000; after subtracting from which the sum total of the expenditures, which amounted by the reductions proposed to £ 15,811,000, the permanent income would exceed the permanent expence, including the million annually appropriated to the extinction of the national debt, by no less than £ 400,000. The supplies wanted for the present year would amount to £ 5,654,000, for which the means provided constituted a sum that exceeded the former by £ 37,000. From the foregoing

Prosperous state of commerce and revenue.

* February 17th.

statement

ſtatement, Mr. Pitt was of opinion, that the ſurplus would enable government to take off ſuch taxes as bore chiefly on the poorer claſſes, to the amount of one half of that ſum; and to appropriate the other half to the diminution of the public debts. By the methods projected for the redemption of this debt, £ 25,000,000 would be paid off in the ſpace of fifteen years; towards which the intereſt of the ſums annually redeemed would be carried to the ſinking fund, till the annual ſum to be applied to the redemption of that debt amounted to £ 4,000,000. This favourable ſtate of the finances aroſe from the actual proſperity of the nation, which, though arrived at an eminent degree, had not yet attained that ſummit of grandeur and felicity, that lay within the reach of its induſtry and manifold abilities. During the diſcuſſion on the ways and means, ſeveral ſevere ſtrictures were made on the miſchiefs of lotteries, in waſting the property and corrupting the morals of the lower claſſes. Miniſters replied, that the lottery was a tax upon adventure, which would exiſt though it were not taxed, it was no reaſon to forbear a productive ſource of revenue, that its ſubject might be abuſed. Near the cloſe of the ſeſſion Mr. Dundas laid before the houſe his annual ſtatement of the income and expenditure of Britiſh India. In the preceding ſeſſion the ſurplus, after deducting all charges, was £ 1,409,000, applicable to the reduction of the company's debt, and to purchaſe an inveſtment. The actual revenues of Bengal, Madras, and Bombay, he ſtated at £ 7,350,000; the ſum remaining, together with that which aroſe from the ſale of imported goods, amounted

Proſpect of farther reducing the debt and taxes.

Flouriſhing ſtate of India finances.

to

CHAP. XLVIII. 1792.

to £ 591,000, from which deducting the interest paid at Bengal, Madras, and Bombay, the surplus of the whole was between three and £ 400,000. From a general review it appeared, that war with Tippoo Saib, and the interest of the debt, had nearly exhausted the whole revenue of India, and the profits of the sales; and that a debt had been contracted of £ 1,782,328, arising from the purchase of investments. Notwithstanding the increase of the India debt, Mr. Dundas stated the affairs of the company to be on no worse a footing at the commencement of 1792, than at the commencement of 1791; and they had been improved at home by the payment of debts to the amount of £ 694,000, and by an increase of money in their treasury, amounting to £ 541,400. Thus after a war of eight months, the company's finances were only the worse by £ 276,000. On the 15th of June, the session terminated with a speech from the throne, in which his majesty, mentioning the state of affairs in Europe, declared his own intention to observe a strict neutrality.

Political transactions in India.

While so many important concerns both internal and continental interested the British nation, a war breaking out in India, engaged a considerable share of the public attention. The peace of Mangalore, caused by the reduction of Tippoo Saib's strength, endured no longer than his deficiencies lasted. Inheriting the views and passions of his father, he sought the empire of India, and as a step to its attainment, the expulsion of the English, his most powerful rivals. For several years he had been collecting and difciplining large armies; and though hopelefs of affiftance, either from France or the native powers, was not afraid fingly to provoke England to war. The Englifh government in India, well informed of his defigns, was fufficiently prepared for counteraction. Mr. Pitt's plan for the adminiftration of the Indian territories, executed under the direction of Mr. Dundas, had corrected abufes, reftored profperity, and extended revenue through Britifh India. Sir John Macpherfon fucceeded Mr. Haftings as governor general, and imitated in peace the plans of economy which his predeceffor had concerted and executed, as firmly and conftantly as was poffibly confiftent with the neceffary expenditure of multiplied wars: he thereby furmounted the pecuniary difficulties in which the executive government was unavoidably involved. He liquidated the civil and military debts which had been incurred, and eftablifhed fuch a fyftem for reducing expenditure and improving income, as greatly facilitated the beneficial adminiftration of the board of controul. Lord Cornwallis being fent out to India, in fpring 1786, and with the double appointment of governor general and commander in chief, arrived at Calcutta in September, and found the different prefidencies in rifing profperity. He availed himfelf with moderation, firmnefs, and temper, of the beft arrangements of his predeceffors, and introduced feveral new regulations that contributed farther to the public welfare, including the fecurity and happinefs of the natives. In Madras and Bombay, affairs were proportionably flourifhing; the Britifh prefidencies were alfo fecured

Beneficial effects of Mr. Pitt's legiflative meafures, and Mr. Dundas's executive management.

Sir John Macpherfon Governor General, able and fuccefsful adminiftration of.

He is fucceeded by Lord Cornwallis, who proceeds in plans of comprehenfive improvement.

CHAP. XLVIII. 1792.

secured by a very powerful military force. The Nizam and the Mahrattas, as well as less considerable powers in the southern parts of the peninsula, were in alliance with the English. Such was the state of India when Tippoo Saib commenced hostilities by attacking our ally the Rajah of Travancore, whose dominions the English had guaranteed with Tippoo's consent, at the late peace. The council of Madras remonstrated, and attempted amicable mediation, but to no purpose. Bound in honour and justice to protect our ally, the supreme government of Bengal declared war against the sultan of Mysore. In June 1790, general Meadows from the Carnatic, invaded Tippoo's dominions, while general Abercrombie from the west, having conquered Cannamore, advanced towards Seringapatam. Tippoo, with masterly skill, eluded all Meadows' ablest efforts to bring him to battle, and after a long and tiresome succession of marches and countermarches, with several skirmishes, the English general was obliged by the rainy season to return to Madras. Nor were Abercrombie's exertions after the reduction of Cannamore during the first campaign, attended with any decisive efforts. Though the campaign in all its operations, very honourably displayed British valour and conduct, yet it did not answer expectations, and Lord Cornwallis himself judged it expedient to take the field the following year. In March 1791, he proceeded to Mysore by the Eastern Ghauts; and having surmounted the passes, he attacked Bangalore, the second city of the Mysorean empire. Tippoo marched to its relief: for so important an object ventured a

Tippoo Saib recruits his strength. He attacks the Rajah of Travancore.

War, and invasion of Mysore.

Campaign of 1790, indecisive.

1791, Lord Cornwallis invades Mysore, and comes within sight of Seringapatam;

pitched

1792.

pitched battle, was defeated, and the town was taken by ſtorm. Lord Cornwallis now proceeded towards the capital of Myſore, whither Abercrombie was alſo advancing with the weſtern army. In the month of May he arrived in the neighbourhood of Seringapatam, where he found Tippoo very ſtrongly poſted, and protected in front and flank by ſwamps and mountains: not deterred by theſe difficulties, the Britiſh general attacked the enemy, and though the Myſoreans made a very gallant reſiſtance, entirely defeated them, and compelled them to ſeek ſhelter under the guns of the capital. The ſun was about to ſet when the victorious Engliſh, purſuing the enemy, firſt beheld Seringapatam, riſing upon an iſland, in all the ſplendor of Aſiatic magnificence, decorated with ſumptuous buildings, encircled by moſt beautiful gardens, and defended by ſtrong and extenſive fortifications. The grand object of their purſuit now appeared to the Engliſh within their immediate graſp; but diſaſters which no foreſight could have anticipated, and no wiſdom could have prevented, now obſtructed its attainment. A covering army was neceſſary while they were carrying on the ſiege, both for ſupporting their operations, and for commanding the country, to ſecure the conveyance of proviſions. When Lord Cornwallis ſet out on this expedition, he had truſted to the co-operation of the Mahrattas, but was diſappointed. Still expecting General Abercrombie, he marched up the Cavery, to ſecure and facilitate the advance of the weſtern army; but the river ſuddenly ſwelling, rendered the junction of the two armies impracticable. The troops from Bombay re-

is prevented by the floods of the Cavery from inveſting the metropolis of Myſore.

CHAP. XLVIII. 1792.

luctantly yielding to neceſſity, departed for the weſtern coaſt, expoſed to all the fury of the monſoon which was then raging on the Malabar ſide of the mountains. Cornwallis having halted ſome days to cover the retreat of the other army, deemed it expedient to defer the ſiege of Seringapatam till the following campaign, and ſpent the remainder of the ſeaſon in reducing the interjacent country and forts, ſecuring communication with the allies, preparing plentiful ſupplies of proviſion, and making other diſpoſitions for commencing the inveſtment as ſoon as the monſoon ſhould be over. The moſt difficult and moſt important acquiſitions during the remainder of this campaign, were Nundydroog, the capital of a rich diſtrict, and Savendroog, or the Rock of Death, a fortreſs which commanded a great part of the country between Bangalore and Seringapatam. Early in 1792, the Nizam and the Mahrattas joined the Britiſh army, now on its march; and on the 5th of February, the Britiſh hoſt once more appeared before Tippoo's capital. On the 7th, ſoon after midnight, they attacked the ſultan's lines, forced his camp, gained a complete victory, and compelled him to confine himſelf within the city. The Bombay army now arriving, a junction was effected between Abercrombie and the commander in chief, and the city was inveſted on every ſide. Seringapatam has the form of a triangle almoſt iſoſkeles: two ſides are waſhed by the river, while the third is joined to the country. On this, the weſtern ſide, as naturally the moſt acceſſible, the fortifications are the ſtrongeſt: aware of this circumſtance, the Britiſh general inſtead of directing

In 1792, he beſieges Seringapatam.

his

his main attack from the island, resolved to make his assault across the river. The trenches were open, the siege was advancing with great rapidity, and dispositions were made for commencing an immediate assault. The sultan seeing himself hemmed in on every side, importuned by the people to terminate the war, and fearing sedition if he refused, at last sued for peace, which was granted him on the following conditions: first that he should cede one half of his dominions to the allied powers; secondly, that he should pay three crores, and thirty lacks of rupees *; thirdly, that he should unequivocally restore all the prisoners which had been taken by the Mysoreans from the time of Hyder Ally; and fourthly, that two of his three eldest sons should be delivered up as hostages for the due performance of the treaty. Agreeably to these terms, the treasure began to be carried to the British camp, and on the 26th, the young princes were conducted to Lord Cornwallis. This ceremony was performed with great pomp: meanwhile Tippoo made some attempts to retard the execution of the treaty, but Lord Cornwallis issuing orders for recommencing the siege, he submitted to all the British demands; and the peace was finally concluded on the 19th of March. Thus ended a war which delivered the company from the dangers to which it was exposed, by the inveterate hostility of the most powerful of its neighbours; constantly inclined from interest and connection, to unite with France. The territories of which Tippoo was divested, were divided between the three allied powers, in three equal portions.

Tippoo sues for peace, and obtains it at the dictation of Lord Cornwallis.

* About £4,125,000.

 This

CHAP. XLVIII.

1792.

Generous conduct of his lordship respecting prize money.

This act of good faith to our allies, and the separate arrangements made by Lord Cornwallis with the nabobs of Oude and the Carnatic, as well as the principal native rajahs, left a very honourable and advantageous impression of British justice on the memory of the natives. Lord Cornwallis and General Meadows, with great generosity, resigned their share of the plunder to the rest of the army. His lordship having reduced this potent enemy, turned his attention to the improvement of the territory which had been ceded by the sultan of Mysore.

Measures of for the improvement of India.

Several British gentlemen had applied themselves to the study of the oriental languages, and by this means had become acquainted with the history and customs of the natives. Among other valuable information, they had learned the ancient mode of collecting the revenues throughout India. By conversancy in the Persian and Indostan tongues, both civil and military officers discovered that the system of collection in Mysore was extremely productive, without oppressing the inhabitants; and that its chief advantage arose from the imposts being fixed, so that accounts were simplified, and the oppressions of intermediate agents were not suffered to exist. His lordship, from the knowledge which he had acquired concerning Indian systems of finance, extended his improvements to Bengal, and other settlements in India*.

* See Annual Register, 1792.

CHAP. XLIX.

The French revolution chiefly engages the attention of the continent and of Britain.—The British government still resolved not to interfere in the internal affairs of France.—Catharine's views respecting Poland—she desires to embroil her powerful neighbours in war with France.—Cautious prudence of Leopold.—Convention at Pilnitz between the chief powers of Germany.—The parties disavow hostile intentions against France.—The French king notifies to foreign princes his acceptance of the new constitution—answers of the different powers.—Circular note of the Emperor.—Sweden and Russia urge the German powers to active hostilities, but without effect.—Proceedings in France.—Meeting of the second National Assembly—they conceive internal revolution a reason for changing the law of nations—Seizure of Avignon—Operations of the French exiles at Coblentz.—The king urges them to return—rapid diminution of the king's power.—General character of the French nation.—violent passions, ardour of pursuit, and energy of action—the same character appears in their religious, loyal, and democratical enthusiasm—progress of republicanism.—Intrigues between the royalists and republican leaders—from the emptiness of the royal coffers are unavailing.—The king refuses to attempt his escape.—Different views of the emigrant princes and of the nobles—of foreign potentates.—Disputes between the French government and the elector of Treves.—The princes of the empire headed by the Emperor and supported by Prussia form a confederacy for defending their rights.—Sudden death of the Emperor.—Preparations of the king of Sweden.—Assassination of that heroic prince.—The French government demands of Austria and Prussia the disavowal of a concert hostile to France.—Basis of tranquillity proposed by Francis and Frederic William.—French declare war against Austria and Prussia.—Counter declarations.

tions.—The Duke of Brunswick is appointed general of the combined armies of Germany.—Preparations of France and distribution of the armies.—The French invade the Austrian Netherlands—their first operations are desultory and unsuccessful—unprovided state of their armies—is imputed to treachery.—Dispositions of government to remedy this defect. The Duke of Brunswick arrives at Coblentz.—The allied powers misinformed concerning the disposition of the French nation—under this misinformation they concert the plan of the campaign—they propose to invade France and restore monarchy—Manifesto of the duke of Brunswick—threatens more than its authors can execute—unwise and hurtful to the cause.—State of parties in France—the manifesto combines diversity of sentiment into unanimous determination to resist foreign interference—hurries the downfal of kingly power—and completely defeats the purposes of its framers.—Proceedings at Paris—power of the jacobins—the sanscullottes—decrees for raising a jacobin army and punishing refractory priests—the king refuses his sanction.—La Fayette repairs to Paris—but is obliged to fly—he leaves the French army and surrenders to the Austrians.—French enthusiasm on the approach of the combined armies.—Anniversary of July 14th.—The Marseillois—passive citizens.—The mayor of Paris in the name of his constituents demands the deposition of the king.—Proceedings of the 10th of August—a banditti assault the Thuilleries—valour of the Swiss guards—they are overpowered and massacred by the savage mob.—The royal family carried prisoners to the Temple—deposition of the king—plan of provisionary government drawn up by Brissot—manifestoes to the French and to foreign powers—plan of a convention—persecution of the unyielding priests.—Church plate is sent to the mint and the bells are turned into cannon.—Domiciliary visits.—Massacres of September—atrocious barbarity towards the Princess Lamballe.—Meeting of the national convention.—English societies address the convention with congratulations and praise—accompany their commendations with a gift of shoes.

shoes.—The corresponding society by its secretary Thomas Hardy shoemaker, invites the French republic to fraternity with Britain.—The convention believes the boasts of such reformers, that they speak the voice of the British nation—this belief influences their political conduct.—Schemes of the convention for procuring the property of other countries.—Proceedings of the Duke of Brunswick.—He enters France and advances towards Champaign.—Dumourier the French general, occupies a strong position.—The Duke of Brunswick retreats.—Elation of the French.—Dumourier enters the Netherlands, defeats his enemy at Jemappe, and reduces the country.—The French propose to conquer and revolutionize all neighbouring states.—Noted decree of November 19th, encouraging foreign nations to revolution.—The French open the Scheldt, contrary to treaties with Britain.—Effects in Britain from French doctrines and proceedings.—Anti-constitutional ferment during the recess of 1792.—English republicans confidently hope for a change.—Alarm of many friends of the constitution.—Mr. Reeves's association against republicans and levellers—is very generally joined—and gives an important turn to public opinion.—The king embodies the militia—and at such a crisis summons parliament before the appointed time.

CHAP. XLIX. 1792.

WHILE lord Cornwallis thus effected so great a change in Indostan, the eyes of all Europe were fixed on the revolutions of Poland and France. From the admiration of virtue, or from the enmity of ambition, princes and subjects were warmly interested in the concerns of the gallant, moderate, and discriminating votaries of rational liberty in Poland, but they were still more universally and vigilantly attentive to the furious proceedings of democratical and anarchical licence in France. Every friend of human rights regarded the Polish establishment of diffused freedom

The French revolution chiefly engages the attention of the continent and of Britain.

CHAP. XLIX. 1792.

with complacency and satisfaction; but he rejoiced at it on account of the Poles themselves, without considering his own security or interest as likely to be affected by the acts of men who confined their views to their own country. In contemplating France, whether with a friendly, hostile, or impartial regard, every neighbouring beholder saw that the conduct of the Gallic revolutionists would and must influence other nations. The principles and proceedings, whether deserving praise, reprobation, or a mixture of both, were general in their object, and energetic in their operation; and their effects, happy or miserable, evidently must be extensive. The monarchs of the continent, conscious that even moderate and rational liberty was by no means consistent with their own respective governments, regarded with alarm a system, tending not merely to restrain, but to crush and annihilate monarchy.

The British government still resolved not to interfere in the internal affairs of France.

Britain declared her resolution not to interfere in the internal affairs of France; but the other sovereigns by no means concurred in disclaiming such intentions; indeed some of them were severally predisposed to a very contrary policy. Since the peace of Werela, a close intercourse had subsisted between Catharine and Gustavus. The ambitious empress foiled in the expectations with which she had begun the Turkish war, saw a fresh barrier rising against her power in the establishment of Polish independence, which, if suffered to acquire strength and stability, would counteract her future projects; she therefore resolved to crush the new-born freedom. Austria and Prussia only possessed the power of obstructing her designs; and though they

Catharine's views respecting Poland.

were

were at present upon amicable terms, yet she wished to have a stronger security for the forbearance of their interference: the most effectual, she well knew, would be, if she could occupy them in another quarter. As a sovereign she was, no doubt, inimical to doctrines so unpalatable to crowned heads, and in some degree entered into the sympathies of her neighbours. But the prevention of republicanism, not very likely to make its way among the slavish boors of Russia, was by no means her principal or immediate object. Concealing, however, her real intentions, she expressed not only the strongest indignation against the French revolutionists, but openly and publicly was the first to declare herself determined to protect and restore the ancient government of France. She applied to the king of Sweden, who very readily listened to her suggestions, and promised to co-operate. Catharine and Gustavus expressed the warmest approbation of the emperor's letter *. The empress dispatched a minister to the French princes at Coblentz, assisted them with money, and pressed them to enter on their expedition. Though determined to avoid all active interference herself, she assumed the † appearance of the most ardent zeal against the French revolutionists.

She desires to embroil her powerful neighbours in war with France.

Leopold proceeded in his plans with a caution and coolness which the more ardent advocates of a counter-revolution considered as dilatory. In August 1791 a convention was held at Pilnitz between the emperor, the king of Prussia, and the elector of Saxony. The friends of the French revolution

Cautious prudence of Leopold.

Convention at Pilnitz between the chief powers of Germany.

* See Chapter xlvii. † Bouillé's Memoirs, 457.

formed

CHAP. XLIX. 1792.

formed an hypothesis that at this meeting a treaty was concluded for two great purposes; the restoration of absolute monarchy, and the dismemberment of the French empire *. The real object of this convention is now found to have been to preserve the public tranquillity of Europe, and for that purpose to endeavour, by combined influence, to effectuate the establishment of a moderate and limited monarchy in France. The conference at Pilnitz was attended by the Count d'Artois, the Marquis de Bouillé, and Mr. de Calonne. These illustrious exiles and the contracting sovereigns, stipulated that they would support the establishment of order and moderate liberty; and that if the king of France would concur, and other potentates accede to their designs, they would exert their influence and power to obtain to his christian majesty freedom of action; Leopold, publishing this engagement, disavowed hostile intentions towards France.

The parties disavow hostile intentions against France.

The French king notifies to foreign princes

In the month of September a notification was sent by the French king to all the crowned heads in Europe,

* On this fiction, the vindicators of France in other countries, and especially in Britain, in conversation, speeches, and writings, during the first five years of the war, rested their principal arguments to prove, that innocent and unoffending friends of liberty and of the human race, were driven by necessity to defend themselves against the confederation of despots which met at Pilnitz. A paper was actually published as an authentic copy of this treaty of Pilnitz, not only supported by no evidence, but carrying, in its intrinsic absurdity, the clearest proofs that it was a forgery. Another fabrication of the same kind was also published as a state paper, and long referred to under the title of the treaty of Pavia. These forgeries are very fully and ably exposed in the Anti-jacobin newspaper, by a writer under the signature of DETECTOR.

1792.

rope, that he had accepted the new conſtitution. Britain ſent a very friendly anſwer: in his reply, Leopold expreſſed his hopes that this meaſure might promote the general welfare, remove the fears for the common cauſe of ſovereigns, and prevent the neceſſity of employing ſerious precautions againſt the renewal of licentiouſneſs. The anſwers of ſome of the other powers expreſſed their diſbelief of the king's freedom, and therefore forbore any opinion concerning the notification; but the greater number ſent friendly replies *. In November the emperor ſent a note to the different powers of Europe, declaring that he conſidered the French king as free, and the prevailing party to be diſpoſed to moderate counſels, from which his majeſty augured the probable eſtabliſhment of a regular and juſt government, and the continuance of tranquillity. But leſt the licentious diſorders ſhould be renewed, the emperor thought the other powers ſhould hold themſelves in a ſtate of obſervation, and cauſe to be declared by their reſpective miniſters at Paris, that they would always be ready to ſupport in concert, on the firſt emergency, the rights of the king and the French monarchy†. About the end of November his imperial majeſty wrote a note to the king of France, declaring that he had no intention to interfere with the affairs of his kingdom as long as the French ſhould leave to their king all the powers ‡ which they had voluntarily ſtipulated,

His acceptance of the new conſtitution.

Anſwers of the different powers.

Circular note of the emperor.

* See in State Papers of October and November 1791 the reſpective anſwers.

† State Papers, November 19th, 1791.

‡ This declaration certainly was an interference, as it preſcribed bounds beyond which they were not to go in the arrangement of their own affairs.

and

CHAP. XLIX. 1792.

and thofe which he had voluntarily accepted, in the new conftitutional contract. Leopold, indeed, manifefted in every part of his proceedings a difpofition to maintain peace with the French nation. He difcouraged the emigrants from affembling within his territories to concert projects inimical to the revolutionary government. This conduct was by no means agreeable to the French princes, who ftrongly expoftulated with him on the meafures which he was purfuing. The king of Sweden and the emprefs of Ruffia ftrenuoufly urged both the German potentates to active hoftilities *, but without effect: and long after the meeting at Pilnitz, the princes who conferred proved themfelves inclined to peace.

Sweden and Ruffia urge the German powers to active hoftilities, but without effect.

Proceedings in France.

Meeting of the fecond national affembly.

Meanwhile the fecond national affembly met in October 1791: having fworn to maintain the conftitution of the kingdom decreed by the conftituent affembly, they immediately exhibited a fpecimen of their legiflative juftice by paffing a law to rob the pope of the territory of Avignon, which had been ceded to that prince by the moft folemn treaties. This act was a farther illuftration of the principle already exemplified by the revolutionifts in their aggreffions on the German fovereigns, that becaufe France had made a change in her internal conftitution, fhe was alfo to alter the law of nations according to her convenience or pleafure, and to vio-

They conceive internal revolution a reafon for changing the law of nations.

* The Marquis de Bouillé, who was in the confidence of the king of Sweden, quotes feveral letters which prove Guftavus to have been very anxious to take an active part in the reftoration of monarchy; but the zeal of Catharine, he fays, never extended beyond profeffions. Page 457.

late the rights of independent ſtates. Their next project of rapacious injuſtice was againſt the biſhopric of Baſle *. Thither they ſent commiſſioners to ſettle certain differences which they pretended to have ariſen amongſt the inhabitants, and between Avignon and Carpentras. They began the ſyſtem of their operations by inſtituting a club, and gaining partizans among the people: after maſſacring the moſt peaceable and reſpectable inhabitants, they compelled the remainder to meet, and vote their union with the kingdom of France. The French royaliſts were forming an army under the prince of Condé; and, from the continued junction of the nobles and their adherents, they were become very numerous. On the 14th of October the aſſembly decreed, that emigrants thus collected ſhould be from that time conſidered as traitors againſt their country; and that, from the 1ſt of January 1792, ſuch as ſhould be known to be aſſembled ſhould be puniſhed with death; that all the French princes and public functionaries who ſhould not return before the 1ſt of January, ſhould be adjudged guilty of the ſame crimes, and ſuffer confiſcation of their property. The king refuſed to ratify this decree, but endeavoured to reconcile the exiles to the French government by admonition and perſuaſion: he repeatedly diſpatched letters to all the princes, earneſtly intreating them to return: he uſed his endeavours by a public proclamation, as well as

Seizure of Avignon.

Operations of the French exiles at Coblentz.

The king urges them to return.

* See French Journals of the proceedings of the aſſembly, which the Engliſh reader will find with conſiderable accuracy, in the Gentleman's Magazine, and the hiſtorical ſubſtance in the Annual Regiſters; but in fuller and more minute detail in the Moniteurs.

all

CHAP. XLIX. 1792.

all the private influence he poſſeſſed, to recal the emigrants to the boſom of their country, and to retain thoſe who were inclined to emigrate. The French princes, in anſwer to the king's repeated letters, perſiſted in their refuſal to acknowledge the conſtitution accepted by the king, and declared their views to be the re-eſtabliſhment of the Roman catholic religion, and the reſtoration to the king of his liberty and legiſlative authority. The republican party, profeſſing to think that the king ſecretly inſtigated the princes, endeavoured to excite in the nation a general miſtruſt of his intentions; and found their efforts ſo ſucceſsful, that they were encouraged to proceed in executing their deſign of leſſening the power of the king, and exalting their own on its ruins. The firſt ſtep they took for the accompliſhment of this end was, by all means to get rid of the uſual marks of reſpect to his majeſty's perſon. On the 6th February 1792, Condorcet, appointed preſident, was ordered to write a letter to the king, in which he was directed to lay aſide the title of "Your Majeſty." The loweſt rabble were permitted, and even encouraged, to reſort to the palace, and revile the royal family in the moſt groſs and profligate terms.

Rapid diminution of the king's power.

The national character of Frenchmen appeared totally changed: that people which for ſo many ages had been diſtinguiſhed for loyalty and religious zeal, now eagerly trampled on every remnant of monarchy or hierarchy. But the change was really much leſs in the conſtituents than in the direction of their character. The French nation has ever been diſtinguiſhed for ardour of ſenſibility to the paſſion of the times: whatever objects, prevailing opi-

General character of the French nation, violent paſſions, ardour of purſuit, and energy of action.

nions or ſentiments propoſed, they purſued with an energy, rapidity, and impetuoſity, which naturally and neceſſarily produced exceſs. In whatever they ſought, eager for pre-eminence, they ran into extremes: the ſame ſpecies of character which, in the ſixteenth century, took the lead in augmenting the domination of prieſts, in the ſeventeenth century in extending the power of kings, in the eighteenth was pre-eminent in enlarging the ſway of atheiſts and levellers. Prompt in invention, and powerful in intelligence; fertile in reſources, and energetic in execution, the efforts of the French, whitherſoever directed, never failed to be efficacious. Readily ſuſceptible of impreſſion, they were alive to ſympathy. Sentiments and opinions were very rapidly communicated: what Frenchmen ſeek, they ſeek in a body. The ſame national character which ſupported the catholic league, and ſpread the glory and power of Louis XIV. now overthrew the monarchy.

The ſame character appears in their religious, loyal, and democratical enthuſiaſm.

To render the king obnoxious, as well as to increaſe the means of force, the republicans repeated the reports of a confederacy of deſpots, declared their diſbelief of Leopold's pacific profeſſions, and procured a decree of the aſſembly, demanding ſatisfaction for the alleged treaty of Pilnitz. The Jacobin clubs, their pamphleteers, journaliſts, and other agents of confuſion and anarchy, rang the changes on the treaty of Pilnitz, and affirmed that there was in the palace a junto, which they called an Auſtrian committee; and of which De Geſſan, the king's miniſter for foreign affairs, was alleged to be a leading member. At a public trial of one of the journaliſts for aſſerting the exiſtence of ſuch a committee, he could bring no proof to ſupport his aſſertion; nor

Progreſs of republicaniſm.

was

CHAP. XLIX.

1792.

Intrigues between the royalists and republican leaders, from the emptiness of the royal coffers are unavailing.

was there ever any evidence adduced to give the smallest colour to the allegation. The royalists now counteracted the designs of the republicans with openness and boldness; they formed several projects for rescuing the king through the agency of Danton, and some other outrageous democrats, who manifested a disposition to betray their cause, if they found treachery more lucrative than their present violent adherence. Danton, that furious republican, received a hundred thousand crowns * for supporting motions really favourable to the king, though professedly inimical; but finding the resources of the court inadequate to his desires, resumed his republicanism. It is also affirmed that Brissot offered to betray his cause for a large sum of money, but that the court being either unwilling or unable to afford the bribe required † by this patriot, he persevered in his republican career ‡. A plan was concerted for effecting the king's escape to the coast of Normandy, which province was attached to his majesty. His flight, it is believed, would have been practicable; but the character of the king, mild and benevolent, without active enterprize, was little fitted to profit by these opportunities. His departure from Paris would, he thought, annihilate the monarchical constitution which he had sworn to protect; and expose all his adherents, declared or even suspected throughout France, to the infuriate cruelty of dominant licen-

* See Playfair's History of Jacobinism. † Ibid.

‡ Persons thoroughly acquainted with Brissot, declare that avarice was no part of his character; and as Mr. Playfair brings no proofs of his assertion, disbelieve it as improbable.

tiousness.

tiousness. From these considerations the king refused to attempt his escape. Understanding reports to have been circulated that he was projecting to leave Paris; to contradict these he wrote a letter to the national assembly, in which he fully explained his sentiments, views, and intentions *. The friends of the king, and even of limited monarchy, regretted his unwillingness to venture any step that might rescue him from a situation in which he was so degraded and insulted. They conceived that the object was well worthy of the risk; and that the danger of flight was only doubtful, whereas the danger of continuance was, if not immediate, at least certain. Of the emigrants, the princes desired the restitution of the old government, but the majority of the exiled nobles and gentry desired the establishment of a moderate and limited monarchy. Foreign powers were also divided on this subject. Russia, Spain, and Sweden, proposed to restore the ancient monarchy. Prussia was somewhat favourable to this opinion, but would not interfere actively without the co-operation of Leopold. The emperor continued friendly to peace until the conduct of the French government proved to him its determination to disturb tranquillity. They still withheld satisfaction for their usurpations in Lorrain and Alsace. They threatened with hostility the elector of Treves, and alleged various pretexts for their displeasure; but chiefly, his expression of doubts respecting the freedom of the king, and permission given to French emigrants to assemble in his dominions. French troops having approached the fron-

1792. The king refuses to attempt his escape.

Different views of the emigrant princes and of the nobles;

of foreign potentates.

Disputes between the French government, and the elector of Treves.

* State Papers, February 17th, 1792.

 tiers

CHAP. XLIX.

1792. The princes of the empire, headed by the emperor, and supported by Prussia, form a confederacy for defending their rights.

tiers of Treves, and menacing his territories, the elector applied for protection to the emperor. This prince, as head of the Germanic body, proposed to the other princes of the empire an extensive plan of defensive confederation, for mutual and reciprocal security against French aggression, and ordered marshal Bender to march to the defence of Treves. The French government, in a style rather menacing than conciliatory, demanded an explanation of the emperor's intentions. The answer of Leopold, though firm, was still pacific, and disavowed every intention of aggressive hostility. Meanwhile the emperor died very suddenly * at Vienna. Francis, his son and successor, declared his intention to persevere in the pacific plan of his father, but to be prepared for defensive war. The French government categorically demanded a declaration of Francis's intentions, and received a reply announcing the existence of a concert for the purposes of defence, but not invasion. As the discussion proceeded, it became progressively more hostile †, and both sides prepared for war. Catharine, operating on the heroic mind of the Swedish king Gustavus, had induced him, so early as the summer of 1791, to join in a project for the relief of Louis, even if the emperor and Prussia kept aloof; and Spain soon after had acceded to this design. Gustavus, betaking himself to Coblentz, conferred with the

Sudden death of the emperor.

* After an illness of two days, which by many was ascribed to poison; but there was never any proof of this assertion.

† See State Papers, from January to March 1792. Correspondence between the ambassadors and ministers of France and Austria, at Paris and Vienna; especially the letters to and from Count Kaunitz.

exiled

1792. Preparation of the king of Sweden.

exiled princes and nobility; and, encouraged by Catharine, prepared an army which he was to head. He consulted Leopold and Frederic William, but found both unwilling to embark in so very hazardous a project. He, however, made dispositions for proceeding in his undertaking without their co-operation, and was preparing to conduct an armament which should make a descent on the coast of France, and co-operate * with the royalists, when, on the 16th of March 1792, being at a masquerade in his capital, from the hands of Ankerstroem, a disaffected nobleman, who, with others, had plotted against his life, he received a wound which proved mortal. He for twelve days languished in agonizing pain; but retaining the use of his faculties, very ably and completely arranged his affairs; left wise and beneficial directions to his youthful son, and breathed his last on the 28th of March, in the forty-eighth year of his age, and twenty-first of his reign †; a prince for genius and heroism rarely surpassed, and not often equalled, even in the glorious annals of Swedish kings. The confederacy of princes which Gustavus and Catharine first proposed for modelling the government of France, without regard to the voice of the people, did not actually take place, yet a different concert, originating chiefly in the imperious and violent conduct of France herself, was unavoidably formed. Dumourier, now foreign

Assassination of that heroic prince.

* Bouillé, chapters 12 and 13.

† On the sudden fall of these two princes, Tom Paine exultingly observed, "See how kings are melting away!"

CHAP. XLIX.

1792.

The French government demands of Austria and Prussia the disavowal of a concert hostile to France. Basis of tranquillity proposed by Francis and Frederic William.

minister, in dictatorial terms required both from the courts of Berlin and Vienna the disavowal of any concert inimical to France, and the discontinuance of protection to the French emigrants. The answers of Prussia and Austria proposed a general principle as the basis of tranquillity; *that the French should not consider themselves, as from their revolution, entitled to violate the rights of other powers.* They therefore stated three subjects, on which they demanded satisfaction; first, that a compensation should be given to the princes possessioned in Lorraine and Alsace. Secondly, that satisfaction should be rendered to the pope for the county of Avignon. Thirdly, that the government of France should have a sufficient power to repress whatever might give uneasiness to other states*. Dumourier replied that the king of Hungary had no concern in these discussions, repeated in still stronger terms the demand of the French government, and denounced war unless the answer was categorical and speedy.

French declare war against Austria and Prussia.

The two German potentates adhering to their former replies, the national assembly, on the 20th of April, declared war against the king of Hungary and Bohemia†, and soon after, against the king of Prussia. In the decree denouncing hostilities, the national assembly repeated the imputation of a hostile confederacy against the liberties of France.

Counter declaration.

The court of Vienna, in its counter manifesto‡, disavowed as before, all offensive intentions. The princes of

* See State Papers, April 5th, 1792.

† State Papers, April 20th, 1792.

‡ State Papers, July 5th, 1792.

the

the German empire had formed a concert for reciprocal protection against the unjust pretensions of France, which had considered her internal changes as reasons for deviations from the faith of foreign treaties. The king of Prussia, as member of the confederation for securing Germany against the aggressions of France, declared himself compelled to take an active share in the war. But besides the defensive objects avowed by Francis, the king of Prussia's manifesto declared, that one of his purposes was to put an end to anarchy in France, to establish a legal power on the essential basis of a monarchical form, and thus give security to other governments against the incendiary attempts and efforts of a frantic troop*.' Thus the repression of French principles was the chief object which, by his own avowal, induced the king of Prussia to join in hostilities against France; while the protection of the Germanic empire was ostensibly the principal motive of Francis. From the time that Leopold and Frederic William had concluded their alliance, they had joined in deeming the duke of Brunswick, the fittest general for directing the force of the defensive confederacy. An intercourse had been opened between them confidentially on this subject; and the duke was fully apprised, and approved of the enterprize of Leopold. When, from the aggression and declaration of France, war was become absolutely necessary, his serene highness accepted the command, and preparations were made for opening the campaign with the combined forces.

The duke of Brunswick is appointed general of the combined armies of Germany.

* See State Papers, July 24th, 1792.

CHAP. XLIX.

1792. Preparations of France, and distribution of the armies.

Immediately after the declaration of war by France, the French forces were set in motion. The king had established four armies, in order to protect and cover his country, and to be in readiness to act as the existing circumstances might direct. The first army was assembled on the northern confines of France, under the command of the Marshal de Rochambeau, an experienced officer, who had served in the French armies during the American war. This force was destined to cover the frontier towards the Austrian Netherlands, from the German Ocean at Dunkirk, to Maubeuge, in French Hainault, with their right extending to the Meuse. The marquis de la Fayette, appointed to command the second army, fixed his head quarters at Metz, and occupied Nancy, Thionville, and Luneville. By this means was the cordon extended from the banks of the Meuse to the Moselle, and retained in check the important fortress of Luxemburg. The third army was formed on the Rhine, under Luckner, and extended from Landau, by Strasburg, towards Montbeliard, and the pass of Porentrui into Switzerland. The possession of this important defile, aided by the favourable position of the mountains of Jura, rendered the extensive frontier of Franche Compte entirely safe. A fourth army was assembled on the side of Savoy, to watch the motions of the king of Sardinia, who was expected to join the hostile confederacy. The army of the north, commanded by Rochambeau, amounted to above fifteen thousand men; the centre army, commanded by La Fayette, to seventeen thousand; the army of the Rhine, to about twenty-two thousand; the fourth,

to

1792.

to twelve thousand men. The reduction of the Low Countries was the object of this campaign; and the disaffection to the house of Austria still subsisting in the provinces, afforded probable expectations of success. The army under Rochambeau occupied the direct road to Brussels, without any impediment but the garrison of Mons. Fayette commanded the county of Namur, and the navigation of the Meuse; but the armies were found very imperfectly provided and disciplined: the French soldiers were deficient in military experience, in ammunition, and stores of every sort. Many of the officers warmly attached to the king were not eager in promoting a cause which they by no means deemed the cause of their sovereign. The war was begun with an attack on the cities of Mons and Tournay; but the soldiers being impressed with an idea that they were betrayed by their generals, retreated in great confusion; in their savage rage they murdered several officers, and among the rest Dillon, the lieutenant general. They trampled upon his body, and having lighted a fire, threw the corpse into the flames. The infuriated soldiers danced round the remains of their commander: so ferocious and hardened had they become from the influence of the revolutionary enthusiasm. Rochambeau, finding the army totally loosened from subordination and all honourable principles of duty, resigned in the highest disgust. Luckner, appointed commander of the army of the north, found the troops in a much worse situation than even his predecessor had represented. La Fayette made the same complaints of the unprovided state of the force entrusted to his command, as deficient in camp equipage, artillery,

The French invade the Austrian Netherlands.

Their first operations are desultory and unsuccessful.

Unprovided state of their armies.

 ammunition,

CHAP. XLIX.

1792. Is imputed to treachery.

ammunition, and stores of every kind: in short, at the commencement of the war the armies of the French government were in so very unprovided a state, as could hardly arise even from negligence, without the co-operation of treachery. In such a condition of the forces it was found necessary, if not to abandon, to postpone the invasion of the Austrian Netherlands, until discipline were better established, magazines formed, and other dispositions made, proper for a campaign.

Dispositions of government to remedy this defect.

The Austrian force then in the Netherlands was not very considerable; and during the months of May and June the operations of both sides were desultory and unimportant. On the 3d of July, the duke of Brunswick arrived at Coblentz, with the first division of the Prussian army, and in the course of the month being joined by fresh troops, he prepared to commence the campaign. His serene highness, with very great talents, the deepest military skill, and eminent political abilities, is extremely diffident*. From that cause, joined to a gentle and delicate disposition, he frequently treated very inferior capacities with excessive deference, and did not with sufficient vigour maintain in deliberation the dictates of his own excellent understanding. Fitted to lead in council and in war, in the former the duke of Brunswick too frequently followed. In concerting the plan of the campaign 1792, he left the formation chiefly to Francis and Frederic William. These princes were impressed with an opinion, so naturally adopted, and studiously spread by the emigrants, that the greater number of Frenchmen

The duke of Brunswick arrives at Coblentz.

The allied powers mis-informed concerning the disposition of the French nation.

* This is the account given of him by various gentlemen who have visited Germany.

were

1792. Under this mis-information they concert the plan of the campaign. They propose to invade France, and restore monarchy.

were attached to the old government, and would join the standard of monarchy if they found themselves properly supported; and on this supposition they formed the plan of the campaign. It was proposed that the duke of Brunswick should set out from Coblentz with an army of Prussians, fifty thousand strong, and march by Treves and Luxemburg to Longvy. After reducing this fortress, and also if possible Montmedi, the next object was to establish magazines, continue the march, and invest Verdun. In support of these, as well as of subsequent operations, the court of Vienna engaged to bring into the field two armies; the one to act between the Rhine and the Moselle, and to be of sufficient strength for the purpose of at once menacing Landau and Saar-Louis, and carrying on the siege of Thionville; while the other, of much superior force, should be engaged in the Low Countries; their positions were to be as near the Meuse as possible. Should the expectations of a general rise in France be disappointed, the duke of Brunswick was not to cross the river with his main body, but to detach a considerable portion of his army to co-operate with the Austrians in French Hainault, in reducing Verdun, Sedan, and Meziers. Thus the allies establishing themselves upon the French frontier, would be able to winter in security, and commence the following campaign with great advantage. To oppose this invading force, the entrenched camp at Maubeuge, and another at Maulde, with the strong fortress of Valenciennes, formed the principal points of defence on the part of the French. Previous to the march of the duke of Brunswick, a mani-

CHAP. XLIX.

1792. Manifesto of the duke of Brunswick,

a manifesto was composed under the authority, and according to the sentiments of Francis, now emperor of Germany, and the king of Prussia; proclaiming the objects of these two princes in their projected invasion, and issued in the name of the duke of Brunswick, commander in chief of the expedition. This celebrated manifesto was founded on the same misinformation concerning the disposition of the French themselves, in which the plan of the campaign had originated. The proclamation declared, that the intention of the combined princes was neither to conquer any part of France, nor to interfere with the internal government of that kingdom, but simply to deliver the king and queen from captivity. It invited all the French soldiers and other Frenchmen, to join the combined army in executing this design, promised protection and security to all who should accept these proffers; and denounced vengeance against the persons and property of all who should oppose the efforts of the confederates. It declared the present governors responsible for every evil that should accrue to the country from their refractory resistance; called on the people to submit to their sovereign, and promised to intercede with the king to grant his gracious pardon to penitent offenders. It warned other towns, but especially the city of Paris, that if they refused to comply, they should be delivered up to military execution. This proclamation was extremely unwise in its principles and tenor, and no less hurtful in its effects. The hopes of co-operation which the invaders might reasonably entertain, rested on the divisions which subsisted in France.

threatens more than its authors can execute.

Unwise and hurtful to the cause.

The

1792.

State of parties in France.

The parties continued reducible to four general classes; first, the royalists or abettors of the old government, votaries of an absolute power, much more slavish than the most bigotted English tory of the seventeenth century would practically endure. Secondly, the feuillants, votaries of limited monarchy, desiring a mixture of liberty and order, and not much differing from English whigs. Thirdly, the constitutionalists, a still numerous, though decreasing body, friendly to the system which had been established by the late national assembly. Fourthly, the republicans, with great diversity of particular scheme, but concurring in desiring the total abolition of monarchy. If skilful means had been employed to unite the three former parties in defence of monarchy, perhaps the republicans and jacobins might have been repressed. The proclamation tended to unite those who were before divided; and by requiring implicit submission to the king, and declaring that all constitutional changes should originate in his will, it inculcated principles which only the slavish class would admit; and which every monarchical votary of liberty must reject as indignantly as the most outrageous jacobin; besides, it not only was contrary to the sentiments of every French friend of liberty, but of every French supporter of national independence. Two foreign sovereigns declared themselves judges between the members of the French internal government. It could not be reasonably expected that the national spirit of a Frenchman would suffer such an assumption of power by Germans. This manifesto in its effects most materially injured the cause which its framers

The manifesto combines diversity of sentiments into unanimous determination to resist foreign interference.

CHAP. XLIX. 1792.

framers professed to promote: it afforded a simple and comprehensive principle of union in the abhorrence of despotism to be imposed by foreign powers: and combined the friends of moderate and rational liberty, with the most furious partizans of uncontrouled licentiousness. By inducing many to believe that the king approved its sentiments and principles, it rendered his personal safery insecure; and hurried the downfal of the kingly power in France. It totally deviated from the defensive system which the emperor had professed to support, and appeared to justify the imputation of a concert of kings to crush Gallic liberty. Instead of intimidating, it enraged the French nation; threats, without the power of execution, recoiled in indignant scorn upon the menacers. The apprehension of a confederacy formed to dictate to an independent nation the plan of internal government which it should adopt, roused the pride of Frenchmen, and turned the energy of their character to military efforts, invincible in defence, and as it afterwards proved, irresistible in attack.

hurries the downfal of kingly power, and completely defeats the purposes of its framers.

Proceedings at Paris.

Meanwhile proceedings at Paris were hastening the destruction of monarchy, and in effect co-operating with the dictatorial menaces of the confederated invaders. The friends of monarchy absolute or limited, fast continued to emigrate: the king was forced to dismiss ministers of his own choice, and to receive republicans * in their place. The principal

* They consisted of members of a party known by the name of Girondists, from the Girond department, along the banks of the Garonne, which district the principal members of this party represented.

cipal direction was possessed by the jacobin clubs: their system of government was simple and obvious, to overawe and overrule the legislative assembly by the national guards, and the mob of Paris, nor did they seem to have any greater or more fixed object in the exercise of their power, than the subversion of all order, and the confusion of all property. There still remained a diversity of condition, notwithstanding all their advances in the levelling system. The proprietors of estates, the merchants, and the manufacturers, were in a better situation than their respective day labourers, and also than many others, who though possessing no property, did not choose to be labourers. The disposition to idleness was greatly increased by the revolution: many of the inhabitants of Paris had chiefly subsisted by the employment which they received from the nobility and other landed proprietors. These sources no longer flowing, numbers became idle from want of industrious occupation. The sovereignty of the mob was not friendly to productive industry; it could not reasonably be expected, that men taught to conceive themselves kings would vouchsafe to dig ditches or pave the streets. Besides, these sovereigns, even if disposed to manual labour, had no time to spare. They were engaged in politics: hence a very numerous body

---

represented. They had been constitutionalists, but were now become republicans, though less violent in their professions than the Jacobins. Among the Girondists were the chief literary men in France.

of

CHAP. XLIX. 1792.

of citizens, who before their elevation had been useful handicrafts men, were now in their sovereign capacity extremely idle, and extremely poor; and as the new liberty included an exemption from moral and religious restraint, they were also extremely profligate. To the poverty of the idle and profligate, order and tranquillity, which preclude them from their principal means of subsistence, are naturally obnoxious. The meanest and most beggarly citizens sought a more general equalization of property, and assumed the supreme executive authority. A ragged coat was deemed an honourable testimony of the wearer's political principles; the lowest rabble, denominated from their dress sans culottes, or ragamuffins, took a lead in public affairs. The national guards were now become somewhat moderate: the jacobin club, the sans-culottes, and the violent republicans of every kind, determined that an army should be formed, composed of twenty thousand men, under the controul of the republicans. Without any order from the king, the war minister proposed that the desired force should be raised and encamped under the walls of Paris. The assembly, to gratify the sans culottes, passed the decree: under the same influence they also enacted another law against refractory priests. The king firmly refused to sanction these laws, which were respectively inimical to his executive authority, and to justice. The republican ministers urged their master, not without threats, to comply with the desire of the people; but his majesty with becoming dignity dismissed these insolent servants. These and other republicans, as the decree was not passed, embodied

Decrees for raising a jacobin army, and punishing refractory priests.

The king refuses his sanction.

embodied a jacobin army for themselves. An immense multitude assembled from different quarters of Paris, and, armed with pikes, axes, swords, muskets, and artillery, marched in a body, on the 20th of June, towards the Thuilleries, that they might force the king to sanction the two decrees. Appearing before the palace they demanded admittance, and the gates being thrown open, the rabble violently entered into the apartment of their king. His majesty received this banditti with calmness and moderation; but though not without a dread of being assassinated, he firmly refused to comply with their insolent demands. The fury of the mob at length subsided, and they departed without effecting their purposes. Numbers of the populace who had not been engaged in the outrage, expressed their indignation against the rioters, and their admiration of the king's courage and conduct; and the various other parties were extremely incensed against the jacobins. The new minister for the home department taking advantage of this disposition, published a proclamation on the subject of the recent tumult, which gave such satisfaction, that many of the departments sent addresses to the king and to the national assembly, demanding that the authors and abettors of the insurrection might be punished with the utmost severity. It appeared on enquiry that Petion the mayor, and Manuel the procurator, might have easily either prevented or quelled this insurrection; they were therefore both suspended from their offices. The constitutionalists highly approved of this sentence, which the royalists thought too moderate, while the jacobins breathed vengeance against

CHAP. XLIX.

1792.

La Fayette repairs to Paris,

against the punishers of a magistrate who instigated insurrection. La Fayette, finding the tide of popular opinion to run somewhat less against monarchy, repaired to Paris to remonstrate concerning the late outrages; but he possessed neither ability, decision, nor intrepidity to intimidate his enemies; firmness or consistency to give confidence to his friends. After being favourably received by the constitutionalists, he was severely censured by the Girondists and jacobins, for leaving the army without permission, and attempting to govern the assembly by intimidation. He left Paris privately; commissaries were sent from the assembly to arrest the general; he gave orders to have these deputies apprehended; finding however no disposition in his army to afford him support, he withdrew in the night to Liege; there falling into the hands of the enemy, and refusing to join the standard of the French princes, he was sent a prisoner to Namur.

but is obliged to fly; he leaves the French army and surrenders to the Austrians.

Intelligence now reached Paris, that the combined armies were preparing to take the field; the national assembly endeavoured to inspire the people with an enthusiastic eagerness to oppose a confederation of despots; and with the assistance of the jacobin clubs they were successful. They decreed the country to be in danger, and published two addresses *, the one to the people of France, the other to the army, which were skilfully adapted to their respective objects, powerfully stimulated the enthusiasm of both; and demonstrated that however deficient the republican leaders might be in virtuous principles, they could ably call into action the pas-

French enthusiasm on the approach of the combined armies.

* See State Papers, July 1792.

sions

CHAP. XLIX. 1792.

ſions and energies of men. They ſoon iſſued a decree, declaring that all citizens qualified to bear arms, ſhould be in a ſtate of perfect activity. By this meaſure the whole order of things was completely changed; and the French became a nation of ſoldiers. The German potentates threatening the ſubjugation of a powerful people, drove the objects of their invaſion, to the ferocious energy of a military democracy. On the 14th of July, vaſt bodies of federates arrived in the metropolis, at the invitation of the jacobin leaders, to celebrate the third anniverſary of the revolution. Among others a troop from Marſeilles repaired to Paris, to participate of the uproar and confuſion, which they expected to ariſe from the celebration. They happened to arrive too late for the anniverſary, but in ſufficient time to produce diſorder and tumult. They rendered their firſt homage to Petion who was now reſtored to his office, and were received with great kindneſs by that magiſtrate, whoſe duty it was to drive them from the metropolis. They commenced their operations with attacking a party of national guards who were dining at a tavern, and whom they ſuppoſed to be attached to the king; killing one and wounding five, they paid their reſpects to the national aſſembly *; and were very graciouſly received by the republicans. Viſiting the jacobins they partook of the fraternal embrace, and were admitted members of the club. Small as the qualification of voters denominated active citizens was, yet the number of thoſe who were not included was very

Anniverſary of the 14th of July.

The Marſeillois.

* Otridge's Annual Regiſter, 1792, chap. 11.

CHAP. XLIX. 1792.

Passive citizens.

great, and fast increasing from prevalent idleness and profligacy. These consisting of beggars, vagabonds, and the meanest classes of ruffians, thieves, robbers, and assassins, under the name of *passive citizens*, assumed to themselves the chief portion of the executive power, in the exercise of which they were instigated and guided by their friends of the jacobin clubs. The passive citizens most joyfully received the Marseillois strangers, as a co-ordinate estate, but which was soon consolidated into one body with themselves, and their supporters, while the jacobins by their affiliations, and adherents, governed the whole mass. The republicans now denominated the mountain, because they occupied the higher benches in the assembly-room, began to govern the legislature, and from this time the acts of the national assembly are to be considered as the acts of the jacobins. They proceeded in their efforts for destroying regal power; they imputed the king's refusal to sanction the two decrees, to a correspondence with the exiles and the enemy. His majesty having in a letter expressed his reprobation of the duke of Brunswick's manifesto, the assembly would not suffer this expression of his sentiments to be communicated to the public. On the 3d of August Petion demanded, in the name of the forty-eight sections into which Paris was divided, that the king should be excluded from the throne, and that the management of affairs should be entrusted to responsible ministers, until a new king should be chosen by a national convention; and on the 7th of August, Collot d'Herbois a play-actor headed a great body of passive citizens, who made the same demand to the

The Mayor of Paris in the name of his constituents, demands the deposition of the king.

the national assembly. They were answered that the assembly would take the requisition into consideration. The king informed of these proceedings addressed a proclamation to the people of France, stating his own conduct and its reasons; the malicious artifices by which it was misrepresented; the situation of affairs; the union and vigour required at the present crisis*; but the assembly studiously prevented the proclamation from being dispersed. On the 9th of August†, the day appointed for considering the proposed deposition of the king, bodies of armed men surrounded the assembly-hall, menaced ‡ and insulted the members whom they conceived inimical to the republican proposition. As an insurrection was threatened, the constitutional party urged Petion to employ the municipal force in preventing tumult, but no precautions were adopted. At midnight the tocsin sounded, the Marseillois joined by other insurgents marched with such arms, as they could collect, towards the Thuilleries. The council of state made vigorous and prudent dispositions for repelling the attack. The Swiss guards amounting to about a thousand, joined by other loyal and gallant men, formed themselves to resist the insurgents. In the morning the banditti broke in ||; and the officers of the household encouraged the valiant defenders of the king: at first the brave champions of their sovereign repulsed the insurgents, but the rebels having corrupted the national guards,

Proceedings of the 10th of August,

a banditti assault the Thuilleries.

* State Papers, 17th of August, 1792.

† Annual Register 1792, chap. 11. ‡ Clery, page 4.

|| See a very interesting and pathetic detail of these dreadful atrocities in Clery's journal, page 2 to 16.

CHAP. XLIX.

1792.

Valour of the Swiss guards; they are overpowered and massacred by the savage mob;

the gallant Swiss were overpowered and fell under the murderous hands of the banditti. The king was strongly importuned to send for a large body of Swiss guards stationed near Paris, which, joining their heroic countrymen, by steady and disciplined valour might have repelled the infuriate assassins. But the virtues of Louis were not those that were most fitted for encountering the very arduous situations in which he was placed. His gentle disposition was averse to the employment of greater force, as it must cause the farther effusion of blood. In his case wisdom dictated and self-presevation required stern and unyielding firmness; desperate resolution might perhaps have extricated him from his humiliating state; concession to so infuriate atrocity, was certain destruction. Louis still hoping to preserve his family sought refuge from the national assembly, the rulers of which, he well knew were seeking his ruin. The royal captives were now confined in the Temple; the palace which they had left became a scene of pillage, carnage, and desolation. The jacobins elated with their victory, proceeded to the deposition of the king; and on the 10th of August a decree was passed, suspending him from his royal functions, and retaining him as an hostage in the hands of the nation. Brissot one of the chief supporters of this revolution, proposed a provisionary government until a national convention assembling should determine whether the king was to be restored or dethroned. The executive power was to be lodged in a council of the jacobin ministers lately displaced. Brissot wrote a manifesto addressed to citizens, and a declaration addressed to foreign powers, justifying the decree of the 10th of August;

the royal family carried prisoners to the temple.

Deposition of the king.

Plan of provisionary government drawn up by Brissot.

Manifestoes to the French people, and to foreign powers.

August; these papers were dexterously executed, and conveyed a high idea of the ingenuity of the author; skilfully various in its efforts; the declaration to his own countrymen appealed to all their prejudices, and feelings, and passions; and through the very susceptibility of their minds, imposed on their judgment; his memorial to foreign nations employed plausible sophistry to mislead their understandings, as he could hope for less sympathy from their hearts. The first manifesto is misrepresentation in the shape of impressive eloquence; the second in the form of logical deduction; and both shew the author to have in a high degree united declamation and subtlety. While thus exerting himself for the dethronement and imprisonment of the king, this patriot was said to be carrying on a correspondence for betraying the republican party, by suffering the king to escape; but it was alleged that the bribe which he required, half a million sterling, was more than the royal coffers could afford *.

The municipality or common council of Paris, which had been lately constituted and was composed of the very dregs of the people, assumed a large share of the direction of public affairs. By their influence the chief acts of the deliberative body were determined, and through their protection and operation the executive government in a considerable degree was administered. A party of these appearing as the deputies of the people, at the bar of the assembly, demanded in the name of the people, that a national convention should be immediately called. The assembly received these counsellors very graciously,

* See Playfair's Jacobinism.

 and

CHAP. XLIX. 1792.

and in obedience to their mandates, resolved to invite the French to form a national convention.

Plan of a convention.

A plan of a convention drawn up by the Brissotines, was disseminated and recommended through the nation. Meanwhile the jacobins and the sansculotte rabble proceeded in their operations. Hitherto they had not entirely crushed the ecclesiastics, or eradicated christianity, but they rapidly proceeded in the attempt. All who continued to refuse perjury were by an act of the assembly ordered to quit the kingdom. The Council General next ordered, that all the vessels, images, and other moveables in the churches of Paris, whether gold or silver, should be sent to the mint; the church bells were turned into cannon. From monuments of religion they proceeded to monuments of monarchy: the brazen statues of the princes were converted into ordnance, and thus, it was said, were drawn over from the cause of tyranny to the cause of liberty. The next object after religion and monarchy was property. Confiscation hitherto grasping lands had not extended its rapacity in an equal degree to moveables. To supply this deficiency, they instituted what they called *domiciliary visits*, officers employed by the municipality, and accompanied by *passive citizens*, visited private houses, to search for arms; for refractory priests, or other aristocrats. According to their good pleasure they plundered the houses, arrested or even hanged the owners. Brissot in his professional capacity as editor of a newspaper, very strongly recommended and ardently promoted these *domiciliary visits*: Petion as mayor was still more effectually active: nor was Danton as minister

Persecution of the unyielding priests.

Church plate is sent to the mint, and the bells are turned into cannon.

Domiciliary visits.

1792.

Walking commissaries.

minister of justice wanting with his assistance. He proposed, and by threats extorted a decree, for *walking commissaries*, who were to co-operate with the domiciliary visitors. Whoever should refuse to give up his arms, or to serve in the army at the requisition of the said commissaries, was to be declared a traitor and punished with death, without any further enquiry. The visitors and commissaries did not murder all those whose houses they inspected; but in many instances contented themselves with sending the owners to dungeons. The prisons were become extremely full; the rulers thought it expedient to rid themselves of the captives by stirring the populace to another insurrection and massacre. For this purpose it was alleged, that as the duke of Brunswick's approach would compel the majority of the inhabitants to take the field, it would be dangerous to leave the prisons so full of aristocrats and suspected persons. By these representations the murderous rabble was easily excited to assassination. On the 2d of September the tocsin was sounded, the cannon of alarm were fired; and bands of ruffians were sent to the different prisons. They commenced their carnage with priests; two hundred and forty-four clergymen were murdered before the evening. The assassins from the ministers of religion, proceeded to the gallant defenders of fallen monarchy, and murdered the Swiss officers, that having been spared at the last massacre were now in prison. From these murders the savages betook themselves to more indiscriminate barbarity, searched the common prisons and even hospitals, butchered felons, sick, and lunatics*, as well as those who were charged with disaffection to go-

Massacres of September.

* See Annual Register for 1792, chap. 3.

 vernment.

CHAP. XLIX.

1792. Atrocious barbarity towards the princess Lamballe.

vernment. Among the cases which most strongly mark the enormous depravity of those brutalized barbarians, none can exceed the massacre of the princess Lamballe: this lady sprung from the house of Savoy, was distinguished for personal charms, and a character at once amiable and estimable, and had been superintendant of the queen's household. Married to a man whom she loved, she had been deprived of her husband, through the duke of Orleans*; and was now principally distinguished for her ardent and invincible attachment to her royal mistress, and her detestation of her husband's murderer. She with other attendants on her queen had been sent to prison on the 10th of August; the murderers about eight in the morning of the 3d of September, entered the apartment in which this unfortunate lady was immured. They offered to save her life, if she would fabricate charges against the queen. The heroic princess returned a resolute negative; they demanded that she should take the oath of liberty and equality, also an oath of hatred to the king, to the queen, and to royalty; the first she consented to take, but refused the last: an assassin said, swear or you are a dead woman; she looked in his face but made no reply. In an instant she was assassinated with pikes and bayonets; her cloathes were torn off, and the naked corpse exposed to the most abominable insults. With religion, justice, order, and humanity, decency and modesty fled. The head and body of the massacred lady were exposed before the windows of the royal captives, with every circumstance of brutalism, that diabolical malignity maddened to frenzy could suggest†. The murders continued for a

* See this volume, p. 74. † See Otridge's Register, 1792.

week;

week; in which time the numbers of the maſſacred exceeded five thouſand. Meanwhile the elections of the national convention were carried on under the influence of this terrible ſyſtem. A circular letter from the municipality of Paris, counterſigned by Danton was ſent to all the other municipalities, required the approbation of the whole people to the maſſacres, and even recommended them to imitation; and under ſuch controul the election proceeded. The clergy were baniſhed; the higher and the moſt honourable of the nobility had fled, or fallen by the hands of the aſſaſſins; the royal family in priſon expected their fate; all who favoured royalty or diſtinction of rank were held in abhorrence, and thoſe who had been called paſſive as well as the active citizens had been declared to be eligible to all honours and offices of the ſtate. The convention was chiefly choſen from the moſt violent and deſperate republicans in the kingdom. The members aſſembled on the 20th of September; and the next day they ſanctioned the law for aboliſhing royalty. Having thus proſcribed monarchy, and eſtabliſhed what they termed the French republic, their next object was, to prepare for the murder of their dethroned king.

Meeting of the national convention.

While the French were thus occupied, their proceedings and projects afforded the higheſt ſatisfaction to democratic republicans in other countries. From England many individuals flocked to Paris, as the centre of liberty and happineſs. The ſocieties eagerly tranſmitted their approbation of the French revolutioniſts; during the ſucceſſive degradations of monarchy they had in their own country publiſhed their applauſe of its invaders, but when the acts of the 10th of Auguſt had depoſed and impriſoned the king,

English ſocieties addreſs the convention with congratulations of praiſe;

CHAP. XLIX. 1792.

king, murdered his defenders, and prostrated his power; when the busy week of September extending the massacre of aristocrats, shed the blood of the nobility, gentry, and clergy; when the national convention doing honour to its own composition, had abolished the kingly office, the English societies eagerly testified their joy and congratulations on the success of those with whose principles they declared their own to coincide, and with whose feelings they avowed the most cordial sympathy. The chief democratical clubs of England, were then *the revolution club*; *the society for constitutional information, both in London; and the London corresponding society affiliated with divers places through the kingdom.* The address of the first to the national convention, the shortest of the three, restricted its applause to the 10th of August; augured happiness from the establishment of a republic on the downfall of monarchy; repeated the opinions of the late Dr. Price; to refresh the memory of revolutionists concerning the treatment of dethroned kings, alluded to the history of Charles I.; and expressed their hopes that peace and constant alliance should be established between Britain and the French republic. The address of the society for *constitutional information* approved of the deposition of the king; expressed hopes that the *same doctrines would be received, and the same example generally followed in other countries.* Having declared their sentiments in the most pompous phraseology, they accompanied their eloquence with a donation of shoes *; but the most explicit of the

accompany their commendations with a gift of shoes.

* The conveyance of these shoes was entrusted to Mr. John Frost attorney, who having attained notoriety by professional atchievements, had become a very zealous reformer.

addresses

1792.

The correfponding fociety by its fecretary Thomas Hardy fhoemaker invites the French republic to fraternity with Britain.

addreffes was the production of the London Correfponding Society, and its affiliated friends; which praifing the fucceffive and various proceedings of the French republicans, reprobated the policy and conftitution of Britain*. This addrefs fubfcribed by Thomas Hardy fhoemaker, and Maurice Margarot knife-grinder, ftated divers and manifold bleffings which Britons might attain by following the counfels of the faid Thomas Hardy fhoemaker, Maurice Margarot knife-grinder, and other politicians equally enlightened, inftead of being guided by thofe who had fo long governed Britain: the fentiments of the correfponding fociety devoted openly to the caufe of mankind, exifted, they were convinced, in the hearts of all the free men of England; they enjoyed by anticipation and with a common hope, that epoch (not far diftant), when the interefts of Europe and of mankind, fhould invite the two nations to ftretch out the hand of fraternity. The convention received the addreffes with very great fatisfaction, and ftrongly expreffed their expectations of a fimilar change in England, and their confident hopes, that they fpeedily would have an opportunity of congratulating their correfponding friends, on a national convention eftablifhed in England: the convention conferred the honour of citizenfhip on various individuals belonging to other countries, and fome of the departments chofe for their reprefentatives fuch Englifhmen as they conceived proper delegates for expreffing their doctrines and fentiments. Of thefe the moft noted was Thomas Paine, and the moft eminent was Dr.

The convention believes the boafts of fuch reformers, that they fpeak the voice of the Britifh nation.

* See the refpective addreffes Appendix of Otridge's Annual Regifter 1792, pages 70, 72, 73.

Prieftley;

CHAP. XLIX. 1792.

Priestley; this gentleman was so greatly pleased with the two-fold honours conferred on him, by being thus naturalized by the anarchists, and even deemed worthy of a place in their convention, that he wrote letters both to the convention and individual members, manifesting and declaring the warmest approbation of their principles, as displayed in the suppression of monarchy and the privileged orders, and the whole series of revolutionary proceedings: though his age and other circumstances prevented him from accepting a seat himself, he with the greatest thankfulness and joy accepted it for his son. The convention flattered with the approbation of one whom they conceived to be as great in political philosophy, as he really was in physical, ordered his letter to be transcribed into their records, as a testimony of the applause bestowed by foreign illumination on their powerful efforts for the destruction of establishments; they charged their president to inform their panegyrists that they would with pleasure receive any reflections which he, from the stores of his wisdom, might transmit to an assembly whose sentiments coincided with his own. With these testimonies of approbation from British democrats, the convention fancied, as indeed did many of the democrats themselves, that the voice of the British nation was in their favour, and that Joseph Priestley dissenting minister, Thomas Hardy dissenting shoemaker, Thomas Paine cashiered exciseman and deist, Maurice Margarot knife-grinder and deist, in conveying their own praises of the destruction of rank, property, and monarchy, including the massacres

This belief influences their political conduct.

of

of August and September, echoed the feelings of all free Britons, and that they might soon expect through the British people, the co-operation of the British force. Pleased with attestations, of which they so much over-rated the value, the convention proceeded in a series of measures no less conformable to their own sentiments, than those of their panegyrists. Their operations were directed principally to two objects, plunder and regicide.

The first head comprehended the farther extension of confiscation, and also the convertibility of the objects thus seized into gold and silver; which they found much more current than the assignats. The second consisted of resolutions, decrees, charges, and witnesses, which they were preparing, that in the eyes of their deluded votaries they might give some colour of legality to the murder of their king.

Schemes of the convention for procuring the property of other countries.

In order to accumulate gold and silver, they saw other countries might be rendered extremely productive; for that purpose it was deemed expedient to combine fraud with robbery. Agents were sent to London, Amsterdam, Madrid, and other opulent cities, with orders to negociate bills on Paris, payable in assignats. Those bills being discounted in foreign countries, the value in specie was remitted to France: when they became due, they were paid according to the course of exchange; but before this could be converted into cash, assassins were hired to patrole the streets, and threaten all those who sold gold and silver *; thus

* The gold and silver were sold by porters in the streets, some of whom sold for their own account, but most of them for monied men, who did not appear. See Playfair's History of Jacobinism.

the

CHAP. XLIX. 1792.

the payers were either obliged to take their paper money or a much leſs ſum in coin than that which had been remitted from the diſcount; and by every operation of this kind the quantity of ſpecie of France was increaſed. In managing this traffic, the jacobins, proceeding with their uſual energy and rapidity, rendered it extremely extenſive and productive, before merchants and their bill-brokers diſcovered its hurtful reſult, and before political cauſes put an end to the neutrality through which it was effected. The convention, with much eaſe, amaſſed immenſe quantities of gold and ſilver, both into the public treaſury, and into the private coffers of the leaders. The other chief object, the murder of the king, they purſued with the moſt iniquitous vigour and perſeverance.

Progreſs of the duke of Brunſwick.

Meanwhile, the Pruſſian army advanced on the left towards Thionville, and the Auſtrian army on the right through Luxemburgh, in order to join it on the confines of France. The Auſtrian general reduced Longvy: the armies, after their junction, captured Verdun, and beſieged Thionville. The French executive government diſplayed great vigour and judgment in its exertions and diſpoſitions for reſiſting and repelling the invaſion. The frontier fortreſſes, which, not without probable reaſon, they deemed purpoſely neglected by the royal officers, they ſtrengthened as well as time and circumſtances would permit, but truſted their principal defence to more inland poſts. Dumourier being appointed general, undertook to defend the paſſes between Lorrain and Champaign, with a force much inferior to the German hoſt. Roland, miniſter for the home department, iſſued a

proclamation

CHAP. XLIX. 1792.

proclamation for carrying off provision and forage, cutting down trees, and forming abbatis to impede the march of the enemy. Leaving the sieges to detachments, the combined troops advanced towards Champaign, and found that the people, far from co-operating, were unanimous and zealous in annoying the invaders. Sickness and want of provisions began to pervade the combined armies: still, however, they persevered in advancing. They found Dumourier posted at St. Menehoud, a strong defile in Champaign. They attacked his front division, but were repulsed. A negociation was opened on the 22d of September, between Dumourier and the king of Prussia, but news arriving of the abolition of monarchy, it was broken off. Dumourier now received daily reinforcements. The duke of Brunswick and the king of Prussia perceiving the strength of the enemy before them, and knowing every thing behind them was hostile, fearing to be hemmed in, proposed to retreat. The Austrian general deprecated this movement, but as his command was only subordinate, he was obliged to comply. On the 30th of September these denouncers of conquest were compelled to measure back their steps; and, on their rout, being annoyed by the French army, lost numbers of their men, and a great part of their baggage. Abandoning their conquests, by the 18th of October they completely evacuated France. Thus ended the confederate invasion, which excited great hopes, poured out splendid promises and imperious threats, but performed nothing. It was soon found to have materially injured the cause of the allies: the flight of the enemy, after such boasts, operating on the susceptibility of the

He enters France, and advances towards Champaign.

Dumourier, the French general, occupies a strong position.

The Duke of Brunswick retreats.

Elation of the French.

CHAP. XLIX. 1792.

the French character, elevated their spirits, and turned the military energy which defence had excited to offence and invasion. It was speedily resolved to enter Belgium. Dumourier made rapid and effective preparations in provisions, artillery, and troops elated with recent success. In the beginning of November he entered the Austrian Netherlands; on the fifth of the month attacked the Austrian army in its camp at Jemappe, gained a complete and decisive victory. He successively reduced the various cities of Flanders and Brabant; before the middle of the month was master of Brussels; and in less than another month had totally subdued the Austrian Netherlands, except Luxemburg. General Custine having invaded Germany, captured the cities of Worms, Spires, and Mentz; subjugated all the country between the Rhine and the Moselle, except Coblentz; crossing the Rhine, he also reduced Frankfort.

Dumourier enters the Netherlands, defeats his enemy at Jemappe, and reduces the country.

These rapid acquisitions operating upon the volatile minds of the French, inspired them immediately with the desire of unbounded conquest. They became as eager to sacrifice the rights and properties of other nations to their ambition and rapacity, as they were to seize the rights and properties of their fellow-subjects. They resolved to preserve or annul treaties, without regard to national faith or to justice, as best suited the boundless advancement of their power. Such being their end, their means were at once simple and comprehensive: with their own immense force, to employ in their service the disaffection, caprice, and folly of individuals and bodies in other countries. The susceptibility so often remarked in the French character, appeared in credulity,

The French propose to conquer and revolutionize all neighbouring states.

dulity, or the ready admiſſion of aſſertions and allegations, as well as in ſympathic acceſſibility to ſentiments and doctrines. A deſire of indefinite change had gone abroad through the world; and prevalent as this paſſion really was, the French both conceived and believed it to be univerſal. In Germany and the Netherlands, where it was actually frequent, they ſuppoſed it paramount and irreſiſtible, from hatred to arbitrary power and oppreſſion; in England they apprehended it to be equally dominant, as an emanation from the national ſpirit of liberty. The praiſes beſtowed by eminent ſtateſmen on their efforts to overthrow deſpotiſm, they conſtrued into an unqualified approbation of their levelling ſyſtem. Hearing of the rapid diſſemination of the work of Paine, they imputed the reception of theſe new theories to a deſire of applying them to practice. The addreſſes which they received from obſcure clubs, they, on the authority of the addreſſers, believed to ſpeak the voice of the Britiſh people. The three laſt panegyrics of the reforming ſocieties more ſpecifically expreſſing a deſire of copying the example of France, ſtrengthened their aſſurance of Britiſh ſympathy. The laſt and ſtrongeſt of theſe baniſhed all doubts that Britain deſired to fraternize with France, in eſtabliſhing democracy, and levelling ranks and diſtinctions. So little proportion is there often found in political hiſtory between the importance of inſtruments and effects, that a great ſcheme of French policy, directly hoſtile to all eſtabliſhed governments, and one of the chief cauſes which involved Britain in a continental war, is to be traced to the ignorant vanity of the meaneſt mechanics, ſeeking importance

 out

CHAP. XLIX. 1792.

out of their respective spheres. Believing that Thomas Hardy a shoe-maker, and other worthies of equal political consequence, represented the people of Great Britain, and that the people of other nations concurred to encourage and stimulate subversion of establishment, on the 19th of November 1792, in direct and open contradiction to their former professions, not to interfere in the internal government of other states, the convention passed, by *acclamation*, a decree*, "That the national convention declare, in the name of the French nation, that they will grant fraternity and assistance to all those people who wish to procure liberty; and that they charge the executive power to send orders to their generals to give assistance to such people as have suffered, or are now suffering, in the cause of liberty." This decree confirmed a suspicion which had been entertained from their preceding conduct, that the fomentation of sedition and insurrection in foreign countries, was a systematic principle † of the French republic, immediately produced jealousy and caution in neighbouring nations, and determined most of them to prohibit all intercourse with the French revolutionists. The course of French conquests having led Dumourier to the Scheldt, soon manifested their principles of justice. Their first act, after the reduction

Noted decree of November 19th, encouraging foreign nations to revolutionize.

* See Proceedings of the National Convention, November 19th, 1792.

† Most of our readers will probably recollect the noted saying of Brissot, that they must set fire to the four quarters of the globe. I am assured, by a gentleman who was then at Paris, and very intimate with the Girondists, that this was the general language and intent.

of

of the Auſtrian Netherlands, was to open the navigation of the Scheldt, in contravention to the moſt facred treaties, guaranteed by Britain, France herſelf, and the neighbouring powers. As Holland was ſo intimately connected with Britain, their conduct was a peculiar attack upon this country, and ſhewed that they were reſolved to include Britain in a general ſyſtem of aggreſſive hoſtility. With the deſigns of France, ſo inimical to the Engliſh government, a ſpirit of diſaffection and innovation at home powerfully co-operated.

CHAP. XLIX.

1792. The French open the Scheldt, contrary to treaties with Britain.

Effects in Britain from French doctrines and proceedings.

During the receſs of 1792, the public ferment greatly increaſed in this country. The efforts of the revolutionary emiſſaries became more ſtrenuous in London, and in the other great cities of England. Government had been ſo completely overturned in France, and the poſſeſſion of power and property had been ſo entirely attained by the revolutionary banditti, that their courage and audacity were beyond all bounds. The retreat of the Duke of Brunſwick; a retreat not diſpleaſing to ſome even of the moderate friends of freedom, to thoſe, at leaſt, who conſidered the good of real liberty more than the phantom that had aſſumed its name in France, greatly emboldened the democratical republicans of England, who admired that phantom. About the capital the approaching downfall of the Britiſh conſtitution became a ſubject of common talk: king, lords, and commons, church and ſtate, were deſcribed as on the eve of diſſolution. The garrulous vanity of ſome of the weak and ignorant members of the democratic ſocieties boaſted of the ſituations they were to attain under the new order which was to be

Anti-conſtitutional ferment during the receſs of 1792.

Engliſh republicans confidently hope for a change.

 ſpeedily

CHAP. XLIX.

1792. Alarm of many friends of the constitution.

ſpeedily eſtabliſhed. From a multiplicity of circumſtances it was evident, that a deſign was formed to overthrow the conſtitution, and that there was great confidence of its ſucceſs. That ſuch proceedings required to be checked, controuled, and puniſhed, could not be denied by any who poſſeſſed juſt notions of the nature of man in his ſocial ſtate: government employed ſuch meaſures as appeared to be the beſt calculated to correct this growing and threatening miſchief. But though the arm of law be ſufficiently ſtrong to reſtrain the open invader of the conſtitution, it was not altogether able to ferret all the ſecret arts of its enemies. It became neceſſary, therefore, to aid the efforts of law by employing their own weapons againſt the adverſaries of our eſtabliſhments. As the approaches were carried on by ſocieties, clubs, and familiar books, ſuited to the meaneſt capacities, it became a public duty to eſtabliſh aſſociations, and prepare literary works, which might oppoſe theſe hoſtile attacks.

Mr. Reeves's aſſociation againſt republicans and levellers,

An aſſociation was accordingly inſtituted in November, by a gentleman of the law named Mr. Reeves, for the avowed purpoſe of protecting liberty and property againſt republicans and levellers. The framer's addreſs, ſtating with great perſpicuity and force the multiplied and pernicious efforts of enemies to our laws and conſtitution, and calling on all loyal and patriotic men to unite in the defence of every thing that could be dear to Britons, made a very deep and rapid impreſſion, and ſpread a general alarm.

is very generally joined, and gives an important turn to public opinion.

Aſſociations for preſerving the conſtitution multiplied in every part of the kingdom, and were joined by far the greater number of reſpectable Britons. Theſe

aſſociations

associations had a most powerful effect in counteracting the seditious societies; they recalled the well-meaning but misguided votaries of innovation, to the recollection of the blessings that were ascertained by experience, diffused a spirit of constitutional loyalty through the country, and brought back the stream of popular opinion into the old and useful channel. Mr. Reeves's exhortations to patriotic and loyal union were accompanied with books explaining the hurtful effects of the Gallic changes; and though some of these, in reprobating levelling democracy, may have urged to the contrary extreme, yet the main operation was highly salutary *: the whole measure prevented or recovered great numbers of Britons from Jacobinism, which was then the impending danger; and its certain consequence, if allowed to flourish, the subversion of the British constitution. Before public opinion had received so salutary a bias, the seditious practices had, in various parts, produced such disorders as to render the interference of the executive government necessary. The king availed himself of his legal power to embody the militia, and to convene the parliament before the time to which it had been prorogued, and to call on the representative wisdom of the people for counsel and aid at so

The king embodies the militia; and, at such a crisis, summons parliament before the appointed time.

* For instance, *A Letter from Thomas Bull to his Brother John*, though it employed some of the exploded sentiments and phraseology of tory bigotry, yet taught the common people the mischiefs of innovating speculations; and that their respectability and happiness depended not upon political theories, but on their practical performance of their professional, moral, and religious duties.

momentous

CHAP. XLIX. 1792. momentous a crifis. At this eventful period fome of the moft diftinguifhed fupporters of oppofition, deeming the prefent a feafon of alarm and danger when all party fpirit fhould fubfide, when all party contentions fhould ceafe, and when all men of all parties fhould unite to fupport the conftitutional government of the country, confidered our external as well as internal enemies to be of a fpecies which never yet had been encountered; and that no weapon could fo effectually oppofe their diabolical defigns as an unanimous and determined fpirit of refiftance: they therefore fupported the prefent meafures of adminiftration.

CHAP. L.

Meeting of parliament.—The king states his reasons for this extraordinary convocation.—The chief subjects of consideration the progress of Jacobinical principles.—The greater number of peers and commoners conceive there is a design to revolutionize Britain.—A small but able band think this alarm unfounded.—Conduct of France comes before parliament.—Peace the interest and wish of Britain, if it could be preserved with security.—Commercial policy of the minister, and unprecedented prosperity of the country.—The British government observed a strict neutrality during the hostilities between France and Germany.—Communication between Lord Grenville and the French ambassador in summer 1792.—On the deposition of the king of the French, our sovereign orders his ambassador to leave Paris.—This order a necessary consequence of our king's determination of neutrality.—Careful avoidance of interference in the internal affairs of France.—Application of the emperor and king of Naples to his Britannic majesty to refuse shelter to murderers.—Strict adherence to neutrality by Britain.—Aggressions on the part of France.—Chauvelin opens an explanatory negociation.—Maret, the French secretary, comes to London to confer with Mr. Pitt.—Maret justifies, on revolutionary principles, the opening of the Scheldt, though contrary to the established law of nations.—Mr. Chauvelin supports the same doctrine in his correspondence with Lord Grenville—professes the decree of November 19th not intended against Britain.—Reply of the British minister.—He declares Britain will not suffer France to annul at pleasure the established law of nations.—Britain requires France to forego her projects of invading and revolutionizing other countries.—Alien bill—is passed into a law.—Augmentation of the army and navy.—Proceedings

ceedings at Paris.—Gironde party—their literary ability, boundless ambition, and wild projects.—The Mountain bloodthirsty and ferocious.—Robespierre, Danton, and Marat.—The Girondists desire to spare the king's life.—The mountain and the mob desire regicide.—Pusillanimity of Brissot and the other Girondists.—A decree is passed for bringing the king to trial.—Attempts to break the spirit of Louis—trial—not the smallest proof of guilt.—Complicated iniquity of the process in principle, substance, and mode.—Self-possession and magnanimity of the persecuted monarch.—Sentence.—Last interview of Louis with his family.—Execution—an awful monument of the doctrines and sentiments that governed France.—Chauvelin demands from the British minister the recognition of the French republic—and the admission of its ambassador.—The British government refuses a recognition which would be an interference in the internal affairs of France.—Chauvelin remonstrates against the alien bill and the preparations of Britain—on the massacre of Louis ordered to leave the country.—France declares war against Britain and Holland.—Review of the conduct of both parties.—Opinions of Messrs. Burke, Fox, and Pitt respectively, on the French revolution—the justice and policy of a war.—Messrs. Burke and Pitt support the war on different grounds.—Mr. Pitt proposes the security of Britain—Mr. Burke the restoration of monarchy in France.—Violent party censures.—Impartial history finds in the conduct of neither just grounds for their reciprocal reproach.—Public opinion favourable to war with France.—In declaring war against France our king spoke the voice of a great majority of his people.

CHAP. L.

1792. Meeting of parliament. The king states his reasons for

ON the 13th of December parliament was assembled; and the king stated his various reasons for his present measures. Notwithstanding the strict neutrality which he had uniformly observed in the war now raging on the continent, he could not, without

without concern, obſerve the ſtrong indications of an intention in the French to excite diſturbances in other countries; to purſue views of conqueſt and aggrandizement inconſiſtent with the balance of Europe; to diſregard the rights of neutral powers; and to adopt towards his allies the States General meaſures neither conformable to the public law, nor to the poſitive articles of exiſting treaties. He had, therefore, found it neceſſary to make ſome augmentation of his army and navy: theſe exertions were demanded by the preſent ſtate of affairs, to maintain internal tranquillity, and render a temperate and firm conduct effectual for preſerving the bleſſings of peace.

CHAP. L. 1792. this extraordinary convocation

Never did more momentous objects engage the attention of a Britiſh legiſlature than in the preſent ſeſſion of parliament. Its many and complicated ſubjects of deliberation, however, chiefly reſulted from two ſubjects which were interwoven together, the operation of Jacobinical principles, and the advances of French power. Miniſters, ſupported not only by thoſe members who for many years approved of their meaſures, but by moſt of the principal nobility of the old whig intereſt, Mr. Burke, the veteran champion of that party, and many other gentlemen of the houſe of commons, alſo, many members of the North part of the coalition, eſpecially Lord Loughborough, now Chancellor, declared their conviction that a deſign exiſted to revolutionize this country; and that notwithſtanding the precautions which were already employed, ſtill conſtant vigilance, prudence, firmneſs, and energy, was neceſſary to prevent its ſucceſs. It had not hitherto,

Chief ſubjects of deliberation the progreſs of Jacobinical principles and French power.

The greater number of peers and commoners conceive there is a deſign to revolutionize Britain.

CHAP. L. 1792.

they admitted, produced such overt acts as to afford grounds for judicial process; but had discovered, and even manifested, such objects and tendencies as demanded the counteraction of deliberative wisdom. There were intentions and schemes openly avowed, with many more reasonably suspected, for effecting the downfal of the existing establishments; although no specific treasonable plot had been actually brought to light, the evidence for the existence of such projects consisted of conversations, writings, specific proceedings, and general conduct. To repress such views and attempts, preventive and prospective measures were proposed, and not retrospective or penal.

A small but able band think this alarm unfounded.

A small but very able band, headed by Mr. Fox, ridiculed and reprobated this apprehension; they said it was a mere chimera, like the Popish plot of Titus Oates; that it sprang from the eloquent misrepresentations of Mr. Burke's invectives against the French revolution, and was supported by ministers to promote an alarm; divide the whigs; oppose the spirit of liberty and the reform of parliament, and facilitate hostility with France. These were the respective positions of the bodies which now differed in Parliament on the subject of internal danger. Mr. Fox and his adherents called for specific instances of conspiracy; and alleged, that since none were produced, the pretended schemes and projects did not exist; that every general imputation must be an aggregate of particular facts, or must be false; that the deduction of probable practice from speculative theories was inconsistent with sound reason and experience, and totally unworthy of a legislature. Must parliament interfere whenever a hot-brained enthusiast writes or speaks nonsense? for the ostensible purposes of ministry, their arguments were futile; but for their real purposes their assertions and actions were well adapted. At the commencement of the session Mr. Pitt was absent, his seat being vacated by his acceptancy of the Cinque Ports. The chief impugner of these arguments of Mr. Fox and his friends was Mr. Burke, who shewing the connection between opinion and conduct, insisted that the strongest preventive policy was necessary to the salvation of Britain.

Conduct of France comes before parliament.

Meanwhile the conduct of France towards this country, with the part which Britain should act in the present emergency, was a subject of anxious concern to the parliament and nation. To a commercial country deriving its prosperity from its industry and arts, cherished by peace, war was an evil to be incurred from no motive but necessity. The extension of commerce, manufactures, and every other source of private wealth and public revenue, though very far from exclusively occupying the official talents of Mr. Pitt, had hitherto been the most constantly prominent objects of his administration.

Peace the interest and wish of Britain, if it could be preserved with security.

Commercial policy of the minister, and unprecedented prosperity of the country.

He had promoted trade by the wisest and most efficacious means, removal of restraint, and reciprocation of profit. His exertions had been eminently successful where legislative or ministerial effort was necessary, and when no political interference was wanted, the national capital, enterprize, and skill, nourished by freedom, and secured by peace, had done the rest. The prosperity of the country

CHAP. L.

1792.

The British government observed a strict neutrality during the hostilities between France and Germany.

country was beyond the precedent of any former time, and was evidently more abundant from the advantages of neutrality in the midst of surrounding war. The British government was fully aware of the blessings of peace, and the British sovereign had uniformly adhered to the strictest neutrality, and also to a rigid forbearance from any interference in the internal affairs of France. As soon as the king of France had announced to Britain the commencement of a war between the German powers and his dominions, the court of London issued a proclamation, enjoining his majesty's subjects to receive no commission from any enemy of the French king; and in no way to act hostilely to him or his people, under the severest penalties*. His majesty's subjects observed these injunctions, and no complaint of aggression was alleged either by the French king or nation.

Communications between lord Grenville and the French ambassador in summer, 1792.

Chauvelin, the French ambassador, applied to the British secretary on the 24th of May, stating, that the proclamation published a few days before against seditious writings, contained expressions which might, contrary to the intentions of the British ministry, encourage an idea that France was considered as inimical to the internal tranquillity of England, and requested his application might be communicated to parliament. Lord Grenville's reply represented that Mr. Chauvelin had deviated (he was convinced unintentionally) from the rules of this kingdom, in applying to the British minister to communicate to parliament any subject of diplomatic discussion; but assured the

* See Debrett's State Papers, 25th May, 1792.

French

French minister of the cordiality of the British sovereign. Chauvelin acknowledged his mistake, and expressed his satisfaction at the assurances of amity which the British minister's answers had conveyed. On the 18th of June Mr. Chauvelin delivered a note, stating that by the proceedings of the German potentates, the balance of Europe, the independence of the different powers, the general peace, every consideration which at all times has fixed the attention of the English government, was at once exposed and threatened; and inviting his Britannic majesty, for the general security, to interfere with his mediation. His majesty adhering rigidly to the neutrality, replied, that consistently with his impartial determination, he could not propose an intervention when not solicited by both parties.* On the 11th of July 1792, a small fleet sailed from Portsmouth, under the command of admiral lord Hood, to perform naval evolutions in the channel. The whole squadron consisted only of five ships of the line, besides frigates and sloops: it had but a fortnight's provision on board, and had manifestly no other destination than a sea review. The matter, however, was so magnified in France, and was represented in such a false light, that on the 26th of July, an immediate armament of thirty ships of the line was proposed in the national assembly, and the marine committee was ordered to draw up a report on the subject, and present it within a few

* See the series of correspondence between Lord Grenville and Mr. Chauvelin, in Debrett's state papers, from May 24, to July 8th, 1792.

days.

CHAP. L.

1792.

days*. But Mr. Chauvelin having enquired into the object and circumstances of this squadron, was satisfied that its purpose was not hostile; and the French government and nation were convinced that Britain had no design of taking any part with their enemies†. His Britannic majesty being informed of the suspension of the king's executive power by the decree of the 10th of August, directed his secretary of state||, Mr. Dundas, to write to lord Gower the British ambassador at Paris, that the exercise of the executive power having been withdrawn from his Christian majesty, the credentials of the ambassador were no longer valid, and that he should return to England. This order his majesty deemed a necessary consequence from his determination of neutrality‡; because the continuance of his representative at Paris, treating as the sovereign power that party which had overturned the constitution recently established, would have been an interference in the internal affairs of France, by an acknowledgement of the republican party, in preference to the loyalists and constitutionalists. Our king, conformably to the same cautious and discriminating policy, which would not pledge to the one side his virtual support, repeated his decla-

On the deposition of the king of the French, our sovereign orders his ambassador to leave Paris.

This order a necessary consequence of our determination of neutrality.

Careful avoidance of interference in the internal affairs of France.

* See the Moniteur, 28th July, 1792.

† See Moniteurs of July 1792, and Marsh's History of the Politics of Great Britain and France, chapter 8.

|| Lord Grenville happening to be out of town when this intelligence arrived, that part of his official business was performed by his colleague.

‡ The reader will see the arguments on this subject minutely and accurately detailed in Marsh's history of the politics of Great Britain and France.

rations,

rations, that he would not ſupport the other, or in any way interfere in the internal arrangements of France*. Lord Gower having communicated his royal maſter's orders, and the reaſons wherein they were founded, to Mr. Le Brun, miniſter for foreign affairs, he expreſſed the regret of the executive council that the ambaſſador was to be withdrawn, but its ſatisfaction at his majeſty's continued aſſurance of neutrality, and determination not to interfere in the internal affairs of France†. In the month of September, the emperor and king of Naples ſtated to his Britannic majeſty their apprehenſions, that the atrocities of Paris would extend to the lives of the royal family, and expreſſed their hopes, that ſhould ſuch a nefarious crime be committed, his majeſty would grant no aſylum to the perpetrators‡. With a requeſt ſo conformable to juſtice, humanity, a ſenſe of moral obligation, and an abhorrence of enormous wickedneſs, the king complied, and induced his allies the States General to form the ſame reſolution. Here there was certainly no deviation from neutrality, no interference in the conſtitution of the French polity, unleſs a declared purpoſe to refuſe ſhelter to a party that ſhall commit an atrocious murder, be an interference in that party's private concerns. When the theatre of advancing conqueſt approached ſo near the united Netherlands, the king declared his reſolution to ad-

Application of the emperor and king of Naples to his Britannic majeſty to refuſe ſhelter to murderers.

* See Debrett's ſtate papers, 17th Auguſt, 1792.

† Briſſot and his party deemed the recall of the ambaſſador a hoſtile ſtep; but admitted there had been none before. See Marſh, chap. ix.

‡ Debrett's ſtate papers, September 20th.

here

CHAP. L.

1792. Strict adherence to neutrality by Britain.

here to their mutual alliance, and at the same time expressed his conviction that the belligerent parties would not violate the neutrality of the States General. From the time of the deposition of the king, Chauvelin could not properly be considered as ambassador from the monarch of France. Nevertheless the British government not only permitted him to reside in London, but even negociated with him when he was agent for the executive council; and lord Grenville assured him "that outward forms would be no hindrance to his Britannic majesty, whenever the question related to explanations, which might be satisfactory and advantageous to both parties;" and Mr. Pitt declared to the same gentleman, that it was his desire to avoid a war, and to receive a proof of the same sentiments from the French ministry *. MR. PITT AND HIS COADJUTORS WERE UNIFORMLY CONSISTENT IN MAINTAINING ONE PRINCIPLE, THAT THE INTERNAL CHANGES OF FRANCE DID NOT PRECLUDE AMITY WITH ENGLAND; and therein totally differed from Mr. Burke and his followers. No communications material to the question of aggression passed between Mr. Chauvelin and the British minister, until the decree of the 19th of November, the invasion of the rights of our allies, and the rapid advances of French conquest, aroused and alarmed Britain. There had

Aggression on the part of France.

* These declarations of our two ministers are acknowledged by Brissot, in his report to the convention of the 12th of January 1793; and in the official revolutionary journal, the Moniteur of 15th January, 1793.

hitherto

1792.

hitherto been strict neutrality, as we have seen, on the part of England, while there had been aggression on the part of France; for that aggression satisfaction was due, and the French professed to wish a pacific adjustment. Chauvelin was instructed to open an explanatory negociation, conformable to those professions. Ostensibly to promote this purpose, Mr. Maret, now foreign minister of France, came himself to England, to confer with Mr. Pitt. In the uniform spirit of neutrality which Britain observed, his majesty avoided discussing the diplomatic capacity of the ministers who were sent by the executive council of France; because an admission of their official character would import the admission of the executorial competency of their employers; would have been a declaration in favour of a party, and consequently an interference in the internal arrangements of France. Mr. Pitt therefore did not meet Mr. Maret as the minister of England the minister of France; however they did meet, and their conversation, as detailed from Mr. Maret's communication*, shewed on the one hand, that MR. PITT EARNESTLY DESIRED TO PRESERVE PEACE WITH FRANCE; and on the other, that the French agent endeavoured to explain the obnoxious decree as not intended to apply to Britain. On the subject of the Scheldt, Maret stated that the order of the council, and the decree of the national convention concerning that navigation, founded on the most sacred principles of

Aggression on the part of France. Chauvelin opens an explanatory negociation. Maret, the French secretary comes to London, to confer with Mr. Pitt.

Maret justifies on revolutionary principles the opening of the Scheldt,

* By Mr. Miles, in a work entitled *Authentic correspondence*. Mr. Miles was the intimate and confidential friend of Mr. Maret.

CHAP. L. 1792.

though contrary to the established law of nations.

Gallic liberty, were irrevocable, and thus admitted that the internal change in France was by its votaries considered as authorizing them to violate the rights of foreign and independent nations; and that they were resolved to make no satisfaction for an injury inflicted, in conformity to this principle*.

Mr. Chauvelin supports the same doctrine in his correspondence with Lord Grenville,

The same questions were agitated with much greater particularity of detail, and reciprocation of argument, between Monsieur Chauvelin and Lord Grenville, in the latter end of November, and during the month of December. Chauvelin maintained the right of the French to open the navigation of the Scheldt: he however declared, by order of the executive council, that if at the end of the war the Belgians were unfettered, and in full possession of their liberty relinquished this navigation, the French would decline all opposition. This answer evinced a firm and unalterable resolution of adhering not only to the infraction of the treaty of Utrecht, but also of dismembering the Netherlands from the Austrian dominions, and making them dependent on France; he obstinately

and professes the decree of 19th Nov. not intended against Britain.

contended that the decree of the 19th of November could have no reference to Great Britain, and declared that if Holland continued to observe neutrality, France would not invade her dominions. These professions the British minister would not believe, because they were totally contradicted by actual conduct. Concerning the decree of the convention, the application of these principles to the British

* See Maret's letter to his colleague. Debrett's state papers, 2d December, 1792.

king's

king's commiſſions was unequivocally ſhewn, by the public reception given to the promoters of ſedition in this country, and by the ſpeeches made to them preciſely at the time of this decree, and ſince on ſeveral different occaſions. At the very time France declared ſhe would not invade Holland, ſhe had already attacked that nation by opening the Scheldt.

Reply of the Britiſh miniſter.

France, (ſaid the Britiſh miniſter) can have no right to annul the ſtipulations relative to the Scheldt, unleſs ſhe have alſo the right to ſet aſide equally all the other treaties, between all the powers of Europe, and all the other rights of England, or of her allies. She can even have no pretence to interfere in the queſtion of opening the Scheldt, unleſs ſhe were the ſovereign of the Low Countries, or had the right to dictate laws to all Europe.

He declares Britain will not ſuffer France to annul at pleaſure the eſtabliſhed law of nations.

England will never conſent that France ſhall arrogate the power of annulling at her pleaſure, and under the pretence of a pretended natural right, of which ſhe makes herſelf the only judge, the political ſyſtem of Europe, eſtabliſhed by ſolemn treaties, and guaranteed by the conſent of all the powers. This government, adhering to the maxims which it has followed for more than a century, will alſo never ſee with indifference that France ſhall make herſelf, either directly or indirectly, ſovereign of the Low Countries, or general arbitreſs of the rights and liberties of Europe.

Britain requires France to forego her projects of invading and revolutionising other countries.

If France is really deſirous of maintaining friendſhip and peace with England, ſhe muſt ſhew herſelf diſpoſed to renounce her views of aggreſſion and aggrandiſement, and to confine herſelf within her own territory, without inſulting other governments, diſturbing their tranquillity, and violating

CHAP. L. 1792. violating their rights*; but the French government positively refused to satisfy Britain for the violation of treaties†.

In the consideration of peace or war with the French republic, the proceedings of the French rulers, the negociation between their agents and British ministers, and the conduct of our executive and legislative government, are so much interwoven, that it is frequently necessary to change the scene to review their process of action and re-action, and exhibit cause and effect. Before we follow this negociation to its close, it is necessary to present to our readers, both internal legislative proceedings, and foreign acts, by which the negociation was affected. The great objects of alarm, both to the British government, and to the principal part of the British nation, were the rapid advances of French principles, and the rapid progress of French power. The number of aliens at this time in Britain, far surpassed the usual influx. Of these, many so conducted themselves as to justify a suspicion of their evil intentions towards this country. Agreeably to the system of preventive policy already recorded, the attorney general proposed to parliament to provide for the public tranquillity by subjecting the resort and residence of aliens to certain regulations. All foreigners arriving in the kingdom were, by the plan of ministers, to explain their reasons for coming into this country, to give up all arms except those commonly

Alien bill,

* See correspondence between Lord Grenville and Mr. Chauvelin, in December 1792. State papers for that period.

† See Chauvelin's note to Lord Grenville, Dec. 27th.

used for defence or dress. In their several removals through the country, they were to use passports, by which their actual residence, or occasional movements might be manifest, and their conduct easily observed. Those who received eleemosynary support, were to be distributed in districts where they would be more liable to the vigilance of the civil power. Particular attention was to be paid to foreigners who had visited this kingdom within the present year, who should hereafter come without obvious reasons, and be thus more obnoxious to prudent suspicion. Such were the objects and chief provisions of the law known by the name of the *alien bill.* Those members of both houses who had denied the existence of the dangerous doctrines, consistently with their opinions, opposed a measure, which upon their hypothesis was certainly not necessary. Admitting, however, that there was external danger from abroad, they unanimously agreed to ministerial motions for the augmentation of the army and navy.

Is passed into a law.

Augmentation of the army and navy.

While the British legislature was making these dispositions against internal and foreign danger, an event took place in France, the flagrant injustice and ferocious cruelty of which most fatally manifested the pitch of infuriate wickedness at which the Jacobins were arrived. The republicans now consisted of two parties, the Girondists and the Mountain. The former contained the principal part of the literary class, ingenious, and eloquent enemies of monarchy; the latter, the most daring and bloodthirsty directors of the murderous mobs, the votaries of anarchy. Though men of genius, the leaders

Proceedings at Paris.

CHAP. L.

1792. Gironde party:

of the Gironde were much more brilliant than solid *. Formed to the metaphysical theories long so prevalent in France, they carried their visionary abstractions to practical life. To subtle paradox and ingenious hypothesis, which are commonly the effusions of literary retirement, many of them joined profligate corruption and rapacity, that would grasp all the wealth and power which stimulate injustice in the active world, with an excessive vanity, which represented all the objects of their cupidity as within the reach of their invention and enterprize.

their literary ability, boundless ambition, and wild projects.

This wildness of speculative sciolism, this depravity of principle and pursuit, and this overweening self-estimation dictated their internal and external politics; impelled them to seek a republic not suitable to the human character; in which levelling others, they might themselves enjoy boundless riches and unlimited sway; and to fancy that their talents and address could employ both the weakness and strength of various parties, in their own and other countries as instruments for the execution of their designs. To extend the circle of their proposed dominion, and also that pre-eminence which Frenchmen have always sought, they formed their boundless schemes of national aggrandizement †; of embroiling mankind in war; subjugating all countries by French principles and French power, and thus subjecting the

* The chief philosophical scholar among them was Condorcet. Brissot was animated, enthusiastic, and operative, but by no means profound.

† See Brissot's works passim; also the writings of other Girondists.

the whole to themſelves; new as theſe men were in ſome part of the compoſition of their characters, yet in others as old as vanity, avarice, and profligacy, they tranſcended every bound of morality or religion. Poſſeſſing great energy they in a conſiderable degree attained, and for a ſhort time preſerved the objects of their deſire; but wanting profound wiſdom, and over-rating their own talents of managing tools, they ultimately fell by the inſtruments of their exaltation. As the great operators in the ſeveral changes of the revolution were the Pariſian rabble, the demagogues who could moſt readily and effectually direct the mob, poſſeſſed a formidable power either inſtrumental or ſupreme according to the ability and ſkill of its poſſeſſors. The members of the legiſlature, moſt ferociouſly violent againſt the king, were the Mountain. Theſe, leſs literary in their acquirements, leſs metaphyſical in their harangues, exhibited in their manners a coarſeneſs which the others, educated as gentlemen, had not been able completely to attain, and were much more popular among the governing ſanſculottes. The head of this party was Robeſpierre, a man much inferior to the Girondiſts in cultivated underſtanding, poliſhed eloquence, and thoſe talents which would have had weight with an ingenious and refined audience; but by the uncouth plainneſs of his ſpeeches, and the energy of his invectives, he was well fitted to govern a mob at any time; and by his ſtern and ſanguinary diſpoſition peculiarly ſuited to the Pariſian mob, panting for regicide. Next in power was Danton, equally blood-thirſty and ambitious, leſs ſtrong and direct in his means, but more dexterous. Subordinate

The Mountain blood-thirſty and ferocious.

Robeſpierre, Danton, and Marat.

CHAP. I. 1792.

to these was Marat; a half-lettered editor of a newspaper, hideous in appearance, loathsome by disease*, and squalid in attire; he was passionately desirous of reducing all eminence and distinction to the same low level with himself; and long the hireling of Orleans, he imbibed against the king that rancorous gall which he had been paid for disseminating through the populace. Bloody in his disposition, ardent in his cruel exhortations; he was the delight of the murderous mob, because in so many points coinciding with themselves. By these leaders chiefly, assisted by many others of the Mountain members, the Parisian rabble was directed. The Gironde party saw the character of these demagogues, but in their eager efforts to subdue the constitutionalists, and overthrow kingly power, had co-operated with the Mountain; intending, and for a considerable time appearing, to use them as tools. The insurrection of the 10th of August was the work of the Girondists for the subversion of monarchy: Danton was a most powerful auxiliary in the massacres of that bloody day. So effectually instrumental to the execution of the Girondist designs, the mob, and the leaders of the Mountain, more sensibly felt their own resistless power. The Gironde party were totally unrestrained by conscience from seeking their ends through means however wicked; yet they do not appear to have had a desire of shedding blood merely for pleasure. Blood they would not spare where they conceived it to answer their purpose; the butchery of their fellow-creatures, however, they did not seek as a *pas-*

* See Adolphus's Memoirs. Life of Marat.

time.

time. Not so the sansculottes, who manifestly sought massacre for its own sake *. Before the beginning of September the power of the Mountain was very greatly increased. Marat and his associates, under Danton and Robespierre, were the ringleaders in the September carnage. Brissot had formed the plan of a national convention, and a republic: the leaders of the Mountain were contriving that the republic, which they had been instrumental in creating should be directed by themselves, and that the national convention should contain a majority of their creatures. When the assembly which he had projected met, Brissot found that the Mountain was becoming very strong. The executive council, however, still consisted of Girondists, and, the army being commanded by officers of that party, they remained formidable. The Gironde party, desirous of establishing democracy, appeared to have had no intention of attacking the life of their sovereign, unless they conceived it to interfere with the preservation of the republic and their own power. From the German retreat, and the subsequent success of the French arms, they entertained no apprehensions of the restoration of monarchy, and wished to save the king's life: the opposite party, not merely murderers from policy, but sanguinary from the infuriate disposition of the multitude, desired the blood of Louis. The jacobin clubs, now leagued with the Mountain, promoted the savage barbarity. Their leaders, es-

The Girondists wish to spare the life of the king.

The Mountain and the mob desire his massacre.

* What but the mere delight in human carnage could have prompted the greater part of the September massacres? See details in Playfair's Jacobinism.

pecially

CHAP. L. 1792.

pecially Robespierre, had formed views of the most unbounded ambition, and conceived that, by involving the people in the guilt of regicide, they would bind them entirely to their system, and overpower their adversaries the Gironde and all other parties. The Girondists, superior as they were in genius and literature to the Mountain, were less daring and intrepid, and besides, had more to dread, as their adversaries were supported by the governing mob*. There were, however, still great numbers throughout the provinces, and even in Paris itself, who ardently desired to spare the blood of their king. By firmness and magnanimity, the Girondists, possessing the executorial functions, might have rallied round the metropolis a sufficient force for saving innocent blood; but they did not display the courage of resolute determination, without which lawless ambition will not retain newly usurped power. The proceedings were pusillanimous half measures, more contemptible in their inefficacy than the diabolical conduct of their adversaries; and though less detestable in their operation, equally noxious in the result. The Mountain persuaded the populace that Louis had betrayed his country, and conspired against France with its enemies: on these grounds they instigated the mob to demand his trial†. After various preliminary discussions, the Girondists being afraid to express their sentiments, a decree was passed for bringing to trial a personage whose life, by every principle of expediency and policy, ought to have been sacred under any well-regulated constitution; and whose person was inviolable according to the polity existing in France at the

Pusillanimity of Brissot and the other Girondists.

A decree is passed for bringing the king to trial.

* Segur vol. iii. page 6. † Ibid, page 7.

time

time when the acts charged were alleged to have been committed. To prevent the public mind from hearing innocence calling for justice, they suffered not the king to know that his life was sought. From the fidelity of a zealous domestic * Louis of France first learned that a perjured banditti prepared publicly to destroy their monarch's life, which every federate Frenchman had sworn to protect. To break down the soul of their sovereign by accumulated misery, they debarred him from the sight and converse of his wife and children. They hoped that the strength of his benevolent affections, thus deprived of their dearest objects, would crush the faculties of his mind, and would disable him from vindicating his innocence, and exposing the enormity of their blood-thirsty guilt; but their purpose was frustrated. The dreadful situation in which their wickedness had placed him, roused the energies of a mind which manifested itself not unworthy of the descendant of Henry. With every circumstance of degradation that the upstart insolence of unmerited power could bestow, he was brought to the bar, and his charges were read. They consisted of two general heads; first, of crimes committed before his acceptance of the constitution; secondly, of crimes committed after his acceptance of the constitution. The evidence was composed of interrogatories put to the accused himself, and of documents charged to have been written with his privity and concurrence. The charges before his acceptance of the constitution he successively an-

Attempts to break the spirit of Louis.

Trial.

* See Clery.

swered,

CHAP. L. 1793.

swered, by declaring what every hearer well knew, that the power then vested in him authorized the several acts, and consequently could now be no subject of question: the accusations for conduct subsequent to the acceptance he either shewed to be agreeable to his constitutional powers, or denied to be such as were represented. In every particular case he protested he had acted according to the best of his judgment for the good of his subjects. The allegation of conspiracy with the enemies of his country he firmly denied. The written evidence on which he was accused contained neither proof nor grounds for probable presumption that he was culpable, much less guilty: the assertions rested upon no evidence *. When the charge for the prosecution was finished, the king applied for permission to be allowed counsel. Various emigrants †, informed of the charges, proffered exculpatory testimony: Louis's judges would hear no evidence but on one side: the accusation was totally unsupported by proof. His defence was conducted, first by himself, with great magnanimity and ability, and afterwards by his counsel. It was glaringly manifest, that his accusers had totally failed in making out their case; that there was not a shadow of foundation to justify an arraignment, much less evidence

Not the slightest proof of guilt.

* For the proof of this assertion we refer to the reports of the trial.

† Lally Tollendal, Bertrand, Narbon, Caza'es, and Bouillé, offered, at the risk of their lives, to go to Paris, and bear testimony to the falsity of the principal charges against the king, wherein they respectively were said to have been agents. Otridge's Annual Register, 1793.

5 to

to authorize a penal sentence, even against the meanest subject. Before judgment was passed, it was proposed to appeal to the people. The national convention, it was said, was not a tribunal of judges, but an assembly of lawgivers; and in assuming a judicial power they were usurpers. The people, their constituents, had not delegated to the national convention the power of trying causes. This objection, though unanswerably valid, had no weight with men determined to commit murder: for the appeal there were two hundred and eighty-three, against it four hundred and twenty-four. It being resolved by such a majority that the king should suffer punishment, it was strenuously contended by one party that he should be confined, by the other that he should be put to death. In a meeting of seven hundred the bloody verdict was passed by a majority of five! The iniquitous sentence being delivered after midnight, on the 20th of January, it was that day, at two o'clock, announced to the king, that the following day he was to be executed. With unmoved countenance hearing the decree read, he requested permission to see his family. The hardened hearts of his murderers did not refuse him this last boon *. He himself first conveyed to his queen, sister, and children, the agonizing intelligence. During the dismal interview, retaining his firmness, he inculcated on his son the transient nature of sublunary grandeur; called to his mind what his father had been, and then was; bid him trust for happiness to that virtue and religion which no human

Condemnation and sentence.

Self-possession and magnanimity of the persecuted monarch.

Last interview of Louis with his family.

* Clery's Journal, 235.

CHAP. L. 1793.

efforts could efface. Late in the evening his family left him, trusting * to see him the next morning once more. Prepared by conscious innocence, uprightness, and piety, for meeting death, neither guilt nor fear disturbed his rest. He slept soundly † till five o'clock, the hour at which he ordered his faithful valet to awaken him for the last time ‡. His family he now resolved to forbear again pressing to his arms. The bitterness of death the tranquil resignation of the christian regarded with complacency; the bitterness of parting grief the brother, father, and husband could not endure. He sought from religion, in his last hours, that consolation which, in the zenith of power, splendor, and magnificence, as well as in humiliation and captivity, she had never failed to afford. The attendance of a clergyman, a favour refused him ever since his imprisonment in the Temple by his atheistical oppressors, was, at his earnest intreaty, granted him on the day of his massacre. Being now assisted in the external rites, as well as encouraged in the internal sentiments of devotion, and having opened his soul to a priest whose sanctity he revered, he, for a short interval, returned to the concerns of this world; delivered to his faithful servant his last charges and commissions ‖ to be conveyed to

* Clery's Journal, 239. † Ibid. 242. ‡ Ibid.

‖ At seven o'clock (says Clery), the king, coming out of his closet, called to me, and taking me within the recess of the window, said, "You will give this seal to my son, this ring to the queen, and assure her that it is with pain I part with it: this little packet contains the hair of all my family; you will give her that too. Tell the queen, my dear children, and my sister,

to his family and friends. The messengers of murder arrived; and he was conducted from the Temple. When he was ascending the scaffold his executioners seized his hands in order to tie them behind his back: as he was not prepared for this last insult, he appeared disposed to repel it, and his countenance already beamed with indignation. Mr. Edgeworth, his clerical attendant, sensible that resistance would be vain, and might expose the royal sufferer to outrages more violent, intreated his sovereign to submit *. He presented his hands to the ministers of blood: they tied them with so much force as to call forth another remonstrance. He now mounted the scaffold amidst the noise of drums: bound and disfigured as he was, he advanced with a firm step, and requesting the drums to cease, was obeyed. He then, with a steady voice and in a distinct tone, addressed the people to the following purport. "Frenchmen, I die innocent of all the crimes which have been imputed to me; and I forgive my enemies. I implore God, from the bottom of my heart, to pardon them, and not take vengeance on the French nation for the blood about to be shed." As he was proceeding, the inhuman Santerre,

sister, that although I promised to see them this morning, I have resolved to spare them the pangs of so cruel a separation: Tell them how much it costs me to go without receiving their embraces once more!" Clery 249.

* The words of the priest were, "Sire, this added humiliation is another circumstance in which your majesty's sufferings resemble those of that Saviour who will soon be your recompence.

CHAP. L. 1793.

terre *, who presided at the execution, ordered the drums to beat, and the executioners to perform their office. The king's voice was drowned in the noise of drums, and the clamours of the soldiery. As the fatal guillotine descended on his head, the confessor exclaimed, " Son of St. Louis, ascend into heaven !" The bleeding head was exhibited to the populace, some of whom shouted, *Vive la repub-lique!* but the majority appeared to be struck dumb with horror, while the affection of many led them to bathe their handkerchiefs in his blood. That every barbarous insult might be offered to the remains of the murdered prince, the body was conveyed in a cart to the church-yard of St. Madelaine, and thrown into a grave, which was instantly filled with quick-lime, and a guard placed over it till the corpse was consumed.

The execution of Louis XVI. violated every principle of justice, and every rule of law, which affords security to men bound together in society. By the established constitution, and which subsisted during all the time that he had any power to act, his person was inviolable †. By the law of the land he was amenable to no criminal court : the most tyrannical of all decrees only, a law passed after the alleged guilt could subject him to penal enquiry, whatever might have been his crime. But if his person had not been by law inviolable, the assembly which presumed to try him was not a competent court. The national convention, even though admitted to

* Annual Register, 1793. † Chap. xlvii.

be

be the delegates of the people fairly chosen, were not delegates beyond the extent of their commissions: they were chosen by the people as their legislative representatives only. In exercising a judicial power, they were not a lawful tribunal, but a banditti of usurpers *. If the national convention had been a competent court, the charges adduced were principally irrelevant; some of the acts alleged referred to a period in which the constitution had been different, and in which Louis had simply exercised the powers which were then vested in the king: his former conduct they had sanctioned by conferring on him the supreme executive authority by the new constitution. Most of the accusations against him subsequent to his acceptance were constitutional exertions of his prerogative. The charges of corresponding with emigrants and foreign powers for the purpose of overturning the liberties of France, were supported by no authentic evidence. Thus, a personage criminally responsible to no French tribunal, was tried by a set of men that were not a legal court, for charges not criminal by the law of the land, if proved; or charges which, if criminal, were not proved. Condemned and executed in those circumstances, he presented to France an awful monument of the ferocious disposition by which it was now governed. The massacre of Louis demonstrated that liberty, law, and justice, were vanished; and exhibited the prevalence of a system which terror only could maintain.

Complicated iniquity of the process in principle, substance, and mode.

An awful monument of the doctrines and sentiments that governed France.

* This argument was very forcibly and eloquently employed by the constitutionalists and Girondists against the murderous Mountain. See speeches of the convention passim.

CHAP. L.

1793. Chauvelin demands from Britain the recognition of the French republic, and the admission of its ambassador. The British government refuses.

While the French government was preparing this dreadful catastrophe, it instructed its agent at London to demand the virtual recognition of its establishment and authority, in the acceptance of an accredited ambassador. His Britannic majesty, considering the present rulers as only one party, and from the rapid vicissitudes of sway, a temporary and short-lived party, in conformity to his principles of neutrality, would not receive an ambassador, because such admission would have acknowledged as the rulers of France a particular junto; and violated his resolution and promise not to interfere in the internal affairs of France. But though he would not recognize the paramount faction of the day, as the firmly established and permanent rulers of France, yet while these powers did exist, and menaced England with hostility, he did not forbear to repeat his statements of the injuries which he had received, and the satisfaction he demanded; and since that continued to be refused, to prepare the means of enforcing redress. Chauvelin, by the instructions of the executive council, still persisted to refuse satisfaction for their aggressions, demanding the recognition of the republic, and the acceptance of an ambassador. He farther remonstrated against the alien bill, and the naval and military preparations, imputed hostile intentions to England, and notified that if the preparations continued, France would prepare for war. In conformity to the principles and objects of the decree of the 19th of November, he intimated an intention to appeal to the people of England against the government. His Britannic

Chauvelin remonstrates against the alien bill.

Britannic majesty, persevering in his former conduct, declared he would continue his preparations until France should relinquish her ambitious aggression*. On the 24th of January 1793, intelligence arrived in London of the melancholy catastrophe of Louis XVI. His majesty immediately directed a notification to be sent to Mr. Chauvelin, that the character with which he had been invested at the British court, and of which the functions had been so long suspended, being now entirely terminated by the fatal death of his most Christian majesty, he had no longer any public character here. The king, after such an event, could permit his residence here no longer: within eight days he must quit the kingdom, but every attention should be paid him that was due to the character of the ambassador of his most Christian majesty, which he had exercised at this court. A negociation was still open on the frontiers of Holland, between Lord Aukland and General Dumouriez, but the French persisted in refusing to relinquish their invasion of our allies, and in demanding the recognition of the republic; which requisitions being totally inadmissible, matters were not accommodated. The French rulers, finding Britain inflexibly determined on adherence to the rights of independent nations, by a decree of the convention, declared war against Great Britain with acclamations, and soon after against Holland, which their

CHAP. L. 1793.

On the massacre of the king he is ordered to leave Britain.

France declares war against Britain and Holland.

* See series of correspondence between Mr. Chauvelin and Lord Grenville. Debrett's state papers of 27th December 1792, to 27th January 1793, both inclusive.

forces

CHAP. L. 1793.

forces were ready to invade. Britain and Holland, in their own defence, returned a declaration of hostilities; and thus commenced the war between Great Britain and the French republic.

France the aggressor.

The hostile advances of France, and the refused satisfaction for an aggression totally inconsistent with the law of nations, and existing treaties upon rights which we were bound to protect, combined with their attempts to excite insurrection in our own country, and followed by their declaration of war, render it evident that the French were the aggressors, and that Britain had a just RIGHT to go to war. The EXPEDIENCY of that measure, however, is a different question, and perhaps few subjects have occurred in political history, which have produced stronger arguments on both sides; in which men of the most patriotic hearts, and wisest heads, drew more opposite conclusions, according to the light in which they viewed this immense and complicated subject. Never was there a question in which candour, founded on cool and comprehensive reflection, examining the mass of evidence and reasoning on both sides, would more readily allow laudable and meritorious motives to total diversity of opinion and conduct. Yet never did there occur a contest in which party zeal generated more illiberal constructions, and more malignant interpretation of intentions.

Opinions and sentiments of different parties.

The sentiments of Britons on the subject of the French revolution, may be divided into two classes; those who wished the establishment in England of a system resembling the French republic, to the utter subversion of the British constitution; and those who,

who, varying in their plans and measures, desired the preservation of the British constitution. Most of the British democrats and jacobins were inimical to a war with France, because it interrupted the communication by which they expected to establish their favourite system; but some of them were said to have rejoiced at the hostilities, because they conceived war would excite such discontent as would lead to a revolution. But far was opposition to the war from being confined to democrats, jacobins, and the enemies of our polity. Of those who disapproved of hostilities, many, in the general tenor of their conduct, evinced themselves the firm friends of constitutional liberty, and monarchy. They sought the same ends, the preservation of the British constitution, and the maintenance of British security, but deemed them attainable by peace instead of war. The friends of the British constitution, both without and within parliament, for and against the war, in a great measure took the tone of opinions advanced and maintained by three of the highest parliamentary characters; Edmund Burke, Charles James Fox, and William Pitt. Burke continued to deem the French revolutionists, of every opinion, kind, and succession, the determined and inveterate enemies of religion, virtue, civilization, manners, rank, order, property, throughout the world; and eagerly and resolutely bent on disseminating disorder, vice, and misery; to regard them as pursuing these ends, not only in the ardent violence of infuriate passion, but also in the principled and systematic constancy of depraved, but energetic and powerful reason. He reckoned them totally incor-

Views of Messrs. Burke, Fox, and Pitt respectively on the French revolution, and the war with France.

 rigible

CHAP. L.

1793. Messrs. Burke and Pitt support the war on different grounds.

rigible by any internal means; and therefore strenuously inculcated an external force to overwhelm an assemblage of beings, who, in his estimation, unless conquered, would destroy and devastate mankind. Long before* the commencement of hostilities between France and Germany, he had suggested a confederation of the European powers for the subjugation of men whom he thought revolutionary monsters; and had uniformly written and spoken to the same purport. He eagerly promoted war, not merely for the purpose of procuring satisfaction for a specific aggression, which, in both plain and figurative language, he described as comparatively insignificant, but for the restoration in France of the hierarchy, aristocracy, and monarchy, the downfal of which, was, he thought, the cause of French ambition and encroachment, menacing the destruction of all Europe. Mr. Burke desired war with the French revolutionists, to overthrow the new system, and to crush the new principles. Mr. Fox continuing to impute the increasing outrages of the new votaries of liberty to glowing enthusiasm, still conceived that the enthusiasm would subside if left to its own operation. External force, he predicted, would not only preserve, but increase the vehement heat, which might otherwise cool. The recent experience of the effects of the German invasion, confirmed him in this opinion. He thought that an attempt to force the establishment of monarchy, would drive France to become a military democracy: the project was unwise, because it was

* See his posthumous works, memorial written in autumn, 1791.

impracticable

impracticable in its object, as well as pernicious in its means. Criminal, Mr. Fox said, as the French republicans were in their various confiscations and massacres, and in the murder of their king, their acts were no crimes against England; if the French nation choose to abolish existing orders, and to annihilate monarchy, they were not invading the rights of England; such a purpose of going to war was totally unjust; our efforts would spill the blood of our brave countrymen, would overwhelm us with additional debts; we might wage war year after year against France, as against America; we should make no progress, we should in the end be obliged to conclude a peace, recognizing the form of government which should then be established in France. The aggressions alleged against the French were too inconsiderable to justify war as a prudent measure, and if these were the sole causes of contest, they might be easily compromised, were Britain in earnest. We ought to receive an ambassador from the ruling powers of France, because they were the ruling powers *. With all foreign nations we considered neither the history of the establishment, nor the justice of the tenure, but the simple fact that the government with which we treated was established; such also was the conduct of other nations respecting England; France, Spain, and other monarchies, negociated with Cromwell; England ought now to pursue the same course: we ought to treat with those who possessed the power of doing what we wanted, as for the same reasons we frequently negociated with Algiers, Turkey, and Mo-

* See speeches of Mr. Fox on war with France, in January and February 1793. Parliamentary Debates.

 rocco,

CHAP. L. 1793.

rocco, however much we reprobated their respective governments. Mr. Pitt was far from coinciding* with Mr. Burke, in proposing to carry on a war for the restoration of the monarchical government. France had manifested schemes of unbounded aggrandizement, actually invaded our allies, and declared her resolution to encourage revolt in other countries. By the reciprocal action and reaction of her principles and power, she sought the unlimited extension of both. Attacking us in such a disposition, and with such views, she compelled us to go to war for the repression of principles, and the reduction of power endangering our security. We ought not to recognize a government consisting merely of a faction, and not having the marks of probable stability, in the cool and deliberate approbation of the people. From a party so uncertain and changeable, we did not choose to receive a regular ambassador, as if it were firmly fixed in the supreme power; but we did treat with the existing government. The source of war was not our refusal to treat, as many believed, or pretended to believe, but the refusal of the French leaders to make satisfaction for injuries and insults. Not the restoration of monarchy in France, but the security of Britain, being our reason for going to war, we should carry on hostilities no longer than

* See Mr. Burke's two memorials, written respectively in November 1792, and October 1793, published in his posthumous works; and also his regicide peace, wherein he severely censures the objects of the allies, and the little confidence they reposed in the emigrants.

we

1793.

The objects both of the ministerial party and opposition in parliament constitutional, though sought under different impressions, and by different means.

we were in danger from the conduct and dispositions of France. As the republicans and democrats in opposing the war, coincided with Messrs. Fox, Erskine, Sheridan, and other able men who were inimical to hostilities, on patriotic and constitutional grounds, many of the other party classed them, and more affected to class them, with democrats and jacobins. As on the other hand, the votaries of war were presumed, by its opponents, to seek the re-establishment of despotism in France, they were called crusaders against liberty. On the one side party zeal represented Messrs. Burke and Pitt, and their respective adherents, as the abettors of tyranny; on the other, Mr. Fox and his adherents as the abettors of jacobinism and anarchy. Impartial history, viewing the individual acts and chain of conduct of these three illustrious men, finds no grounds to justify so injurious an opinion; but the strongest reasons for concluding that they and their supporters and adherents, through different means, sought the same end, the constitutional welfare of their country.

Public opinion favourable to war with France.

Many as were averse to war, both on the constitutional grounds of Mr. Fox, and on the unconstitutional grounds of democrats and jacobins, that great engine of politics in a free country, public opinion, was on the whole favourable to hostilities. A sense of the actual aggression of the French republic; but much more the alarming apprehension of French principles, rendered the country desirous of a total interruption of communication with France. It was not the war of the court, of the ministers,

CHAP. L.

1793. In declaring war against France, the king spoke the voice of the nation.

ministers, of the privileged orders; it was A WAR OF THE GREAT MAJORITY OF THE PEOPLE OF BRITAIN. IN DECLARING WAR AGAINST FRANCE IN FEBRUARY 1793, HIS BRITANNIC MAJESTY SPOKE THE VOICE OF THE BRITISH NATION.

CHAP. LI.

Objects of Britain—the repression of French principles, and the prevention of French aggrandizement.—Sir John Scott the attorney general introduces a bill for preventing traitorous correspondence— arguments for and against—modified, passes into a law.—Motion for peace.—Reasonings of Mr. Fox respecting the war and its probable effects.—The propositions are negatived by unprecedented majorities.—Mr. Sheridan proposes an enquiry into the alleged sedition.—His motion rejected.—Motion for parliamentary reform by Mr. Grey—arguments for.—Mr. Whitbread.—Arguments against.—Proposition reprobated as peculiarly unseasonable at such a period—and rejected.—State of commercial credit, and causes of its being affected.—Mr. Pitt proposes an advance of public money on the security of mercantile commodities.—The proposition is adopted, and revives mercantile credit.—East India company's charter on the eve of expiration.—Mr. Dundas presents a masterly view of the prosperity of India under the present system.—He proposes the renewal of the charter.—His plan is passed into a law.—Measures adopted to render British India farther productive.—Plan of agricultural improvement.—Sir John Sinclair—enquiries of in Scotland and England.—Result that agriculture is not understood and practiced in proportion to the capability of the country—proposes the establishment of a board of agriculture—the proposal adopted.—Lord Rawdon's motion respecting debtors.—Increase of the army and navy.—National supplies.—A loan.—Taxes.—Session closes.—Commencement of campaign 1793.—French invade Holland—reduce Breda.—Hundart and Gertruydenburgh surrender.—Dumouriez besieges Williamstadt and Maestreight.—The British forces arrive in Holland.—The French raise the siege of Williamstadt.—Attacked by the Austrians at Winden

Winden—defeated.—French generals accuse each other.—Dumouriez evacuates the Netherlands—disapproved by the convention—privately proposes to make peace with the allies and restore monarchy—suspected by the French government—summoned to return to Paris to answer for his conduct—sounds the dispositions of the army—finding them unfavourable, deserts to the Austrians.

CHAP. LI.

1793.

Objects of Great Britain—the repression of French principles and the prevention of French aggrandizement.

THE grand purposes of the British government in its conduct respecting France were to repress the operation of revolutionary principles in this country, and to prevent the French system of aggression and aggrandizement from being longer carried into successful execution on the continent. In this two-fold object originated the measures of external policy adopted by parliament during the remainder of the session, and also some of those that were confined to internal regulation.

Sir John Scott, the attorney-general, introduces a bill for preventing traitorous correspondence.

War having been declared against a foreign country, it was obviously expedient to prevent correspondence between British subjects and the hostile party. To render this prohibition effectual, Sir John Scott, attorney-general, on the 15th of March introduced a bill for preventing, during the war, all traitorous correspondence with the king's enemies. The law of treason was founded upon a statute of the 25th of Edward III. which had been the subject of legislative exposition in different laws, enacted since that period. The acts declared treasonable in that statute were principally reducible to two heads *; to compass, that is, to intend or project the king's death; to levy war against the king, and

* See vol. iii. 232.

to

to abet or assist his enemies. Since that period, during wars, parliament had repeatedly passed laws which applied the general principle to the existing case; by specifically prohibiting adherence or assistance to nations at enmity with our sovereign *. Agreeably to the original statute, and the consequent explanatory acts the present bill was framed. Former laws had, in such circumstances, prohibited British subjects from sending military stores, arms, ammunition, and provision, of various enumerated kinds. The present bill, besides interdicting these articles, prohibited purchases of French funds or French lands. The reason of this prohibition was, that, as the French government proposed to carry on war against this country by the sale of lands, British subjects, if allowed to purchase such land would not only feel an interest in the property which they had thus acquired, but furnish the enemy with the means of carrying on war against ourselves. It was further proposed that no persons should be allowed to go from this country into France, without a licence under his majesty's great seal; and that their neglect of this clause should be deemed a misdemeanour; and that no persons, though subjects of this country, coming from France, should be allowed to enter this kingdom without a passport or licence,

Arguments for and against.

* An act had passed in the reign of Queen Anne, to prevent all traitorous correspondence, which prohibited any person from supplying the enemies with arms, naval or military stores, or from going out of the kingdom to the enemy's country without licence. A similar act of William and Mary had carried the regulation farther; it prohibited goods and merchandizes of every sort. See Statutes at large.

CHAP. LI. 1793. licence, or giving to a magiſtrate ſuch ſecurity as he ſhould require. The laſt regulation was to prevent the inſurance of veſſels which ſhould traffic with France.

The bill was oppoſed as inconſiſtent with the treaſon laws of Edward III. the principles of the Britiſh conſtitution, with juſtice and commercial policy. The proviſion againſt Engliſhmen returning to the country, was the beſtowal of a power on the king to baniſh, during the war, every Britiſh ſubject now in France. Though he might return, in certain caſes, by giving ſecurity, who were to be the judges of the amount of that ſecurity? This was to be left to a magiſtrate: here one man was to be put under the diſcretion of another, who might render his return impoſſible, by exacting ſecurity to an amount that could not be given *. The reſtriction upon the purchaſe of lands was repreſented as extremely impolitic: it was alleged to be founded upon an abſurd ſuppoſition, that Britons having here the moſt permanent ſecurity for their money, would ſend their capital to France, where they could have no ſecurity. Frenchmen, on the other hand, found property expoſed to the revolutionary graſp in their own country; and, to eſcape ſpoliation, had ſent many and large ſums of money to Britain to be veſted in our funds, and alſo great quantities of other precious moveables: as proſcription advanced they muſt wiſh to ſend more to the place of ſafety. If the preſent regulation were adopted, France

* See ſpeeches of Meſſrs. Erſkine and Fox. Parliamentary Debates, 1793.

would

would no doubt follow the example: we ſhould render her government the moſt eſſential ſervice, by forcing Frenchmen to employ their money in their own funds. Inſtead, therefore, of preventing, as propoſed, the efflux of money to the country of our enemies, we would prevent its influx into our own; and by the project of withholding reſources from the enemy, we ſhould add to his ſtrength. The bill was defended as conformable both to the general law, and to ſpecial acts paſſed in periods of war. The particular proviſions moſt ſtrongly combatted were ſupported as neceſſary in the preciſe and ſpecific nature of the preſent war; the circumſtances in which it was founded, and the projected reſources of the enemy. After many debates, the two clauſes moſt ſeverely reprobated, concerning the return of Britiſh ſubjects, and the purchaſe of property in France, were abandoned. Undergoing theſe important changes, and ſeveral much leſs material modifications, the propoſed bill was paſſed into a law.

Modified, it paſſes into a law.

Motions for peace.

Repeated motions were made in the houſes of parliament in order to procure peace. Of theſe the moſt important was a propoſition of Mr. Fox, after the firſt ſucceſſes of the allies, and the retreat of the French armies from the Netherlands *. Intelligence having arrived, that the French, leaving the ſcenes of recent invaſion and aggreſſion, had retired within their ancient frontiers; Mr. Fox, profeſſing to con-

* The hiſtorical narrative of theſe events is ſomewhat ſubſequent: I here only mention a reſult on which Mr. Fox founded part of his reaſoning.

ſider

CHAP. LI. 1793.

Reasonings of Mr. Fox on the inexpediency of the war, and predicting its effects.

sider the avowed objects of the war as now attained, proposed an enquiry into the reason of its continuance; and moved an address to his majesty praying him to make peace. Supposing, for the sake of argument, the present a just, prudent, and necessary war at the beginning, he contended that the alleged reasons no longer existed. Holland, our ally, was not now exposed to any attack: France would willingly purchase peace by insuring the continuance of that safety, whereas he was afraid perseverance in carrying on war along with the combined powers, would again expose her to danger. The French had, no doubt, manifested designs of aggrandizement, but these had arisen from the successful repulsion of confederate attack. Besides, must England go to war with every continental power that perpetrates injustice? Was not the conduct of the partitioners of Poland equal in infamy and iniquity to the aggressions of France? Were the people of England to suffer all the miseries of war because the people of France were unjust, when that injustice, be it ever so atrocious, was violating no right of Englishmen? They had, indeed threatened the security of his majesty's allies; but now confined within their own territories, they were occupied in defending their frontiers against the combined powers. The danger apprehended from their former conquest was no longer a subject of just uneasiness and alarm. The French were, at present, in great internal confusion and distress; and Britain could form no views of aggrandizement from the situation of her adversary. Even were justice and humanity out of the question, would policy

licy and prudence authorize this country to seize the possessions of France? What advantage could we derive from promoting the conquering and encroaching plans of other powers? Having driven France from the territories of her neighbours, for what purpose were we to persevere in a war, unless to invade her dominions? If we did make an inroad into her territories, could such a movement be to attain our professed objects, security and defence? By continuing the war we should manifest an intention of either dismembering her empire, or interfering with the government which her people chose to establish. These objects our government had uniformly disavowed, and the declared ends of hostilities had been compassed. The most favourable season for offering peace was in the midst of success; when the enemy were sufficiently humbled to feel the evils of war, without being driven, by the haughtiness of the conquerors, to desperate efforts, which might turn the tide of victory. Those, who calculated probable exertions of men fighting for conceived liberty and independence by the usual course of military events, fundamentally erred in expecting similar effects from totally dissimilar causes. Inspired by such animating motives, men had, in all ages and countries, displayed valour, prowess, and policy, astonishing to the rest of mankind. Pressed by continued and invading war, which excited such motives, the ardent spirit and inventive genius of the French would, Mr. Fox predicted, no less exert themselves; WE SHOULD DRIVE THEM TO BECOME A MILITARY REPUBLIC. Let us therefore endeavour, while opportunity

CHAP. LI. 1793.

was favourable, to procure an honourable and secure peace. To this a common objection is, with whom shall we treat? The answer is obvious: with any men who possess the power of doing what we want: the French are desirous of peace, and the present rulers are as competent to conclude peace as to carry on war. Shall we be at peace with none whose form of government we shall not have previously approved? We have formerly made peace with tyrants; not because we approved their maxims and constitution of government, but because they had the power of making and observing conventions. Peace with any ruler or rulers implies approbation of their character no more than of their government. The French republicans have been guilty of cruelty and atrocious murders; so was Louis XIV. No British statesman refused to treat with the bigotted banisher of his most valuable subjects, nor with the sanguinary devastator of unoffending provinces. The statesman treats not with the virtue * but with the power of another party; and in expecting performance, looks for his best security, not in the integrity but the interest of the contractor. These were the arguments by which Mr. Fox inculcated the restoration of peace; and this was the strain of reasoning which he and other votaries of amity employed repeatedly at various stages of the contest †.

Messrs. Pitt and Burke oppose Mr. Fox on different grounds.

In opposing the address, Messrs. Burke and Pitt argued conformably to the different views which they had respectively adopted concerning the French

* Parliamentary Debates, 17th June, 1793.

† See also his Letter to the electors of Westminster.

revolution

revolution and the war. Mr. Pitt persevered in urging the impracticability of any treaty with the persons that at present exercised the government of France; and in supporting his position, exhibited a very eloquent view of their individual and collective atrocities: therefore he would not treat with them *now*. Reprobating the French principles as manifested in their present operation, he still disavowed every design of forcible interference in the internal government of France: he sought only security. This security was to be effected in one of three modes: first, by obtaining an assurance that the principles should no longer predominate; secondly, that those who were now engaged in them should be taught that they were impracticable, and convinced of their own want of power to carry them into execution; or, thirdly, that the issue of the present war should be such as, by weakening their power of attack, should strengthen our power of resistance. Without these we might indeed have an armed truce, a temporary suspension of hostilities, but no permanent peace; no solid security to guard us against the repetition of injury and the renewal of attack. The present situation of affairs not being such, in Mr. Pitt's estimation, as to admit these means of obtaining security, he and his votaries opposed the address for the discontinuance of the war. Mr. Burke clearly and expressly combatted the principle asserted by Mr. Fox, that England had no right to interfere with the internal government of France. If (he said) by the subversion of all law and religion, a nation adopts a malignant spirit to produce anarchy and mischief in other countries, it is the right of all nations to go

CHAP. LI. 1793.

to war with the authors of ſuch attempts. In ſupport of this doctrine he quoted the authority of Vattel, who lays down a poſition, "that if any nation adopt principles maleficent to all government and order, ſuch a nation is to be oppoſed from principles of common ſafety." This was the ſpirit of France; and what was to keep the effects of it from England? War, and nothing elſe: therefore war with the French republic, *on account of her ſyſtem and principles*, Mr. Burke recommended; and explicitly declared his opinion, that while the exiſting ſyſtem continued, peace with France was totally inadmiſſible. The propoſed addreſs to the king was negatived by a majority equally great as that which had voted for the war; and throughout the nation perſeverance in hoſtilities was as generally popular.

The propoſitions are negatived by unprecedented majorities.

Miniſters, and many others who had been formerly inimical to their meaſures, having expreſſed their conviction that there exiſted in the country diſpoſitions and deſigns to ſubvert the conſtitution, and to follow the example of the French innovators, Mr. Sheridan propoſed that an enquiry ſhould be inſtituted into the alleged ſedition. He declared his diſbelief of the miniſterial repreſentations upon any evidence that had been adduced, but avowed himſelf open to proofs, if ſuch ſhould be eſtabliſhed: he therefore propoſed a committee of the whole houſe to inveſtigate the aſſertions, that it might be aſcertained whether there was really a plot againſt the country, or if it was merely a falſe and miſchievous report to impoſe on the credulity of the nation; to attach obloquy to the opponents of adminiſtration,

Mr. Sheridan propoſes an enquiry into the alleged ſedition;

administration, and to facilitate the continuance of the war. In answer to Mr. Sheridan's requisition it was argued, that government had not asserted the existence of plots to be established by proof for judicial animadversion, but of a seditious spirit and operations, which required deliberative precaution and the most vigilant care to prevent them from maturing into plots and insurrections. From a combination of various and disconnected circumstances a man might receive a moral certainty of a general fact which ought to regulate his conduct, though he might have no proof of such a fact * sufficient to establish it before a magistrate. The active circulation of seditious writings, the proceedings and declarations of the innovating societies †; the public and avowed sentiments ‡ of great numbers in favour of the French system as a model for this country, concurred in manifesting the existence of a spirit which it became the legislature and government to repress; and Mr. Sheridan's motion was negatived by a very numerous majority. his motion is rejected.

Great and powerful as the body was which now supported administration in both houses, the small band which in parliament abetted contrary measures was not discouraged from persevering in an opposition which appeared very unlikely to attain any of their objects in parliament; and out of parliament

* Mr. Windham's speech on Mr. Sheridan's motion, 4th March 1793. See Parliamentary Debates.

† Ib. see ib.

‡ Speech of Sir James Sanderson the Lord Mayor. See ib.

CHAP. LI.

1793. Motion by Mr. Grey for parliamentary reform.

was not gratified by that popularity which has so often encouraged and elevated parliamentary minorities. Mr. Grey, agreeably to the intimation which he had given the preceding year in the house, and to the promise which he had made to the friends of the people, proceeded in his resolution to move a reform in parliament. Various petitions were presented to the house from inhabitants of towns, villages, and districts, both in England and Scotland, who joined for that purpose. Of these, some were moderate and respectful, but others wild and violent. One petition, of a very great length, was read from persons calling themselves *friends of the people* *: this representation, repeating the usual arguments, endeavoured to illustrate them by facts and instances†; and earnestly, though temperately, urged a change. Mr. Grey, having presented this petition, seconded its prayer by a proposition of parliamentary reform.

Arguments for.

Besides the usual arguments which, on a subject discussed so often in parliament, must necessarily be

* Not the association of which Mr. Grey was at the head, but a society that appears to have sprung from the addresses of that body.

† A work was published about this time, presenting an abstract of counties and boroughs, especially the latter, asserted to be in the nomination of peers, commoners, and the treasury, and not of the ostensible electors. The alleged result was, that seventy-one peers nominate eighty-eight, influence seventy-five; that the treasury nominate two, influence five; that ninety-one commoners nominate eighty-two, influence fifty-seven; that in England and Wales the whole number of members returned by private patronage amounted to three hundred and nine. See *Report on the state of the representation, published by the society of friends of the people.*

repetitions,

repetitions, and personal animadversions on the affirmed change of Mr. Pitt's conduct, Mr. Grey endeavoured to obviate objections to the seasonableness of the requisition. Forcibly urging the vast mass of influence which, though before known as a general fact, had never been so explicitly demonstrated by particular enumeration, he contended that the greater part of the influence in question was under the controul of ministers; that thence they had been enabled, at different periods of history, to establish systems and execute measures which were totally inconsistent with the country's good. Whatever evils did or might threaten our country, there was no preventive so certain, no safe-guard so powerful, as a pure and uncorrupted house of commons, emanating fairly and freely from the people. The national debt, in its present accumulation, was owing to the corruption of parliament: had a reform in the representation of the people taken place at the conclusion of the peace of 1763, this country would, in all likelihood, have escaped the American war: if it had been accomplished last year, probably it would have saved us from our present distresses. If ever there was danger to be apprehended by this country from the propagation of French principles, the danger was now completely at an end. No set of Britons, without being bereft of their senses, could after recent events propose the French revolution as a model for British imitation. But were such principles ever to threaten danger, the surest way of preventing it from being serious was, by promoting the comfort and happiness of the people *, to gratify their reasonable

* Mr. Grey's speech on reform, 6th May 1793. See Parliamentary Debates.

 wishes,

CHAP. LI. 1793.

Mr. Whitbread.

wishes, and to grant a parliamentary reform, which was so essentially necessary, and so ardently desired: the effectual preventive of violent and forcible alteration was timely reform. This last position was still more warmly urged by Mr. Whitbread. Metaphysical opinions (he said) have never, in any instance, produced a revolution: the engine with which Providence has thought fit to compass those mighty events has been of a different description: the feelings of the governed, rendered desperate by the grinding oppression of their governors. What brought about that great event the reformation? Not the theories or speculations of philosophers, but the impolitic avarice and injustice of the church of Rome. What produced the catastrophe of Charles the first? What produced the revolution in this country? The oppressions of the executive government; and to the same cause America owes her freedom. Lastly, what produced the revolution in France? The misery of the people; the pride, injustice, avarice, and cruelty of the court *. The great characters who acted in these different scenes had but little power in producing their occasions. Luther, Cromwell, or Washington, the illustrious persons who appeared at the æra of the English revolution, or the wild visionaries of France could never have persuaded the people to rise, if they had been unassisted by their own miseries and the usurpations of power. When the feelings of men are roused by injury, then they attempt innovation; then the doc-

* Mr. Whitbread's Speech on reform. See Parliamentary Debates.

trines of enthusiasts find ready access to their minds. This general reasoning was not controverted by the opposers of parliamentary change in the present circumstances. No one pretended to assert that seasonable reform was not better than perseverance in profligate corruption and tyrannical oppression; but the existence of these mischiefs was denied: no evil had been demonstrated that called for such a corrective. The persons associated to petition for a reform in parliament (their opponents said), after a year's consideration, and, as it appears, repeated meetings, do not produce any specific plan whatever; it is therefore reasonable to infer, that they have not been able to ascertain the evil, much less to produce a remedy. The supporters of reform have asserted that the national debt originated in the corruption of parliament; and that a reform would have prevented the many burdensome wars in which this country has been engaged since the revolution. Instead of theory examine fact: all these wars have been agreeable to the people; the proposers and supporters of them spoke in unison with the sentiments of the people. Was not a great majority of the nation favourable to the wars of William and Anne, for humbling the pride and reducing the power of Louis XIV.? Was not the Spanish war of 1739 popular?—undertaken at the express requisition of the people, and even contrary to the known opinion of the government? Consider the war of 1756: was that unpopular? Never was any country engaged in a war more universally popular. The American war was equally approved by public opinion until within a year and a half of its

1793. Arguments against.

CHAP. LI. 1793.

its conclusion: nothing could be more marked than the approbation which the public gave of that measure. No new system of representation could have spoken the voice of the people more plainly and strongly than the house of commons expressed it in approving these wars. That there might be improper influence in elections could not be denied; such influence, however, arose not from the political constitution, but from the imperfections, prejudices, and passions of human nature. If you are to reform, begin with moral reform * : but if political reform be wanted, this certainly is not the time to agitate subjects so likely to inflame the passions of the people, and to excite a public ferment. Though there may be some defects, abide by the constitution rather than hazard a change with all the dreadful train of consequences with which we have seen it attended in a neighbouring kingdom. These arguments made a deep impression, and the proposition of Mr. Grey was rejected by a very great majority, as totally inadmissible in the present state of affairs, opinions, and sentiments.

The proposition is reprobated as peculiarly unseasonable at such a period,

and is rejected.

State of commercial credit, and causes of its being affected.

One of the most important objects of parliamentary consideration during the present session was the state of mercantile credit. A spirit of commercial speculation and enterprize had been for some years increasing in every part of the kingdom, and was now risen to such an height, as to threaten public credit with very serious danger. The circulating specie being by no means sufficient to answer the very greatly augmented demands of trade, the

* The reasoning in the text is in substance taken from the speech of Mr. Jenkinson. See Parliamentary Debates, May 6th, 1793.

quantity

quantity of paper currency which was brought into circulation as a ſupplying medium, was ſo large and diſproportionate, that a ſcarcity of caſh was produced which threatened a general ſtagnation in the commercial world. In conſequence of the diſtreſs and alarm which this ſtagnation had cauſed, Mr. Pitt propoſed that a ſelect committee ſhould be appointed to enquire into facts, and explore their cauſes; and the ſubject being inveſtigated, it was found that the embarraſſments aroſe from the precipitation, and not the inability of Britiſh merchants. The multiplication of paper currency, and ſcarcity of coin, induced banks and bankers to ſuſpend the uſual diſcounts in expectation of which, merchants had formed engagements that were far from exceeding their property, but in the preſent ſtate of pecuniary negotiation, ſurpaſſed their convertible effects. To extricate commercial men from theſe difficulties, Mr. Pitt propoſed that government ſhould advance money on the ſecurity of mercantile commodities, by iſſuing exchequer bills, to be granted to merchants, on the requiſite ſecurity, for a limited time, and bearing legal intereſt. Oppoſition expreſſed their apprehenſions that the propoſed mode would be ineffectual, that the failures aroſe from the preſent ruinous war, and that every remedy but peace would be futile. The projected plan, beſides, would open a path to the moſt dangerous patronage, ſince government could afford or withhold the accommodation according to the political conduct of the applicant. Theſe objections being over-ruled, the bill was paſſed into a law: the temporary embarraſſment was removed; and manufactures and trade again became flouriſhing.

Mr. Pitt propoſes an advance of public money on the ſecurity of mercantile commodities.

The propoſition is adopted, and revives mercantile credit,

Another

CHAP. LI.

1793. East India Company's charter on the eve of expiration.

Another subject, of the highest commercial magnitude, at the same time occupied legislature. The charter of the East India Company being on the eve of expiration, a petition for its renewal was presented to parliament; and on the 23d of April the subject was taken into consideration. The very general reception of Smith's commercial philosophy, especially his doctrine of free trade, and the known admiration in which Mr. Pitt, and many of his coadjutors and votaries held the popular system of political economy, had given rise to expectations and apprehensions that the exclusive privileges of the East India merchants would last no longer than the period which was pledged by the public faith. Many supposed that the commercial monopoly would be for ever destroyed, and that the trade to India would be opened to the whole energy of British enterprize.

Mr. Dundas presents a masterly view of the prosperous state of India under the present system.

To scrutinize this subject was the peculiar department of Mr. Dundas; and though thoroughly acquainted with the views of theoretical economists, that able minister regarded the question as a practical statesman. Without undertaking to controvert the doctrines of speculative writers concerning the productive efficacy of a free trade, or even denying the probability of its profitable effects, if extended to our intercourse with India, he laid down a sound and prudent proposition, that legislators ought not rashly to relinquish a positive good in possession for a probable good in anticipation. The advantages which experience had proved to accrue from the present system were immense, varied, and momentous. The shipping employed by the East India Company amounted to 81,000 tons; the seamen navigating those ships were about seven thousand

ſand men, who had conſtant employment: the raw materials imported from India, for the uſe of the home manufactures, amounted annually to about £700,000. British commodities annually exported to India and China, in the company's ſhips exceeded a million and a half ſterling, including the exports in private trade which were allowed to individuals. The fortunes of individuals annually remitted from India amounted to a million. "The induſtry of Britain thus, (ſaid Mr. Dundas) on the one hand is increaſed by the export of produce and manufactures; and the conſumption of thoſe manufactures enlarged by the number of perſons returning with fortunes from India, or who are ſupported by the trade and revenues of India; and on the other, it is foſtered and encouraged by the import of the raw materials from India, upon which many of our moſt valuable manufactures depend. So that, on the whole, the trade adds between ſix and ſeven millions to the circulation of the country. Such is the benefit accruing from the monopoly of the company, exercised under the controul of the legiſlature. The experience of nine years has juſtified this ſyſtem! British India is in a ſtate of proſperity which it never knew under the moſt wiſe and politic of its ancient ſovereigns. The Britiſh poſſeſſions, compared to thoſe of the neighbouring ſtates in the peninſula, are like a cultivated garden contraſted with the field of the ſluggard*. The revenues of India have been increaſed, and the trade connected with them is in a ſtate of progreſſive improvement. A neceſſary war has been conducted with vigour, and brought to an honourable and advantageous concluſion. A ſyſtem ſo effectually

* See Parliamentary debates, April 23d, 1793.

conducive

CHAP. LI. 1793.

conducive to all its important purposes; the prosperity of Britain, the welfare of India, its internal good government, and security from foreign aggressors, ought still to be supported. The benefits to be derived from a free trade may be still greater; but they must be contingent, whereas the present are certain. Before a change can be digested and executed many great difficulties are to be surmounted. Would it not create an interruption in the discharge or liquidation of the company's debts? Would it not derange the regular progress of their increasing commerce? and would there not be a serious danger, that while these innovations were proceeding, rival European powers might seize the occasion, renew their commercial efforts, and divert into a new channel those streams of commerce which render London the emporium of the Eastern trade? On these principles, illustrated through a vast variety of important detail, he moved that the company's monopoly should be continued, under the present limits, for twenty years. He farther proposed regulations tending to promote a free trade, which should not interfere with the company's charter, and should embrace only such articles as did not employ the capital and enterprize of the East India Company, that should bring this surplus commerce into the ports of London instead of the continent of Europe, to which it had been chiefly diverted *. The most important measure which he proposed for this purpose was, that the company should annually provide

He proposes the renewal of the charter.

* See Sir George Dallas's letter to Sir William Pulteney, in which the origin, history, and nature of this free trade is very ably explained; and the means of making it to centre in British ports is clearly demonstrated.

three

three thousand tons of shipping for conveying to and from India such exports and imports as it did not suit themselves to include in their own commercial adventures, that thus British sailors might be employed in this private trade instead of foreign sailors; and British subjects might be enriched by this employment of British capital instead of aliens. After considerable discussion, the plan of Mr. Dundas was digested into a law; the charter was renewed, and the clauses respecting the promotion of free trade inserted into the act.

This plan is passed into a law.

Measures adopted to render India farther productive.

While commercial arrangements so much occupied the attention of our statesmen and lawgivers, a kindred subject was submitted to their consideration. Agriculture has never occupied a share of legislative attention proportioned to its momentous value as a branch of political economy, since Britain became so eminent for manufactures and commerce. This is an omission the consequences of which have been often fatally experienced from recurring scarcity in a country, by the fertility of its soil and the talents of its people, so adapted for securing plenty. An evil so frequent was naturally the subject of reiterated complaint; but no effectual measures were employed to prevent it from often occurring again. Among the many ardent enquirers into political economy, one of the most active and indefatigable whom an age supremely addicted to such studies has produced, is Sir John Sinclair. This gentleman, of a vigorous and acute understanding, enriched with knowledge and methodized by erudition, had bestowed great industry of research on various branches of political philosophy. He had traced, investigated, and presented to the public, the history of revenue. In the progress of his pursuits, agriculture

Plan of agricultural improvement.

Sir John Sinclair.

CHAP. LI. 1793.

agriculture presented itself to him as an object most deserving of promotion. He saw that very much remained to be done; but before he could set about propositions of improvement, he thought it wisest and most expedient to ascertain the facts; and therefore sought information where useful information was most likely to be found. In Scotland, his native country, he applied himself to the clergy, the best informed of any class of men of fixed rural * residence, and addressed certain queries to the members of that numerous and respectable body. These queries, embracing the physical, moral, religious, and political situation of the respective parishes, in the result of the answers produced an immense body of statistical knowledge; especially on pastoral and agricultural subjects. He afterwards, less systematically and extensively executed, through different means, a similar plan in England. He advanced, however, so far as to ascertain a general fact, of the very highest importance; that though in some particular districts improved methods of cultivating the soil are practised, yet, in the greater part of these kingdoms, the principles of agriculture are not yet sufficiently understood; nor are the implements of husbandry, or the stock of the farmer, brought to that perfection of which they are capable. To promote so desirable a purpose, Sir John Sinclair projected the establishment of a board of agriculture, to be composed of gentlemen perfectly acquainted

Enquiries of in Scotland, and England.

Result, that agriculture is not understood and practised in proportion to the capability of the country—

proposes the establishment of a board of agriculture.

* From the towns also the reports were extremely valuable; but these were not all executed by clergymen. The most important—the account of the city of Edinburgh, came from the pen of Mr. Creech; and with the state of the metropolis, very happily united the progress and variation of national manners.

with

with the ſubject, and conſiderably intereſted in the ſucceſs of the ſcheme, and who ſhould act without any reward or emolument. An addreſs was propoſed to the king, praying him to take into his royal conſideration the advantages that might accrue from ſuch an inſtitution. His majeſty directing the eſtabliſhment of the board; the commons voted the neceſſary ſums for defraying the expences, and the board of agriculture was accordingly eſtabliſhed *.

CHAP. LI. 1793.

The propoſal is adopted.

Certain diſtricts of Scotland, on the coaſt, were moleſted with heavier duties upon coals than other parts of the country. This evil had been often and ſtrongly ſtated in the ſtatiſtical reports; and the duty actually amounted to a prohibition. In the North of Scotland, from the high price of coals, the people were obliged to truſt almoſt entirely to their peat moſſes for a ſupply of fuel. In preparing this article a large portion of the labour of that part of the country was expended, which might be beneficially employed in fiſheries and manufactures, and by this means a great part was loſt to the revenue, which would have ariſen from the induſtry of the inhabitants. For theſe reaſons Mr. Dundas propoſed the repeal of the duties in queſtion; and that the revenue might not ſuffer, he moved certain impoſts upon diſtilled ſpirits, which, enhancing the price of the article, would benefit health and preſerve morals. A petition was preſented by the cities of London and Weſtminſter, praying for a repeal of a duty upon coals: in the reign of queen Anne a tax of three ſhillings per chaldron had been impoſed upon imported coals, and the amount was to be

* See Otridge's Annual Regiſter, 1793, chap. iv.

CHAP. LI. 1793.

applied to the building of fifty-two churches *. The duty afterwards had been employed in the maintenance of the clergymen of those churches; and lastly, was made a part of the consolidated fund; and ministers alleging it was no longer a local tax, prevailed on the house to reject the petition. Among the classes of subjects who applied for relief this season were the catholics of Scotland: the Lord Advocate stated on their behalf, that his majesty's catholic subjects in Scotland were at present incapacitated by law either from holding or transmitting landed property, and were liable to other very severe restrictions, which could not now be justified by any necessity or expediency. He therefore proposed a bill to relieve persons professing the catholic religion from certain penalties and disabilities imposed on them by acts of parliament in Scotland, and particularly by an act of the 8th of King William: the bill being introduced, was, without opposition, passed into a law †.

Law for the relief of Scottish catholics.

Motion of Lord Rawdon for the relief of debtors and satisfaction of creditors.

Lord Rawdon this year presented a bill for the relief of insolvent debtors, and for amending and regulating the practice with regard to imprisonment for debt. The bill was a compound of that humanity and discrimination which has been already noticed in this benevolent and able character. His lordship deemed the law of imprisonment for debt to be founded in principles at once rigorous and absurd: it was rigorous, because it exacted from the

* This was a quite different impost from that of Charles II. of five shillings per chaldron, now enjoyed by the Duke of Richmond.

† Acts of parliament, 33 of Geo. III.

victims

victims of its operation, while doomed to inaction, that which, in the free exercise of their faculties, they were not able to perform; and was absurd, because ineffectual to its avowed purpose; for it was calculated to defeat, not to attain, its object. If the debtor be guilty of a fraud, said his lordship, punish him as a fraudulent agent; if not guilty of a fraud, do not punish insolvency as a crime, which should rather be commiserated as a misfortune: to punish insolvency as criminal, and to doom fraud to the same punishment as mere insolvency, is to confound all moral distinctions. As the law now stands between debtor and creditor, in the very commencement of an action the fundamental principle of justice is violated. What is the great object of the institution of government, but to prevent individuals from being even the judges, far more the avengers, of their own wrong? Yet, by the existing laws of the land, the creditor is enabled to deprive the debtor of his liberty upon a simple swearing to the debt. The proposed bill, however, for the present, did not intend a general change of the law which he reprobated as so severe and unjust: what he now desired, was a modification of arrests and of bail, so as to prevent oppression and distress for inconsiderable sums. The bill was opposed by Lord Thurlow and by others, as striking at the whole system of the law of England; and the Lord Chancellor proposed that it should be referred to the judges to examine the state of the debtor and creditor laws, to consider the subject, and prepare a bill to be introduced early the next session: Lord Rawdon agreeing, it was, for the present, withdrawn.

CHAP. LI.

1793. Increase of the army and navy. National supplies. Loan and taxes.

These were the principal subjects that came before parliament this session, except the supplies. The army and navy were increased to a war establishment, and a considerable body of Hanoverian troops was employed in the service of Britain. Besides the ordinary national funds, a loan of four millions five hundred thousand pounds was required. The high estimation in which the minister stood with the monied capitalists induced the public to expect that the loan would have been negotiated on very favourable terms: but the stagnation of mercantile credit was felt by the minister as well as others who had occasion to borrow money. There was actually a great scarcity of cash, and the public was obliged to pay a premium of eight per cent. For defraying the interest of the loan the provisions were, ten per cent. on assessed taxes; an additional duty upon British spirits, on bills, receipts, and on game licences.

Session closes.

On the 21st of June the session was closed by a speech in which his majesty expressed the highest satisfaction with the firmness, wisdom, and public spirit, which had distinguished the houses during so very important a session, and testified his approbation of the successive measures which they had adopted for the internal repose and tranquillity of the kingdom; for the protection and extension of our commercial interests both at home and in our foreign dependencies, and for their liberal contributions towards those exertions by which only we could attain the great objects of our pursuit, the restoration of peace on terms consistent with our permanent security, and the general tranquillity of

Europe. The signal successes with which the war had begun, and the measures that were concerted with other powers afforded the most favourable prospect of a happy termination to the important contest in which we were engaged *. CHAP. LI. 1793.

Campaign of 1793.

Having brought the parliamentary history of this session to a close, the narrative now proceeds to military transactions, some part of which passed at the same period; including certain events to which allusion has already been necessarily made.

From the disposition of their forces the French were enabled first to commence hostilities; and as soon as war was declared against Great Britain and the States General, Dumouriez proposed to invade the United Provinces. There the democratic party, which, as we have seen, the aristocratical faction had cherished and abetted to co-operate in their enmity to the house of Orange, still subsisted. Though cautious in their proceedings since the re-establishment of the stadtholder, they were increasing in number and force from the Belgian commotions, and still more from the French revolution; especially after the republicans had become masters of the Netherlands. With the disaffected Dutch Dumouriez maintained a close correspondence, carried on chiefly by emigrant Hollanders assembled at Antwerp: these, formed into a kind of Batavian committee, were the channels of communication between the Gallic leaders and the malcontents residing within the united provinces. The malcontents recommended eruption into Zealand, but the general himself thought it more adviseable to ad-

* State Papers, June 21st, 1793.

vance

CHAP. LI. 1793.

vance with a body of troops posted at Mordyck, and masking Breda and Gertruydenberg on the right, and Bergen-op-Zoom, Steenberg, Klundert, and Williamstadt, on the left, to effect a passage over an arm of the sea to Dort, and thus penetrate into the very heart of Holland *. The design was adventurous, but not unlikely to succeed, if executed with such rapidity as to anticipate the arrival of assistance from England. The army which Dumouriez commanded on this occasion consisted of twenty-one battalions, which, including cavalry and light troops, amounted to about thirteen thousand men. He was accompanied by the skilful engineer D'Arcon, who had invented the floating batteries at the siege of Gibraltar, and a considerable number of Dutch emigrants. A proclamation was published, inveighing against the English government and the conduct of the stadtholder, and calling upon the Dutch to assist their democratic brethern in destroying the power of their aristocratic tyrants†. On the 17th of February the French army entered the territories of the States General. Breda being invested surrendered by a capitulation, in which it was stipulated, that the garrison should retain their arms, and continue to fight for their country during the war. On the 26th Klundart opened its gates to the French army; and on the 4th of March, Gertruydenburg having stood a bombardment of three days, surrendered. The same terms were granted to these two fortresses as to Breda. The strength of the captured towns was so great, that military critics, convinced they might have

The French invade Holland. Breda, Klundart, and Gertruydenburg surrender.

* Memoirs of Dumouriez.

† State Papers, February 1793.

resisted

1793. Dumouriez besieges Williamstadt and Maestreicht.

resisted much more effectually, did not hesitate to conclude that their easy submission arose from treachery. Dumouriez now proceeded towards Williamstadt. While he was himself making such progress on the left, General Miranda, advancing on the right, invested Maestreicht with an army of twenty thousand men. Having completed his works, he summoned the garrison to surrender; but the Prince of Hesse, commander of the fortress, refused to capitulate, and avowed his determination to defend such an important post to the last extremity. The French general bombarded as well as cannonaded the town; while, on the other hand, the besieged made two sallies, though without material success. General Miranda continued his investment of Maestreicht; and a covering army of French was encamped at Herve under the command of General Valence. Meanwhile General Clairfait, with the Austrian army, having crossed the Roer, attacked the French posts on the 1st of March, and compelled the army to retreat as far as Alderhaven, with the loss of two thousand men, twelve pieces of cannon, thirteen ammunition waggons, and the military chest: the following day the archduke attacked several French batteries, and took nine pieces of cannon. On the 3d of March the Prince of Saxe Cobourg obtained a signal victory over the French*, and drove them from Aix la Chapelle even to the vicinity of Liege, with the loss of four thousand killed, one thousand six hundred prisoners, and twenty pieces of cannon. In consequence of this

* New Annual Register 1793, p. 159.

CHAP. LI. 1793.

defeat of the covering army general Miranda raised the siege of Maestreicht. Dumouriez, following the career of his successes in the west, laid siege to Williamstadt, and to Bergen-op-zoom*; but the course of his victory was arrested; for now he had a new enemy to encounter in the British army.

The British forces arrive in Holland.

The first object of the British military plans for this campaign was the defence of Holland, and a body of troops was in February sent, consisting of about six thousand British, commanded by the duke of York. A brigade of British guards was thrown into Williamstadt, who animating the Dutch to vigorous defence, and leading their efforts, made so gallant a resistance, that Dumouriez saw that perseverance would be unavailing; he therefore raised the siege, ordered his troops to retire from Bergen-op-zoom, evacuated the towns and forts which had surrendered, and returned to take the command in the eastern Netherlands, where the declining fortunes of the French required the presence of an able general. The Austrians had continued advancing to Brabant; and several skirmishes of posts had taken place, in which the Germans were generally superior. On the morning of the 18th of March, an engagement commenced at Neer Winden, on the confines of Brabant and Liege. General Dumouriez attacked the centre of the imperial army with great vigour, but suffered a repulse; and he yielded to the same superior efforts from the imperial right wing. In the afternoon, however, the French right wing gained some ad-

The French raise the siege of Williamstadt.

They are attacked by the Austrians at Neerwinden, and defeated.

* See Dumouriez's Memoirs.

vantage;

vantage; but the corps de reserve, commanded by general Clairfait, decided the day. The army of Dumouriez retreated for some time in good order, but were at length entirely routed by the Austrian cavalry. The slaughter was great; the French lost four thousand men, and soon after six thousand deserted to the enemy. The French generals, by mutual crimination, endeavoured respectively to remove from themselves the blame of disaster. Dumouriez imputed the defeat to general Miranda, who, he asserted, both fought feebly, and fled unnecessarily. In his memoirs, indeed, he admits that general La Marche committed the first error, by an injudicious movement which threw his troops into confusion; but Miranda is the subject of his principal censure*. Miranda, on the other hand, imputes the discomfiture to treachery on the part of Dumouriez†. But wherever the blame lay, if there was any, the battle of Neer Winden decided the fate of the Belgian Netherlands. The Austrians continued to pursue the republicans; on the 21st, Dumouriez judged it proper to take post nearer Louvain, and on the following day he was attacked by the enemy. The action was bloody, and lasted the whole day; but the Imperialists were compelled to retreat with great loss; the Austrians, however, rapidly advancing in other quarters, the French general judged it expedient to evacuate all his conquests, and re-enter France. Dumouriez thoroughly knew the disposition of the convention; and foreseeing

French generals accuse each other.

Dumouriez evacuates the Netherlands.

* See Dumouriez's Memoirs.

† In a letter to Petion, dated 21st March 1793.

the

CHAP. LI.

1793. He privately proposes to make peace with the allies, and restore monarchy.

the fate which the suspicious republicans prepared for a vanquished general, he resolved to make his peace with the allies, to march with his troops against Paris, there to effect a counter-revolution, and re-establish monarchy. On this subject he conversed with colonel Mack, an Austrian officer of great eminence; and it was agreed that the Imperial troops should act merely as auxiliaries for the attainment of this object; and should remain on the frontiers, unless he wanted their assistance. If Dumouriez should find it impracticable to effect a counter-revolution without the aid of the Austrians, then he should indicate the number and kind of troops of which he should stand in need to execute his design. The Austrian forces to be furnished in that event, should be entirely under the direction of Dumouriez. The executive government suspecting the dispositions of Dumouriez, sent deputies to investigate his conduct. Confident of the assistance of his army, he did not disguise from them his project to annihilate the national convention, and fix a king upon the throne. Informed of his design, the convention sent commissioners to supersede his command, and summoned him to appear at Paris to answer for his conduct. Dumouriez ordered these delegates to be seized, and conveyed to general Clairfait's head quarters, to be kept as hostages for the safety of the royal family. But the army soon shewed the vanity of Dumouriez's expectations; they not only refused to follow him to Paris, but gave him reason to doubt his personal security; and he was compelled to seek safety by flight. Having reached the imperial territories, he had an interview with

He is suspected by the French government, and summoned to return to Paris, to answer for his conduct.

He sounds the disposition of the army; but finding them unfavourable, deserts to the Austrians.

with colonel Mack, and with the prince of Saxe Cobourg. Two proclamations were digested, one by Dumouriez himself, the other by the prince of Saxe Cobourg. The manifesto of General Dumouriez contained a recapitulation of his services to the French republic; a statement of the cruel neglect which his army had experienced in the preceding winter, and of the outrages which were practised by the Jacobins towards the generals of the republic, and particularly himself. It states the reasons why he arrested the commissioners; exhibits a vivid picture of the evils which might be apprehended from the continuance of the anarchical system in France; and expresses his confident expectations, that as soon as the Imperialists entered the territory of France, not as vanquishers, and as wishing to dictate laws, but as generous allies, come to assist in re-establishing the constitution of 1790, great numbers of the French troops would join in promoting so necessary a purpose. He protested upon oath, that his sole design was to re-establish constitutional royalty; and that he and his companions would not lay down their arms until they had succeeded in their enterprize. These protestations, interspersed with a considerable portion of gasconading promises which he could not perform, and threats which he could not execute*, constituted the declaration. A mani-

* In the last paragraph, in which he introduces his oath under the head "*I swear* (he says) that we will not lay down our arms until we shall have succeeded in our enterprize; and our sole design is to re establish the constitution, and constitutional

CHAP. LI. 1793.

A manifesto * was also published by the prince of Saxe Cobourg, announcing that the allied powers were no longer to be considered as principals, but merely as auxiliaries in the war; that they had no other object but to co-operate with general Dumouriez, in giving to France her constitutional king, and the constitution she formed for herself. He pledged himself that he and his army would not enter the French territory to make conquests, but solely for the end now specified. He declared farther, that any strong places which should be put into his hands, should be considered as sacred deposits, to be delivered up as soon as the constitutional government should be established in France, or as soon as general Dumouriez should demand them to

tional royalty; that no resentment, no thirst after vengeance, no ambitious motive, sways our purposes; that no foreign power shall influence our opinions; that wherever anarchy shall cease at the appearance of our arms, and those of the combined armies, we will conduct ourselves as friends and brothers; that wherever we shall meet with resistance, we shall know to select the culpable and spare the peaceable inhabitants, the victims of the infamous wiles of the Jacobins of Paris, from whom have arisen the horrors and calamities of the war;—that we shall in no way dread the poignards of Marat and the Jacobins;—that we will destroy the manufacture of these poignards, as well as that of the scandalous writings by which an attempt is made to pervert the noble and generous character of the French nation;—and finally, in the name of my companions in arms, I repeat the oath, that we will live and die free. The general in chief of the French army, Dumouriez. See State Papers, 1793.

* See State Papers, April 5th, 1793.

be

be ceded. It was at this period that Mr. Fox * and many others thought that the combined powers might have proposed such terms of peace to France, as would have been accepted with equal readiness and gratitude. The allies, it was alleged by the votaries of peace, ought to have declared themselves to the national convention to the following purport. Arrange your internal government according to your own inclinations: the present confederacy is formed for purposes of defence, not of aggression; we shall not therefore interfere in the constitution of France. We only desire you to re-establish the ancient boundaries of the Netherlands, to restore your other conquests; to liberate the queen and the royal family; and to allow the emigrants a moiety of their property: we will then withdraw our forces, and be your friends. Had such propositions been made, these politicians affirmed that a stop might have been immediately put to the effusion of blood; and that France would at this time have been under a regular and established government, and Europe would have been at peace. It is difficult to say with any degree of probability, what would have been the result in a very problematical question, of an experiment that never was tried. The probable success of such an attempt proceeded upon an assumption that either the French were not originally the aggressors; or, if the beginners of the war, were from recent discomfiture tired of its continuance.

Hypothetical reasonings on the practicability and expediency of peace at this period of victory to the confederates.

* It was in consequence of the present posture of affairs, that he made the motion for peace, which has been already mentioned in the parliamentary history.

CHAP. LI. 1793. continuance. Perhaps if the offer had been made, in their present circumstances they might have received it with delight; and for a time have continued pacific; but afterwards might have resumed invasion, when the confederation was broken. But it belongs not to history to state possible, or even probable consequences, which might flow from measures that were not adopted. If as some able statesmen argued, the hour of victory was the hour of offering peace, the confederates against France were of a totally different opinion. They conceived France to have been the aggressor; to have manifested views of ambitious aggrandizement; that it was the policy of her neighbours to prevent her encroachments, and in her present condition to reduce her strength so as effectually to prevent the future accomplishment of her projects; that therefore they ought now to press upon her in her weakened state. On this view they regulated their policy, and formed the plan of the rest of the campaign. A congress was held at Antwerp, wherein representatives attended from the several powers that formed the combination, which had now been joined by Spain and Naples. At this congress were present the prince of Saxe Cobourg, counts Metternich, Starenberg, and Mercy d'Argenteau, with the Prussian, Spanish, and Neapolitan envoys. It was determined that the fortresses on the frontiers of France should be invested by the armies of the confederates, that the enemy's coasts should be beset on every side by the fleets of the maritime powers, and that every encouragement and practicable assistance should be afforded to the royalists

royalists within France*. A second proclamation was now published by the prince of Saxe Cobourg, annulling the first, and declaring a design of keeping whatever places he should capture, for the indemnification of his sovereign. Dumouriez, when he was informed of this change in the Imperial system of military operations, declared to the prince de Cobourg, that he could not with honour serve against France. Receiving a passport, he therefore retired into Germany †.

By the plan of operations concerted for attacking the frontiers of France, the British, Dutch, Austrian, and Prussian troops were to press on to the Netherlands; an army of Prussians and other Germans from the Rhine. Joined to the confederate armies were great bodies of emigrants, commanded by the princes of the blood, and other refugees of high rank and distinction. The chief part of the exiles was attached to the army of the Netherlands; and on all sides dispositions were made for invading the French dominions.

* New Annual Register, 1793.

† He first came over into Britain, but was desired by ministers to quit the kingdom; and in his visit nothing passed of any historical importance. See Annual Register, 1793.

CHAP. LII.

Overtures of the French government for peace with Britain.—Le Brun the minister proposes to send an ambassador to England.—Letters containing his propositions are delivered to Lord Grenville—but receive no answer.—Alarming state of France—at war with all her neighbours.—Intestine war in La Vendee.—The victorious allies invade the French dominions.—Battle at St. Amand between the allies and the French.—The Duke of York and the British troops take a share in the action.—British soldiers supremely excellent in close fight—in spite of French numbers and artillery by the bayonet decide the fate of the day.—Battle of Famars and the defeat of the French.—Blockade and surrender of Conde.—Siege of Valenciennes—strength of the fortress—operations—taken after a siege of six weeks.—Successes on the Reine.—Mentz taken by the Prussian army.—France torn by dissentions.—Mountain excite a clamour against the Brissotines.—Establishment of the revolutionary tribunal.—Brissotines, with distinguished speculative ability, deficient in practical talents.—Mountain superior in decision and daring atrocity.—Brissot, Roland, and their supporters, seized and committed to prison.—Robespierre and his associates become rulers of France.—System of terror reigns.—Constitution of 1793.—Singular absurdity and anarchy.—Committees of public and general safety.—Combination in the South for overthrowing the frightful tyranny.—Toulon puts itself under the protection of Lord Hood and the British fleet.—Comprehensive and efficacious malignity of the governing junto.—Robespierre and his band abolish Christianity—publicly and nationally abjure the Supreme being—proscribe genius, destroy commerce, confiscate remaining property—debase every kind of excellence—attempt to level all civil, political, and moral distinctions.

distinctions.—The pressure of the war facilitates their atrocities.—Forced loans—requisitions.—Bold scheme of the war minister to raise the nation in mass.—Efficacy of this system—confounds all calculations of the allied powers—overcomes the insurgents of La Vendee—forces the British to seek safety by evacuating Toulon.—Netherlands.—Activity and progress of the Duke of York and the British troops.—Victory at Lincennes—invests Dunkirk with reasonable hopes of success.

CHAP. LII.

1793.

Overtures for peace by Le Brun the French minister.

ABOUT the time that Dumouriez engaged in a negotiation with Cobourg for the re-establishment of monarchy, the existing government of France made an attempt to procure the restoration of peace. The proposals were conveyed through a very unusual channel: Le Brun, the French minister, employed Mr. James Matthews, an Englishman of whom he had no knowledge but what Matthews gave himself, to carry to London two letters * addressed to Lord Grenville, and a third to Mr. John Salter, attorney, then a vestry clerk to the parish, since a notary public in Penny's Fields, Poplar, recommended by Matthews, requesting him to deliver the two letters to the British secretary. The purport of the first was, that the French republic desired to terminate all differences with Great Britain, and that he demanded a passport for a person to repair from France to Britain for that purpose. The second mentioned Mr. Maret as the person who was to be deputed, and claimed a safe conduct for him and his necessary attendants. Mr. Salter accepted the commission, as he had probably agreed with Matthews; and on the 26th of April 1793, delivered the two letters to Lord Grenville, at his office, Whitehall.

He proposes to send an ambassador to Britain.

Letters from him are delivered to Lord Grenville,

* Dated at Paris April 2d, 1793, and delivered to lord Grenville 26th April 1793. See State Papers.

CHAP. LII.

1793. but receive no answer.

Whitehall. The letters procured no attention, and produced no effect: they never, like other overtures for negotiation, were the subjects of parliamentary discussion; and the literary notice which they excited was inconsiderable. The partizans of war regarded the uncommonness of the agency as a sufficient reason for overlooking the propositions *. The votaries of peace did not view the advances in that light, but from their general and cursory account, appear to have thought the transaction of little importance †, and are totally unacquainted with the causes and circumstances of a mode of conveyance so different from the established etiquettes of diplomatic communication. The real history of this mission the kind information of Mr. David Williams has enabled me to lay before the reader.

Circumstances and history of these proffers of conciliation.

The literary celebrity of Mr. Williams, and the use which the French reformers had made of his "Letters on political liberty," induced the Girondists to invite him to France, that he might assist them in the formation of a constitution ‡. Brissot, whom he describes as an honest but a weak man, he had known in England, had corresponded with him, and warned him of the danger which he was incurring by his violence. Repairing to Paris, he be-

* See Otridge's Annual Register for 1793; a volume which, having evidently taken a side, I prize less as an authority than any of the other volumes of the same work, which loyally and patriotically supporting our constitution, record and estimate measures with the dignified impartiality of authentic history.

† See Belsham's history, vol. v. p. 47.

‡ See Madame Roland's Appeal, and Public Characters for 1798, page 472.

came intimate with Condorcet, Roland, and other political leaders of the times. He continued to admonish them of the evils which they would encounter, unless they could moderate the licentiousness of the populace, and suppress the faction of the jacobins. He saw the wildness and extravagance of the Girondists themselves, and strongly represented to Brissot the impracticability and madness of rousing and uniting the nation by war. He powerfully inculcated the necessity of peace and moderation, to the welfare of the people, and the security of any constitution which might be formed for that purpose: he particularly recommended the maintenance of peace with England, and strongly reprobated the prosecution and death of the king, as giving the populace a taste of blood. Eager as the Brissotines were for war, yet they were conscious that France was not prepared for hostilities with England: patriotic policy sometimes overcame revolutionary fury, and then they would listen to the pacific counsels of Mr. Williams. When the discussions between Mr. Chauvelin and Lord Greaville were evidently tending to hostility, they asked Mr. Williams to undertake a mission to the British court, in order to effect an accommodation. Regarding such an office as not altogether suitable to a British subject, especially in the fluctuation of sentiment which the French government exhibited on the questions of peace and war, he declined the mission. Still, however, he conceived that peace might be preserved: the same opinion was expressed to him by members of the Girond; and it was with great surprize, on the 1st of February, that he heard the convention declare war by *acclamation* against Britain and Holland. Mr.

 Williams

CHAP. LII. 1793.

Williams now resolved to return to his country: still Le Brun and other members of the French government professed to him their wishes for the restoration of peace; and since he would not himself undertake a mission, that minister asked him to bear a letter to Lord Grenville, which requested the British government to open the ports of Dover and Calais; in the postscript declared the French government to desire the re-establishment of peace, proposed to send a minister, and stated that Mr. Williams was empowered to explain their principle and project of conciliation, so as to be satisfactory to the British government. Mr. Williams returned to Britain, repaired to the secretary of state's office, delivered his letter*, and mentioned his readiness to wait on Lord Grenville whenever his lordship should appoint; but he was never sent for by the secretary, and there his commission ended. Mr. Williams himself appears to me to think that the French were already convinced of their precipitation in declaring war, and would have willingly agreed to the terms which Lord Grenville had required from Chauvelin, if they found the British government equally disposed to return to amity; but as no opportunity was afforded him of an audience from Lord Grenville, neither his statements nor deductions could be of any avail to the purpose of the commission with which he was charged.

Correspondence between Britain and France being now precluded, Le Brun heard nothing from Mr. Williams. While Mr. Williams had been at Paris, there went thither a Mr. James Matthews,

* See State Papers.

who

who professed great regard and veneration for Mr. Williams, was frequently in his company, and had thereby opportunities of knowing the names and persons of some members of the French government, but was not introduced to any of these rulers. The inauspicious commencement of the campaign between France and the allies disappointed the republicans; and the desertion of Dumouriez added treachery as a fresh ground of alarm to the apprehensions that were entertained from the British and Austrians. Perhaps these considerations rendered the French government more anxious for peace, or perhaps they might profess anxiety without being sincere: whatever was the motive, they certainly did repeat the attempt; and this Mr. Matthews was the person, on the mere pretence of being Mr. Williams's confidant, that was appointed to carry the second overtures to England. Why Mr. Le Brun chose Mr. Salter to be the deliverer of the dispatches sent by Mr. Matthews I have not learned, or why Mr. Matthews did not deliver them himself, he not being in a state of mind to answer such questions. Indeed, the whole transaction; Mr. Matthews's application to Le Brun as the confidant of Mr. Williams; the appointment of Mr. Salter, then vestry-clerk of the parish of Poplar, to convey the letters to Grenville; and the assurances of Matthews, who brought the letters, that he should instantly make peace, and provide for all his friends (in which, however, Mr. Williams was not mentioned), can be accounted for only from an incipient derangement of mind, the symptoms of which soon appeared, and for which he has been ever since confined.

CHAP. LII. 1793. confined. Mr. Matthews was chosen to be the bearer, not as an obscure and unconnected individual, but from being conceived by the French government to have the confidence of Mr. Williams. Mr. Williams they had first wished, in their extravagant manner, to be, in effect, an ambassador; and finding he would not accept that general mission, they prevailed on him to be the bearer of specific proposals, which they professed to think conducive to peace. Thence came Mr. Matthews to be employed in the SECOND application which the French government, within the first three months of the war, made for the re-establishment of peace. That the republicans were sincere in these proffers it would be very rash to affirm.. Against their sincerity there were the series of Brissotine menaces of universal warfare; the tendency and character of the revolutionary enthusiasm: for their sincerity there were the actual disappointments which they were experiencing, and the farther disasters which they *then* appeared likely to suffer. Perhaps they might be sincere in desiring peace with Britain, in order to facilitate their schemes of ambition against other countries; but those schemes of ambition had been formed in the exultation of unexpected success, and might not be cherished at the season of discomfiture and retreat. From the correspondence between Grenville and Chauvelin, they well knew that no proposal would be admitted by Britain which did not renounce the navigation of the Scheldt, forbear interference with the internal affairs of other countries, and forego their projects of aggrandizement: if they intended to offer less, their overtures,

overtures, therefore, would have been futile; but it cannot † be aſcertained whether their offers would or would not have been ſatisfactory, according to our requiſition of ſatisfaction, ſince they were not *heard*. The intervention of a veſtry clerk has been ſtated as ridiculous; but Le Brun did not propoſe Mr. Salter as a negociator, he employed him as a courier for carrrying an offer of ſending as ambaſſador Mr. Maret, who had a few months before conferred and negociated with Mr. Pitt.

Alarming ſtate of France; at war with all her neighbours.

The ſituation of France was at this time extremely alarming; ſhe was at war with her three moſt powerful neighbours, Pruſſia, Auſtria, and Britain. A body of her braveſt ſons, ſtimulated by the ſtrongeſt reſentment, was joined to her formidable enemies. The ſtates of Holland, and principalities of Germany, though not very important in their ſeparate force, yet added to the impulſe which was already ſo great. Sardinia, Naples, and Spain, were embarked in the ſame cauſe. From the Texel to the ſtraits of Gibraltar, from Gibraltar to Shetland, there was a circle of enemies encompaſſing France*. Within

† On this part of my enquiries Mr. W. declined any particular explanation. He is writing on the ſubject himſelf.

* The people, from having ſuch a multiplicity of enemies, conceived themſelves at war with the whole world: the following incident that occurred to a captain of the navy, a near relation of mine, is a curious illuſtration of theſe ſentiments. On the 22d of March arrived at Portſmouth from Jamaica, the Falcon ſloop of war, captain Biſſet, having captured off Uſhant a French privateer. Captain Biſſet was not apprized of a war between this country and France, till he fell in with the above privateer, who bore down upon the Falcon, but perceiving her to be a ſloop of war, ſhe immediately hauled her wind, and fired

CHAP. LII. 1793. Within her territories there were numerous bodies eagerly desirous of co-operating with her foes from without: a formidable rebellion was broken out in La Vendee, and the French government, divided into two violent factions, appeared on the eve of destruction by an intestine war. These concurring circumstances seemed to justify the hopes of the confederacy, that France, surrounded by so many enemies, and rent by such convulsions, would be unable to resist their separate and united efforts: but the French republicans were not overwhelmed by the multiplicity of dangers. The national convention, informed of the arrestation of their commissioners, and the defection of Dumouriez, manifested that rapid energy which ever distinguished the French revolutionists in emergency and danger, and adopted efficient measures to preserve the tranquillity of the metropolis, and defend the frontiers against the invading host. The northern army was re-organized, and general Dampierre being re-appointed provisional commander in chief, re-occupied the camp at Famars in French Hainault, near the right bank of the Scheldt. The confederate army was posted at Kieverain on the frontiers of Austrian Hainault,

---

fired her stern. Captain Bisset, astonished at this conduct, instantly stood after her, and coming up with her, demanded the reason of such conduct; when he was told by the commander of the privateer, "*that France had declared war against all the world.*" The Falcon then fired a few guns, and the French ship struck her colours, and was taken possession of by the Falcon.

with

with their right extending to St. Amand, and their left to Bavie, ſo as to blockade Conde, threaten Valenciennes, and even to overawe Maubeuge. The French general propoſed to drive the allies from ſo advantageous a poſition, and to relieve Conde. On the 1ſt of May he began the execution of this deſign, by attempting to diſlodge the Auſtrians from ſeveral villages which they poſſeſſed, but was repulſed with the loſs of near a thouſand killed and wounded. Dampierre undiſmayed by this check, and encouraged by reinforcements which were juſt arrived, marched on a ſecond time, with three formidable columns againſt the Pruſſian lines at St. Amand, and maintained a long, ſevere, and bloody conteſt, till ſuccours from the Auſtrians under Clairfait, obliged him to make a precipitate retreat, after leaving two thouſand men on the field of battle. His immediate object being to relieve Conde, he ſtill threatened the Pruſſians, who were now joined by the Britiſh troops under the duke of York. Intending to confine his attack to the right wing, he feigned an intention of aſſailing the whole line; and advancing to the wood of Vicoigne, he began the charge. On his left were conſtructed ſeveral ſtrong batteries, where were poſted ten thouſand men drawn from the garriſon of Liſle. Againſt this numerous force the Coldſtream guards, with ſome other Britiſh troops, were diſpatched. This heroic band, regardleſs of numbers, checked the enemy's batteries with their field pieces; and after one diſcharge of muſketry, ruſhed forward with fixed bayonets. Terrible in every ſpecies of warfare, Britiſh ſoldiers are irreſiſtible in cloſe fight; when

British ſoldiers ſupremely excellent in cloſe fight,

CHAP. LII. 1793.

when no dexterity can elude the force of personal prowess; and hence the opportunity of charging bayonets has rarely failed to assure victory to our countrymen. Our combatants made an impression on their antagonists, which the French soon saw they could not withstand man to man; they had, therefore, recourse to their chief excellence, missiles; with rapid activity they wheeled round artillery from the front to the flank, and opened with grape shot upon the gallant English. Dreadfully annoyed, the British forces disdained to fly: they kept their ground, repulsed the multitudes of the enemy, and in the conflict mortally wounded Dampierre*. The French had gone forth to battle in the most assured confidence, thinking they had only Prussian tactics and intrepidity to oppose their rapidly active genius and valour; but finding it was a very different undertaking to combat the energy of British heroism, they retreated within their lines, nor afterwards attempted offensive operations in a quarter secured by so formidable champions. From this period to the 23d of May, the French did not venture out of their lines; the allies, on the other hand, encouraged by the impression which was made by the action of the 8th, resolved to make a general attack on the camp at Famars, that covered the approaches to Valenciennes. The dispositions for this grand object being finished, the 23d of May was fixed for executing the design. At day break the British and Hanoverians assembled under the command of the duke of York, and the Austrians and German auxiliaries under the prince of Cobourg and general Clairfait. Great pains had been employed to conceal

in spite of French numbers and artillery, by the bayonet decide the fate of the day.

* New Annual Register, 1793.

conceal the projected attack, until its execution should be commenced. A fog somewhat retarded the advance of the troops, but at the same time concealed their approaches; until the sun penetrating through the mist, displayed to the astonished French the allies in four columns, proceeding towards their camp. A tremendous fire of artillery began the action on both sides: the contest soon became closer; and one of the Austrian columns was nearly overpowered, when the Hanoverians and British repulsed its assailants: at length the combined troops, led by the British, and headed by the duke of York and general Abercrombie, entirely defeated the French army. During night the duke of York refreshed his forces, resolved to attack the enemy's fortifications the next morning; but in the night the republicans abandoned the entrenchments which they had formed with such pains and expence, and left the way open to Valenciennes. About the same time bodies of Dutch and Austrian troops employed in the maritime Netherlands, drove the French invaders on that side within their frontiers.

Battle of Famara.

Condé, as we have seen, was in a state of blockade: the town was not provided with a sufficient quantity of provisions to sustain a long siege: the governor (General Chancel), therefore, about this period ordered the women and children to quit the place. As the diminution of consumers tended to prolong a blockade, the Prince of Wirtemberg, who commanded on that service, would not suffer their departure; opposed and prevented repeated attempts. The besieged, after a very brave and obstinate

Blockade and surrender of Conde.

CHAP. LII. 1793. obstinate resistance, and enduring with the most persevering fortitude all the rigours of famine, were, on the 10th of July, obliged to surrender at discretion.

Siege of Valenciennes. But a much more arduous enterprize, undertaken by the allies, was the siege of Valenciennes; and the victory at Famars having enabled them to approach, they formed a regular investment. Valenciennes is situate on the left bank of the Scheldt, opposite to the camp which the French had recently occupied.

Strength of the fortress. Its fortifications, among the chief efforts of Vauban's genius, rendered it a post of extraordinary strength. The garrison consisted of about eleven thousand men: Custine, appointed on the death of Dampierre to take the command of the Northern army, found it impossible to relieve the fortress, which was therefore obliged to depend upon its own strength. The allies, conscious of their force, and confident of ultimate success, summoned the fortress to surrender: the summons was disregarded; and being repeated, was still unavailing: the allies, therefore, proceeded with their approaches. A difference of opinion prevailed between the two chief engineers of Britain and of the emperor respectively, Colonel Moncrief and Monsieur Ferasis. The British officer, less regarding customary modes than efficient means, proposed to plant batteries immediately under the walls of the city, instead of approaching it by regular parallels*. The German officer, adhering closely to experimental tactics, proposed to proceed in the manner which had been so long in use; and his opinion was adopted by the council of war.

Operations. On the morning of the 14th of June the trenches were opened; and Farasis directed

* New Annual Register, 1793, page 187.

the

1793.

the ſiege under the ſuperintending command of the Duke of York. The ſucceſſive parallels were conducted with diſtinguiſhed ſkill, and finiſhed with uncommon expedition; this diſpatch being powerfully promoted by the Britiſh guards; who, from their habits of working in the coal barges on the Thames, were enabled to do more work in a given time than an equal number of any other ſoldiers*. In the beginning of July the beſiegers were able to bring two hundred pieces of heavy artillery to play without intermiſſion on the town, and the greater part of it was reduced to aſhes. The ſmallneſs of the garriſon, compared with the extent of the fortifications to be defended, prevented General Ferrand, the commander, from attempting frequent ſorties: in one which the garriſon made on the 5th of July, however, they were very ſucceſsful, killed ſeveral of the enemy, and ſpiked ſome cannon. A conſiderable part of the war was carried on under ground, by numerous mines and counter-mines, which both beſiegers and beſieged conſtructed. The chief of theſe were, one which the beſiegers formed under the glacis, and one under the horn-work of the fortreſs†. Theſe mines were completed and charged on the 25th of July, and in the night, between nine and ten o'clock, were ſprung with complete ſucceſs. The Engliſh and Auſtrians immediately embraced the opportunity to throw themſelves into the covered way, of which they made themſelves maſters. The Duke of York now, for the third time, ſummoned the

* See Macfarlane, vol. iv. page 390.

† New Annual Regiſter, 1793, page 190.

place

CHAP. LII.

1793. Captured, after a siege of six weeks, in the name of the emperor.

place to ſurrender; and the governor ſeeing no hopes from farther defence, capitulated; by the capitulation the troops taken in the garriſon were allowed to retire into France, on ſwearing that they would not during the war, ſerve againſt any of the allied powers; and the Duke of York took poſſeſſion of Valenciennes in the name of the Emperor of Germany.

Sentiments of Burke and his votaries on this ſubject,

Thoſe promoters of war with the French republicans who deſired the reſtoration of monarchy as the chief object of hoſtilities, diſapproved of various circumſtances in the capture of Valenciennes, and indeed in the principle on which the campaign was conducted; as, according to their hypotheſis, the legitimate object of the war in which the confederacy was engaged was the re-eſtabliſhment of monarchy, the emigrant princes and other exiles ought to have had the chief direction in its councils and conduct; whereas theſe were really employed as mercenaries. On the ſame hypotheſis Valenciennes and other towns captured, or to be captured, ought to be poſſeſſed in the name of Louis XVII. as king of France, and of his uncle the Count of Provence, as lawful regent during the young king's minority; and troops capitulating ought to be reſtricted from ſerving againſt French royaliſts, as well as the allied powers. Theſe obſervations were fair and conſiſtent inferences, if it had been admitted that the combined powers were actually, as the Engliſh oppoſition aſſerted, fighting for the reſtoration of the monarchical conſtitution *: but according to Bri-

* The moſt eloquent and illuſtrious advocate of this doctrine, Mr. Burke, exhibits this theory in his remarks on the policy of the allies, begun in October 1793.

tiſh

are different from those of Mr. Pitt and his coadjutors.

tiſh miniſters, and the greater number of their parliamentary votaries, the purpoſe of the war was not a counter-revolution in France, but the attainment of ſecurity againſt the French projects of aggrandizement, and diſſemination of revolt; that the moſt effectual means for this purpoſe was the reduction of her power, without any regard to her internal government; that we were to reduce her ſtrength in the preſent as in former wars, by capturing, according to our reſpective force, her towns and poſſeſſions. Indeed, the confederates at preſent ſeemed to proceed on the ſame principle of conquering warfare which had been practiſed by the grand alliance for humbling the power of Louis XIV. To adopt the language of works leſs ſpecially devoted to the ſupport of miniſterial politics, than to the reſtoration of monarchy in France; they were rather *anti-gallicans*, warring againſt phyſical France, on the general principles of former times, than *anti-jacobins*, warring againſt moral France, on the peculiarly requiſite principles of preſent times. On the one hand, the object of Mr. Burke, however impolitic and impracticable it may have been deemed, was much more definite than the objects of Mr. Pitt, as far as theſe were explained: on the other, the objects of Mr. Pitt being conceived to be merely anti-gallican, were much more agreeable to the prevailing ſentiments of Britons than the avowal of a combination would have been, for interfering in the internal polity of France, and re-eſtabliſhing a government which, in its former exerciſe, Britain ſo very much diſapproved. The capture of French towns in the name of the young prince, as ſovereign

CHAP. LII. 1793.

reign of a country that had renounced its authority, would have been an avowal of a counter-revolutionary project, which the British government disavowed, and which the majority of the British nation would have cenſured. The appropriation and capitulation of Valenciennes were therefore perfectly conſonant to the profeſſed views with which the allies, having completed the purpoſes of defence and recovery, had invaded the French Netherlands. While the allies were thus engaged in the Netherlands in ſtrengthening the power of the emperor on the Rhine, they were occupied in recovering the captures of the French. On the 20th of June the Pruſſian army inveſted Mentz; and after a regular and vigorous ſiege, and a very gallant defence, it capitulated on the 22d of July.

Succeſſes of the Pruſſians. Mentz is taken.

France is torn by diſſentions.

While the confederates were making ſuch advances on the frontiers of France, the republic was entirely torn with diſſentions. The Girondiſts, who had been long declining in authority, and who were more than ever abhorred by the Mountain, ſince their deſire to ſave the king, had conſtantly ſupported Dumouriez againſt the invectives of Marat and the jacobins. As ſoon as Dumouriez was driven into exile, the Mountain raiſed an outcry againſt his late protectors the Girondiſts. They were repreſented to the furious multitude as a band of traitors and counter-revolutioniſts. The municipality of Paris, and the jacobin clubs, reſounded with complaints, threats, and imprecations, againſt the party in the convention which retained ſome ſentiments of humanity, ſome love of order, and ſome regard for juſtice. The Girond party ſtill poſſeſſed

The Mountain excite a clamour againſt the Girondiſts.

conſiderable

considerable influence in the convention; but the Mountain, gratifying the Parisian rabble with blood and plunder, exercised the supreme command in the city. In March was established the revolutionary tribunal for trying offences against the state. This celebrated and dreadful court, consisting of six judges, was wholly without appeal. The crimes on which it was to pronounce were vague, undefined, and undefinable; extending not merely to actions, but to most secret thoughts. On the 1st of April a decree was passed abolishing the inviolability of members of the convention when accused of crimes against the state.

Establishment of the revolutionary tribunal.

The chiefs of the Brissotines appeared to be astonished and confounded at these daring and desperate measures of their inveterate adversaries, confident in their power and popularity; and made no vigorous opposition to decrees which were evidently intended to pave the way to their destruction *. It was now manifest that the Girondists were inferior to their antagonists in vigour and decision; and, notwithstanding the intellectual and literary accomplishments of the leaders of the party, grossly deficient in practical talents for government; that, therefore, they must finally sink under the contest of which they were unequal to the management. The Mountain had not only in its favour the jacobin club and the dregs of the people of Paris, but it knew that the triumphant party in that immense city, from terror or obedience, was able to command, throughout the whole extent of the republic; and whilst

The Girondists possessed a speculative ingenuity, but wanted practical ability.

The Mountain superior in decision and daring atrocity.

* See Belsham's history, vol. 5. p. 62.

CHAP. LII.

1793. The Gironde leaders are committed to prison.

the Girondists were reasoning, deliberating, and menacing, the Mountain conspired, struck, and reigned. On the 31st of May, early in the morning, the tocsin was sounded; the barriers were shut; Brissot, Roland, and many others of the most distinguished Girondists were seized and committed to prison by a force devoted to Robespierre. Terror quickly seized all minds; and the theoretic republic of ingenious, but unwise and unprincipled innovators, became subject to a detestable and bloody tyranny.

Robespierre and his associates become rulers of France. System of terror reigns

Robespierre, Danton, Marat, Collot d'Herbois, Billaud, and Couthon, became rulers of France. They associated with themselves ferocious individuals whose talents were necessary to the administration, and who consented to serve them through fear, ambition, or policy*. They hastily drew up the celebrated constitution of 1793; and no policy ever existed more absurd, or more favourable to anarchy. Legislation was confined to a single council, the members of which were elected without any qualification of property: the executive power was among twenty-four ministers, appointed by the convention, and dismissed at their pleasure. This government, the most absolute and the most ferocious of which there has ever been an example, was confined to two sections, consisting of twelve deputies. The one was called the *Committee of public safety*, and the other the *Committee of general safety*. They were to be renewed every month; but by one of the incalculable effects of fear, which blinds those whom it governs, the convention, divesting itself of its inviola-

Constitution of 1793. Singular absurdity and anarchy

Committees of public and general safety.

* See Segur's History of Frederic William, v. iii.

bility,

bility, entrusted the committees with the formidable right of imprisoning its members; and thus rendered the power of the government as solid as it was extensive. Meanwhile, some of the Girondist deputies who escaped the proscription excited insurrection. Several departments indicated a disposition to avenge themselves, and resist oppression: some of them took up arms. By far the most formidable resistance to the reigning usurpers arose in the South, where the three principal cities, Lyons, Marseilles, and Toulon, formed a combination for overturning the existing tyranny. Toulon opened a negociation with Lord Hood, who commanded the British fleet in the Mediterranean. The English admiral, at the instance of the inhabitants, took possession of the town and shipping, in the name of Louis XVII. The Spaniards advanced into Languedoc, proffering assistance to all those Frenchmen who wished to resist the horrid tyranny of the jacobin faction.

Combinations in the South for overthrowing the frightful tyranny. Toulon puts itself under the protection of Lord Hood and the British fleet.

In comprehensive tyranny, efficacious malignity, deliberative iniquity, affecting the persons, liberties, properties, and minds of their countrymen, the junto which now governed France surpassed all the wickedness ever recorded in history. Their predecessors had progressively promoted infidelity, confiscation, destruction of rank and order; but still there remained a considerable degree of religion, and great masses of property, with a small share of subordination. Robespierre and his band abolished christianity; publicly and nationally abjured the Supreme Being. They proscribed genius, lest its efforts might overthrow their horrible system. They ruined commerce to stimulate the multitude to plunder;

Comprehensive and efficacious malignity of the governing junto.

Robespierre and his band abolish Christianity and abjure the Supreme Being;

CHAP. LII.

1793. attempt to level all civil, political, and moral distinctions.

plunder; and they seized all property. Totally free from every principle of religion and virtue; without humanity, pity, or remorse, they proscribed, they murdered, they plundered; they deemed all mankind merely instruments for gratifying their diabolical passions*. The means by which they were enabled to exercise such a complication of tyranny was the multitude. By the populace conjunctly and aggregately they were able to exercise despotism over the populace themselves severally†. The war facilitated the extension of their power, because it enabled them to accuse all persons obnoxious to themselves as traitorous correspondents with foreign enemies. The war, also, so much engaged the anxious attention of the people, that they had less time to brood over the internal sufferings of their country. Pressed on all sides by invaders, who they conceived were desirous of dictating to them in the arrangement of their own government, an ardent zeal to maintain national independence drew off their thoughts from internal despotism. The same patriotic spirit was inflamed, not only by the fears of foreign interference in their government, but by the belief that the dismemberment of their country was intended.

The pressure of the war facilitates their atrocities.

The pressure of the confederates, and their supposed designs, cherished the ferocious tyranny of Robespierre. Detestable as this relentless tyrant was, yet, in one momentous object, he promoted the first wish of Frenchmen; not to be controuled by foreign invaders. In opposing the confederacy of princes, the revolutionary government displayed

* See Otridge's Annual Register, 1793.

† See Burke on Regicide peace.

an

an energy that triumphed over all obstacles. Much of this energy, no doubt, is imputable to the very wickedness of the system. The understanding, employing its invention and foresight in seeking means for gratifying passions, without the least restraint from conscience, may certainly be more efficacious; than if repressed in its devices by religion and virtue. The extinction of every pious and moral sentiment, and the removal of the sanctions of a future state, prepared minds for every enormity. It paved the way for bearing down all opposition to the executive power proceeding by massacre or any other crime that might most expeditiously effect its purposes. The revolutionary government, in its total violation of justice, found ample resources for military supply. *The terrible system* wanted money: a forced loan placed the fortunes of all men at its disposal. It wanted provisions, ammunition, arms: it put all physical resources under REQUISITION *. It wanted men: its war minister, bold in conception as unrestrained by humanity and justice, said, "let us confound all the calculations of experienced warriors: ours is a new case; raise the whole nation in MASSE: overpower discipline by multitude; bear down tactical skill and experience; and tire out their efforts by fresh and incessant relays: consume your enemies by the fatigue of exertion." Scarcely were the orders given when twelve hundred thousand men † marched out to meet the enemy. Of

CHAP. LII. 1793.

Forced loan.

Requisitions.

Bold scheme of the war minister to raise the nation in mass.

* See decree of August 15th, 1793, requiring all Frenchmen to be in permanent readiness for the service of the armies with every kind of warlike stores, and even every material for making arms, powder, ball, and all other kinds of ammunition or provision for military service.

† See New Annual Register, 1793.

CHAP. LII. 1793.

these, great numbers, no doubt, were propelled by fear, and the assured alternative of massacre if they refused; but whatever might have been the motive, the effect was prodigious. To hasten the operation of such a multitude, vehicles were contrived for carrying both men and cannon with extraordinary dispatch against the enemy. Immense bodies were sent to quell the insurgents of La Vendee, and succeeded in repressing the attempts of these royalists. Marseilles yielded with little contest to the revolutionary arms. Lyons, instead of following the example of Marseilles, made a most resolute resistance, and for two months heroically withstood an active siege. General Kellerman, who commanded the army of the Alps, was ordered to besiege that city; but not answering to the impatience of the convention, he was removed, and General Doppet appointed to succeed him; to whom the inhabitants, who were not only unused to arms, but very ill provided with the means of defence, as well as the necessaries of life, on the 8th of October, were obliged to surrender. A great part of the city was reduced to ashes by a continual bombardment. The victors, who had sustained considerable loss during the siege, were filled with furious resentment, and gratified their revenge by the most savage and atrocious cruelty. The wretched victims, too numerous for the individual operation of the guillotine, were driven in large bodies, with the most brutal and blasphemous ceremonies, into the Rhone; or hurried in crouds to the squares to be massacred by musketry and artillery *. Immense bodies of troops, under General

Efficacy of this system. It overcomes the insurgents of La Vendee.

Murderous cruelties.

* See Otridge's Annual Register for the year 1793, p. 275.

Cartaux,

Cartaux, proceeded to Toulon: an advanced corps having arrived in the neighbourhood of that city, Captain Keith Elphinstone, of the navy, landing from the fleet, and joining a body of English and Spanish infantry, attacked and routed the enemy with considerable loss. Soon after, General O'Hara, arriving from Gibraltar, took the command of the British forces. Attacking the enemy, he defeated and put them to flight; but pursuing the fugitives very eagerly, he unexpectedly encountered a large force entirely fresh. In endeavouring to draw off his soldiers safely to Toulon he was unavoidably engaged in a conflict with superior numbers; and after an obstinate contest he was wounded and taken prisoner. Near a thousand of the British and their allies were either killed or captured. As an immense mass of French was now approaching, against which to defend the town the remaining handful was totally incompetent, it was judged expedient to evacuate the place with all possible dispatch. Accordingly, the allies made dispositions for withdrawing, and saving as many of the inhabitants as could be removed; and for destroying all the shipping, stores, and provisions, that could not be preserved by any other expedient from falling into the hands of the enemy. This service was performed very completely: the troops were carried off without the loss of a man; and several thousands of the loyal inhabitants of Toulon were sheltered in the British ships. Sir Sidney Smith, to whose active intrepidity was entrusted the conflagration of the magazines, store-houses, and arsenals, with the ships in the harbour, most effectually performed this hazardous and extraordinary duty. On this occasion, fifteen ships of the line,

The French force the English to evacuate Toulon.

 with

CHAP. LII. 1793.

with many frigates and smaller vessels, were destroyed, and an immense quantity of naval stores. Three ships of the line, and several frigates, accompanied the British fleet. By this destruction the French navy received a blow very difficult to be retrieved.

Netherlands.

While the French, rising in a mass, crushed revolt and expelled foreign enemies in the South, their gigantic efforts effected in the North a momentous change in the events of the campaign. After the reduction of Valenciennes, the French were compelled to abandon a very strong position which Custine occupied behind the Scheldt, denominated Cæsar's camp. A council of war was now held by the allies to consider the most effectual plans of pursuing their successes. Generals Cobourg and Clairfait proposed *, while the French were under an alarm from the disasters in the Netherlands, to penetrate towards Paris, while a force should be sent, under cover of the British fleets, to co-operate with the loyalists in Britanny: the Duke of York was of opinion that it would be much more adviseable to extend their conquests upon the frontiers. He proposed that the army should divide; that he, at the head of his countrymen, the Dutch and Hanoverians should attack the enemy on the side of West Flanders, while the allies continued their operations in the Eastern Netherlands.

Progress of the Duke of York and the British troops.

It was concerted that the allies should besiege Quesnoy, and that the duke of York marching to the coast where he could receive maritime co-operation, should invest Dunkirk. This port has ever been, in time of war, a very great

* Annual Register, 1793.

receptacle

receptacle for privateers, and extremely troublesome to the English trade in its approach to the Downs. Therefore the British cabinet, as well as the commander in chief, were eager to wrest from the enemy such means of annoyance. Separating from the allies, his highness marched towards Dunkirk; and on the 18th of August he reached Menin *. The Dutch under the hereditary prince of Orange, attacked a French post at Lincelles in that neighbourhood, and were repulsed; but the British troops, though very inferior in force, carried the post with fixed bayonets, and defeated the enemy. The French no longer venturing to obstruct his advances, on the 22d his highness arrived before Dunkirk. On the 24th he attacked the French out-posts, and compelled them to take refuge within the town †. In this engagement, however, he incurred some loss both of men and officers; and among the latter the Austrian general Dalton, so noted, as we have seen during the revolt of the Netherlands from the emperor Joseph. On the 28th of August the siege was regularly commenced by the duke of York, while general Freytag with an army of auxiliaries, was posted to cover the besiegers. A considerable naval armament from Great Britain, intended to co-operate with a military force, by some unaccountable delay did not arrive nearly so soon as was appointed and expected. His highness nevertheless carried on the siege with great vigour and skill. Meanwhile the republican troops, commanded by general Houchard, poured from all

Victory at Lincelles.

His highness invests Dunkirk with reasonable hopes of success. Late arrival of the artillery and naval force. Progress of the siege notwithstanding.

An immense mass of French arrives.

* Otridge's Annual Register, 1793, p. 272. † Ibid. 273.

quarters,

CHAP. LII. 1793.

quarters, in an enormous mass. Attacking the army of Freytag the 7th of September, after several severe actions, in which the Germans made a most vigorous resistance, the French at last overpowered them by numbers, defeated them, and compelled them to make a very precipitate retreat. In this rout Freytag himself, and prince Adolphus of England, youngest son of his Britannic majesty, were taken prisoners, but in a short time rescued. The duke of York, from the defeat of the covering army, found it necessary to raise the siege. Before he had departed, the garrison, informed of Houchard's success, made a sally, in which they were repulsed with great loss; while the besiegers also suffered considerably, and among other officers were deprived of the celebrated engineer colonel Moncrief, who was killed by a cannon ball. Houchard now attacked a second time all that remained of the covering army, gained a complete and decisive victory, and with his daily increasing mass, hastened against the duke of York. The British commander found it absolutely necessary to withdraw from Dunkirk, to prevent his gallant band from being totally overpowered by such an infinite multitude of enemies. The unavoidable hurry of his retreat compelled our prince to leave his heavy artillery, and a great quantity of ammunition, which fell into the hands of the enemy. The military chest was preserved by being hastily put on board a frigate.

The British prince is obliged to abandon the attempt.

The miscarriage of this enterprize produced great censure among those who judge of plans by events; but at the time that the enterprize was concerted,

 there

there were reaſonable hopes of ſucceſs; and the attainment of the object would have been extremely advantageous to Britain. The delay of the gun-boats and artillery, muſt certainly have retarded the execution of the deſign; but the final diſappointment was owing to cauſes which no man judging from military experience could have poſſibly anticipated. The new French expedient of arming in maſs had not yet been known to the allies, and the rapid means of bringing forward their immenſe multitudes were no leſs extraordinary and aſtoniſhing. The prodigious hordes thus carried to the ſcene of warfare, muſt have diſcomfited the Britiſh project, however wiſe the undertaking, well concerted the plan, ſeaſonable and efficient the preparations. Ends were to be ſought, and means to be employed according to probabilities, founded in the experience that then exiſted. From ſo unprecedented a collection of armed multitudes, eſcape without very conſiderable loſs was a great atchievement; ſo great indeed, that the enemy conceived it impracticable: they apprehended that if general Houchard had diſcharged his duty, he might have effectually cut off the Britiſh retreat. Under this impreſſion the French general was afterwards denounced, and ſuffered by the ſentence of the revolutionary tribunal.

The French maſs compels the Auſtrians to retire behind the Sambre.

While the duke of York was engaged before Dunkirk, the allies inveſted Cambray, Bouchain, and Queſnoy; the two former they found impracticable, the latter they executed. Prince Cobourg having repulſed a detachment ſent to the relief of Queſnoy, the fortreſs ſurrendered to general Clairfait on the 11th of September. Soon after this capture the

CHAP. LII. 1793.

the duke of York rejoined the confederates. The French army of the north, after raiſing the ſiege of Dunkirk, took a ſtrong poſition in the neighbourhood of Maubeuge, where they were immediately blockaded by the whole united force of the allies, collected under the prince of Cobourg. The republican armies, after the accuſation of Houchard, were entruſted to the command of Jourdain, who having formerly ſerved in the French army in a humble rank, and afterwards became a ſhop-keeper in a petty village*, but having reſumed the military profeſſion, was by the French government deemed worthy of the ſupreme command; and, as the allies experienced, did ſignal honour to the penetration of his employers. Jourdain, on the 15th and 16th of October, attacked prince Cobourg with ſuch numbers, vigour, and effect, as to compel him to abandon his poſition, and repaſs the Sambre. The French general now freed from blockade, was at liberty to employ offenſive operations. Detachments were accordingly ſent to make inroads into maritime Flanders. They took poſſeſſion of Werwick and Menin, from whence they advanced to Furnes: they proceeded to Nieuport, which they beſieged and greatly damaged; but the place was ſaved by having recourſe to inundation. It was ſome time before the allied forces were able to ſtop the progreſs of the republicans, and their generals even trembled for the fate of Oſtend. A conſiderable armament from England, however, being at that time preparing for the Weſt Indies, under Sir Charles Grey, their

* See New Annual Regiſter for 1793. It is there ſaid he was a haberdaſher.

destination was altered; and by arriving at this fortunate moment at Ostend, they saved the Low Countries for the present campaign.

CHAP. LII.

1793.

They force the Prussians to retreat.

On the Rhine, after the capture of Mentz, a number of petty actions took place, in which the French were generally successful; but no event of importance ensued†. During the month of September, the duke of Brunswick gained several advantages, and the allies invested Landau, the siege of which occupied the remainder of the campaign. A French army commanded by general Landremont, strongly posted on the Lauter, covered and protected this important fortress. On the 14th of October general Wurmser forced the strong lines of the enemy; and Lautreburg surrendered at discretion, after being evacuated by the republicans. The town of Weissembourg made a longer resistance; part of it, however, was unfortunately burned, and the French before they retreated, set fire to their magazines within the walls, as well as those at Alstade. The French, not disheartened by these losses, made repeated attacks on the enemy's lines, and at last were so successful, that the duke of Brunswick deemed it expedient to raise the siege of Landau, and retire into winter quarters. The armies of the Netherlands finished the campaign about the same time.

The campaign terminates much less favourably than its commencement promised.

Although the continental campaign of 1793 was on the whole successful on the side of the allies, yet its termination was by no means equally auspicious as its preceding periods. From its commencement

† See New Annual Register for 1793, p. 192.

to

CHAP. LII. 1793.

to the month of August, it had been progressively successful; then, however, the career of victory was arrested. In point of actual possession, the allies had preserved Holland, and recovered the Netherlands; had retaken Mentz, captured Conde, Quesnoy, and Valenciennes. But it required little discernment to see that the prospect was not now favourable to the confederates, and that the tide of success was turned. The allies never appeared to have established that concert of ends, and consistency of means, without which alliances cannot hope to succeed against a single and well compacted powerful opponent. If it was wise and expedient to seek the restoration of monarchy, their efforts should have been directed to that sole object. Separate aggrandizement, even were it in itself justifiable, necessarily created jealousy and distrust. The king of Prussia began to conceive that the successes of the campaign were advancing the power of Austria, while he had a share only in its expence and disasters.

Gigantic efforts of France, and want of concert among the allies.

From the dismemberment of France he could look for no accession, and was, besides, intent upon dismemberment in another quarter. Catharine having attained her wish of engaging the German powers in a war with France, had executed her intentions, of destroying the new constitution of Poland, which had tended to extricate that country from its dependence on herself. She invaded Poland with an army of a hundred thousand men, forcibly annulled the constitution at the diet, and to secure the concurrence of the king of Prussia, as well as gratify her own ambition,

Catharine prosecutes her designs against Poland:

proposes a second partition of that territory, and invites the king of Prussia to participate.

bition, she proposed a second partition of the Polish territories; that the king of Prussia should for his share receive the cities of Dantzick and Thorn, with Great Poland, while her own portion of the spoilation was nearly half the remainder more contiguous to Russia. The Prussian king was more occupied in securing his spoils in Poland, which a band of patriotic heroes still endangered, than in seconding the emperor. On the other hand, the emperor was extremely jealous of the acquisitions of his Prussian ally; and the bands of the confederacy were evidently loosening.

Frederic William intent on securing the spoils of Poland.

On her own element, Britain, unincumbered by allies, began the war with signal success. In the West Indies, the valuable island of Tobago was captured by a British squadron under admiral Laforey, about the beginning of April. From an early period of the French revolution, the West India islands belonging to France, and particularly St. Domingo, had been agitated and convulsed by the revolutionary spirit, and by premature and injudicious attempts to confer the rights of free citizens, in that part of the globe, upon the "people of colour," who constitute a large proportion of the inhabitants*. From the dreadful internal commotions, St. Domingo was a scene of devastation and bloodshed. In July, Fort Jeremie, and Cape Nicola Mole, being attacked by the British squadron, surrendered themselves. In the gulph of St. Lawrence, the

Rapid success of the British where they fought alone.

Conquests in the West and East Indies.

* See Belsham's History, vol. v. page 101.

islands

CHAP. LII. 1793. islands of St. Pierre and Miquelon, were captured. In the East Indies, the company's troops, in the first campaign of the war, reduced Pondicherry, and all the settlements of the French on the coasts of Malabar and Coromandel.

CHAP. LIII.

Projects of political reform.—Club of united Irishmen.—Institution and objects.—Convention bill.—Britain—great numbers are infected with the desire of change.—Causes ignorance, vanity, and visionary enthusiasm, more than malignant intention.—Propensity in the lower orders to be spokesmen—arises from the free interchange of opinion which Britons enjoy—at this time is abused.—Dangerous tendency of certain political associations and sentiments.—Scotland.—Messrs. Muir and Palmer—trials of for sedition.—They are sentenced to transportation.—The punishment is represented as excessive, and even illegal.—Scotch convention for new modelling the constitution—consists chiefly of persons of low condition—dispersed by the civil power.—Their leaders are tried and sentenced to transportation.—Meeting of parliament.—Mr. Fox and his supporters recommend peace—arguments against and for.—Mr. Pitt's reasoning on the war, and the internal system of France.—Lord Mornington's view of the subject.—A great majority approve of the continuance of the war.—Messrs. Fox and Sheridan impute to the combination the astonishing efforts of France.—Discussion of the question with whom should we treat.—The opponents of the war predict the dissolution of the confederacy, and the triumph of the French.—Mr. Fox complains that the object of the war is indefinite—contrasted with former wars.—He prophecies that the war with France, like the war with America, would terminate in disappointment.—Various motions for peace—rejected.—Questions respecting the trials for sedition in Scotland.—Mr. Adam's proposed amendment of the Scottish criminal law—debate negatived.—Proposed enquiry into the conduct

 of

the Scottish judges.—His speech on that subject.—Reply of the lord advocate.—The motion of Mr. Adam is rejected.—Third proposition of Mr. Adam for assimilating the Scottish to the English criminal law.—Masterly speech of Mr. Adam on that subject.—Answer of Mr. Dundas.—Reply of Mr. Fox—The proposition is negatived.—Progress of the innovating spirit among the lower ranks.—Seditious lectures against the British constitution, and kingly government.—Proceedings of the democratic societies.—Plan of a national convention—discovered by ministers—leaders arrested, and papers seized.—Committees of both houses appointed to examine their papers—from the reports Mr. Pitt proposes a bill for detaining suspected persons without allowing them the benefit of the habeas corpus act—bill passed into a law.—Ministers, including lord Loughborough the chancellor, consider the crimes charged as high treason.—Lord Thurlow asserts, that by the law of England they are not treason.—Supplies, subsidies, and taxes.—Debate on the introduction of Hessian troops.—Apprehensions of an invasion.—Voluntary contributions for levying troops.—Session closes.—Internal proceedings in France.—Jacobin faction and Robespierre paramount.—Iniquitous trial, condemnation, and punishment of the queen.—Brissot and the other Girond prisoners put to death.—Orleans shares the same fate.—Danton overborne by Robespierre.—The Parisian mob adore Robespierre.—Real talents and character.

CHAP. LIII.

1793. Project of political reform.

THE chief internal occurrences of this year regarded projects of political reform. In Ireland a society was established for promoting a complete emancipation of the Catholics; that is a thorough exemption from all legal disabilities, and a *radical* reform of parliament, on the principles of univer-

fal

1793. Club of United Irishmen.

ſal ſuffrage and annual elections. This club, conſtructed on the model of the affiliated Jacobins, took the name of the *United Iriſhmen*, which was afterwards productive of ſuch dangerous conſequences. In the Iriſh parliament an act had been paſſed, granting relief to the Catholics, but by no means ſo extenſive as their ſupporters in and out of parliament deſired. They were allowed to exerciſe all civil and military offices under the crown, except in the very higheſt departments of the law and ſtate; and they were prohibited from ſitting in parliament. The executive government appeared well inclined to extend the relief, but the apprehenſions of the Proteſtant party were ſo deeply rooted, as to render it inexpedient in the legiſlature to proceed any farther at that period. The united Iriſhmen, as a party, were not particularly connected with the Catholics, but conſiſted of the votaries of innovation* in general; held aſſemblies for concerting and preparing means to promote their ſchemes of change. Theſe meetings being conſidered as dangerous in the preſent ferment, a law was paſſed by the Iriſh parliament for preventing ſuch aſſemblies; being ſpecifically deſcribed, both in nature and purpoſe, ſo as to reſtrain innovating cabals: the new act was known by the title of the convention bill. While the legiſlature endeavoured to prevent pernicious aſſemblies in Ireland, projects were formed in Britain by bodies of individuals for holding a convention, which ſhould ſpeak the national voice, and effect ſuch changes as in the judg-

Inſtitution and objects.

Convention bill.

* See Reports of Iriſh Committees in 1797 and 1798.

CHAP. LIII. 1793. Britain. Great numbers are infected with the desire of change.

ments of these politicians should appear necessary for the regeneration of Britain.

The revolutionary doctrines of France spreading into this island, produced a desire of change, which was different in object and extent according to the circumstances, knowledge, and character of their votaries. Men of desperate fortune or reputation might desire a subversion of government, in hopes of profiting by the general confusion, and no doubt there were such men in the clubs which were supposed to seek revolution. These were a kind of associates that revolutionary leaders might be sure to acquire, according to the believed probability of success. But, if their conduct be candidly reviewed, by far the greater number of the associated votaries of indefinite change will appear to have been misled by folly, ignorance, or visionary enthusiasm, rather than prompted by malignant intentions. A passion which produced the addition of many members to these clubs, was vanity. They wished to make a figure in spheres for which their education and condition rendered them totally unfit. The supposed exaltation of the people in France, inspired many well-disposed manufacturers, mechanics, tradesmen, and peasants with a desire of reaching the same distinction, and stimulated them to exercise their talents as orators and lawgivers. There is, indeed, in the lower orders of our countrymen a peculiar propensity to oratory: the free constitution under which they live empowers them to utter their sentiments and opinions with open boldness; the love of social and convivial intercourse very naturally following an unrestrained interchange

Causes—ignorance, vanity, and visionary enthusiasm, more than malignant intentions.

Propensity in the lower orders to be spokesmen; arises from the free interchange

terchange of thoughts and feelings, produces clubs, which at this period were very numerous. These requiring some kind of methodical arrangement, introduced some kind of order and system in addresses and replies beyond the desultory irregularity of conversation. Hence arose debate, which generated emulation to distinguish themselves in their circle of companions; the members respectively tried to be spokesmen. As their oratorial talents, in their own apprehension, increased, they wished for a wider field of exercise; this they found in vestries or other meetings of local arrangement; or sometimes betook themselves to debating societies, where they could exhibit their eloquence and wisdom on subjects of erudition, philosophy, and politics. From these causes there was, especially through the great towns, a pre-disposition in people of low rank, without education and literature, to recreate themselves with speeches and dissertations*. The visions of French equality held out to their fancies and passions pleasing images and powerful incentives; increased the objects of their eloquence and political exertions, proposed so wide fields for exercise, and promised such rewards as stimulated great numbers to seek change, less from dissatisfaction with the present than from sanguine expectations of the future; and rendered them desirous of reforming assemblies, not so much with a view to overthrow the established constitution, to

1793. of opinion which Britons enjoy: at this time is abused,

* At the trial of Hardy, the shoemaker, one Wills a dancing master, who had accompanied the defendant to the Corresponding Society, being interrogated as to his own motives for resorting to that meeting, replied that he had a pleasure in hearing the conversation of *clever* men. See State Trials in 1794.

 crush

CHAP. LIII. 1793.

crush king, lords, and commons, as to distinguish themselves in the proposed conventions. That some of the ringleaders desired the subversion of our existing establishments, admits very little doubt; but that a total misconception of the purposes of their leaders, vanity and the love of distinction, and not treasonable motives, actuated the chief portion of their votaries we may candidly and fairly presume. But, whatever might be the intention of the individuals respectively, the tendency of such assemblages collectively, in a season of revolutionary enthusiasm, was evidently dangerous; and required the unremitting vigilance of government, to restrain and correct delusion and to chastise mischievous deluders.

Dangerous tendency of certain political associations and sentiments.

Scotland.

In Scotland, two active agitators of political change, Messrs. Muir and Palmer, the former an advocate, the latter a dissenting clergyman, were tried for sedition, charged to have been committed in writing and other acts. The following facts were established against Mr. Muir at his trial: he had actively dispersed in and about Paisley and Glasgow Paine's Rights of Man and other books and pamphlets of a similar tendency; in conversation expressed his wishes and hopes of changes on the model of France; and purchased works hostile to the British constitution, especially Paine, for people too poor to buy them themselves and so ignorant as to be easily impressed by his exhortations*. It was farther proved that he was an active

Messrs. Muir and Palmer, trials of, for sedition.

* Such as Thomas Wilson, barber, Ann Fisher, servant-maid, and others in equally humble stations. See Muir's Trial.

and leading member in ſocieties for promoting ſuch doctrines and conduct as Thomas Paine inculcates, and that his rank and ſituation afforded great weight and influence to his exhortations. Mr. Palmer, an Unitarian preacher at Dundee, had been no leſs active in the eaſt than Mr. Muir in the weſt, and indeed much more violent. He had either compoſed or promoted addreſſes, which ſtimulated his votaries to enmity againſt the Houſe of Commons and the exiſting orders, and declared the higheſt privilege of man to be univerſal ſuffrage; inveighed againſt the conſtituted authorities, their counſels and meaſures, as oppreſſive and tyrannical; called on the people to join in reſiſting theſe oppreſſions, and adjured them by every thing that was dear to them, to combine for the preſervation of their periſhing liberty and the recovery of their long loſt rights. Theſe and other publications ſimilar in inflammatory rapſody, were diſperſed with ardent activity by Mr. Palmer, and by a very ſtrenuous agent, George Mealmaker, weaver*. There could be no doubt that ſuch conduct was ſeditious, and no valid objection could be made to the evidence. The jury were therefore bound to bring in a verdict *guilty* in each of theſe caſes. In Scotland the ſentence in caſes of ſedition, reſts with the judges; and in both theſe caſes the puniſhment was, that they ſhould be tranſported for the ſpace of fourteen years beyond the ſeas, to ſuch place as his Majeſty, with the advice of his privy council, ſhould think proper.

They are ſentenced to tranſportation.

* See Trial of Palmer, at the Autumn Circuit at Perth 1793.

CHAP. LIII.

1793.

Both these gentlemen possessed fair and unimpeached moral characters, and were deemed enthusiasts in what they conceived to be right, and not intentionally malignant incendiaries. Though this circumstance did not diminish the mischievous tendency of their conduct, yet lessening their moral guilt, it excited a considerable degree of compassion for their destiny. The punishment, indeed, was by very eminent members of the law of Scotland deemed and represented as an assumption of power by the court, which was not allowed by the statute enacting the penalties consequent on the species of sedition charged in the indictment. They were tried on an accusation of *leasing** *making*, a term, which in the Scotch law means stirring up sedition, by spreading false reports between the king and his subjects. It was asserted by Mr. Henry Erskine and others that the punishment annexed by the law of Scotland to this crime, was outlawry†, and not transportation; that the judges might sentence the convicts to be exiled from Scotland, but that their judgement could not extend to their conveyance to any other place. Others who were neither disposed nor competent to such legal disquisition, censured the judges for adopting the most rigorous mode that even by

The punishment is represented as excessive, and even illegal.

* *Leasing*, a Scotch word, in its general import signifies a *lie*; in law it is applied to the particular species of falsehood described in the text.

† The punishments are three, fine, imprisonment, or banishment: the question respecting the last was whether it meant merely the *exilium* of the civil law (outlawry), or the *deportatio*, (transportation). There were very respectable authorities on both sides.

their

their own hypothesis could be chosen. Many, however, deemed the castigation wholesome in example, and beneficial in tendency.

Scotch convention for new modelling the constitution,

In the end of October, 1793, a club of persons, entertaining similar extravagant ideas of reform as Messrs. Muir and Palmer, meeting at Edinburgh, denominated themselves *the Scotch convention of delegates* for obtaining annual parliaments and universal suffrage. This notable assembly consisted chiefly of tradesmen and mechanics, a few farmers, many of lower situation, and one or two men of abilities and knowledge, who were unfortunately smitten with the revolutionary contagion. These persons having met, adopted the modes and phraseology of the French convention, accosted each other by the term of *citizen*, divided themselves into *sections*, granted the honour of *sittings*, in humble imitation of their model; and proposed to concert measures with the innovating clubs, especially the London corresponding society, for the attainment of their object. It is remarkable that those who sought universal equality of political privileges, claimed this equality as *an inherent right*, and upon this assumption founded all their theories. Now political power is the inherent right of no individual: every man has a natural right to govern himself, but has no natural right to govern others*: government is the creature of expediency. In every society those ought to govern who are most fit for promo-

consists chiefly of persons of low condition.

* See this doctrine very ably explained by the learned and profound Fergusson's Principles of Moral and Political Science, vol. ii. p. 471, on the exercise of legislative power.

ting

CHAP. LIII. 1793. ting the general good. All men are not equally qualified for legislation, therefore it is not expedient that all men should have an equal suffrage, either in legislation or in constituting a legislature: the political inequality which these visionary innovators sought to reduce, arose from unequal means of advancing the general welfare which these levellers professed to pursue. On this absurd theory of human rights, without any proof of expediency, these agitators proceeded; but before they had brought their deliberations to a conclusion, they were interrupted by the civil power*, and dispersed. Skirving, Margarot, and Gerald, three of their most active members, were tried for sedition, and received sentence of transportation; which judgement incurred the same censure as the punishment that was appointed for Muir and Palmer. The conduct of the judges who passed the sentence was very much blamed, not only by democrats, but by the constitutional opponents of government; and was not completely approved by many others who were well affected to ministers; but the merits of the judgements afterwards underwent a discussion in parliament.

dispersed by the civil power.

Their leaders are tried and sentenced to transportation.

1794. Meeting of parliament.

The session opened on the 21st of January, 1794; and the diversities of political opinion continued to resolve themselves into three classes, the same in principle as before, though somewhat varied in detail, from the course of events. A few, at the head

* On this occasion Mr. Elder, the lord provost, peculiarly distinguished himself by his activity, resolution, and prompt decision.

head of whom was Mr. Burke, deemed war against regicides indispensibly necessary, until monarchy should be restored. A small, but greater number, reckoned the war unwise from the commencement, and a peace conducive to its professed purposes, to be at present attainable. The season of important victory, (according to Mr. Fox and others) all wise politicians thought the best opportunity for concluding a peace. The continuance of war, instead of subjugating France, tended to drive her to desperate efforts*. We had seen in her recent exertions arming her people in mass, and hurrying them on to the scene of war with unheard of rapidity, the consequences of invading her territories. Continued attempts to trench upon her dominions, would only drive her to still more extraordinary efforts. Besides, to what purpose was the continuance of war; the professed objects of the British government had been attained in the delivery of Holland, and the expulsion of the French from the Netherlands. Unless we proposed to restore monarchy, which ministers said we did not, we were now fighting without an object. A very numerous body, at the head of which was Mr. Pitt, maintained that the object of the war was and uniformly had been the same; the SECURITY of Britain, and general tranquillity†. The present terrible system of France was totally incompatible with these objects: in its dreadful nature it could not last. The people, if properly seconded and supported, would

Mr. Fox and his supporters recommend peace.

Arguments against and for.

Mr. Pitt's reasoning on the war and the internal system of France.

* See Parliamentary Debates, 21st January, 1794.

† Ibid.

CHAP. LIII. 1794. generally revolt against such an oppressive, rapacious, and desolating government. With the present rulers we could not make peace; but we might expect that their sway would be of short duration: the efforts of the terrible system had far exceeded any reasonable or probable expectation; but the resources from which they arose, so desperate and iniquitous, afforded in themselves the most certain symptoms and indications of the approaching decay of that fabric with which they were connected. The leading feature in the French revolutionary character, (said the minister) is a spirit of military enterprize, exerted not for the purposes of systematic ambition, but every where in its progress spreading terror and desolation. We are called in the present age to witness the political and moral phenomenon of a mighty and civilized people * formed into an artificial horde of banditti, throwing off all the restraints which have influenced men in social life, displaying a savage valour directed by a sanguinary spirit, forming rapine and destruction into a system, and perverting into their detestable purposes all the talents and ingenuity which they derived from their advanced stage of civilization, all the refinements of art, and the discoveries of science. We behold them uniting the utmost savageness and ferocity of design with consummate contrivance and skill in execution, and seemingly engaged in no less than a conspiracy to exterminate from the face of the earth all honour, humanity, justice, and religion. In this state can there be any question but to resist,

* Mr. Pitt's speech, 21st January, 1794. Ibid.

where

CHAP. LIII. 1794.

where resistance alone can be effectual, till such time, as by the blessing of providence upon our endeavours, we shall have secured the independence of this country, and the general interests of Europe. All the succeeding parties which had prevailed from the deposition of the king, however adverse to each other, had agreed in hostility to this country: the alternative of war and peace did not at present exist. Before we could relinquish the principles on which the war commenced, proof was necessary, either that the opinions which we had conceived of the views of France were erroneous, that the war was become desperate and impracticable, or that, from some improvement in the system and principles of the French, the justice and necessity which prompted us to commence the war, no longer co-operated. Lord Mornington spoke on the same side, and displayed very extensive information, and considerable ability. According to the representation of his lordship, the French views of aggrandizement were unlimited. Their desire of conquest sprang from principles which were subversive of all regular government. The avowals and exhortations of their most admired writers fully proved their schemes of boundless aggression, and their determined hostility to this country*. But a still surer proof was their conduct, which was uniformly and consistently hostile to this and every

Lord Mornington's view of the subject.

* To support his argument, his lordship quoted many extracts from French writings, especially from a pamphlet by Mr. Brissot, which had recently reached England, and which breathed hostility to Britain.

other

CHAP. LIII. 1794.

other nation within the reach of its influence. Our cause was originally just; the whole series of events confirmed its justice. But an important point to be considered was the probability of success: the recent efforts of the French arose from causes that could not long exist; these were the atrocious tyranny of the present government, which embraced men, money, liberty, property, and life, within its grasp. The dreadful fire was consuming the fuel by which it was nourished: their expenditure was enormous; their finances must be speedily exhausted*, and leave them no longer the means of so formidable hostilities: they would be compelled to succumb to the just and systematic exertions of the allies. But it was by our warlike efforts only that we could secure ourselves from the inroads of revolutionary France. In proportion as this system of tyranny consumed the property of France, it must endeavour to repair its disordered finances by foreign plunder. It must be the immediate interest of a government founded upon principles contrary to those of surrounding nations, to propagate the doctrines abroad by which it subsists at home, and

* This was an argument often repeated by Mr. Pitt at different periods of the war. It was partly founded on the reports and calculations of sir Francis d'Ivernois, who very accurately and justly explained the sources of finance known to former experience; but in his estimate, not sufficiently allowing for the enthusiastic spirit by which the French republicans were now actuated, did not consider its creative effects. Thence it was that all predictions of French bankruptcy, founded in the application of common rules to a case totally beyond their reach, were completely falsified.

to subvert every constitution which can form a dis- advantageous contrast to its own absurdities. Nothing could secure us against the future violence of the French, but an effectual reduction of their power. That was a purpose which we had the most reasonable prospects of ultimately accomplishing, and the strongest inducements to persevere. But even were the French rulers, instead of being eagerly resolved to persevere in a war indispensibly necessary to their usurped domination, disposed to accede to terms of equitable accommodation, where was the assurance of their stability? What reliance could we repose on the performance of their engagements? What was the purpose of attempting to negociate with a government utterly unable to fulfil its stipulations? Not only the characters, the dispositions, and the interests of those who exercised the powers of government of France, but the very nature of that system they had established, rendered a treaty of peace upon safe and honourable terms impracticable at present, and consequently required a vigorous and unremitting prosecution of the war. A very great majority in parliament, convinced that peace could not be preserved with the present rulers of France, and confident that their extraordinary efforts would speedily exhaust their own source, approved the continuance of the war, and its most vigorous prosecution.

A great majority approves of the continuance of the war.

Mr. Fox and Mr. Sheridan persevered in maintaining the inexpediency of the war, the improbability of success, and the wisdom of peace. They denied that France had been hostile to this country. The chief charge of the present rulers against their predecessors

The opponents of the war impute to the combination the astonishing efforts of France.

CHAP. LIII.

1794. Messrs. Fox and Sheridan predict the dissolution of the confederacy, and the triumph of the French.

predecessors was, that they involved their country in a war with Britain contrary to the interests and wishes of the people. But whencesoever the war had originated, the exertions and events afforded no reasonable ground for expectation that the objects, even if just, were attainable. The efforts of the French arose from the enthusiasm of conceived liberty and patriotism. So devoted (it was said) are the whole people of France to the cause which they have espoused, so determined are they to maintain the struggle in which they have engaged, so paramount and domineering is the enthusiastic spirit of liberty in their bosoms, so insignificant, comparatively, are all other considerations, and finally, so bitter and active is their animosity against the conspiring powers which surround them, that individual property has ceased to be regarded even by the possessor, but as subsidiary to the public cause; and the government which had demanded these unprecedented sacrifices, yet retains its power, and does not appear to have impaired its popularity*. France, by the pressure of the allies upon her frontier, had become a school of military wonder; and if other governments persisted in their design of thus goading her to almost præternatural exertions, we should see a military republic firmly established in the heart of Europe†. Such was the energetic spirit of the French, that we might be sure, with

* See Mr. Sheridan's speech on the first day of the session, 1794. Parliamentary Debates.

† See Marquis of Lansdown's speech, on his motion for peace.

the

1794. Difcuffion of the queftion with whom fhall we treat.

the refources that fpirit would call into action, we could never fucceed. In anfwering the minifterial objection, with whom could we treat, we might negociate with the exifting rulers, and depend for adherence to pacific engagements, neither on the juftice or ftability of the prefent fet, but on their intereft, and the interefts of their fucceffors, whoever they might be, and of the whole French nation. Intereft, and not good faith, had been our fecurity in our various treaties with the defpotic princes of France. The confederacy, in which we endeavoured to make an impreffion upon France, compofed of heterogeneous materials purfuing different objects, Mr. Fox ftrongly and repeatedly predicted, muft be foon diffolved. If the objects of the war had been juft and wife, the plans were disjointed, inconfiftent, and confequently ineffectual. But minifters, faid Mr. Fox, never defined the object: they vaguely told us we were fighting for *fecurity*; but wherein was that fecurity to confift. In former wars our objects had been definite, to prevent the aggrandizement of France*, by the acceffion of one of her princes to the throne of Spain†; to protect our merchantmen from the fearch of Spaniards‡; to defend our colonies from the encroachments of France ||; to refift the interference of foreign nations, in difputes between us and our colonies§. There the objects, whether right or wrong, were definite: but here they were barren generalities, mere abftractions: if, as

* War 1689. † War 1702. ‡ War 1739.
|| War 1756. § War 1778.

 minifters

CHAP. LIII. 1794.

ministers professed, we were not warring for the restoration of the Bourbon princes to the throne of France. From their conduct, however, he was convinced they did propose that restoration which he predicted no foreign force would ever produce. He had spoken, and would always continue to speak, against a war which sought no object beneficial to Great Britain; required exertions that drained her resources, and anticipated the products of future industry. He prophecied that the war with France, like the war with America, would terminate in disappointment. We were incurring an enormous expence, in return for which we had no prospect of advantage or compensation. Such conduct might be varnished by splendid eloquence, or justified by sophistical logic, yet when viewed by common sense and common prudence, it was infatuated blindness that was producing consequences which the present and future ages would have strong reasons to lament and deplore. The minister merely played on the passions which he had himself enflamed, without addressing the reason or consulting the interest of his countrymen. These arguments were repeated both on direct motions for peace*, and various other questions connected with the war, but produced no effect on the majorities in parliament.

Mr. Fox prophecies that the war with France, like the war with America, would terminate in disappointment.

Various motions for peace are ineffectual.

Next to peace and war, questions arising from internal discontent, projects of innovation, and the prosecutions which some abettors of these had un-

* February 17th, by the Marquis of Lansdown: May 30th, by the Duke of Bedford and Mr. Fox, in their respective houses.

dergone,

dergone, occupied the chief ſhare of parliamentary deliberation. Meſſrs. Muir and Palmer, and the ſentenced members of the Scottiſh convention, in conſequence of the power left by the judgment with his majeſty and council to appoint the place of deportation, had been ordered to be ſent to Botany Bay. In the execution of their ſentence they had been ſent on board tranſports at Woolwich, along with other convicts deſtined for the ſame place. Many who admitted the juſtneſs of the judgment, deprecated the ſeverity of the treatment; but a ſtronger ground was taken in parliament: it was maintained, that the ſentence was not legal, and that the criminal juriſprudence of Scotland required a reviſion, which ſhould render it more definite and preciſe, and put it on the ſame footing with the penal law of England. Motions to theſe intents were brought forward by Mr. Adam, a counſellor of great eminence, deeply converſant both in Scottiſh and Engliſh law, with moral and political ſcience, which could appreciate their ſeparate and comparative merits. With this view, he propoſed to bring forward two bills; the one of which ſhould grant an appeal to the lords of parliament from the judgment of the courts of juſticiary and circuit in Scotland, in matters of law: the other ſhould aſſimilate the criminal law of England and Scotland, that crimes and miſdemeanours affecting the ſtate ſhould be on the ſame footing in both countries; that a grand jury ſhould be held in Scotland in the ſame caſes as in England; and that the power of the lord advocate ſhould be the ſame as the power of the attorney general. Theſe objects Mr. Adam had

Queſtions reſpecting the trials for ſedition in Scotland.

Mr. Adam's propoſed amendment of the Scottiſh criminal law.

 in

CHAP. LIII. 1794.

in view before, and in the preceding session had announced his intention of proposing alterations which should assimilate the criminal law of the two countries. But the recent trials in Scotland, in his apprehension, had rendered the discussion of the subject more urgently necessary; and made it adviseable to change the intended form of the propositions so as to include a declaratory and retrospective, as well as an enacting and prospective operation. His first proposition was introduced to the house of commons on the 4th of February. Its purpose was, to establish an appeal from the court of justiciary to the Lords, and to have a clause inserted which should subject the sentences of 1793 to the projected revisal. Having stated historically and juridically the facts and tendencies respecting the law as it now stood, and its administration; he observed, that there was not only a strong analogy between the criminal codes of England and of Scotland in the great purposes of all penal laws, but a striking resemblance also in their respective course of proceedings. Their mode of trial by jury was the same; every thing was the same except one circumstance; a right in the house of lords to revise the sentences of the court of Justiciary and the circuit courts. With regard to the inconvenience that might accrue by bringing cases of criminal law from Scotland to a tribunal that did not understand the system of Scottish criminal law, this was an objection that applied much less to penal than civil cases, subjected by the union to the appeal which he now proposed *. Criminal

* Speech of Mr. Adam, introductory to his motion. Parliamentary Debates, 4th February, 1794.

laws

laws had, in all countries, a confiderable likenefs, becaufe there was in all countries an abhorrence of crimes; whereas civil laws greatly differed under different circumftances, objects, and purfuits of the feveral focieties. Mr. Adam moved for leave to bring in a bill to give an appeal to the lords in parliament from judgments and fentences of the court of jufticiary and circuit courts in Scotland, in matters of law, and that this be referred to a committee of the whole houfe. The motion was oppofed on the following ground: it was a total change in the law, as it had exifted both fince and before the union. No appeal had ever lain from the jufticiary court either to the parliament of Scotland or the parliament of Great Britain; there was no reafon for the propofed innovation, as no evil had been felt under the eftablifhed mode. The greater number of the inhabitants of Scotland were perfectly fatisfied with the adminiftration of law as it now ftood. They were perfuaded of its excellence, and fenfible of the bleffings which they enjoyed under its protection. It was impolitic and hazardous to change a fyftem experienced to be beneficial for a fyftem untried, and confequently of doubtful operation in that country, and not fought by the people for whofe benefit it was intended *. After a great difplay of legal and political ability by the mover, his fupporters †, and his opponents ‡, the motion was negatived by a

* Thefe arguments are to be found principally in the fpeech of Mr. Anftruther. See Parliamentary Debates, February 4th, 1794.

† Chiefly Meffrs. Adair and Fox.

‡ Meffrs. Anftruther, Watfon, and the Lord Advocate. See Parliamentary Debates.

 majority

CHAP. LIII.

1794.

propoſed enquiry into the conduct of the Scottiſh judges:

his ſpeech on that ſubject.

majority of a hundred and twenty-ſix to thirty-one. Defeated on the queſtion of appeal, Mr. Adam propoſed an enquiry which he had intended to have made a part of the ſame bill. He moved for a copy of the record of the trials of Meſſrs. Muir and Palmer, on the 24th of February; and on the 10th of March propoſed the reviſion of the ſentence paſſed upon theſe two gentlemen. He undertook to prove, firſt, that the crimes charged againſt Meſſrs. Muir and Palmer were what the law of Scotland calls *leaſing making*, or public libel; that, by the law of Scotland, the puniſhment annexed to leaſing making was fine, impriſonment, or baniſhment, but not tranſportation: that the acts proved againſt theſe gentlemen did not amount to leaſing making, the crime charged in the indictment. If the mover made good theſe poſitions, the obvious inference was, that the Scottiſh judges had, in the late ſentences, greatly exceeded their power; and if they did ſo, the illegality would be, in impoſing ſuch a puniſhment, extremely tyrannical. The mover ſupported his legal poſitions by very extenſive knowledge, juridical and hiſtorical, reciprocally illuſtrating and enforcing each other; he endeavoured from ſtatute, analogy, and precedent, explained by their civil and political reaſons, to eſtabliſh his doctrines; and attempted to prove that the acts, caſes, and deciſions which he quoted, were not detached or inſulated, but all reſulted from the ſame ſpirit and principles, operating moſt effectually at the beſt times, under the moſt admired authorities and pureſt adminiſtrations of juſtice. He alſo contended, that tranſportation to places beyond

yond ſeas neither was nor could be a part of the Scottiſh law before the union, becauſe there were no places beyond ſeas in the poſſeſſion of Scotland; and no act had ſince the union, been paſſed, allowing Scottiſh courts to tranſport in caſes of ſedition. On theſe grounds he denied the right of the Scottiſh judges to inflict ſuch a puniſhment if the crime had been eſtabliſhed; and farther, aſſerted that the charge was not proved. Having thus endeavoured to ſhew that criminal juſtice had been perverted, he forcibly and eloquently ſtated the evils, moral and political, which muſt ariſe from ſuch perverſion; and concluded with moving the production of the records.

Reply of the lord advocate.

The lord advocate, chief law officer of the crown in Scotland, had officially acted as the leading public accuſer againſt thoſe perſons; and now vindicated the judgments in queſtion as legal and meritorious. He endeavoured to prove, that though baniſhment, by the Engliſh law, might not be the ſame with tranſportation, they were regarded as ſynonimous by the Scottiſh law: this (he ſaid) was their acceptation uniformly in the opinion of criminal courts and lawyers; and he quoted caſes to illuſtrate his doctrine. Such conſtruction, he argued, was perfectly conformable to the practice of the Scottiſh juſticiary courts, and the Scottiſh privy council; and he particularly ſtated inſtances that had occurred in the reign of Charles II. to juſtify his expoſition. After endeavouring to prove that ſuch was the law, he vindicated its recent exerciſe. The perſons in queſtion had been extremely active in ſedition, and deſerved exemplary puniſh-

 ment

CHAP. LIII.

1794.

The motion is negatived.

Third proposition of Mr. Adam.

Masterly speech of Mr. Adam on that subject.

Answer of Mr Secretary Dundas.

ment. The chief speakers * on both sides took a very active share in this debate, which produced a display of legal and political ability that has been rarely exceeded in parliament: the motion was negatived by a great majority. Notwithstanding these repeated disappointments, the manly spirit of Mr. Adam proceeded in the course which he conceived to be right. On the 25th of March he introduced a third motion for regulating the justiciary courts of Scotland: the general object of his proposition was the assimilation of the Scottish to the English criminal law, in its substance, sanctions, rules, and forms of administration. The discussion of this subject necessarily introduced a repetition of certain arguments which had been already used; but also intermingled new matter. The mover endeavoured to prove, by accurate enumeration, the general incompetence of the Scottish criminal system to answer the purposes of substantial justice; he kept his present proposition distinct from the special subjects and enquiries which, at his motion, the house had lately been discussing; and considered the present as a general question, which derived its reasons and importance from the general system of Scottish penal law and its administration. Mr. Secretary Dundas denied the necessity or policy of a change in a system with

* Messrs. Sheridan and Fox on the one hand, and Mr. Pitt on the other, exerted themselves in respectively supporting Messrs. Adam and Dundas. Mr. Dundas's exhibition on this subject was universally allowed to be able, and worthy of the high office which he filled. Mr. Adam's speech was, by all parties, deemed one of the first that had ever been delivered upon a subject of law within that house, and made a very great addition to a character fast rising in eminence.

which

which the people subject to it were thoroughly contented; instituted a comparison between the Scottish and English law, and endeavoured to prove, that in many cases the Scottish penal code was much superior. Respecting sedition, when he saw the attacks that were daily made on the very vitals of the constitution; when he observed this systematically done; when he found that works in their nature hostile to the government of the country, and addressed to the lower orders of society, were spread with indefatigable industry, he must avow his conviction that the punishment annexed to this crime by the law of England was not sufficiently severe to deter persons from this pactice, and that the legislature must adopt a different mode of procedure upon that subject *. The lord advocate, with more minute specification, defended the law of Scotland and its administration. The attorney general, with his usual acuteness and moderation, defended the criminal justice of Scotland, as adapted to the general purposes of penal codes; the sentiments, character, pursuits, and habits of the people; and as firmly fixed by the articles of the union; but he delivered no opinion on the competency of the English penal code, as it then stood, to restrain sedition. The seemingly incidental observations of Mr. Dundas respecting the inadequacy of the English laws, did not escape the penetration of Mr. Fox. He appeared to consider it not merely as an illustiative remark on the subject before the house, but as an indirect intimation of an agitated change, and intended to found the opinion and feelings of the commons: he warned

Reply of Mr. Fox.

* See Parliamentary Debates, March 25th, 1794.

him

CHAP. LIII.

1794. The propofition is negatived.

him to beware how he meddled with the liberties of Englifhmen, and to confider well before he increafed punifhment. This third motion of Mr. Adam experienced a fimilar fate with the two former; and was negatived by a very great majority. Petitions from Meffrs. Muir and Palmer were laid before the houfe, praying the reconfideration of the fentences; but the commons refufed to interpofe in a judgment which had been regularly pronounced by a competent court. Thofe important fubjects which Mr. Adam fubmitted to the difcuffion of the houfe of commons, were alfo introduced before the lords by the Earl of Lauderdale. His lordfhip's motion was negatived without a divifion; and the lord chancellor propofed a refolution, declaring, "there was no ground for interfering in the eftablifhed courts of criminal juftice as adminiftered under the conftitution, and by which the rights, liberties, and properties of all ranks of fubjects were protected." Thus finifhed the parliamentary confideration of fubjects which warmly interefted the public mind. Meffrs. Muir, Palmer, and alfo the condemned members of the Scottifh convention, were fent to Botany Bay. Many out of parliament, who ufually coincided with adminiftration, reckoned this punifhment extremely fevere. Though unable to follow Mr. Adam through the refearches of legal difquifition, or the depths of legal fcience, yet, conceiving the convicts in queftion to be rather mifled by enthufiafm than prompted by malignant intentions, they thought that the punifhment far exceeded the moral guilt. Others, who deemed fevere punifhment neceffary, argued, that whatever the

the intention might be, the tendency was ſo pernicious as to require the moſt rigorous chaſtiſement which the law permitted, for the future prevention of ſo dangerous incendiaries; but this laſt reaſoning proceeding on a ſuppoſition that the law did permit ſuch ſentences, could make no impreſſion on thoſe who denied the premiſes.

Progreſs of the innovating ſpirit among the lower ranks.

The puniſhment of theſe agitators in Scotland did not deter innovating projectors in England from advancing with their ſchemes. During the preceding year clubs had met, both in full aſſemblies and detached committees, to project plans and deviſe expedients for effecting the manifold and radical changes which the Britiſh conſtitution required to ſuit the ideas which theſe perſons had formed of the perfection of political ſyſtems.

Proceedings of the democratical ſocieties.

Of the three ſocieties which we have already recorded to have congratulated the French convention on the downfal of monarchy, the revolution club appears to have ceaſed its collective exiſtence; moſt of its members being probably joined to the other fraternities. The other two, the conſtitutional and correſponding ſocieties, very ſeduloufly made certain reſults of their deliberations known to the world by advertiſements, ſubſcribed with the names, and *ſanctioned by the authority* of Mr. Daniel Adams *, under clerk, and Mr.

* This Mr. Daniel Adams I have ſeen before he betook himſelf to his legiſlative occupations. He then appeared to be a common-place, harmleſs, vain man, deſirous of what, in colloquial language, is called *daſhing*. His chief ſubject of converſation was the high company which he kept, and his own importance in the ſaid company. I have no doubt that the man was actuated

CHAP. LIII.

1794.

Mr. Thomas Hardy, ſhoe-maker, reſpectively, ſecretaries to the conſtitutional and correſponding ſociety. Theſe were ſeconded by hand-bills and pamphlets, ſummoning the people to aſſociate for the attainment of radical reform. In the courſe of their preparations they had called ſeveral meetings; eſpecially one at Chalk Farm, near Hampſtead. There ſeveral intemperate ſpeeches were made; and when feſtivity intermingled with politics, very inflammatory toaſts were propoſed, and the meeting was undoubtedly ſeditious. Some of its moſt active members, not only at that time, but in their habitual conduct, manifeſted themſelves inimical to the Britiſh conſtitution, as far as their enmity could operate; hoſtile to kingly government of all kinds, and deſirous of eſtabliſhing a jacobinical democracy. Among theſe one of the moſt noted was John Thelwal, deſtined to the ſame kind of perpetual remembrance which has followed John Ball, Wat Tyler, Jack Cade, and Kett the tanner, thoſe celebrated votaries of radical reform in their days. This John Thelwal, beſides his joint efforts with others of the correſponding ſocieties, was ſingly and ſeparately inſtrumental to the purpoſes of ſedition by a kind of

Meeting at ChalkFarm.

Lectures of John Thelwal againſt the Britiſh conſtitution and kingly government.

actuated by the ſame love of diſtinction in his reforming projects, and that no inconſiderable motive to his undertaking the office of ſecretary was to read his own name at the bottom of the advertiſements. Indeed, as I have already ſaid, after conſiderable enquiry and reflection, I think no one paſſion produced more votaries of change than vanity. But whatever might be the ſpring that ſet ſuch an engine in motion, the dangerous operation was the ſame when it was actually moved.

periodical

periodical declamations, which he ſtyled *political lectures*. Theſe lectures were chiefly comments on Tom Paine's works and ſimilar performances, with abuſe of the preſent conſtitution and government, more direct and pointed to its ſpecific meaſures than even the efforts of Paine himſelf. With the moſt ſcurrilous invectives againſt eſtabliſhments, which he called uſurpation, his harangues mingled vehement exhortations * to revolution, or, as he phraſed it, to reſume the rights of nature †. Government obſerved the open proceedings of theſe ſocieties and individuals, and ſuſpected the ſecret machinations of the ringleaders: to diſcover the truth they adopted the policy which is neceſſary in apprehended plots ‡; and employed deſpicable inſtruments that are eaſily to be found in all great cities, as ſpies that were to attend the conventicles of ſedition, and to become members of the ſocieties, in order to betray the ſecrets with which they might be entruſted. In conſequence of diſcoveries which were obtained through theſe and other channels, miniſters ordered

* See Thelwal's Tribune, paſſim.

† See Rights of Nature, in oppoſition to the uſurpation of eſtabliſhment, by the ſame, paſſim.

‡ The anti-miniſterial writings of the times ſeverely inveighed againſt government for employing wretches ſo very deſtitute of honour, and thence inferred to be ſo unworthy of belief. But the beſt and wiſeſt ſtateſman, in inveſtigating ſecret and aſſociated villany, muſt often make uſe of worthleſs inſtruments. As well might Cicero be blamed for employing the proſtitute Fulvia in eliciting information reſpecting a conſpiracy which he deemed dangerous to Rome, as miniſters for employing ſuch fellows as Goſlin, Lynham, Taylor, and Groves, to elicit information concerning a conſpiracy which they conceived dangerous to Britain.

CHAP. LIII.

1794.

Leaders arrested, and their papers seized.

Hardy and Adams to be arrefted, and their papers to be feized; and immediately after Thelwal, Loveit a hair-dreffer, Martin an attorney, and two or three others, to be apprehended. In a few days the arreftations extended to men of higher rank and reputation: Mr. Joyce, a refpectable clergyman, chaplain to Lord Stanhope; Mr. Kydd, a barrifter of talents and faft rifing character; the eminent and celebrated Mr. Horne Tooke, were among the numbers of the confined. The papers being examined, it was found that the two focieties had concerted a project for affembling, by their joint influence, a national convention. This defign, in combination with the many other proceedings of the focieties, was conftrued by minifters to be a confpiracy againft the conftitution; and confequently (they inferred), a confpiracy againft the king, amounting to high treafon. His majefty fent meffages to both houfes, announcing the difcoveries which had been made, and referring to their confideration the voluminous papers that had been feized. The minifters propofed a fecret committee for the infpection of thefe documents. Mr. Fox reprobated the projected fecrecy as unconftitutional and unneceffary, tending to promote that fyftem of mifery and delufion with which he had often charged the meafures of adminiftration. Whatever (he faid) the criminality is, drag it openly to light: befides, by a refolution of the houfe, the feizure of papers has been declared to be illegal, unlefs treafon be charged in the warrant, which authorizes fuch feizure. Minifters replied, that treafon was charged in the warrant; that the feizure, therefore, was not illegal; that not only

Plan of a national convention difcovered by minifters.

prudent

prudent policy directed, but the most imperious necessity dictated, secrecy in their inquisitorial proceedings, as the very existence of parliament and the constitution was at stake. On the 12th of March, at the instance of ministers, secret committees were nominated; and on the 16th the first report being read to the commons, Mr. Pitt stated at great length his view of its contents. He traced the history and proceedings of the societies for the last two years: they had adopted (he said) the monstrous doctrines of the Rights of Man, which seduced the weak and ignorant to overturn government, law, property, security, and whatever was valuable; which had destroyed whatever was valuable in France, and endangered the safety, if not the existence, of every nation in Europe. The object of all these societies was the practical inculcation of such doctrines. A correspondence prior to the enormities of France had subsisted between these societies and the French jacobin clubs. When the jacobin faction, which usurped the government, had commenced hostilities against Great Britain, these societies as far as they could, had pursued the same conduct, expressed the same attachment to their cause, adopted their appellations, and formed the design of disseminating the same principles. Their operations were chiefly directed to manufacturing towns. They considered the convention at Edinburgh as the representatives of the people, asserted the innocence of those members who fell under the sentence of the law, and declared they could only look for reform in such a convention. But the chief attention of the house was required in considering a society, though

Committees of both houses appointed to examine the papers. Report of the committees. Mr. Pitt states his view of the substance.

CHAP. LIII. 1794.

though composed of the meanest and most despicable of the people, who acted upon the worst jacobin principles, and had within it the means of the most unbounded extension and rapid increase. This society, comprehending thirty divisions in London, was connected by a systematic correspondence with other societies scattered through the manufacturing towns. It had arrived at such a pitch of audacity as to declare its competence to watch over the progress of legislation; to investigate its principles; to prescribe limits for its actions, beyond which if it presumed to advance, an end was to be put to the existence of parliament itself. Recently this corresponding society had laid before the constitutional society a plan for assembling a convention for all England. The evident object of the proposed meeting, in Mr. Pitt's opinion, was to exercise legislative and judicial capacities, to overturn the established system of government, and wrest from the parliament the power which the constitution has lodged in their hands. This plan was to be speedily carried into execution, and a centrical spot * was chosen to facilitate the meeting of their delegates. An assembly had been held on the 14th of April, and resolutions were passed which arraigned every branch of the government; threatened the sovereign, insulted the house of peers, and accused the commons of insufficiency. Declarations were uttered, that if certain measures were pursued, whether with or without the consent of parliament, they should be rescinded; and that

* Sheffield.

the constitution was utterly destroyed*. The proofs of these allegations were their own records; and it farther appeared from the report, that arms had been actually procured and distributed by the societies; and that, so far from breaking up this jacobin army, they had shewn themselves immoveably bent on their pursuit, and displayed preparations of defiance and resistance to government. From all these facts Mr. Pitt inferred there was a very dangerous conspiracy, which it became them, by seasonable interference, to prevent from being carried into execution†. In times of apprehended rebellion it had been usual to enact a temporary suspension of the habeas corpus law: that act had been suspended when the constitution and liberty of the country were most guarded and respected; and such a suspension was more particularly called for at this crisis, when attempts were made to disseminate principles dangerous to that constitution for the preservation of which the law had been made: Mr. Pitt, therefore, proposed a bill, "empowering his majesty to secure and detain all persons suspected of designs against his crown and government." Mr. Fox expressed his astonishment that the committee should solemnly call the attention of the house to facts so long notorious: the persons in question had for two years openly and publicly avowed the acts now asserted to amount to a treasonable plot. If this was a conspiracy, it was the most garrulous conspiracy

Mr. Pitt proposes a bill for detaining suspected persons without allowing them the benefit of the habeas corpus.

Mr. Fox's view of the alleged conspiracy.

* Report of the secret committee of the house of commons concerning the seditious societies.

† Parliamentary Debates, May 16th, 1794.

that

CHAP. LIII. 1794.

that was ever recorded in history. Plots for overturning government had been published for two years in the daily newspapers; the real transactions reported by the committee were chiefly repetitions of stale advertisements. What was the real amount, taken apart from the comments of Mr. Pitt's eloquence? Societies had been constituted for the purposes of parliamentary reform; these had corresponded together; and they had corresponded with France when at peace with this country. To effect the purposes of parliamentary reform, a convention had been held in Edinburgh: all these facts were notorious and stale; a convention was proposed for the purposes of reform in England; and this was *the only new information*. The project was in itself contemptible and ridiculous, and could not really alarm the minister, or any man in his senses. The remainder was not statement of facts, but inferences either of the committee or minister; containing an imputation of intention to overturn government, without the slightest evidence that such intentions existed. No grounds were adduced that could possibly justify such a momentous intrenchment on the liberties of the subject as this bill proposed. The minister, Mr. Fox believed, was not really alarmed *; but it was necessary for his views to keep up or create some new cause of panic, to gain a continuation of power over the people †. Why had not the law officers of the crown

* Parliamentary Debates, 16th May, 1794.

† This opinion was still more poignantly asserted by Mr. Sheridan.

prosecuted

prosecuted the authors of the writings or acts reported to the house, if they were so very mischievous? The bill underwent a very interesting discussion in both houses: its other supporters agreeing with Mr. Pitt, contended that the facts brought to light evinced the existence of a most dangerous conspiracy, requiring the proposed suspension in order farther to discover its extent, and to prevent its wider diffusion. The other opposers agreed with Mr. Fox that no conspiracy or project of rebellion existed, and that the bill was an unnecessary and destructive infringement of British liberty; but the design of Mr. Pitt prevailed, and the proposition of ministers was passed into a law. By persons who admitted criminalty in the facts charged, different opinions were entertained concerning the degree of guilt which, if proved, they would constitute. The Lord Chancellor Loughborough, and several other eminent lawyers, conceived that the allegations, if established, would amount to a conspiracy against the king and government, and must be considered as intending or compassing the king's death. No less eminent lawyers, and at their head Lord Thurlow, declared, that though proved, they would not amount to high treason; that the interpretation by which they should be denominated high treason, was totally inconsistent with the letter of our statutes, which precisely and accurately defined that crime; and with the spirit of our laws, which rejected circuitous construction. These thought that the allegations amounted to sedition, and that the persons who should be proved actively guilty would well deserve the punishment annexed to sedition by the laws

The bill is passed into a law.

Ministers, including the chancellor, deem the crimes charged to be high treason.

Lord Thurlow asserts, that by the law of England they are not treason.

CHAP. LIII.

1794.

The accused are sent to the Tower.

laws of England. Government having adopted the chancellor's opinion, and resolved to prosecute the persons arrested for high treason, sent them to the Tower, there to be confined until evidence should be prepared for their trials.

Supplies.

These were the principal discussions and measures concerning subjects of internal tranquillity, whether retrospective or prospective, that engaged parliament during the present session. The other objects which chiefly occupied its deliberations were warlike preparations both for defence and attack: the investigation of belligerent measures and events, and schemes of finance.

Debate on the introduction of Hessian troops.

An expedition having been projected to re-animate and assist the insurgents of La Vendee, a body of Hessian troops was hired as part of the force destined for that service: they reached the coast of the Isle of Wight, and, to prevent sickness, were disembarked until preparations should be ready. No objection was made to the employment or destination of those troops; nor was the propriety or necessity of landing them called in question; but it was maintained in parliament, that whenever the introduction of foreign troops became necessary, ministers ought either to obtain the previous consent of parliament, or resort to a bill of indemnity. Without discussing the general question of prerogative, so as to form any precedent for future times, it was determined that the specific exigency justified the measure in the present case.

Bill for the employment of emigrants.

Among the military supplies proposed for the service of the current year, was a corps of emigrant volunteers. Mr. Pitt introduced a bill for that purpose

pose, to enable the emigrant subjects of France to enlist in his majesty's service on the continent of Europe, and to receive native officers. Such a corps must be (it was said by its supporters) of wonderful efficacy, especially if sent to assist the royalists of La Vendee. The great body of the French was inimical to the terrible system, and wanted nothing but the prospect of steady and effectual aid to animate and invigorate them against the convention. The present usurpation of France was incompatible with the existence of other governments; and till we could overthrow their system of politics, we must not hope for peace or security *. In this endeavour he thought it right to unite with us persons who had the same reasons with ourselves, and who called upon the British nation to give them arms. As the present proposition, combined with the reasoning by which it was supported, appeared to approach nearer to interference in the internal affairs of France than ministers had before professed to intend, it was very warmly promoted by Mr. Burke, who seemed at last to conceive hopes that Britain would resolve, and explicitly avow its resolution of carrying on war *for the restoration of monarchy*. Mr. Dundas, indeed, had not stated the restitution of kingly government as synonimous with the overthrow of the existing usurpation. Mr. Burke, however, conceived that the terrible system did not spring from the individual character of Robespierre, but from the revolution which over-

* See Mr. Dundas's speech on the bill for employing emigrants, when before the committee.

CHAP. LIII. 1794. turned the eſtabliſhed orders, enabled and ſtimulated Robeſpierre's ambition to operate. The emigrant corps, he hoped, aſſiſting the La Vendeans, if powerfully and comprehenſively ſupported by this country, would pave the way for a counter-revolution. Meſſrs. Fox and Sheridan, with ſome others, oppoſed the bill: they alleged that it tended to render the war more ferocious, which muſt always be the conſequence of arming citizen againſt citizen; raiſed a force that was totally inefficacious, and that would certainly be overpowered; employed the votaries of the old government againſt the new government; and thus, contrary to the profeſſions of miniſters, really interfered in the internal affairs of France. They farther repreſented the meaſure as inconſiſtent with humanity towards the emigrants themſelves. The French government had declared that no quarter ſhould be given to Frenchmen caught in arms againſt the republic. In its immediate operation it muſt encourage the moſt cruel retaliation and ferocious vengeance; in its ultimate reſult, from the immenſe force of the preſent government, it would expoſe the emigrants to the moſt dreadful butchery. On theſe grounds they oppoſed the bill; but their objections were over-ruled: it paſſed through both houſes with very great majorities, and was enacted into a law.

Apprehenſions of an invaſion.

In the courſe of the ſeſſion a meſſage from the king announced the avowed intentions of the enemy to invade this kingdom. A great augmentation of the militia, and an addition of volunteer fencible corps were accordingly voted: a letter from the ſecretary of ſtate to the lord lieutenants of counties, ſolicited

solicited voluntary subscriptions to levy troops. The solicitation was represented, by members of opposition, as an attempt to raise money without consent of parliament. It was contended by ministers, that voluntary contributions of the subject for the purpose of assisting levies, when they received the sanction of parliament were perfectly legal, and consonant to precedent and practice; and quoted the contributions and levies during the rebellion in 1745; in the beginning of the seven years war; and in the American war, after the capture of Burgoyne. The supplies for the present year were very great and expensive: eighty-five thousand seamen, and a hundred and seventy-five thousand landsmen were voted. Besides the usual ways and means, there was a loan of eleven millions: new taxes on British and foreign spirits, bricks and tiles, slate, crown and plate glass, met with little opposition: duties on paper and on attornies were represented as oppressive, but on the whole it was allowed, that the imposts of Mr. Pitt, affecting the rich or middling classes, displayed financial ability and discrimination. Various subsidies were voted to foreign princes, and justified on the ground of contributing to the great purposes of the war. But the most important of these was the subsidy to the king of Prussia. On the 20th of April his majesty sent to the house of commons a copy of a treaty concluded by him with the States General and the king of Prussia, for the purpose of more effectually carrying on the war. By the stipulations with Frederic William Britain had agreed to pay him £50,000. a month; £100,000. a month for forage; in all, for the re-

1794. Voluntary contributions for raising troops.

Supplies and taxes.

Subsidies to foreign powers—

to the king of Prussia.

 maining

CHAP. LIII. 1794.

maining nine months of the present year, thirteen hundred and fifty thousand pounds: the whole year would amount to £1,800,000., out of which the States General were to pay £400,000. Embarked (said Mr. Pitt) as we were in war so just and necessary, it was material for us to possess the aid of so powerful a force. The king of Prussia was certainly a principal in the war, but unable to carry it on without pecuniary assistance; and his force, for which we were engaged to pay, was to be employed for our advantage, and the conquests to be made in the name of the maritime states. The astonishing exertions of France rendered efforts on our part additionally necessary; and the object of the war being so important, it would be the most preposterous folly to slacken our exertions in order to spare expence*. Opposition reprobated this policy as the height of profusion, and contended, first, that from the efforts of the king of Prussia, no benefit could accrue to this country which would compensate the cost; secondly, that we had no security that when the money was contributed he would perform the engagements which he incurred. The king of Prussia had originally begun the war: this very beginning of his, whether through the French aggression or his own, had ultimately involved us in the contest. Now, the king of Prussia having engaged other powers in the quarrel, desired to withdraw himself, and must be bribed to persevere in a war, which, but for himself, would have never been begun †.

* Parliamentary Debates, 29th April, 1794.

† Parliamentary Debates, 29th April, 1794.

His

His conduct contained such a mixture of perfidy, fraud, and meanness, as was unparalleled in all modern political history. No man of the least prudence could repose any confidence in one by whom he had been deceived yet were the people of this country to pay to such a person one million three hundred and fifty thousand pounds, the return for which was to depend upon his own honour: let us not trust a prince whose good faith we had so much reason to doubt. But if the king of Prussia was to be considered merely as a hirer of troops, why were the soldiers which we paid to be commanded by himself? The direction of mercenaries should belong to the power which purchased their service. These arguments produced little effect: a great majority of the house conceiving the proposed subsidy to the king of Prussia to be conducive to the purposes of the war, the advantage and honour of this country, agreed to the motion which was proposed by ministers.

Bill to prevent sums vested in the British funds by French subjects, from being seized by the French rulers.

While the British government adopted such measures as it thought most likely to strengthen our means of carrying on the war, it also endeavoured to impair the resources of the enemy. As the public funds of Britain afforded the most unquestionable security to the proprietors of money: there very large sums belonging to French subjects were vested. Agreeably to their general principles of converting private property to the use of the revolutionary government, the French rulers had turned their attention to this subject. They had formed a resolution, directing the use of every possible expedient to ascertain the property of French

subjects

subjects in foreign funds, in order that it might be delivered up to the state and become public property; and that when the transfer was made, it should be paid for in assignats estimated at par. Mr. Pitt discerned the object of this scheme, and proposed means to prevent its operation. The purpose, he saw, was, to supply the resources for carrying on the war by plundering individuals of their property deposited in foreign countries, as they had before grasped the property in their own country. A general principle of our laws (he observed) was, that the payment of any debt owing to an alien enemy may be suspended during the war; and the king, if he thought fit, might attach it as belonging to an alien enemy: to continue, however, the benefits of mercantile intercourse, which were for the advantage of individuals, without trenching on public safety, the milder practice of modern times long suffered the rigour of this law to relax. In the present case Mr. Pitt proposed to secure the individuals by withholding their property from the grasp of the revolutionary rulers; and thus, whilst private advantage was promoted, resources sought by the enemy would be arrested. For this purpose he proposed a bill to prevent the application to the use of the present government of France, of all monies and effects in the hands of his majesty's subjects, the property of individuals of that country; and for preserving such money and effects to the use of its owners. The bill, with very little opposition, passing into a law, answered the double purpose of securing their property to individuals, and detaining from the enemy means of carrying on the war.

Repeated motions made in both houses for the restoration of peace, necessarily reiterated the arguments which were before adduced; and indeed, the purposes of the propositions on that subject appear to have been chiefly to procure from ministers some declaration, or at least admission, of the specific objects for which the war was continued *; at least to induce them expressly to disavow every intention of co-operation with the continental powers to dictate her internal government to France: they farther aimed at persuading the houses to disapprove the conduct of the allies, especially of Prussia. Besides these indirect attempts, a direct effort was made to expose as impolitic the principle, system, and series of our foreign treaties. Mr. Whitbread, on the 6th of March, proposed an address to his majesty, expressing the concern of the commons that the king had entered into engagements totally incompatible with the avowed purposes of the present war; that he had made a common cause with powers, whose objects, though undefined, really appeared to be the restitution of monarchy; and earnestly praying his majesty, as far as was consistent with the national faith, to extricate himself from such engagements as might impede the conclusion of a separate peace. Next to the subsidiary treaty with the king of Prussia, a treaty with the king of Sardinia, by which we engaged to continue the war till Savoy was restored, incurred the strongest and most explicit censure. Britain had stipulated a subsidy of two hundred

Treaty with the king of Sardinia.

* See Resolutions moved by the Duke of Bedford and Mr. Fox, May 30th.

thousand

CHAP. LIII. 1794. thousand pounds a-year, to assist the king of Sardinia in his efforts to defend his own dominions. Mr. Whitbread and others maintained, that the advantage which Britain could derive from such exertions was by no means adequate to the expence to be incurred; and that *the integrity of the king of Sardinia's* dominions was not, in the smallest degree, NECESSARY TO THE SECURITY OF BRITAIN; for which, according to ministers, we were engaged in the contest. Ministers endeavoured to prove that the whole system and series of treaties, subsidiary as well as others, were means necessary to promote the grand ends of the war. The address was negatived by the usual very great majority; and a similar motion on the same subject experienced in the house of lords the same fate.

Proposition of an enquiry into the conduct and success of the last campaign.

Having in vain endeavoured to procure the termination of the war, and the dissolution of alliances deemed by government, and the majority in parliament, essentially conducive to its purposes, opposition proposed to enquire how far, in the late campaign, its objects had been attained, and what the probability of success was from perseverance in the contest. Major Maitland, after a detailed review of the measures and events of the last campaign, and an estimate of the result, contended that the attainments of the French had been greater than their losses. They had been forced to evacuate Belgium, but they had suppressed the revolt of La Vendee, a much more important event; since all their dangers arose from internal disturbance. The strength of the allies had been declining ever since the siege of Valenciennes. The empress of Russia made protestations,

testations, but took no active share in hostilities; and the king of Prussia was manifestly meditating a secession. The military plans latterly adopted by the allies deserved severe animadversion. While their armies were united, their efforts had been crowned with success: the separation of the forces he imputed to the influence of the British cabinet, as Britain alone was to be benefited by the capture of Dunkirk. If the attempt upon that fortress by a detached force was expedient, the sole hope of success must arise from promptitude of execution, and the completeness of preparations; but neither of these attended the attack upon Dunkirk: four weeks elapsed from the taking of Valenciennes before the siege of Dunkirk was undertaken. Neither artillery nor gun boats were ready in proper time for covering the operation. To the master-general of the ordnance, and to ministry, the failure of that enterprize must be attributed. The evacuation of Toulon was still more severely reprobated: why were not other troops sent to preserve the conquest of Toulon? or why, when it was found untenable, was not an evacuation at once determined upon, and the fleet brought away to save the unhappy inhabitants from the fury of those whom they had mortally offended? On these grounds Major Maitland "moved a committee to enquire into the causes which led to the failure of the army under the Duke of York at Dunkirk; and to enquire into the causes which led to the evacuation of Toulon under General Dundas and Lord Hood." It was replied, that Dunkirk would have been to Britain a very important acquisition; that it had every probable

CHAP. LIII. 1794.

bable appearance of practicability; that the attempt was therefore wise: that its failure arose from the enormous efforts of the French, which could not have been foreseen or expected. From the same cause proceeded the evacuation of Toulon: those who censured us for leaving that place ought to recollect, that we had there given such an effectual blow to the French navy, that ages would elapse before they would be able to recover their losses as a maritime power. On a general review of the events of the campaign, great glory was due to the British councils and arms. These arguments appearing to the majority valid, the proposed motion was negatived. About the same time a proposition was offered to the house of commons respecting sinecure places and pensions. Since a war was deemed necessary that called for all our resources, it was prudent and expedient to retrench every unnecessary expence: for this reason Mr. Harrison proposed a bill to apply certain parts of salaries and pensions to the use of the public during the continuance of the war; and also to appropriate part of the emoluments of efficient places, so that they should not amount to more than a specific sum. This motion was severely reprobated by Mr. Burke, as similar to the proceedings which had occasioned the ruin of France. It was the peculiar province of the crown to measure and distribute the portion of rewards according to the merits of its servants; and he was astonished the house should be called upon to interfere in a matter not within the scope of their ordinary functions. Mr. Sheridan attacked this doctrine as totally unconstitutional: did the crown possess

Proposition of a tax on places and pensions.

Arguments of Mr. Burke against the proposition

possess the sole right of judging what rewards were to be bestowed upon the public servants? If it did, he would ask who was obliged to pay those rewards? The money belonged to the public: the commons were the servants of the people; and as the people contributed, they had a right to expect and demand that the contributions should be applied for their good. Entering into a detail upon this general principle, he gave a particular account of the emoluments enjoyed by certain individuals, which he appeared to think far surpassing their services; and that it was but fair they should contribute part of the surplus towards the public exigencies caused by a war which they warmly supported. The opposite party replied, that the pension list and sinecure places, during the administration of Mr. Pitt, had been very greatly reduced; besides that it would be extremely unjust to subject one body of men to an exclusive tax: On these grounds Mr. Harrison's motion was rejected.

Mr. Dundas, as president of the board of controul, presented his annual statement of the finances of India; the result of which was, that notwithstanding the late war with Tippoo, and the stagnation of commerce at home until measures were adopted for the support of mercantile credit, the affairs of the company were in a prosperous situation, and he augured great and rapid increase of their prosperity.

The slave-trade was this session again resumed by Mr. Wilberforce; whose efforts, however, for the present were limited to one branch of that traffic. He proposed to abolish that part of the trade which supplied

CHAP. LIII.

1794.

supplied foreign territories with slaves. The supporters of the slave-trade rested their cause on the ground of its being necessary to the well-being of our West Indian possessions, which could not otherwise be supplied with labourers. They who were sincere in this objection to the abolition must warmly defend the present motion; for, instead of abridging that supply it tended to increase it, and to prevent us from raising the colonies of foreigners into a competition with our own. A bill for the purpose being introduced by Mr. Wilberforce, passed the commons, but was rejected by the peers.

The session closes.

These were the chief subjects which occupied the attention of the house during this very important session, which was closed by a speech from the throne on the 11th of July.

Internal proceedings of France.

Before the narrative proceeds to the campaign of 1794, it is necessary to take a short view of the internal affairs of France, which had a powerful influence on military transactions.

Jacobin faction and Robespierre paramount.

We left the jacobin faction triumphant by the downfal of the Girondines; Robespierre paramount by his command over the populace; the system of terror completely established, and producing the most direful effects within the country, but the most gigantic efforts against the enemies of its revolutionary system. The government of France was now become a government of blood, to be sustained by the terrors of the guillotine. This fell engine was employed to remove the obnoxious, to crush the suspected, and to destroy the unsuccessful. Misfortune, though totally blameless, was consummated on the scaffold; thence Custine, a general of great ability and enterprize,

prize, was recalled from the Northern army after the ſurrender of Valenciennes, and inſtantly committed to the priſon of the Abbey. He was accuſed before the revolutionary tribunal of having maintained a traitorous correſpondence with the Pruſſians while he commanded on the Rhine; and of having neglected various opportunities of throwing reinforcements into Valenciennes. No evidence was adduced to prove the allegations; but proof was not neceſſary to ſanguinary deſpotiſm: he ſpeedily ſuffered death. CHAP. LIII. 1794.

The execution of Cuſtine was ſoon followed by the trial of the unfortunate queen. This awful inſtance of the inſtability of human grandeur, after the murder of her ill-fated huſband, had been ſeparated from her family in the Temple. On the 1ſt of Auguſt 1793, ſhe was ſuddenly, and in the moſt cruel and inſulting manner, removed to the Conciergerie, a priſon deſtined for the reception of the vileſt malefactors. In the midſt of a nation recently ſo diſtinguiſhed for loyalty, every effort of invention was employed in the moſt wanton and barbarous inſults to the conſort of their lately adored ſovereign. In a metropolis, within a few years the centre of refinement, and devoted attention to the ſex, the moſt brutal and ſavage ingenuity was exerted in oppreſſion, inſolence, and tyranny, to a poor, helpleſs, and forlorn woman, The cell in which ſhe was immured was only eight feet ſquare; her bed was an hard mattreſs of ſtraw, and her food of the meaneſt kind; while ſhe was never ſuffered to enjoy the privilege of being alone, two ſoldiers being appointed to watch her night and day, Situation of the queen.

 without

CHAP. LIII.

1794. Iniquitous trial and condemnation.

without the intermiſſion of a moment *. Confined in this loathſome dungeon, in ſuch circumſtances of aggravated brutality, on the 15th of October, ſhe was brought before the revolutionary tribunal. The charges adduced againſt her were, that ſhe had contributed to the derangement of the national finances, by remitting, from time to time, conſiderable ſums to her brother the emperor Joſeph: ſince the revolution continued to hold a criminal correſpondence with foreign powers: attempted a counter-revolution, particularly by applying to the officers at Verſailles in October 1789; and at the ſame time, through the agency of certain monopoliſts, had created an artificial famine. According to her accuſers ſhe was the principal agent and promoter of the flight of the royal family in June 1791: induced the king to refuſe his ſanction to the decrees concerning the emigrants and refractory prieſts: in conjunction with a ſcandalous faction (the Girond), perſuaded the king and the aſſembly to declare war againſt Auſtria, contrary to every principle of ſound policy and the public welfare: war being commenced, ſhe had conveyed intelligence to the enemy, and was the cauſe of the maſſacre of the 10th of Auguſt. To theſe allegations, ſome of which were totally indifferent, whether true or falſe, and the reſt ſupported by no proof, one was added for a conſummation to the reſt, as phyſically incredible, as morally infamous: it was affirmed by theſe brutes, in conception as well as in conduct, that

* See Otridge's Annual Regiſter, 1793, p. 276.

ſhe had an inceſtuous commerce with her own ſon, a child of eight years old *. The queen conſidered accuſation by blood-thirſty deſpots as ſynonimous with condemnation: though ſhe diſregarded ſuch accuſers, yet out of juſtice to herſelf, her origin, her family, and her fame, ſhe exerted her abilities in rebutting charges ſo horrid and flagitious. With the dignity of an elevated mind, attacked by the ſcorn and iniquity of the unworthy, ſhe anſwered ſerenely and calmly to all their aſſeverations. Retaining, in this dreadful ſituation, that full poſſeſſion of faculties which magnanimity ſecures to unmerited ſuffering, ſhe, though totally ignorant of the allegations that were to be made, demonſtrated their futility, and confuted the aſſertions of her enemies. Reſpecting the charge of inceſt, ſhe appealed to thoſe who were themſelves mothers for the poſſibility of the crime. Though her defence completely overturned the evidence for the proſecution, it was, as ſhe well knew it would be, totally unavailing: ſhe was pronounced guilty of all the charges, and doomed to die the following day.

The queen heard with reſignation a ſentence which announced her ſpeedy releaſe from a ſituation of ſuch accumulated miſery. She had one conſolation to which the diabolical malignity of her murderers could not reach: ſhe was a CHRISTIAN: ſhe believed in a future ſtate; and therein ſhe looked for happineſs which no revolutionary tribunal could diſturb, no atheiſtical aſſaſſins could deſtroy. Before ſhe was reconducted to her dungeon, it was four in

* Otridge's Annual Regiſter, 1793, p. 276.

 the

CHAP. LIII. 1794. the morning; and twelve the ensuing day was the hour fixed for her decapitation. She was not allowed a clergyman of her own choice, but provided with a constitutional priest. At half past eleven the queen was brought out of prison, and, like the lowest malefactor, was conducted in a common cart to the place of execution. Her hair was entirely cut off from the back of her head, which was covered with a small white cap; she wore a white undress; her hands were tied behind her; and she sat with her back to the horses. They who had seen her in the zenith of magnificence and splendor, could not but contrast her former with her present condition: those who had admired her exquisite beauty, could not but observe the premature depredations of sorrow on a face so fair: but if the changes impaired the gloss of her juvenile charms, they, together with their causes, to feeling spectators (and all Frenchmen were not brutes) rendered her faded countenance more interesting and impressive. She calmly conversed with her priest, exhibiting neither ostentatious indifference nor overwhelming anguish, but resigned submission. Casting her eyes to the Thuilleries, one scene of her former greatness, which called up so many tender associations and melancholy ideas, she indicated a sorrowful emotion; but repelling this last intrusion of wordly recollection, she turned to the instrument of death. Execution. At half past twelve the guillotine severed her head from her body; which the executioner exhibited, all streaming with blood, from the four corners of the scaffold, to an inveterate and insatiable multitude. The body of the murdered

murdered queen was immediately conveyed to a grave filled with quick-lime, in the church-yard called De la Madelaine, where the remains of Louis XVI. had been interred with the same privation of pious regard or decent ceremonial.

Brissot and the other Girond prisoners are put to death.

The murder of the queen was soon followed by the death of the accused deputies. The trial of these persons was deferred from time to time, till the complete overthrow of their adherents should give security to their prosecutors. They were charged with having conspired against the unity and indivisibility of the republic, by exciting a rebellion in the departments of the South, and in Calvados. One article of the charges respecting foreign politics was, they were accused of having caused war to be declared, first against Austria, and afterwards against England and Holland. Thus arraigned, at the instance of the ruling party, they were all doomed to death: many others experienced a similar destiny, either undeservedly or illegally. The detestable and contemptible Orleans suffered the same fate which, at his instigation, had overwhelmed so many others. A decree had been passed under the present rulers for removing the Bourbon family to Marseilles; and Orleans, who had latterly assumed the silly and fantastical name of Philip Egalite, was included in its operation. From Marseilles he was brought to Paris, on a charge of having aspired at the sovereignty from the commencement of the revolution. As this was an accusation which could scarcely admit of any evi-

Orleans shares the same fate.

* See Otridge's Annual Register 1793, p. 278.

CHAP. LIII. 1794.

dence but conjectural, it was not substantiated so far as to justify the sentence of death to which he was doomed. Orleans experienced in his own person the tyrannic cruelty of the revolutionary system which he had been so ardent to promote; and however deserving he might be of capital punishment, he, according to the most probable accounts, suffered *illegally*. Profligate and despicable as the character of this man had been, his sentence excited neither horror nor commiseration in any party: the last period of his life, however, appeared to indicate sentiments less disgraceful than those which had manifested themselves in the invariable tenour of his former conduct. On the 6th of November he was conveyed to the place of his execution, amidst the insults and reproaches of the populace; and met death with a magnanimity less befitting the associate and tool of Robespierre and Marat than the descendant of Henry. Two days after the ignominious catastrophe of Orleans, the lovely and accomplished Madame Roland was brought to the scaffold. To the distinguished talents, varied and extensive knowledge of this celebrated lady, her domestic virtues were not inferior. Her husband, hated by Robespierre on account of his attachment to the Gironde party, was included in the proscription that followed the decree of the 3d of May: he accordingly quitted Paris, but his wife was apprehended and committed to prison. She was at length brought to trial, and the empty charge of a conspiracy was followed by a sentence of death. At the place of execution she maintained that firm undaunted spirit which had hitherto supported her;

and,

and bowing down before the ſtatue of liberty, ſhe exclaimed, "O liberty, how many crimes are committed in thy name."

Dreadful ſtate of France under Robeſpierre.

To take away property, liberty, and life, to inflict anguiſh and torment; to produce to human beings phyſical evil, did not ſatiate the inventive malignity of this extraordinary tyranny. Robeſpierre and his band, more comprehenſive and more thoroughly diabolical, ardently, ſtudiouſly, and ſyſtematically ſought the increaſe of moral depravation. Projects for diſſeminating miſery could not, they well knew, be ſo completely ſucceſsful as by eſtabliſhing the domination of ſin. Sin could never attain ſo extenſive an empire as by the total ſubjugation of religion; therefore to annihilate piety, with all its external forms and aſſiſtances, was one great object of Robeſpierre's devices. To effect this purpoſe, one means was to deſtroy the reverence for all the inſtitutions which are deduced from the ſcriptures, and tend ſo powerfully to cheriſh ſentiments of religion. Of theſe, none had been found more effectual than the excluſive devotion of one day in the week to the ſocial worſhip of God; and the appointment of certain ſtated periods for ſpecific commemorations. The calendar in all chriſtian countries, taking its firſt origin from the birth of our ſaviour, and enumerating the years by an event the moſt momentous to the chriſtian world, had regulated the diviſions of the year by epochs in the hiſtory of our ſaviour's miſſion upon earth, or ſome other ſeaſons connected with ſcripture narratives; and had intermingled religious aſſociations with the ſeveral progreſſions of the ſeaſons. Of theſe, the

CHAP. LIII. 1794. observance of the sabbath recurring most frequently is the most extensively beneficial. The government of Robespierre projected the abolition of these institutions, and actually effected a new calendar which destroyed all reference to christian history and precepts, commenced the æra from the downfal of monarchy, annihilated all terms connected with christian history and establishments, abolished the sabbath; and instead of the seventh day, enjoined by the commandment of God to be kept holy, they appointed the tenth as a period of mere civil respite, to the total exclusion of all religious exercise. Having thus renounced christianity, their new calendar partly adopted the phraseology and arrangement of pagans, denominated every space of four years an olympiad, in imitation of the Greeks, and the extraordinary day of every fourth year an intercalary, in imitation of the Romans*. This innovation therefore, under the government of Robespierre and his agents, tended strongly to promote that impiety which the tribunitian government was so eager to establish. Robespierre and his junto had often declared their disbelief of the christian religion, and even denied the existence of a supreme being; but they had not yet produced a formal and public renunciation of the God and saviour of the world. An act so horible remained for the legislature of a

* They divided the year into twelve months consisting each of thirty days, and distinguished by names expressive of their usual produce, temperature, or appearance; while to complete the year, five supplementary days are added, and denominated sans culotides.

most

most enlightened nation, near the close of the eighteenth century. On the 7th of November, in the phrenzy of impiety, the republican bishop of Paris, and his grand vicars, entered the hall of the convention along with the constituted authorities, abjured the name of Christ, renounced the office of christian priests, their appointments as christian pastors, and their characters as christian men. Now they would own no temple but the sanctuary of the law, no divinity but liberty, no object of worship but their country, no gospel but the constitution. This abjuration was received by the convention with the most rapturous applause. A number of allegorical deities, liberty, equality, indivisibility, and many others, were consecrated as objects of worship. To promote this system of paganism, agents were dispatched to all the departments, to complete the change. In many parts the abjuration of religion, through the efforts of the clergy, was very warmly received, while its various commentators added to the impiety, according to the measure of their invention. One of the most zealous votaries of impiety, was the republican bishop of Moulins. Trampling on the cross and the mitre, he assumed the pike and cap of liberty, and preached the doctrine big with horror to reflecting men, but full of encouragement to diabolic natures, "that death is an eternal sleep." A common prostitute was placed on the altar of the cathedral church of Paris, to receive adoration, as a substitute for Jesus Christ. The convention combined intolerance with atheism and blasphemy, and passed a decree, ordering the churches to be shut. Many of the priests who still attempted

1794. The revolutionary bishops abjure the name of Christ,

and a future state.

The churches are shut.

CHAP. LIII 1794. attempted to officiate at their altars according to the rites of chriſtianity, were thrown into dungeons. Renunciation of religion, as its abettors foreſaw, promoted the moſt enormous crimes. The populace, who in conſequence of theſe proceedings reckoned themſelves authorized to plunder every place of worſhip, public and private, divided with the convention large heaps of ſhrines, figures, and veſſels, hitherto uſed in the offices of religion, while commiſſioners from the convention aided the ſacrilegious pillage. The revolutionary phrenzy had not totally overwhelmed every principle and ſentiment of natural and revealed religion. The decree for ſhutting up the churches was received with ſo general horror and deteſtation, that the government found it neceſſary immediately to reverſe it, and again to admit religious worſhip. Robeſpierre, though moſt active in enmity to religion, yet eagerly deſirous to preſerve and increaſe his popularity, promoted the reſtoration of divine ſervice. By the influence which he eſtabliſhed among the populace, he was able to acquire an aſcendency over his aſſociates. Of theſe, one of the ableſt was Danton: this revolutioniſt, much ſuperior to Robeſpierre in the talents and accompliſhments which would have commanded attention in the Roman or Britiſh ſenate, did not equal him in the arts which conciliate an ignorant rabble. Conſcious of his own powers, he intended Robeſpierre for a tool; and was active in overturning the Briſſotines, in order to elevate himſelf; but at length fell like many of his revolutionary predeceſſors, by the inſtruments of his exaltation. So contrary to the intereſt of an able

Fall of Danton.

man

man it is to aggrandize a rabble that would level all distinctions. The Parisian populace loved and revered Robespierre, because in manners, appearance, and passions, he was one of themselves. His ruling affection was envy*, a desire of reducing all others to the level of his own meanness. This sentiment, together with fear, the natural passion of a despot without high talents and greatness of mind, chiefly prompted all the enormities of this monster. He both hated and feared † the aristocracy of genius, as a superiority over himself, and the means of effecting his downfall. But his tyranny, dreadful as it was to France, by its very terrors produced most gigantic efforts against its enemies.

CHAP. LIII. 1791. The Parisian populace adore Robespierre. His real talents and character.

* See Adolphus's Memoirs of Robespierre.

† Domitian was the most timid of men; the fearlessness of Julius Cæsar, on the contrary, hastened his assassination.

CHAP. LIV.

Jealousy among the allies.—The Emperor tries to raise his subjects in mass—is opposed by the King of Prussia.—Plan of the campaign.—Respective force of the belligerent powers.—The Emperor joins the allied armies.—Energy of the revolutionary leaders in France.—Rebellion is quelled in La Vendee.—The confederates take the field.—Siege of Landreci.—Conflicts between the allies and the republicans.—Battle of the 24th of April, between the duke of York and the republicans.—Our prince and countrymen are victorious.—Landreci is taken.—Testimony of the convention to the heroism of the English.—Pichegru—his new plan of warfare—well suited to the state of his army.—System of incessant attack.—Co-operating line of French armies from the German Rhine to the sea.—The French wisely avoid a close engagement with the British.—Separation of the Confederates. Jourdain advances with an army in mass.—The Prince of Cobourg attempts to oppose him without the assistance of the Duke of York—receives a signal defeat at Fleurus, which decides the fate of the campaign.—Pichegru in West Flanders attacks and defeats Clairfait.—Dangerous situation of the Duke of York—who retires to Antwerp.—Earl Moira is ordered to Flanders with his army.—The Prince of Wales offers to act under him as a volunteer—it is not deemed expedient to risk the person of the heir apparent.—His lordship lands at Ostend—finds the place surrounded by enemies—determines to force his way to the Duke of York—masterly execution and success of his design.—Advances of the French. The Austrians entirely evacuate the Netherlands.—Intrepid stand of the British at Breda.—The Duke of York and the Prince of Orange are obliged to fall back—they retreat behind the Meuse.—Victories of the Republicans on the Rhine.—The German troops cross the Rhine.—Address of the Emperor to the German princes—is totally unavailing. Faithlessness

Faithlessness of the King of Prussia.—Opinions on the operations and events of this campaign.—Suspicions unfavourable to the Prince of Cobourg—are not supported by proof.—Cobourg a man of very moderate abilities.—Victories of the republicans over the gallant Clairfait.—The republicans reduce the whole left bank of the Rhine.—The British gain some advantages.—Winter campaign in Holland.—Sickness and mortality of the British troops,—intrepid efforts of the exhausted remains.—Immense superiority of numbers obliges our reduced army to evacuate Holland—which yields to the French arms.—Campaign of 1794 peculiarly disastrous to the British army.—Strictures of military critics on the plan of operations.—Strictures of political critics on the executive councils of Britain.—Efforts of France beyond all evidence of experience or probable conjecture—the event therefore does not necessarily afford grounds of either military or political censure.—Signal successes of Britain when she fought alone—her fleets paramount in the Mediterranean—reduce Corsica, and protect Spain and Italy—in the West Indies she subdues Martinico, Guadaloupe, St. Lucie, and part of St. Domingo.—Operations of Earl Howe and the Channel fleet—skilful manœuvre to bring the enemy to battle—battle of the first of June—numbers, force, and courageous efforts of the enemy—unavailing against the British fleet—decisive, glorious, and momentous victory.

CHAP. LIV. 1794.

THERE was a great and evident want of concert among the German powers engaged in the combination against France. The Duke of Brunswick was disgusted with the conduct of General Wurmser in abandoning the lines of Wiessembourg without risking a battle, whence his serene highness had been compelled to raise the siege of Landau. He had written a letter to the King of Prussia, complaining of the want of concert, and extending

CHAP. LIV. 1794.

tending his animadverſions to the two campaigns. On the other hand the Emperor, though he was far from blaming the Duke of Brunſwick individually, was by no means ſatisfied with the co-operation of the Pruſſian king. The truth appears to be that the jealouſy which for half a century had ſubſiſted between the houſes of Brandenburg and Auſtria, and which at the commencement of the war ſeemed abſorbed in enmity to the French revolutioniſts, was ſtill alive, and ſtrongly operating*. The King of Pruſſia conſidered the continental efforts of the laſt campaign as aggrandizing Auſtria, without producing any benefit to him which could indemnify his own exertions, or balance the acceſſion to his ancient and neareſt rival. He did not regard the operations on the frontiers of France as neceſſary to the ſafety of the empire and ſecurity of his own dominions, and therefore conceived himſelf not fighting his own battles. If it was wiſe at all to combine againſt France, the expediency of ſuch a confederacy muſt have ariſen from ſome common object, which it imported the ſeveral members of the alliance to purſue; and if it was to be purſued, vigorous meaſures with concert of operations only could be efficient. If the King of Pruſſia apprehended imminent danger from the progreſs of French principles, or of French power, in ſound policy he ought to have made the repreſſion of theſe his ſupreme object; and to have reſtrained for the preſent his jealouſy of the houſe of Auſtria. If he did not apprehend danger from France, prudence required he ſhould withdraw from the confederacy; honour and ſincerity demanded that he

Jealouſy among the allies.

* Segur, vol. iii. chap. 13.

ſhould

should not pretend to be an ostensive member of the alliance, if he was resolved to be inactive in its service, and indifferent about its success. On the other hand, the same unity of object was the real interest of the Emperor, if it was his interest at all to be member of a combination against France. The separate appropriation of fortresses could not indemnify him for his belligerent exertions, must disgust his continental ally, and ultimately contravene the advancement of their common object. In the beginning of this year the Emperor, extremely anxious to oppose fresh numbers of Germans to the republican host, actively endeavoured to induce the Germanic states to arm in mass. This mode the King of Prussia declared he would never sanction, and would withdraw his troops if it were attempted. He however professed himself still an active member of the confederacy, and ready to support every prudent and practicable project for forwarding its ends. The emperor found it necessary to acquiesce in Frederic William's objections to a levy in mass, and to appear satisfied with his professions of zeal in the cause. The subsidiary treaty with England either empowered him to make vigorous efforts or induced him to promise such, and accordingly he was still deemed one of the chief members of the confederacy, and upon the conviction of his co-operation the projects and plans of the campaign were formed. The confederates proposed this year to press upon the frontiers of France with numerous forces on various sides, and also to co-operate with the insurgents on the coast of Brittany. In the

CHAP. LIV. 1794.

The Emperor tries to raise his subjects in mass;

is opposed by the King of Prussia.

Plan of the campaign.

CHAP. LIV. 1794. the month of February the Duke of York, and with him Colonel Mack, came over from the continent to London to hold a conference with the British ministers on the operations of the campaign. Respective forces of the belligerent powers. The emperor undertook to furnish two hundred thousand men, the King of Prussia sixty-four, including thirty-two thousand in British pay, Britain forty thousand, the rest of the allies, the Dutch, German princes, and the Emigrants fifty-two thousand, so that the whole combined force to operate on the frontiers of France should amount to three hundred and fifty-six thousand men, besides the troops intended to be employed by Britain on the coast. The French army it appears at this time amounted to seven hundred and eighty thousand men, of whom four hundred and eighty thousand composed the armies on the frontiers, and the rest were employed either in watching the late scenes of insurrection, or on the frontiers of Spain and the Alps.

On the fifth of March the Duke of York arrived on the continent, to take the command of the British army; on the seventeenth he proceeded with General Clairfait to Valenciennes, where a council of war was held with the Prince of Saxe Cobourg, after which the generals returned to their respective head-quarters. It was determined that the emperor himself should take the field, and should be invested with the supreme command.

The Emperor joins the allied armies. On the ninth of April his Imperial Majesty arrived at Brussels, and was inaugurated Duke of Brabant. This ceremony, performed with great

pomp

pomp and ſplendour, it was preſumed would ſtrike the imaginations and hearts of the people, and ſtimulate them to the moſt vigorous efforts in his and their own cauſe. The ſtates in a body preſented his Imperial Majeſty with the keys of the Louvain; on the gate there was the following inſcription: "*Cæſar adeſt, trement Galli;*" this ſentence was by the courtiers conſtrued to mean the French republicans tremble at the approach of the Emperor Francis. Great numbers of children, decorated with white ſtaves, drew the ſtate coach ſolemnly along; at the principal church *Te Deum* was chaunted; verſes were preſented to the Emperor, congratulating his inauguration, and celebrating the atchievements which he was to perform. His Imperial Majeſty proceeding to Valenciennes, was joyfully received by the allied army; and on the 16th of April he reviewed the combined forces, previouſly to the commencement of military operations.

Energy of the revolutionary leaders in France.

Meanwhile the French government had made the moſt powerful and efficient diſpoſitions for opening the campaign. Horrible as the decemviral ſyſtem was, it poſſeſſed one quality ſo momentous in war, that without it all other qualities ſupported by the moſt abundant reſources are of little efficacy; it was diſtinguiſhed for extraordinary ENERGY. Every latent power was called into action, its immenſe reſources were not only employed, but converged into a focus. The immediate object was to repel foreign invaſions and interference whereſoever they threatened, and whereſoever they were ſeconded; to concentrate all the intellectual and phyſical force of France to this point; to crumble all

 oppoſition

CHAP. LIV. 1794.

opposition to this design and to the existing rulers who were carrying it into execution. Some embers of rebellion rekindling early in spring, troops were sent with the usual rapidity to the scene of reviving insurrection. These speedily subjugated the royalists, and punished them in the most summary and cruel manner. Rebellion was crushed by the dispersion of the Vendeans; faction was extinguished; and hostile operations against foreign powers engrossed the sole attention. General Jourdain was removed from the command of the northern army, and succeeded by General Pichegru, whose uncommon military talents proved him deserving of this confidence. As Jourdain was permitted to retire without disgrace, and indeed, in the express words of the decree, with honour to himself and with the gratitude of his country, his retirement was but short, and he was afterwards appointed to command the army of the Rhine.

Rebellion is quelled in La Vendee.

The confederates take the field. Siege of Landreci.

On the seventeenth of April the confederates advanced in eight columns to invest Landreci, a well fortified town in Hainault, on the right bank of the river Sambre. The first column, composed of Austrian and Dutch troops under Prince Christian of Hesse Darmstadt, advanced upon the village of Catillon, which was forced after some resistance. The second under Lieutenant General Alvintzy, forced the French entrenchments at Mazinguer, Oisy, and Nouviou, and took possession of the whole forest of Nouviou. The third column, led on by the Emperor in person and the Prince of Cobourg, after carrying the villages of Ribouville and Wassigny, detached forwards the advanced guards, which

which took poſſeſſion of the heights called Grand and Petit Blocus. The fourth and fifth columns were entruſted to the Duke of York; the firſt of theſe was under his own immediate direction; and the latter was commanded by Sir William Erſkine. The objects of theſe columns were the redoubts and village of Vaux, and the ſtrong entrenchments of the French in the wood called Bois de Bouchain. The ſixth, ſeventh, and eighth columns, under the hereditary Prince of Orange, were not engaged, being only a corps of obſervation on the ſide of Cambray *. The Duke of York endeavoured, notwithſtanding the ſtrong poſition of the French army, to turn their right, and for that purpoſe ordered the whole column to move forwards under the cover of the high ground, leaving only ſufficient cavalry to occupy their attention. The fire of the republicans was at firſt ſevere, but finding the Britiſh troops eager to preſs them to a cloſe engagement, which they foreſaw would terminate in their diſcomfiture, they thought it expedient to retreat. Theſe ſucceſſes of the Britiſh troops enabled the confederates to commence the ſiege. The French aſſembled in conſiderable force at the camp of Cæſar, near Cambray, which, as we have ſeen, they had occupied the former year. The Duke of York, well knowing the efficacy of the Britiſh force, on the 23d of April ſent General Otto to attack the enemy's poſition. Otto, finding the French ſtrong, and firmly poſted, delayed the aſſault till the arrival of a reinforcement, when, charging them with

C H A P. LIV. 1794.

Conflicts between the allies and the republicans.

* See New Annual Regiſter for 1794, p. 328.

 impetuoſity,

CHAP. LIV.

1794.

impetuofity, he foon broke their line, and after killing twelve hundred drove the reft into Cambray, with the lofs of their artillery *. Pichegru, not difheartened by thefe repeated difadvantages, ftill directed his own movements againft the moft formidable part of his enemies. On the 24th of April he attacked the Duke of York on all fides. The confummate general of the republicans found in the Britifh prince and his army a commander and foldiers not to be overcome even by his ability and efforts. Frederic vigoroufly receiving the affailants in front by grape fhot and mufketry, judicioufly difpatched feveral regiments of cavalry round the right, and of infantry round the left wing of his enemy, while he himfelf oppofed the powerful and numerous hoft in the front of the battle; the two detachments charging the enemy's flanks, broke their lines, and produced a moft deftructive carnage in both wings: fuch a combination of valour and fkill completely defeated the French. This attempt of Pichegru was only part of a general plan of attack, extending from Treves to the fea, although he chofe for himfelf the poft of moft difficulty and danger. On the right, the columns of the French attacking the enemy's army were repulfed with lofs, though not nearly fo great as the lofs which they incurred in their conflict with the Duke of York. On the left, they gained a trifling advantage by the reduction of Menin and Courtray. Other engagements took place during the fiege, without any decifive event. Where the Britifh fought the

Battle of the 24th of April between the Duke of York and the republicans;

our prince and countrymen are victorious.

* See Macfarlane's hiftory, vol. iv. p. 469.

French

French were uniformly repulſed; but in their other conflicts they were more ſucceſsful. Their efforts, however, to relieve Landreci, were not effectual, as that fortreſs was captured after an inveſtment of ten days. The French rulers acknowledged in the convention, that though not the moſt numerous, the moſt formidable opponents to Gallic valour were the Engliſh*.

CHAP. LIV. 1794. Landreci is taken. Teſtimony of the convention to the heroiſm of the Engliſh.

Pichegru, a man of ſtrong and comprehenſive genius, regarded precedented modes of warfare no farther than they could ſerve his purpoſe, and formed a plan of attack at once new and admirably adapted to the character of the French, eſpecially to the ſoldiers under his command. His ſyſtem of tactics conſiſted in purſuing the enemy without intermiſſion; courting opportunities of engagements; and keeping his whole force together, without dividing it for the purpoſe of carrying on ſieges; to reduce only ſuch as were neceſſary in order to ſecure proper poſitions, without ſeeming to be at all concerned about the reduction of ſuch ſtrong places as he had left behind. This ſyſtem was ſuitable to the ſtate of military experience among the greater part of the French ſoldiers, as well as to the character of the people. The troops were moſtly new levied, and although nationally courageous, active, and impetuous, and then inſpirited by enthuſiaſm, yet they were not ſufficiently trained in ſtationary warfare to undertake any ſiege of difficulty. Be-

Pichegru. His new plan of warfare.

* See Barrere's ſpeech in the convention, after the late victory of the Duke of York.

CHAP. LIV. 1794.

ſides, as an annaliſt * of the preſent campaign obſerves, "the French ſoldier is too ardent and impatient to go through with a chain of operations that require perſeverance. In the field he darts forth as an eagle, and fights like a lion. But a long and arduous ſiege repels, and often even diſcourages. In order to have a military body of men perfect and invincible, it would be neceſſary to carry on ſieges with Swiſs troops, and to have French armies of obſervation. But while a general has only Frenchmen under his command, he ought not to let them grow reſtive, by remaining long in one place, but keep them always in breath, and always within view of the enemy." This ſyſtem of inceſſant attack was extended in its operation to the ſeveral armies of the republicans, ſo as to render them really parts of one great hoſt, cloſely connected together, as one army over a wide expanſe of country. From the German Rhine to the ſea, there was one co-operating line of armies. Though the victory of the duke of York, and the capture of Landreci retarded the progreſs of this grand ſcheme of advance and aſſault they did not prevent its final execution and ſucceſs. The exertions and attainments of the Britiſh arms eventually promoted the accompliſhment of the French projects. After the battle of the 24th of April, they cautiouſly abſtained from cloſe engagement with the Britiſh forces, and

Syſtem of inceſſant attack.

Co-operating line of French armies from the German Rhine to the ſea.

The French wiſely avoid a cloſe engagement with the Britiſh.

* Hiſtoire Chronoligique des operations de l'Armée du Nord, et de celle du Sambre et Meuſe, par le citoyen David, temoin des plupart de leurs exploits.

bent

bent their principal efforts, both on the right and left, against the Auſtrians.

Separation of the confederates.

To this plan of partial attack the movements of the allied army were peculiarly auſpicious. Soon after the ſiege of Landreci it was judged expedient to divide the confederates into three parts; the chief army under the immediate command of the prince of Cobourg, and having the emperor himſelf at its head, was poſted near the Sambre; the duke of York with the Britiſh forces, was ſtationed at Tournay; and general Clairfait, with a third army, occupied Weſt Flanders. Pichegru directed his own principal efforts to the left againſt Clairfait, and ſtraitening the quarters of the duke of York; and in attacking Britiſh poſts and detachments, without hazarding a deciſive battle. Several very bloody conflicts, however, took place in this kind of warfare, but without materially impairing his highneſs's force, though freſh numbers were daily joining the French army.

Jourdain advances with an army in maſs.

Jourdain with the army of the Rhine, in the beginning of the campaign, had met with ſevere checks, but had been ultimately ſucceſsful againſt general Beaulieu, whom he compelled to evacuate the duchy of Luxemburg, and to fall back to Namur. Encouraged by their career of ſucceſs, the French now prepared to inveſt Charleroi on the Sambre. The prince of Cobourg with the main army advanced to its relief; but though the undertaking was extremely important, truſted to his own troops, without calling for the aid of the duke of York from Tournay. On the 21ſt of June he reached Ath, and on the 24th he effected a junction

CHAP. LIV. 1794. Battle of Fleurus. with the prince of Orange and general Beaulieu, at Nivelles. The main body of the French army, under General Jourdain, was posted at this time at Templeuve, Gosselies, and Fleurus, for the purpose of covering the siege of Charleroi. A battle ensued: both armies fought with the most intrepid courage, but the impetuous valour of the French succeeded. June 26. The allied army was defeated in every quarter, and forced with immense loss to retreat to Halle, thirty miles from the field of battle*: this victory decided the fate of the campaign. Charleroi, and soon after Brussels, fell into the hands of the victorious enemy. Pichegru in West Flanders attacks and defeats Clairfait. In West Flanders Pichegru was equally successful against Clairfait. Receiving large reinforcements from Lisle, he undertook the siege of Ypres, the key of Flanders. The importance of this place induced general Clairfait to hazard the whole corps under his command for its relief. On the 13th of June he attacked the republicans; and drove them from their first position; but fortune soon changed. The ability, courage, and skill of Clairfait were in vain opposed to the immense host of impetuous republicans. After a series of defeats he was compelled to abandon Ypres, to retire to Ghent, while Pichegru overran West Flanders. Dangerous situation of the duke of York, The geographical reader, by tracing the progress of the French army, and the retreat of the Austrians, and observing the position of the duke of York, will see that he was in a very dangerous situation, surrounded on all sides by the conquering

* New Annual Register, 1794, page 333.

quering multitudes of the French troops. Ever ſince the enemy, by the defeat of Cobourg, were ſo much advanced on his left, the duke's poſition had been very perilous; but ſince the progreſs of Pichegru upon his right, his poſt was no longer tenable; he accordingly retired with great expedition to Antwerp. The emperor deſpairing of ſucceſs, after in vain endeavouring to raiſe the people of the Netherlands in maſs, returned to Vienna.

who retires to Antwerp.

Part of the original plan of the campaign had been, as we have already ſeen, to co-operate with the inſurgents of La Vendee. Britain had undertaken, with that view, to ſend an expedition to France, and propoſed to entruſt the command to the valour, ability, and conduct of Earl Moira*, who as Lord Rawdon had attained ſo high military diſtinction in America. But the ſuppreſſion of the inſurgents, already recorded, prevented this deſign from being carried into execution. His lordſhip's army was therefore ordered to Flanders. One illuſtrious perſonage, ſeeking a wider field for the exerciſe of his vigorous genius and active mind, and wiſhing to learn the military art from ſo able a maſter, deſired to ſerve as a volunteer: this was George prince of Wales. Fitted by natural abilities and acquirements for either the cabinet or the field, the heir apparent from the delicacy of his ſituation, had cautiouſly abſtained from political buſineſs. His preſent propoſition did not, he conceived, interfere with the line of conduct which filial duty had chalked to itſelf. But his royal parents not deeming it expedient to

Earl Moira is ordered with his army to Flanders.

The prince of Wales offers to act under him as a volunteer.

* His lordſhip had ſucceeded to that title in the former year by the death of his father.

CHAP. LIV. 1794.

It is not deemed expedient to risk the person of the heir apparent. His lordship lands at Ostend; and finds the place surrounded by enemies;

risk the person of the heir apparent, the execution of his intention was not permitted. In the latter end of June earl Moira, with ten thousand men, landed at Ostend, just as the Austrians had been obliged to evacuate West Flanders. The French, in the mean time, were advancing upon Ghent in great force, and but little expectation was entertained of general Clairfait's being able to make any effectual resistance in that quarter. In the situation in which the earl of Moira found the affairs of the allies, an alternative occurred, of either defending Ostend, or proceeding to join the duke of York. To succour the confederates, and support the British army, appeared an object of more urgent importance than the precarious possession of a single town; whatever movement was to be made required dispatch, lest the advance of the French armies might completely cut off the communication.

determines to force his way to the duke of York.

A council of war was therefore called by the earl of Moira, and it was determined immediately to evacuate Ostend. This difficult and laborious task was committed to colonel Vyse. On the morning of the 1st of July he began to embark the troops on board the shipping, which lay at single anchor in the harbour, and the baggage and stores were in the vessels before night. The French entered the town as the last detachment embarked. While colonel Vyse was engaged in conducting the evacuation of Ostend, lord Moira with his main army repaired to Malle, about four miles from Bruges, on the great causeway to Ghent.

Masterly execution and success of the design.

The enemy pressing very fast, nothing was left but the most rapid dispatch. For that purpose they marched without tents and baggage. The French general was extremely

tremely eager to attack this corps; but so skilfully had their masterly leader arranged them on their march, that passing through a country overrun by myriads of enemies elated with victory, and eager for combat, encountering numberless defiles, through flats intersected with canals, and lately inundated, he did not afford them a single opportunity of attack. After undergoing incredible hardships, on the 8th of July he joined the duke of York. Having conducted this important accession of strength in safety to the prince, lord Moira returned to Britain. The French generals were now advancing in all directions through the Netherlands, and the allies were apprehensive that Holland would again become the scene of invasion. The duke of York remained at Antwerp, to afford the Dutch time to strengthen their fortifications, and prepare for a vigorous defence. The prince of Orange, in the beginning of the month, had taken post at Waterloo; and here he was at first successful in repelling an advanced guard of the French. He was soon, however, compelled to abandon this post, by the advance of the republican armies to Brussels. He attempted afterwards to make a stand along the canal of Louvain; but the French bringing up continual reinforcements, he was obliged, with considerable loss, to retreat on the 16th across the Dyle, and established, for a short time, his head-quarters at Nyle. The stadtholder solicited the Dutch, by repeated proclamations, to levy one man in ten throughout the United Provinces. But a great portion of the people were disaffected, and the rest were torpid. The French generals advanced in front of the Dyle towards Louvain. At the Iron Mountain,

Advances of the French.

The duke of York and prince of Orange are obliged to fall back.

Mountain, the brave though lately unfortunate Clairfait again attempted an ineffectual reſiſtance, but was completely defeated by general Kleber, with the loſs, in killed, wounded, and priſoners, of ſix thouſand men; while the generals Lefevre and Dubois ſeized on the poſition of the abbey of Florival. It was at firſt the intention of the commanders of the combined armies to make a ſtand at Namur, and to form a line of defence from that city to Antwerp; but theſe ſucceſſes of the republicans, and their rapid movements, totally diſconcerted this plan. Namur was abandoned by General Beaulieu on the night of the 16th, leaving behind him only two hundred men, who ſurrendered both the city and citadel on the firſt ſummons: a large quantity of artillery was found at Namur. On the 20th, the keys of the city were preſented at the bar of the national convention*. In weſt Flanders the important paſs of the Lier was forced about the ſame time: the French on the 23d ſent a trumpeter to inform the inhabitants of Antwerp that they intended to viſit them on the ſucceeding morning, which they did at eleven o'clock, and took quiet poſſeſſion of that city. The allies had previouſly ſet fire to the immenſe magazines of forage which were there collected. Jourdain and his troops entered Liege, which immediately ſubmitted to the victorious republicans. The fortreſſes of Liſle and Sluys were ſpeedily captured†; the four towns taken from the French were ſucceſſively retaken. The Auſtrians entirely evacuated the Netherlands, which were now overſpread

The Auſtrians entirely evacuate the Netherlands.

* New Annual Regiſter, 1794, page 400.

† Ibid. 401.

by

by the republican armies. The British retreated from Antwerp, and in number about twenty-five thousand men proceeded to Breda, which it was determined to defend, and a Dutch garrison was stationed there for that purpose. The right column of the English marched through Breda on the 4th of August, while the left went round the town. They then took a position which had been previously marked out for them, about four miles distant. Having halted several days at Breda, which the prince of Orange was putting into a state of defence, they retreated in the end of August to Bois le-duc, where a Dutch garrison of seven thousand men was posted. In the beginning of September general Pichegru approached with an army of at least eighty thousand men; and the advanced guard of the republicans attacked and stormed the posts on the Dommel, and the village of Boxtel, which though they made a most gallant resistance, found it impossible to withstand the numbers of the enemy. The duke, therefore, with so inferior a force, perceiving his situation totally untenable, on the 16th of September crossed the Meuse, and took a position which had been previously reconnoitred about three miles from Grave. So vigorous had been the resistance of the valiant British, that with twenty-five thousand men they withstood the republicans who were more than eighty thousand, from the beginning of July to the middle of September; in which time they made very inconsiderable advances, where they had the duke of York and his band to combat*. On the Rhine similar

Intrepid stand of the British on the frontiers of Holland, but they are compelled to give way to immense superiority of numbers.

They retreat behind the Meuse.

* See Macfarlane, vol. iv. page 489.

success

CHAP. LIV.

1794. Faithlessness of the king of Prussia.

success attended the energetic efforts of the republicans. The king of Prussia having long manifested the coldest indifference to the confederacy, had early in this year announced to the German princes his determination to withdraw from the alliance. But Britain, judging of his good faith by her own, had conceived that he would bring into the field the forces for which he had stipulated, and for which he had been paid; in short, that a monarch would not descend to an artifice so totally unbecoming a gentleman, or an honest man, *as to procure the money of other people by false pretences.* But our government and legislature had proceeded on the supposition that Frederic William possessed virtues with which they found by experience he was not endued. The force which he furnished was very inferior to that which he promised, and their efforts were not such as might have been expected from a Prussian army, and were of little avail against the sincere, zealous, and ardent enthusiasm of the republican troops.

Victories of the republicans on the Rhine.

On the 12th of July, General Michaud attacked the Prussians near Edickhoffen; and, to favour his operations in that quarter, advanced at the same time upon the Austrians before Spires. The contest was long and bloody, and both parties claimed the victory. On the following day the French renewed the attack on the Prussians with redoubled vigour. The battle lasted from early in the morning till nine at night. They attacked seven times, and at length carried by assault, amidst a terrible fire, the important posts fortified and occupied by the Prussians on Platoberg, the highest mountain

CHAP. LIV. 1794.

mountain in the whole territory of Deux Ponts*. The republicans captured great numbers of prisoners, and nine guns, besides ammunition, waggons, and horses. Continuing their series of attacks, the republicans successively defeated the German troops, and compelled them to seek safety by crossing the Rhine†. The emperor, alarmed by such a multiplicity of successes, endeavoured to stimulate the German princes to join him in efficacious measures to defend the empire against the irruption of the republicans; and for that purpose he addressed a memorial to the circles. His own resources, he stated, were utterly inadequate to the contest: the progress of the French was so rapid, that he must be inevitably obliged to withdraw his troops, and station them for the defence of his own frontiers, unless the empire should think proper to oppose the progress of the French with a sufficient force: these exhortations did not produce the desired effect; and no vigorous efforts were made by the empire to second its chief. The suspicion of treachery often springs from discomfiture; and ideas of this sort were very prevalent during this ill-fated campaign. Many of the Austrian officers incurred the imputation: it was said that a considerable number of these were infected with republican principles; and that not a few were corrupted with French gold. As, however, it would exceed the bounds of history to repeat the various surmises of suspicion, concerning which proof was not adduced

Address of the emperor to the German princes,

is totally unavailing.

Opinions of the operations and events of this campaign.

* New Annual Register, 1794, p. 401.

† Otridge's Annual Register, 1794.

CHAP. LIV. 1794.

to aſcertain the truth of the rumours, the narrative ſhall not follow their details. One reſult however, is, the conduct of the Auſtrians in many inſtances was ſo extremely inconſiſtent with the military ability which the officers of that nation have generally poſſeſſed in a great degree, that it implied either treachery or incapacity. The prince of Cobourg has been ſeverely cenſured for the operations which terminated in the ſignal defeat at Fleurus, and the loſs of the Netherlands. It was ſaid, that knowing the efficacy of the Britiſh troops, he ſhould not have left them at Tournay when he marched to encounter Jourdain: that the addition of ſuch a force would have inſured victory: that the plan of ſeparation in which the poſition of the Britiſh troops originated, was very inimical to the objects of the campaign, and very unfit to oppoſe an enemy whoſe grand ſcheme was an extenſive and cloſely connected line of co-operation: that the allies had ſtationed themſelves at three angles of a triangle, while the republicans, by a ſegment of a circle, at once encompaſſed the whole, and broke the communication of the parts. Theſe allegations, if true, might be all accounted for without any charge of diſaffection againſt Cobourg, and upon a ſuppoſition that will be very generally admitted, that Jourdain and Pichegru, eſpecially the latter, far ſurpaſſed Cobourg in inventive powers which formed new combinations adapted to the caſe. Cobourg, indeed, appears to have been a man of mere tactical experience, without genius, and therefore not fit to cope with ſkilful men of very great genius. This prince, after the evacuation of the Netherlands, was diſmiſſed

Suſpicions unfavourable to the prince of Cobourg, are not ſupported by proof.

missed from his command, not without a rumour of imputed treachery; the truth of which I have no grounds to record as an historical fact; and I myself disbelieve, as his character was fair and honourable; as there is no evidence to support such a charge, and as the disasters of the army under his command appeared to have arisen from the superior ability of the French generals, commanding a much more numerous force, inspired by the most ardent enthusiasm, which, whencesoever it arises, has always inspired men to efforts far beyond diplomatic calculation formed on the experience of common wars. The emperor certainly did not receive in the Netherlands, the assistance from his Belgian subjects, the hopes of which probably had a considerable influence in inducing him to visit these dominions. His exhortation to them to rise in mass was indeed very unlikely to be regarded, as they did not conceive that, like the French, they were fighting their own cause. Their object was naturally their own security, and not the aggrandizement of the house of Austria: they did not chuse to rise in mass to fight for a master, though the French had risen in mass to fight for themselves.

Cobourg a man of very moderate abilities.

After evacuating the Netherlands, general Clairfait, leaving general Latour to cover Maestricht, posted himself at Juliers. Jourdain in the beginning of September prepared to march against Latour; but it was the middle of the month before he was ready for the assault. On the 18th the French in four columns attacked the whole line, from the Aywaille to Emeux. All the passages were forced with the bayonet, and the camps taken

Able efforts of Clairfait.

CHAP. LIV.

1794. Victories of the republicans.

at full charge. The Auſtrians left two thouſand men dead on the field of battle, and ſeveral of their battalions were reduced to one hundred and fifty men. Seven hundred priſoners, twenty-ſix pieces of large cannon, three pair of colours, one hundred horſes, and forty ammunition waggons, were taken, as well as the general's own carriage, his ſecretary, and papers. The remnant of Latour's army was completely routed and diſperſed: general Clairfait having endeavoured without effect to aſſiſt Latour, with great ſkill and ability fortified himſelf at Juliers; and thither the republicans directed their efforts. On the 29th the French advanced from Aix la Chapelle, croſſed the Roer, and attacked all the Auſtrian general's extenſive poſts, from Ruremonde to Juliers and Dureu. The conflict laſted the whole of the 29th and 30th of September, and was renewed on the 1ſt and 2d of October. The battle was extremely fierce on both ſides; but Clairfait having loſt ten thouſand men, found it neceſſary to retreat as rapidly as poſſible. Juliers was abandoned to the French, and Clairfait retreated acroſs the Rhine: the republicans conquered Cologne, Worms, Bonn, and in ſhort reduced the whole left bank of the river. Pichegru, meanwhile was preſſing on towards Holland. He informed the national convention, that with two hundred thouſand men he would ſubjugate the United Provinces; and though the whole force which he required was not immediately ſent, yet ſo numerous an addition was diſpatched to his army, that he deemed himſelf able to proceed with his operations. In the beginning of October he inveſted Bois-le-duc, which

The republicans reduce the whole left bank of the Rhine.

CHAP. LIV. 1794.

which in a few days surrendered. On the 20th of October, a sharp conflict took place between the republicans and the English, in which, though the event was not decisive, the loss was considerable. The duke of York now crossing the Waal, fell back to Nimeguen; and thither the French multitudes soon followed. The British army was posted to the left of Nimeguen, and the enemy in front of the town, where batteries were erected for the purpose of cannonade and bombardment. On the 4th of November a sortie was made in the night. The troops employed in the sally were about three thousand British, Hanoverians, and Dutch; and their object was to destroy the batteries which were newly constructed to annoy the city. It appears that the French were by some means informed of this design, and were prepared to obstruct its execution. The conflict was extremely obstinate, but our troops were victorious, though with considerable loss. The British general, however, from the immense superiority of the enemy, found it necessary to evacuate Nimeguen. Philippine on the Scheld also surrendered: the French army on the right was fast advancing, and after the victories over the Austrians, laid siege to Maestricht. This city stood a regular investment in the beginning of October. During this month the republicans carried on their approaches, and whilst their parallels were forming, constructed their batteries. They repeatedly summoned the town to surrender; this denunciation having on the 30th been made in vain, the besiegers began to pour a most dreadful shower of shot and shells from all their works, with which

The British gain some advantages, but are greatly outnumbered.

CHAP. LIV.

1794.

they had surrounded the place. This fire, lasting during the whole of the night, demolished many public buildings and private houses, wounded and killed great numbers of the inhabitants. During three days this destructive assault continued: the governor at length, moved by the entreaties of the magistrates and people, entered into a negociation with general Kleber, and the city capitulated on the 4th of November. After the capture of Nimeguen and Maestreicht, the operations were inactive during the rest of the month. But the troops, though not engaged in battles, were exposed to the severest hardships. The winter began with extreme severity: the soldiers were in want of clothing and other necessaries for encountering a winter campaign, which had not been foreseen in time to make adequate provision. In a country so much colder and damper than Britain, that season far exceeded its usual rigour. The consequence was sickness and mortality among the soldiers, augmented by the want of remedies and medical assistance sufficient for such an unexpected prevalence of distemper. It is probable, from the inaction of the French at this time, that they laboured under similar evils. Fresh and numerous reinforcements however, arriving, enabled them in December to proceed with their operations. On the 7th of this month they made a fruitless attempt to cross the Waal in four rafts, from Nimeguen; two of the rafts were sunk by the English forces, who were stationed on the opposite side, near the village of Lant; one floated to the side occupied by the Dutch; and only one of the four regained that which was in the possession of the

Winter campaign in Holland.

Sickness and mortality of the British troops.

Intrepid efforts of their exhausted remains.

the republicans. On the 11th the attempt was renewed, and with better succefs: they croffed the river above Nimeguen, and near the canal, in boats and on rafts, to the number of about five thoufand men. Another detachment, however, attempting the paffage, was repulfed with confiderable lofs. About the middle of December the froft became extremely intenfe; and in a few days the Maefe and the Waal were frozen over. On the 27th the army croffed the river; the duke of York had, together with the prince of Orange, endeavoured to roufe the Dutch to fuch energetic refiftance as had formerly faved their country from French invaders; but the circumftances of the times, and the difpofitions of the people, were totally changed. Great numbers of the Dutch were now unwilling to oppofe the French, and moft of the reft conceived oppofition hopelefs. The exhortations of the princes were, therefore, altogether unavailing; and the duke of York confidered all efforts as ufelefs to fave a people not defirous of faving themfelves. Seeing military exertions unlikely to be farther ufeful in that country, he returned to England. The remaining forces were now entrufted to the command of general Walmoden; and an attempt was made to force the enemy to repafs the Waal. For this purpofe ten battalions of Britifh infantry, with fix fquadrons of light cavalry, commanded by major general Dundas, affifted by four fquadrons and four battalions of Heffians, amounting in all to about fix thoufand five hundred infantry, and a thoufand horfe, advanced in three columns. At day break on the 30th of December, attacking a

Attempts of the duke of York and prince of Orange to roufe the Dutch.

CHAP. LIV. 1794.

great body of French at the village of Thuil, they carried it with the bayonet, and drove the republicans acroſs the river. This ſucceſs, however, was only temporary; the Engliſh army was from the dreadful effects of the climate and ſeaſon, rapidly decreaſing. Private liberality was added to public expenditure in ſending plentiful ſupplies of flannel waiſtcoats, and other fences againſt the cold; but the inclemency of the froſts was ſuperior to every expedient: the chief part of the army was overcome with ſickneſs. According to the reports of officers who were engaged in this dreadful ſervice, the profeſſional attention beſtowed upon the ſick was by no means adequate to the effectual diſcharge of that momentous duty*. In the month of January the French again croſſed the Waal with ſeventy thouſand men. This formidable hoſt attacked the remains of the Britiſh army, and compelled them, though ſtill making the moſt gallant reſiſtance, to retire. Without tents, and unable to procure cantonments, the diſtreſſed heroes were obliged to paſs the night, in this ſevere ſeaſon, in the open tobacco ſheds, or under the canopy of an inclement ſky. The Dutch now urged the ſtadtholder to conclude a

* The details on this ſubject, not once or twice mentioned, but very frequently repeated through the periodical works of the time daily, weekly, monthly, and yearly, and never contradicted, charge the medical department with extreme negligence. But candour muſt admit, that the prevalence of diſtemper was much greater than was to be foreſeen or expected when the medical appointments were made, and that therefore a leſs minute attention could be beſtowed on every individual patient, than the caſe required.

peace

CHAP. LIV.
1794.

peace with the French, and finding him unwilling, their provinces and towns successively offered terms to the republicans, which were accepted. Zealand, and soon after Holland, entered into a capitulation. The stadtholder with much difficulty escaped from the Hague with his family, sought and found refuge in England: by the beginning of February the provinces had concluded a treaty with the French. As the republicans now possessed all the country between the British army and the coast of Holland, it was impossible to retreat in that direction; they, therefore, were obliged to take a much more circuitous rout towards the north coast of Germany. They repeatedly occupied strong positions, not with the vain intention of making a stand against three times their number, but to secure their retreat. Therein they had also to encounter many other difficulties. The partial thaws which occasionally took place only served to aggravate the misery of the troops, from the floods which succeeded these alterations in the temperature, and either impeded their progress, or obliged the soldiers to wade through torrents of mud and water, which sometimes reached even to their knapsacks. In this dreadful situation they were obliged to continue their march, or to be overwhelmed by the enemy. After a rout perhaps unequalled in the annals of military hardship, the exhausted remains of our army arrived at Bremen; and, having halted for some weeks, they embarked for England.

Immense superiority of numbers forces the English to evacuate Holland, which yields to the French arms.

Such was the melancholy termination of the British expedition to the continent; so little did the

Campaign of 1794 disastrous to the British army.

expences,

CHAP. LIV. 1794.

expences, preparations, and military equipments of two years anſwer the purpoſes for which they were undertaken. Britain had gone to war to prevent an attack upon the rights of Dutch navigation: inſtead of one river, the whole ſeven provinces were now commanded by the republicans. She had gone to war to prevent French aggrandizement: one campaign had given France an acceſſion of territory fertile, productive, and opulent, far ſurpaſſing all the conqueſts of her moſt ambitious and ſucceſsful monarchs.

In Italy and Spain the republicans were ſucceſsful as far as they employed their efforts: their exertions, however, in Piedmont, were not important. On the confines of Spain they made rapid advances: the Spaniſh government attempted to raiſe the ſubjects in maſs; but this was an expedient that could ſucceed only in countries where the people, either being or conceiving themſelves free, were inſpirited by the ardour of liberty.

From ſuch an iſſue to the efforts of the confederation, perſons that did not exactly conſider the ſpecific caſe might very naturally draw unjuſt inferences. Such might conclude, that becauſe the combination in queſtion had been unſucceſsful, that no future union for ſuppreſſing dangerous ambition could be ſucceſsful, and therefore that the attempt would be vain, Were a concert to be propoſed for reducing the exorbitant power of France, the events of 1794 might be quoted as warnings that the ſcheme would be impracticable; and aſſuredly the ſame means and conduct in ſimilar circumſtances would be unavailing. If the continental powers, pretending

ing to join, were really to purſue different and even contrary objects; and if the French were inſpired by the ſame ſpirit which, during their republican enthuſiaſm, animated and invigorated their exertions, the iſſue would certainly be diſcomfiture to the nominal coalition of really diſcordant parts. But if they were to unite in head, heart, and hand, to purſue an object which many might think more important for their ultimate ſafety than paltry indemnities; and if it were to happen that they had not to contend againſt enthuſiaſm, but torpid indifference, it would by no means follow that the events of 1794 would be repeated. Even reſpecting Holland ſingly, it would be extremely haſty to deduce a general concluſion from the untoward iſſue of this diſaſtrous campaign. The reduction of Holland did not ariſe merely from the arms of Pichegru, but in a great degree from the Dutch themſelves. The majority of them were democratical, and received the French not only without oppoſition, but with gratitude and joy, as their deliverers and brothers. They might have withſtood Pichegru when aſſiſted by the gallant Engliſh, as without any aſſiſtance they withſtood Turenne and Conde; and with much leſs aid they diſcomfited Alva and Parma. The Dutch have clearly manifeſted, that, if they exert themſelves, no foreign power can keep their country in ſubjection, or even dependence. Should it ever happen that they chuſe to aſſert their independence, there is little doubt that they will be ſucceſsful: whenever they have the will they have the power to be free.

Signal ſucceſſes of Britain where ſhe fought alone.

Signal as had been the diſaſters of the Britiſh armies on the continent, where ſhe acted alone, unincumbered

CHAP. LIV. 1794.

incumbered with allies, and on her appropriate theatre, her success was momentous, and her glory transcendant. In the choice of naval commanders, our minister, through the war, has uniformly considered instrumentality; fitness for discharging the duties, and accomplishing the purposes of the appointment. The various commands, supreme and subordinate, were conferred on professional ability and character. Three powerful armaments were prepared for the campaign of 1794: one under Lord Hood commanded the Mediterranean, reduced the island of Corsica, and protected the coasts of Spain and Italy: a second, under Sir John Jervis, with a military force headed by Sir Charles Grey, reduced Martinico, Guadaloupe, St. Lucia, and some parts of St. Domingo. But the most illustrious monument of British naval glory was raised by Earl Howe. During the preceding part of the war, France, conscious of her maritime inferiority to Great Britain, had hitherto confined her exertions to cruizers and small squadrons for harassing our trade. In the month of May, the French were induced to depart from this system of naval warfare. Anxious for the safety of a convoy daily expected from America, conveying an immense supply of corn and flour, of naval stores and colonial productions, the Brest fleet, amounting to twenty-seven ships of the line ventured to sea under the command of Rear-admiral Villaret. Lord Howe expecting the same convoy, went to sea with twenty ships of the line. On the 28th May he descried the enemy to windward. Admiral Pasley in the evening gave signal to the vanmost ships to attack the enemy's rear.

Her fleets paramount in the Mediterranean.

Acquisitions in the West Indies.

Operations of Earl Howe and the channel fleet.

Lord

Lord Hugh Seymour Conway attacked the Revolutionaire of 120 guns, and being soon supported by Captain Parker of the Audacious, so damaged the enemy's ship that she struck; but escaping during the night, she was towed into Rochfort. The next morning the fleets resumed the conflict, but the intermission of a thick fog prevented its continuance. The fog lasted that and the greater part of the two following days. The sun occasionally breaking through the mist, shewed to each other the direction of the fleets; and Lord Howe employed this time in most masterly manoeuvres to obtain the weather-gage, that he might compel them to fight when the atmosphere should clear, and at length he succeeded.

Skilful manœuvre to bring the enemy to battle.

On the 1st of June, the fog being dispersed, our admiral, from his former excellent dispositions, found an opportunity of bringing the French to battle.

Battle of the 1st of June.

Between seven and eight in the morning, our fleet advanced in a close and compact line: the enemy finding an engagement unavoidable, received our onset with their accustomed valour. A close and desperate engagement ensued, presenting the French as combatants worthy of occupying the naval heroism of England.

Numbers, force, and courageous efforts of the enemy; unavailing against the British fleet.

The Montague of 130 guns, the French admiral's ship having adventured to encounter the Queen Charlotte of 100, was, in less than an hour, compelled to fly: the other ships of the same division seeing all efforts ineffectual against British prowess, endeavoured to follow the flying admiral; ten, however, were so crippled that they could not keep pace with the rest: but many of the British ships were so damaged that some of these disabled ships of the enemy effected their escape. Six

Decisive, glorious, and momentous victory.

CHAP. LIV. 1794.

remained in the possession of the British admiral, and were brought safe into Portsmouth, viz. La Juste of 80 guns, La Sans Pareille of 80 guns, L'America 74, L'Achille 74, L'Impetueux 74, and Northumberland 74: these, with Le Vengeur, which was sunk, made the whole loss of the French amount to seven ships of the line. The victorious ships arrived safe in harbour with their prizes: the crews, officers, and admiral were received with those grateful thanks and high applauses which Britain never fails to bestow on her conquering heroes. Earl Howe was by all ranks and parties extolled for his tactical skill, steady perseverance, and determined courage; first, in forcing the enemy, after every evasion, to a close action; and then in obtaining so signal an advantage over a fleet superior in its number of ships and of men, as well as in size and weight of metal *. The year 1794, surpassing in disaster by land the unfortunate 1777 † or 1781‡, by sea equalled the glories of 1759.

* See Macfarlane's history, vol. iv. p. 461.

† Capture of Burgoyne's army. ‡ Cornwallis's army.

END OF THE FIFTH VOLUME.

Printed by A. Strahan,
Printers-Street, London.

Lightning Source UK Ltd.
Milton Keynes UK
UKHW020207260219
337978UK00012B/1260/P